D1452637

# EARLY MODERN LITERARY GEOGRAPHIES

*General Editors*

JULIE SANDERS   GARRETT A. SULLIVAN, JR.

# EARLY MODERN LITERARY GEOGRAPHIES
Oxford University Press

*Series Editors*: JULIE SANDERS, Newcastle University and
GARRETT A. SULLIVAN, JR., Pennsylvania State University

*Early Modern Literary Geographies* features innovative research monographs and agenda-setting essay collections that engage with the topics of space, place, landscape and environment. While focussed on sixteenth- and seventeenth-century English literature, scholarship in this series encompasses a range of disciplines, including geography, history, performance studies, art history, musicology, archaeology and cognitive science. Subjects of inquiry include cartography or chorography; historical phenomenology and sensory geographies; body and environment; mobility studies; histories of travel or perambulation; regional and provincial literatures; urban studies; performance environments; sites of memory and cognition; ecocriticism; and oceanic or new blue studies.

# The Absence of America

## The London Stage, 1576–1642

GAVIN HOLLIS

OXFORD
UNIVERSITY PRESS

# OXFORD

UNIVERSITY PRESS

Great Clarendon Street, Oxford, OX2 6DP,
United Kingdom

Oxford University Press is a department of the University of Oxford.
It furthers the University's objective of excellence in research, scholarship,
and education by publishing worldwide. Oxford is a registered trade mark of
Oxford University Press in the UK and in certain other countries

© Gavin Hollis 2015

The moral rights of the author have been asserted

First Edition published in 2015

Impression: 1

Published in the United States of America by Oxford University Press
198 Madison Avenue, New York, NY 10016, United States of America

British Library Cataloguing in Publication Data

Data available

Library of Congress Control Number: 2014957922

ISBN 978-0-19-873432-1

Printed and bound by
CPI Group (UK) Ltd, Croydon, CR0 4YY

Links to third party websites are provided by Oxford in good faith and
for information only. Oxford disclaims any responsibility for the materials
contained in any third party website referenced in this work.

# Acknowledgements

As befits a project that looks back across oceans, my debts of gratitude are on both sides of the Atlantic. I was fortunate while at the University of Michigan, Ann Arbor, where this project began, to be surrounded by a crack squad of early modernists, who read drafts of my work and provided expert commentary and feedback, frequently over a glass of wine or three. I am grateful to the Early Modern Colloquium, and in particular Kentston Bauman, David Lavinsky, Amy Rodgers, Chad Allen Thomas, Marjorie Rubright, Laura Williamson Ambrose, Aaron McCullough, Holly Dugan, Ari Friedlander, Steven Mullaney, Linda Gregerson, William Ingram, Michael McDonald, and especially Barbara Hodgdon. The project was shaped with the considerable help and expertise of Michael C. Schoenfeldt, Susan Scott Parrish, Susan Juster, and my chair, Valerie Traub. Valerie in particular has been and continues to be an incredible mentor, a model of scholarship of the highest order and a fabulous teacher too. I am humbled to be among the company of fine scholars who have been guided by Valerie. This project has evolved in the years since I left Michigan, but I hope it still carries the stamp of the "Tribe of Val".

Research for this book was conducted thanks to travel awards and Rackham dissertation grants while at the University of Michigan, and with support from CUNY's Research Foundation and Faculty Fellowship Publication Program. I was able to take advantage of archival material at the British Library, the University of Michigan (especially the William L. Clements Library), the Newberry Library, and the New York Public Library (especially the George Arents Collection). Thank you to all the librarians at these institutions, but especially to Karl Longstreth, Mary Pedley, Jessica Pigza, and Jay Barksdale. This project has benefitted from Shakespeare Association of America seminars imagined and expertly coordinated by Mary Floyd-Wilson and Daryl Palmer, Catherine Richardson, Mary C. Fuller, Jonathan Gil Harris, and Helen Smith and Matthew Dimmock, and from feedback from audiences at Columbia University, the CUNY Graduate Center, the New York Public Library, and Hunter College.

I feel so very fortunate that moving to New York brought me into the orbit of Patricia Akhimie, Allison Deutermann, András Kiséry, Vimala Pasupathi, Marie Rutkowski, Andrea Walkden, and Matt Zarnowiecki. I have not only benefited from their thorough and generous critiques of my work and their generosity in suggesting sources and indeed whole new kinds of argumentation; I have also learned so much from reading their work. It is fair to say that this book could not be what it is without their guidance and influence (I freely acknowledge that the errors and missteps are all my own, and that there could have been many more without their input).

I am grateful to my students at Hunter College, CUNY, especially those who took my "Shakespeare's New Worlds" seminars at the undergraduate and graduate level; and to my colleagues in the English department, in particular to Sarah Chinn, Tanya Agathocleous, Jeremy Glick, Lynne Greenberg, Ramesh Mallipeddi, Mark Miller, Gary Schmidgall, Thom Taylor, and especially Cristina Alfar, to whom I am eternally grateful. In 2013, I was fortunate to be accepted into CUNY's Faculty Fellowship Publication Program. My group, led by Moustafa Bayoumi, read two chapters of the book at a crucial point in its development. Moustafa and Siraj Ahmed, Sandra Cheng, Frank Crocco, Shereen Inayatulla, Claudia Moreno-Parsons, and J. Paul Narkunas were marvelous colleagues and co-conspirators, and I thank them for all of their input and their CUNY camaraderie.

I have had inspiring readers of my work, in particular Gil Harris, Jean E. Howard, Valerie Forman, Craig Rustici, Mark Netzloff, and Julie Sanders and Garrett Sullivan, my wonderfully supportive general editors. Julie in particular gave me feedback at a crucial stage of the project that helped shape it in is final moments. I am very proud that this book is the first in the Early Modern Literary Geographies series. My editor at Oxford University Press, Jacqueline Baker, has been a marvelous advocate of this book. She has been extremely responsive (especially as the tenure clock sands were trickling down the hourglass), and approached insightful reviewers who helped develop the project no end. And I'd also like to thank Rachel Platt, Lucy McClune, Mohana Annamalai, Dawn Preston, and Denise Bannerman for their help in putting this book together.

Finally, and closer to home(s), I am grateful for the love, patience, and support of my friends and family on both sides of the Atlantic who have had their ears bent by me wittering on about London drama and the New World. Thank you to Erin Davis and John Davis; Dan Neill; Elspeth Healey, Tamara Bhalla, John Cords, Emily Lutenski, Ji-Hyae Park, Ben Stroud, and Korey Jackson; Evens Go East, Leslie Paris Viking, and Silver Rocket; Richard and Sarah Manton-Hollis; Patricia Hollis; Charlie Hayes and Angela Baggetta; and my parents, Andrea and Malcolm Hollis.

Portions of Chapter 4 of this book have appeared in print elsewhere: "'He would not goe naked like the Indians, but cloathed just as one of our selves': Clothing, Conversion, and 'the Naked Indian' in Massinger's *The City Madam*," in *Renaissance Drama* 39 (2011); and "Enter Orlando with a scarf before his face": Indians, Moors, and the Properties of Racial

Transformation in Robert Greene's *The Historie of Orlando Furioso*," in *Indography: Writing the "Indian" in Early Modern England*, edited by Jonathan Gil Harris (New York: Palgrave MacMillan, 2012). I am grateful to the publishers and editors of these volumes for their permission to re-use portions of my work. Thanks also to Amguedffa Cymru/National Museum of Wales, the Chatsworth Settlement Trustees, the Folger Shakespeare Library, the Huntington Library, the John Carter Brown Library, and the Society of Antiquaries of London for permission to reprint illustrations in their collections.

# Contents

# List of Illustrations

# Introduction

## *"Where America, the Indies?" London Theater and the New World*

Do ye snarl you, black Jill? She looks like the picture of America!

John Fletcher, *The Knight of Malta*

I begin with a prayer:

And whereas we have by undertaking this plantation undergone the reproofs of the base world, insomuch as many of our own brethren laugh us to scorne, O Lord, we pray thee fortifie us against this temptation: let Sanballat, & Tobiah, Papists & players, & such other Ammonites & Horonites the scum & dregs of the earth, let them mocke such as helpe to build up the walls of Jerusalem, . . . let them that feare thee, rejoice & be glad in thee, & let them know, that it is thou O Lord, that raignest in England, & unto the ends of the world.[1]

Uttered twice daily by the court of guard manning the garrisons of Jamestown and printed twice in London in the 1610s, the prayer gives us insight into the embattled state of the Virginia project on both sides of the Atlantic in the first decades of the seventeenth century. The colony found itself repeatedly on the verge of collapse—haggard, half-starved, poorly governed, and beset by foes from within and without. The Virginia Company in London found it hard to attract sufficient funds and competent settlers to support and populate the nascent colony. It was dogged with rumors, "the reproofs of the base world," about the prospects of the colony and the behavior of the colonists—rumors which had come to England thanks to disaffected returnees and were being disseminated by, among others, the professional playing companies. The Virginia

---

[1] "A Praier duly said Morning and Euening vpon the Court of Guard, either by the Captaine of the watch himselfe, or by some one of his principall officers," in William Strachey, *For the Colony in Virginea Britannia, Lawes Diuine, Morall and Martiall* (London: for Walter Burre, 1612), N4.

Company condemned the players (a term which encompasses both actors and playwrights) as part of an unholy trinity, alongside the papists and the Devil, which was hell-bent on bringing about the end of English transatlantic interests and, by extension, the destruction of the English nation itself.

When we look at the plays written and performed in the period, these accusations seem at first like the ramblings of paranoid cranks. Shakespeare's *The Tempest*, so often heralded as *the* American play of the period, is, lest we forget, set on a magical island located (if it is really located anywhere) in the Mediterranean somewhere between Naples and Tunis. Otherwise, no extant English play of the early modern period is set in the Americas until 1658's *The Cruelty of the Spaniards in Peru* by William Davenant. Few plays make transatlantic trade and colonization central to their plots or even subplots. No play stages a Native American character, although there are three that feature Europeans wearing Indian costumes to disguise themselves and test or deceive other characters.

There are, to be sure, allusions to the Americas—whether it be to specific places, or to a vaguely imagined "Indies"—spread out across a number of plays of the period, but the allusions tend to be fleeting and draw more on generalized associations with the New World (its fabled size, wealth, and wildness) than specific associations with the English mission. Virginia, England's first American colony, is only alluded to a few times directly in the commercial drama of the period, and while several allusions are mocking in tone, they are contained within a few lines of dialogue and are for the most part inconsequential to the plot. In sum, while Thomas Platter, the Swiss traveler who visited England in the autumn of 1599, bore witness to how the English "pass their time, learning at the play what is happening abroad; . . . since the English for the most part do not travel much, but prefer to learn foreign matters and take their pleasures at home," it seems that playgoers would not have learnt much about the matters of the New World.[2]

It is tempting, therefore, to dismiss the anti-theatricalists as lashing out at the players to deflect attention from the failings of English transatlantic trade and settlement. It may, however, be more fruitful to think of them as astute playgoers. Even though, from our vantage, we find it difficult to locate an "American play" in the era of the professional playhouse pre-1642, and are forced for the most part to scavenge at the edges of otherwise distinctly "un-American" plays, playgoers may not have found any such difficulties in encountering New World foreign matters on the

---

[2] Thomas Platter, *The Travels of Thomas Platter*, trans. Clare Williams (London: Jonathan Cape, 1937), 170.

stage. Indeed, by exploring the ways in which Londoners experienced the theater, we can begin to see the emergence of a "picture of America," and a picture of the Virginia colony in particular. This picture emerges across a number of plays performed for London audiences, transmitted through (following Louise George Clubb) "theatergrams"—"those elements of dramatic composition such as character, situation, genre, and scene out of which narrative arcs and climaxes, catastrophes and dénouements of plays are assembled"—and through what I call "theatermemes," that is, things like shared allusions, "tunes, ideas, catch-phrases" which "can be said to propagate [themselves] from brain to brain," and, in the case of early modern London, from playhouse to playhouse (and beyond).[3] We can glean the significance of these theatergrams and theatermemes and the picture that they collectively formed, not only for the troubled Virginia Company, but also for London theater audiences. When approached this way, we can see that the picture that was beginning to form was, as the anti-theatricalists surmised, often slanderous and condemnatory, and, as it were, anti-American.

In this book I limn the picture of America that was constituted and circulated in the drama of London's commercial playhouses through the medium of the theatergram and the theatermeme between 1576 (the date of the opening of the first permanent playhouse, The Theatre) to 1642 (the closing of the playhouses by parliamentary decree at the beginning of the first English Civil War).[4] I do so by comparing the playhouse "picture" with that which was being circulated in London as part of the Virginia Company promotional machine. We will see that the Virginia Company repeatedly stressed the transformative possibilities of the New World: through expansion across the Atlantic, England's economy would be rescued; through resettlement, England's itinerants would become productive colonists; through the religious mission, Virginia's indigenous population would be converted to Christians loyal to the English crown.

---

[3] William N. West, "Introduction: Italy in the Drama of Europe," *Renaissance Drama*, 36/37 (2010): ix–xiv, at x; see also Louise George Clubb, "Theatergrams," in *Italian Drama in Shakespeare's Time* (New Haven: Yale University Press, 1989), 1–26. My term "thea-termeme" derives from Richard Dawkins' famous definition of memes. See Dawkins, *The Selfish Gene* (Oxford: Oxford University Press, 1976), quotation at 192.

[4] John Brayne's The Red Lion in Stepney preceded The Theatre by nearly a decade and has good claim to be the first purpose-built playhouse, but is often discounted from the dating of commercial Renaissance drama on account of its very short existence. James Burbage's The Theatre has two advantages: first, Burbage's outsized personality as both carpenter and actor (and head of an acting family) draws attention to his contribution to English drama over that of his brother-in-law, Brayne; and second, because The Theatre survived until 1598, when it was reconstituted as The Globe. See Janet S. Loengard, "An Elizabethan Lawsuit: John Brayne, His Carpenter, and the Building of the Red Lion Theatre," *Shakespeare Quarterly*, 34(3) (1983): 298–310.

By contrast, the theater's -grams and -memes denied that any such transformations were possible. In plays the only economic benefits that Virginia would seem to provide are for bankrupts looking to escape debtors' prison, while those intent on settling in the New World show no signs of likely transformation into productive colonists, but rather seem allured by the idea of the New World as a get-rich-quick scheme or as a place where they can indulge their erotic fantasies. Indeed, if the settler is imagined as transforming, it is into a cannibal (that is, someone either driven or inclined to consume the colony) rather than a productive settler (that is, someone driven or inclined to perpetuate the colony). And the indigenous population remained unconverted, either living in a state of heathen worship and indifferent to the religious mission or intent on using it to cover up their own diabolical aims.

The absence of America refers to the playing companies' refusal to parrot the Virginia Company's promotional machine and celebrate the possibilities of colonization, their choice to mock and undermine the promotional matter, and, as result, how they established the playhouses as alternative news outlets. The absence of America refers to a lack of material relations between England and the New World, and the general lack of public knowledge about the Americas, in comparison to other world regions, despite the best efforts of advocates of transatlantic trade and settlement. The absence of America refers to the theater's own trade in absence, presence, and substitution, which seems markedly apparent when it comes to the Americas, which are represented either through quips and allusions or through surrogate spaces, most notably the city of London itself. To fully comprehend the absence of America, that is, we need to reconsider what we mean by the New World, the Americas, the Indies, and even more specific places like Virginia, and what place they held in the early modern English cultural imaginary; and we need to reconsider what we mean by dramatic representation by considering the place and space of the stage in early modern London life.

All of this is to come. For the remainder of this Introduction I set out to establish the critical parameters of the project in relation to the centrality of the idea of the New World to new historicism and its marginality in subsequent critical examinations of drama's representation of the foreign and the strange. I examine the ways in which the theater was implicated in the New World, by tracing the networks of affiliation that connected the playhouses and playing companies to investors and interest groups and to other sites of knowledge where the matters of the New World were disseminated (primarily the bookstall and the pulpit, both of which were in close proximity to London's theaters). I then examine how London theater catered towards and cultivated a sense of its playgoers as knowledgeable of foreign matters, including news from the New World; and how it did so through London comedy, by attaching New World tropes to London types. In closing I return to the Jamestown prayer, using it as a gateway to explore the ways in which theatrical representation was troubling for advocates of transatlantic colonization—this despite the absence of America on the London stage.

## NEW HISTORICISM AND THE NEW WORLD

For new historicists of the 1980s and 1990s the New World was the quintessential foreign matter of English Renaissance literature. In work by Stephen Greenblatt, Steven Mullaney, and Jeffrey Knapp the Americas catalyze the emergence of the (early) modern English subject.[5] Their work builds around the idea that the English came to know themselves as a nation on the verge of empire, as a culture on the verge of enlightenment, and as persons with (at least semi-coherent) selves and interiorities through the physical, intellectual, and psychological expansion of their known world, and that this expansion was the result of the encounter with and emblematized through the image of the New World (in, for example, the westward voyage depicted on the cover of Bacon's *Instauratio Magna*, 1620, and reprinted on the title-page of Knapp's *An Empire Nowhere*) (see Figure 1.1).[6] While new historicism has pressed various literatures and genres into service as evidence for these transformations, drama has regularly been at the forefront: to quote Rebecca Ann Bach, "most early modern drama is involved with producing English subjects who understood themselves in relationship to that new world."[7] As Walter Cohen has pointed out, "the European conquest of the New World, which seems in retrospect like one of the decisive events of the age and arguably of the last half-millennium, proved remarkably unpropitious for literary

[5] Stephen Greenblatt, *Renaissance Self-Fashioning: From More to Shakespeare* (Chicago, IL: University of Chicago Press, 1980); Stephen Greenblatt, "Invisible Bullets," in *Shakespearean Negotiations: The Circulation of Social Energy in Renaissance England* (Berkeley: University of California Press, 1988), 21–65; Stephen Greenblatt, "Learning to Curse: Aspects of Linguistic Colonialism in the Sixteenth Century," in *Learning to Curse: Essays in Early Modern Culture* (New York: Routledge, 1992), 22–51; Stephen Greenblatt, *Marvelous Possessions: The Wonder of the New World* (Chicago, IL: University of Chicago Press, 1992); Jeffrey Knapp, *An Empire Nowhere: England, America, and Literature from Utopia to The Tempest* (Berkeley: University of California Press, 1992); Steven Mullaney, *The Place of the Stage: License, Play, and Power in Renaissance England* (Chicago, IL: University of Chicago Press, 1988; reprinted Ann Arbor: University of Michigan Press, 1995).

[6] Francis Bacon, *Instauratio Magna* (London: for John Bill, 1620).

[7] Rebecca Ann Bach, *Colonial Transformations: The Cultural Production of the New Atlantic World 1580–1640* (New York: Palgrave, 2000), 113.

**Fig. 1.1.** Title page, Francis Bacon, *Francisci de Verulamio, Summi Angliae Cancellaris Instauration Magna* (or *Novum Organum*), 1620. By permission of the Folger Shakespeare Library.

representation." Yet this has not perturbed "studies of culture and imperialism in the wake of Columbus," which have "danced around this void" without ever quite resolving what Cohen calls the "embarrassment of America."[8]

New historicism places great emphasis on the margins, following through the logic articulated by Allon White and Peter Stallybrass, that that which is socially marginalized within a culture may be symbolically central to that culture.[9] Yet by making marginality symbolically central, new historicism has also tended to assume that a few references amount to an underlying structural pattern within a literary work, which in turn leads to conclusions about the underlying structure of the culture within which that work emerges. How can we tell when something marginal is actually symbolically central and when it is just marginal? To which culture is that marginality central: early modernity or our own cultural moment? Of course, new historicism was right about the eventual centrality of the Atlantic world to English life (as was the Virginia Company for that matter). We know that from the late seventeenth century onwards the Atlantic world became central to English geopolitical and cultural life. We can see all kinds of Anglo-American modernities in this later period—the horrors of the Atlantic slave trade, for example, or the English Revolution of the mid-seventeenth century and the American Revolution of the eighteenth—and these modernities can be traced back to their earlier formulations in the sixteenth and early seventeenth centuries. But if we want to understand how the Americas registered in late sixteenth- and early seventeenth-century London, that is, how it registered *for* sixteenth- and early seventeenth-century London*ers*, we need to be careful lest we presume that our history was their future.

If we understand the drama to be a metric of interest in foreign matters, then we might conclude that the stage was concerned with Ireland, European locales, the Mediterranean, the territories dominated by the Ottoman Turks, or even further afield in Persia and Indonesia. Tudor and early Stuart geopolitical and commercial interests were only haphazardly focused on the New World—Elizabeth I was never seriously interested in transatlantic colonization, despite the antics of Drake, Hawkins, Frobisher, and Raleigh, while James I's granting of the first Virginia Company charters in 1606, 1609, and 1612 should not be taken as proof of any great commitment towards its cause: Ireland was the western frontier that

---

[8] Walter Cohen, "The Literature of Empire in the Renaissance," *Modern Philology*, 102(1) (2004): 1–34, at 4.

[9] Peter Stallybrass and Allon White, *The Politics and Poetics of Transgression* (Ithaca, NY: Cornell University Press, 1986), 5.

dominated Tudor and Stuart foreign policy, while the Americas were paid little more than lip service other than by select (albeit powerful and important) statesmen like Lord Burleigh, Francis Walsingham, John Dee, and Henry, Prince of Wales. England's merchants for the most part saw far greater benefits in investing in eastern trade: the Virginia Company and the New England Company were small fry in comparison to the overseas trading company behemoths, the Merchant Adventurers, the Muscovy Company, the Levant Company, and the East India Company.[10] Many more English men and women had direct contact with the Mediterranean—whether through travel, or even more likely through encounters in England's port cities, of which London was the largest. By contrast, barely a few thousand had experience of life on the other side of the Atlantic until the mass migrations in the 1630s, and the numbers of Native American visitors to England pales in comparison to the number of visitors (and migrants) from Europe, North Africa, and the Levant.

The greater volume of English points of contact with these locations has been reflected in postcolonial approaches to literary study. While the Americas seemed to dominate the critical moment of the 1980s and early 1990s (around, that is, the run-up to the quincentennial), as Barbara Fuchs points out, in twenty-first century critical work on early modern literary geographies and encounters that moment has begun to feel like a "brief excursus."[11] Significant work has been done on drama and its presentations of various European peoples, most notably perhaps on the figures of the Spanish, the Irish, and the unlocatable figure of the Jew.[12]

---

[10] On the relationship between the large trading companies and the transatlantic companies, see Robert Brenner, "The Company Merchants and American Colonial Development," in *Merchants and Revolution: Commercial Change, Political Conflict, and London's Overseas Traders, 1550–1653* (Princeton, NJ: Princeton University Press, 1993), 92–112.

[11] Barbara Fuchs, "No Field Is an Island: Postcolonial and Transnational Approaches to Early Modern Drama," *Renaissance Drama*, 40 (2012): 125–33, at 125. Influential work on early modern literary geographies and encounters includes John Gillies, *Shakespeare and the Geography of Difference* (Cambridge: Cambridge University Press, 1994); essays in Jean-Pierre Maquerlot and Michèle Willems (eds), *Travel and Drama in Shakespeare's Time* (Cambridge: Cambridge University Press, 1996); essays in Andrew Gordon and Bernhard Klein (eds), *Literature, Mapping, and the Politics of Space in Early Modern Britain* (Cambridge: Cambridge University Press, 2001); Claire Jowitt, *Voyage Drama and Gender Politics 1589–1642: Real and Imagined Worlds* (Manchester: Manchester University Press, 2003).

[12] See Eric J. Griffin, *English Renaissance Drama and the Specter of Spain* (Philadelphia: University of Pennsylvania Press, 2009); essays in Margaret R. Greer, Maureen Quilligan, and Walter Mignolo (eds), *Rereading the Black Legend: The Discourses of Religious and Racial Difference in the Renaissance Empires* (Chicago, IL: University of Chicago Press, 2008); Christopher Highley, *Shakespeare, Spenser, and the Crisis in Ireland* (Cambridge: Cambridge University Press, 1997); essays in Brendan Bradshaw, Andrew Hadfield, and Willy Maley (eds), *Representing Ireland: Literature and the Origins of Conflict, 1534–1660* (Cambridge: Cambridge University Press, 1993); David J. Baker, *Between Nations: Shakespeare, Spenser,*

There has been, to quote Gerald MacLean, a "Re-Orienting" of the Renaissance in early modern literary studies, precipitated by critical work by Lisa Jardine, Jerry Brotton, and Nabil Matar.[13] This re-orientation urged a belated revisiting of Samuel Chew's influential exploration of the east–west, Christian–Muslim encounter in *The Crescent and the Rose*, which was first published in 1937 but left to stand as the unquestioned authority on dramatic representations of Islamic figures until the 1990s, long after the publication of Edward Said's *Orientalism* and its articulation of European "imaginative geographies" of "the Orient."[14] Since 2000 or so a number of critics have responded to these promptings, writing influential work on stage representations of Turks, Moors, Persians, and East Indians;[15] on anxieties of contact, conversion, and bodily and

*Marvell, and the Question of Britain* (Stanford, CA: Stanford University Press, 1997); Bernhard Klein, *Maps and the Writing of Space in England and Ireland* (New York: Palgrave MacMillan, 2001); Stephen O'Neill, *Staging Ireland: Representations in Shakespeare and Renaissance Drama* (Dublin: Four Courts Press, 2007); James Shapiro, *Shakespeare and the Jews* (New York: Columbia University Press, 1997); Janet Adelman, *Blood Relations: Christian and Jew in The Merchant of Venice* (Chicago, IL: University of Chicago Press, 2008).

[13] Gerald MacLean, "Introduction: Re-Orienting the Renaissance," in *Re-Orienting the Renaissance: Cultural Exchanges with the East* (London: Palgrave MacMillan, 2005), 1–28. See also Lisa Jardine, *Worldly Goods: A New History of the Renaissance* (London: MacMillan, 1996); Nabil Matar, *Islam in Britain, 1558–1685* (Cambridge: Cambridge University Press, 1998); Nabil Matar, *Turks, Moors, and Englishmen in the Age of Discovery* (New York: Columbia University Press, 1999); Lisa Jardine and Jerry Brotton, *Global Interests: Renaissance Art between East and West* (London: Reaktion Books, 2000); Jerry Brotton, *The Renaissance Bazaar: From the Silk Road to Michelangelo* (Oxford: Oxford University Press, 2002); and Nabil Matar, *Britain and Barbary 1589–1689* (Gainesville: University Press of Florida, 2005).

[14] Samuel Chew, *The Crescent and the Rose: Islam and England during the Renaissance* (Oxford: Clarendon, 1937); Edward W. Said, "II. Imaginative Geography and Its Representations: Orientalizing the Orient," *Orientalism: Western Conceptions of the Orient* (New York: Vintage, 1979), 49–73. On Chew's influence, and the "quite remarkable . . . lack of interest following the wide-ranging impact and influence of Edward Said's *Orientalism*," see Mark Hutchings, "Shakespeare and Islam: Introduction," *Shakespeare*, 4(2) (2008): 111–20, at 112; and Matthew Dimmock, *New Turkes: Dramatizing Islam and the Ottomans in Early Modern England* (Aldershot: Ashgate, 2005), esp. 5–13.

[15] See Richmond Barbour, *Before Orientalism: London's Theatre of the East, 1576–1626* (Cambridge: Cambridge University Press, 2003); Dimmock, *New Turkes*; Gerald MacLean, *Looking East: English Writing and the Ottoman Empire before 1800* (New York: Palgrave MacMillan, 2007); Jack D'Amico, *The Moor in English Renaissance Drama* (Tampa: University of South Florida Press, 1991); Michael Neill, "'Mulattos,' 'Blacks,' and 'Indian Moors': *Othello* and Early Modern Constructions of Human Difference," *Shakespeare Quarterly*, 49 (1998): 361–74; Michael Neill, "Material Flames: The Space of Mercantile Fantasy in John Fletcher's *The Island Princess*," *Renaissance Drama*, 28 (1999): 99–131; Emily C. Bartels, *Speaking of the Moor: From Alcazar to Othello* (Philadelphia: University of Pennsylvania Press, 2008); Ladan Niayesh, "Shakespeare's Persians," *Shakespeare*, 4(2) (2008): 137–47; Shankar Raman, *Framing India: The Colonial Imaginary in Early Modern Culture* (Stanford, CA: Stanford University Press, 2002).

spiritual contamination in east–west encounter;[16] and on the primary dramatic genre of encounter, tragicomedy (or romance).[17] The New World, once so fundamental to academic thinking about England's relationship with the world, has itself come to be marginalized in scholarship about early modern drama and the representation of alterity.[18]

Yet while it may be true that the theater seems to have been more inclined to represent other "foreign matters," that doesn't mean it was ultimately disinterested in the New World. Indeed, the three lost plays, *The New World's Tragedy*, *The Conquest of the West Indies*, and *The Plantation of Virginia*, suggest that the Americas were sufficiently interesting in the years of their performance (1595, 1601, and 1623 respectively) to merit theatrical productions.[19] These numbers are dwarfed by the sixty or so Turk and Moor plays: but this in and of itself does not mean that the New World was *un*interesting, even if the New World was *less* interesting. The Renaissance has (quite rightfully) been re-oriented, in acknowledgment not only of the considerable debt that so-called "Western" science, arts, and thought owe to "the East" but also of the place of Turks, Moors, Persians, and East Indians in English material and imaginative life. If the Americas were marginal and, *pace* Stallybrass and White, not necessarily symbolically central to English imaginative life, what place did they have? Indeed, when we are talking about the "wooden O"

---

[16] Daniel Vitkus, *Turning Turk: English Theater and the Multicultural Mediterranean, 1570–1630* (New York: Palgrave, 2003); Jonathan Gil Harris, *Sick Economies: Drama, Mercantilism, and Disease in Shakespeare's England* (Philadelphia: University of Pennsylvania Press, 2004); Jonathan Burton, *Traffic and Turning: Islam and English Drama, 1579–1624* (Newark: University of Delaware Press, 2005); Jane Hwang Degenhardt, *Islamic Conversion and Christian Resistance on the Early Modern Stage* (Edinburgh: Edinburgh University Press, 2010).

[17] Cyrus Mulready, "Romance on the Early Modern Stage," *Literature Compass*, 6(1) (2009): 113–27; Benedict Robinson, *Islam and Early Modern English Literature* (New York: Palgrave MacMillan, 2007); Zachary Lesser, "Tragical-Comical-Pastoral-Colonial: Economic Sovereignty, Globalization, and the Form of Tragicomedy," *English Literary History*, 74(4) (2007): 881–908; Michael Neill, "Turn and Counterturn: Merchanting, Apostasy and Tragicomic Form in Massinger's *The Renegado*," in Subha Mukherji and Raphael Lyne (eds), *Early Modern Tragicomedy* (Woodbridge: D. S. Brewer, 2007): 154–74; Valerie Forman, *Tragicomic Redemptions: Global Economics and the Early Modern English Stage* (Philadelphia: University of Pennsylvania Press, 2008).

[18] Bach's *Colonial Transformations*, Jowitt's *Voyage Drama*, and Jonathan Hart's *Columbus, Shakespeare, and the Interpretation of the New World* (along with more recent work by Jonathan Gil Harris and Jean Feerick) have been rare examples of scholarly work in early modern English literary studies with a considerable, albeit not exclusive, Atlantic and/or New World focus. Jonathan Hart, *Columbus, Shakespeare, and the Interpretation of the New World* (New York: Palgrave Macmillan, 2003).

[19] See David McInnis, "Lost Plays from Early Modern England: Voyage Drama, a Case Study," *Literature Compass*, 8(8) (2011): 534–42.

playhouse, or the disparate-yet-interconnected forms of daily life, what even constitutes centrality and marginality anyway?

## "WITH THESE AND MANY MORE AMUSEMENTS": LONDON'S NETWORKS, NEW WORLD KNOWLEDGE

To determine the place of the New World in English culture in the early modern period, we need to refine Stephen Greenblatt's influential but vague notion of "the circulation of social energy."[20] To do so, we need to determine the networks of knowledge and affiliation that connected the several publics invested in New World matters, and how London's theaters were situated within them.[21]

Within easy walking distance of the theaters were sites where Londoners could gain access to information about the various colonial projects— sites where we find intersections between the playing companies, the playhouses, and the transatlantic trading companies.[22] The bookstalls, especially those in St. Paul's Churchyard, situated right next to the Paul's Boys' playhouse, around a quarter of a mile west of the Blackfriars Theatre, just over a mile south of The Red Bull, and just the other side of The Thames from The Globe, The Rose, The Hope, and The Swan, were periodically littered with New World reading matter. This matter included the prestige publications of Richard Hakluyt and Samuel Purchas, in which accounts of travel to the Americas had a prominent place, alongside a range of tracts, ballads, and broadsides concerning and often promoting the New World. Many of these stalls housed both accounts of the New World and playbooks. In 1604, one year before publishing *Eastward Ho!* with Thomas Thorpe, William Aspley co-published the

---

[20] Stephen Greenblatt, "The Circulation of Social Energy," in *Shakespearean Negotiations*, 1–20.

[21] My use of the word "public," while having its origins in the work of Jürgen Habermas, is indebted to Bronwen Wilson and Paul Yachnin's definition of the emergent forms of public association in the early modern period as "the active creation that allowed people to connect with others in ways not rooted in family, rank, or vocation, but rather founded in voluntary groupings built on shared interests, tastes, commitments, and desires of individuals." Bronwen Wilson and Paul Yachnin, "Introduction," in *Making Publics in Early Modern Europe: People, Things, Forms of Knowledge* (New York: Routledge, 2010), 1–22.

[22] The connections I draw in this paragraph are drawn from my trawl through Edward Arber (ed.), *A Transcript of the Registers of the Company of Stationers of London 1554–1640 A.D*, 5 volumes (London, privately printed, 1875–94). But this approach to thinking through the contiguities of the bookstall, the print house, and the playhouse is heavily indebted to Zachary Lesser's work, especially *Renaissance Drama and the Politics of Publication: Readings in the English Book Trade* (Cambridge: Cambridge University Press, 2004).

first English translation of José de Acosta's *Historia natural y moral de las Indias*; thus browsers at his stalls at the signs of the Parrot and of the Tiger in 1605 could read a true account of a voyage to the New World alongside a fictional (and heavily satirical) one. Aspley's co-publisher of *Historia natural y moral* was Edward Blount, whose fame rests primarily in his involvement with Shakespeare's First Folio in 1623 but who was selling playbooks in the first decade of the seventeenth century, including George Chapman's *Sir Giles Goosecap* in 1605. A browser at Nathaniel Butter's bookstall at the sign of the Pied Bull, at the eastern end of St. Paul's Churchyard, in 1608 would have encountered Shakespeare's *King Lear*, Heywood's *If You Know Not Me, Part* 1, and Dekker's *The Whore of Babylon*, alongside John Nicholl's *An Houre Glasse of Indian Newes*, an account of the disastrous attempt to found a plantation in Guiana in 1605. A browser at Walter Burre's shops at the sign of the Crane or the sign of the Fleur-de-Luce in St. Paul's Churchyard in 1613 would have found William Strachey's *For the Colony of Virginea Britannia, Lawes Divine, Morall and Martial* (1612) alongside Beaumont's *The Knight of the Burning Pestle* (1613). Burre also published travel accounts and playbooks to be sold by John Stepney or Stepneth at his stall at the West End of St. Paul's Churchyard, including *A True and Sincere Declaration of the Purpose & End of the Plantation begun in Virginia* (1610), which attempted to set the record straight about the Virginia project, and Jonson's *The Alchemist* (1612), which included the dreamily erotic imaginings of "*novo orbe*" of Sir Epicure Mammon (2.1.2).[23] These books may have appealed to very different markets, but their co-existence on the same stalls indicates, at the very least, that many of the most prominent booksellers in London deemed both playbook and travel account marketable.

From the pulpits, located close by, and at most a few miles away from the theaters, famous preachers espoused the spiritual underpinnings of transatlantic investment and settlement. Daniel Price, chaplain to Prince Henry, delivered a sermon praising Virginia on May 25, 1609 at Paul's Cross, as part of a promotional campaign around the time of the Company's second charter. The following year, William Crashaw, preacher at Temple Church and father of the poet Richard, delivered a sermon to the assembled Virginia Company entitled *A New Yeeres Gift to Virginia*, prior to the departure of Lord de la Warr, the new governor of the colony. In an ill-timed sermon delivered at Bow Church in Cheapside on April 18, 1622, Patrick Copland prayed in thanks for the safe arrival of nine ships at

---

[23] Ben Jonson, *The Alchemist*, in David Bevington, Martin Butler, and Ian Donaldson (eds), *The Cambridge Edition of the Works of Ben Jonson*, vol. 3 (Cambridge: Cambridge University Press, 2012). All subsequent citations are from this edition.

Virginia the previous year, and concluded that there was "no Danger after their landing [at Jamestown], either through *warres*, or *famine*, or *want of conuenient lodging*."[24] Little did Copland know that on March 22 of the same year those new arrivals whose safe passage he celebrated had been decimated in the so-called "Indian massacre." John Donne delivered his impassioned sermon about the colony from the pulpit of St. Paul's on November 13, 1622, willing the assembled Company not to forget its religious mission, and to "[o]nely let your principall ende, bee the propagation of the glorious Gospell" despite the attacks of earlier in the year.[25] St. Paul's, Blackfriars, and Cheapside are adjacent to one another; Whitechapel Church is close to the Shoreditch Theatre: and all of the sermons mentioned here were printed and sold at the stalls of St. Paul's Yard.

The playhouse, the print house, bookstall, and pulpit all intersected with one another. Geographically they were proximate, but they also shared overlapping publics: the book-buyer, churchgoer, and playgoer were not necessarily all the same person, but all three sites marketed themselves towards all three types of consumer (with some notable exceptions, as we'll see in Chapter 1), and envisaged the possibility that all three types of consumers could be found in the same person, at the same place, and at the same time.

## "A REFORMATION IN ALL THEIR OTHER PLAYES": PLAYING COMPANIES, "FOREIGN MATTERS," STAGE CENSORSHIP

The connection between playhouse and New World matters can also be traced through the numerous points of intersection between playing company personnel and the Virginia Company. Sir Walter Cope, Company member, statesman, and curiosity collector was master to the actor Richard Burbage's brother Cuthbert, who along with his brother took a half-share in The Globe. Cope mounted a production of Shakespeare's *Love's Labour's Lost* for the entertainment of Queen Anne.[26] William Strachey, colonist and Secretary of the Virginia Company, was also a shareholder in the Children of the Revels, and in 1605 wrote

---

[24] Patrick Copland, *Virginia's God Be Thanked* (London: for William Sheffard and John Bellamie, 1622), 9.

[25] John Donne, "A Sermon Preached to the Honourable Company of the Virginian Plantation, November 13, 1622," in Neil Rhodes (ed.), *John Donne: Selected Prose* (Harmondsworth: Penguin, 1987), 197.

[26] See H. R. Woudhuysen, "Introduction," to William Shakespeare's *Love's Labour's Lost* (London: Thomson Learning, 2000), 83–5.

commendatory verse for the front matter of the quarto of Ben Jonson's *Sejanus*. Captain John Smith was a friend of the actor, playwright, and theatrical impresario Richard Gunnell; Gunnell wrote commendatory verse, "To that Worthy and generous Good Gentleman, my verie good friend, Captain Smith," for *A Description of New England* (printed in 1616), and also staged an early episode of Smith's life in *The Hungarian Lion* (1623; now lost).[27] The Sireniac Club, the group of intellectuals so often associated with Ben Jonson, also included Virginia Company members Edward Phelips, Christopher Brooke, and John Donne. Later in the century "The Wits," the group of courtier-poets who assembled in the orbit of Queen Henrietta Maria, included among their number playwrights and masque-writers William Davenant, Aurelian Townsend, and the future Governor of Virginia, William Berkeley, himself a playwright.

Many patrons of the playing companies and of individual playwrights were invested in New World settlement in one way or another. Prince Henry's Men (formerly the Admiral's Men) were named for one of the most prominent proponents of Virginia at court: known as "Patron of the Virginia Plantation," according to one observer he had put "some money in" the Virginia Company "so that he may, some day, when he comes to the crown have a claim over the colony."[28] George Chapman and Inigo Jones' collaboration *The Memorable Masque*, performed to honor the wedding of Henry's sister Elizabeth in 1613, also marked the young prince's passing the year before by incorporating Virginian themes, as Chapter 3 will explore in more detail. The Virginia Company's aristocratic members included Henry Wriostheley, the Earl of Southampton and patron of Shakespeare, William Herbert, 3rd Earl of Pembroke and patron of Jonson and one of the dedicatees of Shakespeare's First Folio, and the patron of John Fletcher, Francis Beaumont, and John Marston, Henry Hastings, 5th Earl of Huntingdon.

There were also connections between the overseas trading companies and the theaters. London's guilds hired playwrights like Thomas Middleton, John Webster, and Anthony Munday to pen their annual Lord Mayor's Shows, and many such guilds were prominent backers of the Virginia Company. Shows mounted at the inauguration of mayors from

---

[27] Richard Gunnell, "To that Worthy and generous Gentleman, my verie good friend, Captaine Smith," in John Smith, *A Description of New England*, reprinted in James Horn (ed.), *Capt. John Smith: Writings with Other Narratives of Roanoke, Jamestown, and the First English Settlement of America* (Washington, DC: Library of America, 2007), 128. On the various arguments about the play's representation of Smith's life, see <http://www.lostplays. org/index.php/Hungarian_Lion,_The>.

[28] Quoted in Tristan Marshall, *Theatre and Empire: Great Britain on the London Stages under James VI and I* (Manchester: Manchester University Press, 2000), 93, 136 n. 49.

the Company of Grocers incorporated New World themes, a reflection of the fact that the company was the highest contributor of all the London guilds to the Virginia Company to the tune of £487 10s.[29] Middleton's *The Tryumphs of Honor and Industry* (1617) was performed for the accession of Grocer George Bowles, a Virginia Company member, listed among the membership in 1609 while he was Sheriff of London: the pageant featured "A company of Indians, attired according to the true nature of their country, seeming for the most part naked."[30] Other pageants for mayors who were prominent in the Virginia Company, or whose companies had historic links with the New World (such as the Drapers, through their most famous son Sir Francis Drake) similarly incorporated American themes and Indian figures.[31]

These connections between courtly and civic authorities may make it seem surprising that there was no play mounted in support of the Virginia Company. After all, the East India Company—with whom the Virginia Company shared management personnel, including its Treasurer Sir Thomas Smyth—was behind two professional theatrical productions, Walter Mountfort's *The Launching of the Mary* (1632) and the anonymous, and eventually aborted, *Amboyna* (1625). That there is no Virginia equivalent may also make it tempting for us to imagine that (a fear of, or a realized) censorship was the reason for the absence of America. Early modern drama, subject to censorship (at state level, at company level, at personal levels), had to engage in absence by necessity, interweaving topical allusions into drama not otherwise obviously engaged with the world elsewhere.[32] But ultimately censorship seems an unlikely

---

[29] See Susan M. Kingsbury (ed.), *Records of the Virginia Company*, vol. 3 (Washington, DC: United States Government Printing Office, 1933), 80–90.

[30] Thomas Middleton, *The Tryumphs of Honor and Industry*, in Gary Taylor and John Lavagnino (eds), *Thomas Middleton: The Collected Works* (Oxford: Oxford University Press, 2007), lines 43–4. As editors David Bergeron and Kate D. Levin point out, the Indians could also signify the East Indies, as Bowles was prominent in the East India Company too.

[31] Sir Francis Drake featured in three Middleton shows, *The Sun in Aries* in 1621, *The Triumphs of Integrity* in 1623, and *The Triumphs of Health and Prosperity* in 1626. In Middleton's *The Triumphs of Honor and Vertue* (1622) the procession ended with a presentation of "the Throne of Virtue, and the Globe of Honour," the outermost parts of which showed "the world's type in countries, seas and shipping, whereon is depicted or drawn ships that have been fortunate to this kingdom by their happy and successful voyages; as also that prosperous plantation in the colony of Virginia, and the Bermudas, with all good wishes to the governors, traders and adventurers unto those Christianly reformed Islands." Thomas Middleton, *The Triumphs of Honor and Vertue*, in Taylor and Lavagnino, *Thomas Middleton: The Collected Works*, lines 239–70.

[32] On censorship and the English stage, see Annabel Patterson, *Censorship and Interpretation: The Conditions of Writing and Reading in Early Modern England* (Madison: University of Wisconsin Press, 1984); and Richard Burt, *Licensed by Authority: Ben Jonson and the Discourses of Censorship* (Ithaca, NY: Cornell University Press, 1993).

explanation for the absence of America. After all, we know that there were plays that touched on New World subject matters and, while they are now lost, there is little evidence to suggest that they were suppressed. The anonymous *The New World's Tragedy* was performed eleven times by the Admiral's Men at The Rose between September 1595 and April 1596, and *The Conquest of the West Indies* by John Day, William Haughton, and Wentworth Smith was performed six times by the Admiral's Men at The Fortune between April and September 1601. Even with *The Plantation of Virginia*, likely a dramatic representation of the 1622 attacks on the colony, which according to the records of the Master of the Revels was censored so that the "prophaness [was] left out," we find no evidence to suggest that the play was actively suppressed. We have no record of an actual performance, only that it was intended for The Curtain, but that in and of itself is no proof of suppression.[33] Indeed, the records state that the censor "founde fault with the lengthe" and "commanded a reformation in all their other playes" (i.e. the repertoire of whatever company it was that mounted *The Plantation of Virginia*).[34] That these plays existed, were performed, and even, in one case, attracted the attention of the Master of the Revels, would seem to argue against the idea that playwrights were actively self-censoring or that talk of the Americas was attracting state censorship.

Moreover, as A. B. Worden has argued, cases of censorship on the early modern stage were derived either from "an individual entertaining a personal grievance against a playwright, or holding the belief (not invariably devoid of vanity) that he had been mocked on stage," or from public entertainment becoming "entangled with the vagaries of international diplomacy."[35] The first cause could apply to the Virginia adventurer, whose behavior was mocked in a number of plays. The second cause would only apply if Virginia had been seen to be a matter of international diplomacy. For example, the aforementioned *Amboyna* was "stopped" when, according to Thomas Locke (in correspondence with Sir Dudley Carleton), "the [Privy] Council was appealed to by the Dutch

---

[33] N. W. Bawcutt (ed.), *The Control and Censorship of Caroline Drama: The Records of Sir Henry Herbert, Master of the Revels 1623–73* (Oxford: Oxford University Press, 1996), 141.

[34] Bawcutt, *Control and Censorship of Caroline Drama*, 42. G. E. Bentley speculates that the troupe "could have been one of those which normally played in the provinces but which was trying a London season." G. E. Bentley, *Jacobean and Caroline Stage*, 7 vols, vol. 5 (Oxford: Oxford University Press, 1956), 1396. See also the Lost Play Database entry: <http://www.lostplays.org/index.php/Plantation_of_Virginia,_The>.

[35] A. B. Worden, "Literature and Political Censorship in Early Modern England," in A. C. Duke and C. A. Tamse (eds), *Too Mighty to Be Free: Censorship and the Press in Britain and the Netherlands* (Zutphen: Walburg Pers, 1987), 45–62, at 49–50.

ministers."[36] So sensitive was the issue that "inflammatory references to the Amboyna massacre and other unfriendly acts of the Dutch" were removed from Mountford's *The Launching of the Mary* at Herbert's behest, even though the play was staged many years after the Amboyna massacre.[37] That references to Virginia were allowed to stand—even those in *Eastward Ho!*, which was subjected to changes in its second printing following complaints about anti-Scottish slurs—suggests that, unlike the East Indies, Virginia was not a foreign policy matter but rather an extension of domestic policy.

Allusions to Virginia appear despite the intersections between playing companies, overseas trading companies, and colonial advocates. While the figure of the Virginia adventurer resembled the spendthrift gallant and the bankrupt knight, as we'll see in Chapter 1, it did not resemble any particular figure, but rather drew on stage traditions that were evolving out of London-based comedy. If Sir Walter Cope, William Strachey, John Smith, the Earl of Southampton, the Earl of Huntingdon, the Earl of Pembroke, Mayor George Bowles, or Sir Thomas Smyth felt themselves to be personally slighted by the characterization of the Virginia Company adventurer in the theaters, they kept it to themselves. And, as Worden suggests, domestic topicality was not subject to censorship. Worden's observation here is especially useful when we consider how often Virginia is invoked in terms of London, often in London-based plays.

## VIRGINIA AND THE LONDON CITY COMEDY

The theaters were part of London's networks of New World knowledge and interest, but they were not merely passive receptors of this knowledge. As a number of critics have argued, the theater cultivated a sense of itself both as a gathering place for an informed public and as an information hub for its gathered public. Through asides, inside jokes, and shared allusions it presupposed an audience that was knowledgeable about the life of the city, about the city's relationship to "foreign matters"—matters of state, matters of trade—and about "the world elsewhere." That is to say, it presupposed an audience able to decipher its deployment of theater-grams and theatermemes.

[36] Mary Anne Everett Green (ed.), "Locke to Carleton, Feb 12, 1625," *Calendar of State Papers, Domestic Series, of the Reign of James I. 1623–1625, with Addenda* (London: Longman, Brown, Green, Longmans, and Roberts, 1859), 481.

[37] Bentley, *Jacobean and Caroline Stage*, vol. 4, 924. See also <http://www.lostplays.org/index.php/Amboyna>.

That is not to say that playgoers were necessarily *au fait* with such foreign matters. As Jean Howard suggests, theater appealed because it was a site where playgoers could familiarize themselves with London, with a great many plays operating as instructional guides for navigating a city in constant flux.[38] Also, by going to the theater, the playgoer formed part of a public that performed a sense of its own knowledgeability through its ability to interpret theatergrams and theatermemes (even if that knowledge was acquired on attending the playhouse, or even if that sense was cultivated without any actual acquisition of knowledge). Different theaters and different playing companies attracted and cultivated different kinds of public. As Mary Bly has argued, the King's Revels Children at Whitefriars performed plays constituted around its queer public through the deployment of homoerotic puns across its repertoire.[39] While the King's Revels provides us with a rare instance of a company whose repertoire has survived in its entirety, the cultivation of a house style can be detected in other theaters and with other playing companies too, as we've seen in vital work by (among others) Roslyn Knutson, Scott McMillin and Sally-Beth MacLean, Andrew Gurr, and Lucy Munro.[40] Moreover, different genres were also involved in the cultivation of the knowledgeable playgoer. As Adam Zucker argues, "Dramatic comedy always depends on the distances separating those in the know from those who stand in definitive contrast to them;" the genre navigates "the increasing complexity of sociability," and assumes an audience that will get the distinctions between and within certain types of persons.[41] That is, kinds of drama distinguished between their public (who got the joke) and their non-public (often the butt of the joke).

It would be difficult to claim with any surety that any one playing company or any one playhouse was associated with New World matters. Theatermemes on the prodigality of Virginia adventurers can be found in Cooke's *Greene's Tu Quoque* at the relatively inexpensive outdoor venue The Red Bull (1611) and Jonson's *Epicene* at the more expensive indoor

---

[38] See Jean E. Howard, *Theater of a City: The Places of London Comedy, 1598–1642* (Philadelphia: University of Pennsylvania Press, 2007).

[39] Mary Bly, *Virgin Queers and Virgin Queans on the Early Modern Stage* (Oxford: Oxford University Press, 2000).

[40] Roslyn Knutson, *The Repertory of Shakespeare's Company, 1594–1613* (Fayetteville: University of Arkansas Press, 1991); Scott McMillin and Sally-Beth MacLean, *The Queen's Men and Their Plays* (Cambridge: Cambridge University Press, 1998); Andrew Gurr, *The Shakespeare Company* (Cambridge: Cambridge University Press, 2004); Lucy Munro, *Children of the Queen's Revels: A Jacobean Theatre Repertory* (Cambridge: Cambridge University Press, 2005).

[41] Adam Zucker, *The Places of Wit in Early Modern English Comedy* (Cambridge: Cambridge University Press, 2011), 1.

Whitefriars (1609). Theatermemes on the lustiness of Virginia adventurers can be found in Middleton and Dekker's *The Roaring Girl* (The Fortune, 1611), in Taylor's *The Hog Hath Lost His Pearl* (Whitefriars, 1613), and in Fletcher's *The Loyal Subject* (Blackfriars and The Globe, 1618). The New World, then, was not associated with a particular house or company style. Rather, there seems to have been a vocabulary of American reference points shared through theatergrams and theatermemes by writers, playing companies, and with the audiences, and, by extension, across London itself.

Genre, however, seems to be more of a common link between these plays. As a number of critics have pointed out, the dramatic genre that most seemed to engage with "the nature of the early modern economy in an age of increasing globalization" was romance or tragicomedy.[42] Interestingly enough, two of the three lost New World plays, *The New World's Tragedy* and *The Plantation of Virginia*, were tragedies. However, a great many of the plays that feature New World theatergrams and theatermemes are London-based comedies. Jonson, Chapman, and Marston's *Eastward Ho!* (1605), Jonson's *Bartholomew Fair* (1614), Massinger's *The City Madam* (1632), and Jasper Mayne's *The City Match* (1639) are set in London; their Virginian coordinates mark out certain London character types (the *nouveau riche* merchant, the prodigal, the citizen wife, the bankrupt knight). Even plays which feature New World theatergrams and theatermemes that are not London-set but instead seem to draw more on the traditions of tragicomedy and romance seem to attach these reference points to London, in episodes that recall certain London phenomena (such as Trinculo's remembrance of the dead Indian in *The Tempest* or the Porter's recollection of the visit of an Indian in *Henry VIII*), in references to London prodigality, or in characters that seem to draw heavily on the types of London comedy (in particular the bankrupt knight, versions of which can be found in Massinger and Fletcher's *The Sea Voyage* and alluded to in Fletcher's *The Noble Gentleman*). All of which is to say that, while the theater cultivated a sense of a playgoer knowledgeable about the New World—voicing allusions and jokes that were shared across the playhouses and outside the playhouse—it attached this knowledge to an emergent sense of London itself.

That London city comedies, or plays that invoke the genre of London city comedy, engaged in the Americas and Virginia in particular, reflects

---

[42] Lesser, "Tragical-Comical-Pastoral-Colonial," 883. See also Mulready, "Romance on the Early Modern Stage," Neill, "Turn and Counterturn"; Forman, *Tragicomic Redemptions*.

the city's increased interest in New World foreign matters and the ways in which the theater was a place where such information could be circulated. But the fact that London city comedy seems so closely involved in New World foreign matters, and that London comedy seems so markedly invested in troubling desires of personal transformation, allows us to understand why the Virginia Company found so much to object to in the conduct of the players. On the one hand, the move towards the New World—imagined as spatial and sociological movement—becomes emblematic of the kind of transformation that London city comedy habitually satirizes and oftentimes rejects. That is, the spatial and socio-logical movement of many London types to whom New World tropes are attached signifies their undoing or unmaking, in ways that are analogous to the undoing and unmaking that was rumored to be occurring in the New World. On the other, while there are those characters to whom Virginia memes are attached and who are successful in their scheming, the form of their success counters the transformative capacities of Virginia—as promoted by the Company—because it does not rely on hard work and religious contemplation but on quick wits and a flexible moral compass. They succeed, that is, not because of any internal transformation, but often because of some outward transformation, frequently via some form of theatrical turn.

There may be no extant play *about* the New World, but there are several plays which allude to London's *relationship* to the New World. While Londoners may have been preoccupied with New World dream-ings, or dismissive of New World realities, few had any direct contact with life on the other side of the Atlantic. Thus the New World, for all that it was a distant and almost fantastical place, was imagined in localized terms and invoked as a way of understanding the city as much as the colony. By placing the New World within the context of London life, the theater made the New World familiar. It attached tropes of the New World to already recognizable types that had their origins in London city comedy of the late 1590s. Even if these types were exaggerated, they were also legible as types, drawn from the social life of the city at least to the extent that audiences recognized and laughed at them. The theater did not make the New World the desirable place that its proponents wished—the types attached to the Americas in the theater were both undesirable and also not capable of or interested in the transformations that were projected for the colonists in Virginia Company propaganda. But the theater did bring the New World across the Atlantic and, arguably, made it possible for its audiences to imagine it not as a site that conformed to the Virginia Company's imaginings but rather as a site that looked a lot like home.

## THE WALLS OF NEHEMIAH

For all the information swelling around London about the Americas, to an early modern public the New World was not a clearly defined or "mapped" space. Contact was mediated by a variety of forms of cultural production or by displays of peoples and things removed from their context. In a sense, then, America was *already* absent to the English public—even moments of contact were disassociated from their contact zones and reconstituted. The word "America" had considerable elasticity, skating up and down the eastern seaboard and sometimes the western coast too, as did the nominally more geographically specific Virginia, New England, Guiana, and Norumbega; and the other name most often applied, the Indies, was even baggier, taking in south, east, and west cardinal points. This looseness of terminology may in part explain why the word America (or Virginia, New England, Guiana, Norumbega, or even the Indies) was so unstable in the period—after all, what point on the map were audiences expected to imagine when these places were invoked? To limn "the picture of America" becomes a troubled undertaking—indeed, the phrase "the picture of America" that I have been using in this introduction comes from John Fletcher's *The Knight of Malta* and is used to describe Abdella, a Moorish waiting woman (also described as "Black Jill") who is the play's chief antagonist, which should give some idea of the promiscuity of terms.[43] Moreover, the sheer enormity of the Americas reflected their unknowability. They were, to borrow from Justice Overdo in *Bartholomew Fair*, associated with "wonders of enormity" (2.2.95).[44] In their multiple, overlapping, sometimes contradictory iterations, they were conceived of as being so vast and unfathomable (in terms of corruption, vice, folly, wealth, plenitude, and sensual and sexual pleasures) that they could not be comprehended, let alone represented. Indeed, the Americas often stand as a metaphor for an excess in scale or for an unattainable longing.

When we think about the representation of alterities and geographies in early modern drama, we immediately stumble over the following question: how can we tell what constitutes representation? At least sixty plays and dramatic entertainments featured Islamic characters and staged

---

[43] John Fletcher, *The Knight of Malta*, in Fredson Bowers (ed.), *The Dramatic Works in the Beaumont and Fletcher Canon*, vol. 8 (Cambridge: Cambridge University Press, 1992), 5.2.186–7.

[44] Ben Jonson, *Bartholomew Fair*, in Bevington et al., *The Cambridge Edition of the Works of Ben Jonson*, vol. 4. All subsequent citations are from this edition.

Christian–Islamic conflict, yet to speak of a Turkish and Islamic "presence" on stage is oxymoronic, since (as Dympna Callaghan reminds us) no Turks were required to play themselves, nor were Africans, the indigenous Irish, or any other non-English figure to the best of our knowledge.[45] There are plays set in far-flung places—Europe, the Mediterranean, the Levant, Persia, Africa, to name but a few—yet even the most geographically specific of plays repeatedly reminds its audiences of its location in a London playhouse. Early modern drama oscillates between presence and absence, bringing onto the stage what is clearly *not there* by means of words, bodies, and things that *are there*. We would probably be right to conclude that all drama, regardless of the period of its first performance, engages in this oscillation of absence and presence: nevertheless, we might safely say that early modern drama repeatedly and self-consciously engaged in this oscillation.

Just because America was by and large absent from the early modern stage does not mean that early modern drama—and by extension early modern culture—was not informed by America: just because the effect of America on drama is not obvious does not mean that there was no effect whatsoever. I am guided here by Walter Cohen, who argues, "For Renaissance literature a crucial meaning of European imperialism—especially intercontinental or overseas imperialism *and above all American imperialism*—was accordingly registered in nonrepresentational terms. Rather than directly depicting distant lands, the literature of the time often drew implicit lessons from the enlarged theater of European operations in its treatment of ostensibly unrelated matters."[46] I steer in Cohen's wake in this book by applying his approach across a whole genre, drama, particularly plays which were performed in London playhouses by professional playing companies in the sixteenth and seventeenth centuries up until the outbreak of the English Civil War. I question what is meant by representation by applying Cohen's notion of "the logic of imperial nonrepresentation" to a theater that employed minimal scenery—that is, one which did not employ mimetic visual representation and relied instead on words, bodies, costumes and prostheses, properties, and the theater itself to structure its geographies.

By privileging drama as a "site of absence" in this study I do not mean to dismiss the importance of other forms of cultural production. I focus on drama because of its mass appeal in the late sixteenth and seventeenth centuries and its capacity to reach multiple publics—people invested in early colonial enterprise, people fascinated by overseas exploits, and people

---

[45] See Dympna Callaghan, *Shakespeare without Women* (London: Routledge, 1999), 2.
[46] Cohen, "The Literature of Empire in the Renaissance," 4–5. The italics are Cohen's.

hostile to or unmoved by events in the Atlantic world. I focus on drama as well because of the ways in which the theater staged its own theatricality and foregrounded its own ability, and inability, to represent things, people, and places. As Jean-Christophe Agnew writes, in the early modern period "theatricality itself had begun to acquire renewed connotations of invisibility, concealment, and *mis*representation, connotations that were at once intriguing and incriminating."[47] The theater was "a laboratory of representational possibilities": its drama employed theatrical tropes such as disguise (cross-cultural, cross-gender, cross-rank), featured characters who broke out of the scene of action to comment on that scene or on events that had no connection with that scene, and constructed settings in such a way that a single play could gesture to a variety of (often incongruous) locations simultaneously, as well as foreground the fact that it was taking place in a theater in London.[48]

To explain further, let us return to the prayer with which this introduction began, and in particular its articulation of anti-theatrical fervor in relation to "Sanballat, & Tobiah, Papists & players, & such other Ammonites & Horonites," a reference to figures from the Book of Nehemiah in the Old Testament. Nehemiah's account of his governorship of Judea under the benign rule of the Persian king Artaxerxes, and his reconstruction of the walls of Jerusalem, forms an obvious corollary with the Virginia Company, who operated under the patronage of James I and were attempting to build the Holy City anew in the swamps of Jamestown. The siege mentality evinced by Nehemiah's account—the Jews were plagued both by heathen outsiders and by their own numbers, some of whom were less than sure about the wisdom of Nehemiah's plans for urban renewal—resembles distinctly the "us against them" rhetoric that pervades much colonialist propaganda. The Virginia Company also found important corollaries in the examples of Nehemiah's opponents, Tobiah the Ammonite and his servant Sanballat the Horonite, who, upon hearing about the rebuilding project, were "grieved . . . exceedingly that there was come a man to seek the welfare of the children of Israel" and "laughed us to scorn, and despised us, and said, What [is] this thing that ye do?" (2.10.19).[49] Rather than launch a military campaign against the city, they attempt to infiltrate it: "They shall not know, neither see, till we come in the midst among them, and slay them, and cause the

---

[47] Jean-Christophe Agnew, *Worlds Apart: The Market and the Theater in Anglo-American Thought, 1550–1750* (Cambridge: Cambridge University Press, 1986), 40.

[48] Agnew, *Worlds Apart*, 54.

[49] Stephen Pritchett and Robert Cornwall (eds), *The Bible: Authorized King James Version* (Oxford: Oxford University Press, 1997). All citations to the Bible are from this edition.

work to cease" (4.11). The violence threatened is quelled repeatedly during the construction project—when the city and its inhabitants are at its most vulnerable—and upon completing the walls, Nehemiah and the prophet Ezra pointedly exclude the Ammonites from Jerusalem because of their enmity towards Jews. However, after a period of absence Nehemiah returns to find that Eliashib, a priest, has consorted with Tobiah and allowed him into the temple, and that the Jews have inter-married with Ammonites and Moabites. Nehemiah casts them out: "Thus cleansed I them from all strangers, and appointed the wards of the priests and the Levites, every one in his business" (13.30).

To extend the Jamestown prayer's metaphor, the jealousy driven Ammonites and Horonites who plot against the Jews and attempt to infiltrate and take over the Holy City—all defused by Nehemiah's actions—are like the players, who have been driven to badmouth the colony because they have been excluded from its holy mission. This parallel is made explicit by William Crashaw in his sermon of 1610, in which he accused the players of being jealous because while the Virginia Company "send of all trades to Virginea" they "will send no Players" (this will be explored further in Chapter 1).[50]

The parallel between the Ammonites and Horonites and the players, and the underpinning logic of the Book of Nehemiah, has even greater resonance if we consider the importance of walls to Nehemiah's project, and the repeated desires of his opponents to surmount them, destroy them, or render them obsolete. Rather than lay siege to the walls, Nehemiah's enemies try to pass as Jews, attempting to sneak past the barrier erected to keep them out rather than acknowledging that barrier by attacking it from without. The transgressions committed by Eliashib, and by the men and women who intermarried, were intolerable to Nehemiah because they broke down the symbolic valence of the walls. While they remained erect during his absence from the city, in effect they had decayed to the same extent as from before the building project, because strangers had been let in. In all instances, then, Tobiah, Sanballat, and the other opponents were attempting to destroy the wall—not by tearing it down brick by brick but rather attacking it with scorn and then by polluting the stock and hence disregarding the power of the wall to signify distinction between inside and out.

Consider, then, the relationship between players and walls. As Steven Mullaney argues in *The Place of the Stage*, early modern drama made considerable cultural capital out of the relationship between London's

[50] William Crashaw, *A New-Yeeres Gift to Virginea* (London: for William Welby, 1610), H4. All subsequent citations are taken from this edition.

walls and the liberties in which the majority of the theaters were located. London comedies regularly fixate on the relationship between the city and its emergent environs—Jonson, for example, sets the majority of his London comedies in areas immediately adjacent to the walls and, in the case of *The Alchemist*, in the liberty of Blackfriars.[51] Yet as Garrett A. Sullivan, Jr. suggests, Mullaney's influential interpretation of the relationship between the city and its liberties fails "to accommodate the wide range of sociospatial practices that constitute a city."[52] As Janette Dillon argues, however much "Cities... want to be worlds apart, ... the boundaries are never as firmly fixed as cities want them to be, and individuals experience the spaces of the city and not-city in ways that are more fluid than walls, laws and rituals might seem to indicate."[53] If we emphasize the symbolic resonance of London's walls, and the theater's relationship to those walls, we can overlook the ways that spatial practice (to channel Henri Lefebvre, as do both Sullivan and Dillon) undermines that symbolic power and "renders its purported coherence increasingly illusory."[54] We see the symbolic coherence of civic space, represented through walls (of the house or of the city), come undone repeatedly in a range of plays from this period in which characters scale, cross, or walk right through walls.[55] Even *The Alchemist*, so bound up in its setting within the city walls in Lovewit's house closed up against the plague, can't help but represent the ways in which the boundaries of civic space are systematically transgressed in the process of daily life.

At its very core, drama has to ignore walls—how else can you begin a play without someone puncturing the space by entering it? And more particularly, early modern drama reveled in the fact that it had no fixed points of demarcation between play and playgoer—to employ an anachronism, it had no fourth wall. Both anti-theatrical and pro-theatrical debaters shared the idea that words in drama ran between "stage world" and "non-stage world" through the liminal space of the "*platea*," to use Robert Weimann's famous formulation, so that even those words spoken at the margins of the play outside the context of the immediate stage world (which may seem rather incidental, especially to our ears) had an effect in

[51] See James Mardock, *Our Scene Is London: Ben Jonson's City and the Space of the Author* (New York: Routledge, 2008).

[52] Garrett A. Sullivan, Jr., *The Drama of Landscape: Land, Property, and Social Relations on the Early Modern Stage* (Stanford, CA: Stanford University Press, 1998), 201–2.

[53] Janette Dillon, *Theatre, Court, and City 1595–1610: Drama and Social Space in London* (Cambridge: Cambridge University Press, 2000), 97.

[54] Dillon, *Theatre, Court, and City*, 206; Henri Lefebvre, *The Production of Space*, trans. Donald Nicholson-Smith (Oxford: Blackwell, 1991), at 33.

[55] See Dillon, *Theatre, Court, and City*, esp. chapter 5, "Placing the Boundaries," 96–109.

shaping the attitudes and even behavior of the auditors.[56] Indeed, early modern drama's active engagement of its audience's capacity to "piece out" with its "thoughts," most famously voiced in the first chorus of Shakespeare's *Henry V* (Prologue, 23), but implicit throughout much of the drama of this period, meant that what we might now consider at the periphery was in some senses the point of contact between the world invoked by a play and the world outside that play.[57]

It is in this periphery where theatergrams and theatermemes transmit knowledge to and/or cultivate a sense of the knowledgeable playgoer. As we'll find over the course of this book, the most damning invective directed against colonization circulated in theatergrams and theatermemes that breached the walls of the stage world and penetrated the non-stage world. The allusions to Nehemiah that we find in the prayer and elsewhere in Virginia Company propaganda strike me as not coincidental. That the players were Ammonites and Horonites, both scorning the walls and performing their insignificance, seems fitting: as far as the advocates of colonization were concerned, the Virginia Company, from investors like William Crashaw to the court of guard manning the Jamestown garrison, were attempting to set down the walls of the colony. The colony was being established (at least rhetorically) through the setting of the boundary and the building of the wall between "theirs" and "ours."[58] By contrast, the players, no strangers to dissolving fixed barriers, did not so much tear down these walls as deny their very existence, and speak instead from the place between the walls about the follies of the Company, the settlers, the investors, and of the very idea of the colony itself.

## THE WORK AHEAD

This book places dramatic, non-dramatic, "literary," and "non-literary" texts in contact with one another both to see what knowledge about America circulated between various genres of writing and performance

[56] Weimann articulates the relationship between the *locus* and *platea* in "Shakespeare's Theater: Tradition and Experiment," in *Shakespeare and the Popular Tradition in the Theater: Studies in the Social Dimension of Dramatic Form and Tradition*, ed. Robert Schwartz (Baltimore, MD: Johns Hopkins University Press, 1978), 208–60.

[57] Stephen Greenblatt, Walter Cohen, Jean E. Howard, and Katherine Eisaman Maus (eds), *The Norton Shakespeare*, 2nd edition (New York: W. W. Norton, 2008). All subsequent citations to Shakespeare plays are taken from this edition, unless specified otherwise.

[58] See Patricia Seed, "Houses, Gardens and Fences: Signs of English Possession on the New World," in *Ceremonies of Possession in Europe's Conquest of the New World 1492–1640* (Cambridge: Cambridge University Press, 1995), 16–40.

and also to reconstruct, where possible, what was lost as this knowledge was transmitted. It views its materials through a range of theoretical lenses that evolve out of interpretations of absence, in particular work on gender, sexuality, and race. It is indebted to work on early modern conceptions of the body, and argues that advocates of colonization claimed that the masculine English body would thrive in the New World, by displaying various native masculine bodies "of great stature"—arguments that were frequently undone by stories about the devolution of English colonists into "worse-than" New World savages. As its interest in the display of native bodies suggests, the book also reads these texts through the lens of race and ethnic studies, in terms of how indigenous bodies were read in comparison to English bodies, in terms of how those bodies were gendered, and in terms of how pigmentation and coloration were interpreted in the period as markers both of similitude and difference. The manifestation of American Indians on stage only through the trope of native disguise points us to the relationship between matter and ethnicity. Dramatic difference was constituted in terms of property and prostheses, which could be detached and removed from the body once the use had been served. As this last example suggests, the book is informed by work on the ways in which clothing and material culture both constitute and de-constitute identity.

The book is in two parts: Part I emphasizes the figure of the Virginia Company adventurer; Part II emphasizes the figure of the Virginian Indian. In Chapter 1, entitled "The Devil, the Papist, the Player: The Virginia Company's Anti-Theatricalism," I analyze the Virginia Company's accusations that the players were the enemy of Virginia on a par with the Devil and the papist. Since the Company's work was God's work, the players were automatically in league with the Devil and the papists. Since the Company emphasized the necessary labors of the colony, the players' encouragement of idleness was anathematic to its work ethic. While heavily indebted to the anti-theatrical tradition, the Company's insistence on the players being diabolical, papist, and idle takes on renewed significance in the context of Virginia, precisely because the image of the adventurer as craven bankrupt, as perpetuated in theater-memes across a range of plays, chimed with two other types that were invested in New World exploration: the Spaniard, who like the Virginia adventurer was allured by the promise of riches and ease, and who was both Catholic and, in English eyes, diabolical; and the player, who debunked the Virginia Company imagining of adventurer as transformed "new man." That is, while the Virginia Company distinguished between the ideal adventurer and the unholy trinity of Devil, papist, and player, plays collapsed the adventurer, Devil, papist, and player into one another.

Through analyses of both Jonson's *Bartholomew Fair* (1614), which unfavorably compares Virginia adventuring and the experience of play-going, and of the promotion and ubiquity of tobacco in playhouse drama, we might begin to think of the playing companies as constructing and even celebrating a vision of the New World as anti-Virginian, albeit not anti-colonial.

Chapter 2, "Plantation and 'the Powdered Wife,'" traces the dissemin-ation of rumors of cannibalism during Virginia's "starving time," and in particular a story of a husband who killed, dismembered, and ate his wife, and places them in conjunction with the commonplace of "never marry-ing as if you were going to Virginia." The chapter analyzes the voicing of this aphoristic theatermeme in Dekker and Middleton's *The Roaring Girl* (1611), in which the title character's warning to a suitor that he should choose his wife with more consideration is surrounded with cannibalistic imagery. It argues that this moment draws parallels between the plight of women in the colony and the intemperance of the colonial project itself. It also analyzes the iteration of the theatermeme in Jonson, Chapman, and Marston's *Eastward Ho!* (1605), where a female character is an unwilling guest at a ritual feast for Virginia-bound voyagers which threatens to turn into a cannibal slaughter; and in Massinger and Fletcher's *The Sea Voyage* (1622), where momentarily both shipwrecked gallants and shipwrecked women turn to cannibalism, a re-imagining not only of the starving time but also of recent colonial policies regarding marriage, shareholding, and plantation. Chapter 2 concludes by considering what happened to the story from the 1620s onwards following the 1622 "Indian massacre": following the attacks on the colony, the rhetoric of cannibalism came to be grafted onto the figure of the Indian, while the marriage dyad came to operate as a guarantee of the colony's survival rather than a source of anxiety about whether it would consume itself.

Chapter 3, 'The Dead Indian," focuses on the impact of George Chapman's *Memorable Masque* of 1613, in particular how its display of Christianized "Virginian priests and princes" (actually Englishmen in costume) was parodied in three plays performed in the same year, all of which circulated the theatermeme of the displayed Indian. Fletcher and Field's *Four Plays, or Moral Interludes, in One* employs the same motifs and characters as Chapman's masque, but excises its conversion plot, staging Indians in thrall to lucre and the converting colonist as a lost soul. Shakespeare and Fletcher's *Henry VIII* re-imagines Chapman's Vir-ginian princes when it invokes the "strange Indian with the great tool," a figure who instead of inspiring charity invokes only lust and greed—his evocation forming part of a chain of signification in the play where India and Indians are both desired and abhorred. Finally, Chapter 3 analyzes *The Tempest* (which was revived at court in 1613), and in particular Trinculo's recollection of the "dead Indian" that wowed England. Trinculo's memory forms part of the play's satire of both *The Memorable Masque* and the Virginia Company's rhetoric of conversion as embodied in their display of Virginian bodies, and reveals both as serving up little more than dead metaphors.

Chapter 4, "He would not goe naked like the *Indians*, but cloathed just as one of our selves," analyzes drama which employs the theatergram of European males dressing up and disguising themselves as American Indians (what I call "alterity-as-disguise"). The Indian disguise theatergram drew attention to the colonial project of clothing (a metaphor for conversion) while also stressing the impossibility of converting the infidel, because clothing (both attachable and detachable) was both a marker of identity and an index of the inscrutability of identity. While Robert Greene's *Orlando Furioso* seems to suggest that the Indian could be co-opted by the English and become a civilized advocate for imperialism against the Spanish, Philip Massinger's *The City Madam* and the anonymous *The Fatal Marriage* argue for the futility of this mission, because the Indians used clothing to mask their allegiances rather than as a token of their allegiance to the English.

In the book's Afterword, "Scene: Virginia," I explore commercial drama from the interregnum and early Restoration periods, when colonies and colonizers began to be staged in the London playhouses. While these staging practices were innovative—indeed, William Davenant sold his compendium play, *The Playhouse to Be Let* (1663), on the strength of its ability to represent multiple locations in lavish detail—these plays also show the persistence of certain New World memes that we first see in drama pre-1642. We find talk of cannibalism, talk of Indian display and the futility of the religious mission, and talk of the prodigal Virginia adventurer, which suggests that such preoccupations had a considerable afterlife. Here also we find a genre shift: if the plays before the Civil War that tackled New World foreign matters were London comedies, or drew on associations with that genre, from Davenant's *The Cruelty of the Spaniards in Peru* onwards, New World drama drew from the emerging "heroic drama" genre, as defined by John Dryden. Yet when drama represented the English in the New World, it either prophesized their arrival in some imagined future (and did not stage them) or fell back on London comedy typologies. Thus Aphra Behn's depiction of Virginia, *The Widow Ranter* (1689), with which this book closes, combines both the Dryden model of heroic drama—in its depiction of its anti-hero,

Nathaniel Bacon, and of the Susquehanna Indians—and the London comedy model—in its depiction of the Virginian colonists, many of whom are venal and corrupt. While the earlier drama used Virginia as a way of explaining or enhancing certain London types, in Behn's play, London types are employed, with subtle variations, as a way of making legible a new type of character: the Virginian.

# PART I

# ADVENTURERS AND CANNIBALS

# 1

# The Devil, the Papist, the Player

## The Virginia Company's Anti-Theatricalism

Why are *The Players* enemies to this plantation and doe abuse it?

> William Crashaw, *A New-Yeeres Gift*

So, this goes better forward than the plantation in Virginia—but see, here comes half the west Indies, whose rich mines this night I mean to be ransacking.

> Robert Tailor, *The Hog Hath Lost His Pearl*

The Virginia Company regarded religion as both integral to its mission and what distinguished its allies from its enemies. In his sermon to the assembled Virginia Company in February 1610, William Crashaw defined the Company's friends as those who supported its mission of conversion ahead of their own "*priuate ends*" and "*priuate plots*."[1] He grouped its enemies in an unholy trinity of Devil, papist, and player:

> [F]or who but the *Diuell*, and *Papists*, and *Players* doe mocke at religion, and abuse the holie Scriptures? That the *Diuell* doth, who doubts? that the Papists doe, their many bookes doe witness, especially their damnable and hellish *Prurit-anus*: that *Players* doe, too many eyes and eares can witnesse, some to their content, and many to their hearts griefe. Seeing then they will not be separated, let them goe together: the rather seeing they bee all enemies to this noble action.[2]

In Crashaw's estimation, the players mocked Virginia's religious underpinnings to the amusement of some, to the despair of others, and above all to "too many" spectators and auditors. Their mockery amounted to an assault on the godly enterprise that was the Virginia project, in alliance with its other (im)mortal enemies, and was intended to bring about the destruction of the colony and, as a result, the diminution of the English nation.

---

[1] Crashaw, *New-Yeeres Gift*, G2v.
[2] Crashaw, *New-Yeeres Gift*, Hv. *Pruritanus* was a Catholic libel against English royalty since the Act of Supremacy, in circulation in 1609.

While complaints such as Crashaw's about the players' mockery are prevalent in the early seventeenth century, allusions to Virginia in the drama of the same period (few that they are) do not seem to target religion. Instead, Virginia is imagined in a series of theatermemes as a colony that attracted adventurers (a term that could be applied to both investor and settler) who were driven thither out of financial desperation, sexual desire, or a combination of the two. Adventurer theatermemes appear in a number of plays, as we will see, and first collect in Jonson, Chapman, and Marston's *Eastward Ho!* (1605), the play often understood to have been in Crashaw's crosshairs.[3] In the play Sir Petronel Flash, Seagull, Scapethrift, and Spendall attempt to escape their financial woes in London by voyaging to Virginia: they have heard tell that in Virginia "gold is more plentiful than copper is" (3.3.18), that there "you may come to prefer-ment" (38), and that there they will be afforded a generous welcome by the Indians who are "so in love" (15–16) with the English.[4] To be sure, mocking adventurers as gold-hungry desperadoes derogated the Com-pany's work. Examples such as the *Eastward Ho!* adventurers could have been seen to encourage investment and settlement in Virginia solely for financial and social advancement and discourage those who might support its proselytizing agenda. However, it does not seem immediately obvious how the playing companies were targeting the religious aspects of colon-ization through propagating these theatermemes. Indeed, the religious mission seldom features in the early modern drama of this period: it is a focal point of Philip Massinger's *The City Madam*, but this play was not performed until 1632, over two decades after Crashaw delivered his sermon against the players. So what was it about the adventurer theater-memes that antagonized the likes of William Crashaw and made them believe that the players were attacking the Virginia Company mission on religious grounds? What did they hear in the mockery of the adventurers that we do not?

If we attend closely to the rhetoric of the Virginia Company anti-theatricalists, and William Crashaw in particular, we can hear that what upset them was not just that the adventurers were being mocked but also

---

[3] Louis Wright, for example, wonders whether "Crashaw may be referring to *Eastward Hoe*...for it has a scene satirizing Virginia," but also notes that "whether the players had committed some overt act against Virginia at the time of Crashaw's outburst is not clear from surviving evidence." Louis B. Wright, *Religion and Empire: The Alliance between Piety and Commerce in English Expansion, 1558–1625* (Chapel Hill: University of North Car-olina Press, 1943), 101–2.

[4] Ben Jonson, George Chapman, and John Marston, *Eastward Ho!*, in Bevington, Butler, and Donaldson (eds), *The Cambridge Edition of the Works of Ben Jonson*, vol. 2. All citations are to this edition.

that the whole transformational agenda of the colony was being undermined. Theatermemes about the adventurer circulated the idea that the people most attracted to Virginia were far from the ideal adventurer as articulated in the Company's propaganda—English men who would be transformed into steadfast and hardworking "new men" and take on the religious mission of conversion, having, in a sense, been converted themselves through the colonial experience. Instead, the theatermeme adventurer (that is, the figure to whom these theatermemes were attached) was like the Spanish *conquistador*, attracted by tales of vast wealth and excess and willing to go to desperate ends to acquire it; or the adventurer was like the player, trying to gain preferment in the world not by labor and devotion but by theatrical stratagems (often forms of disguise), "*priuate ends*" to meet his own "*priuate plots*," without undergoing a lasting spiritual transformation of his own. In adventurer theatermemes, therefore, Virginia investors and settlers were rendered indistinguishable from the Devil, the papist, and the player, because both *conquistadores* and players were papists, behaved diabolically, and were engaged in the wrong kinds of transformation, if they transformed themselves at all.

After deconstructing Crashaw's answer to "Why are *The Players* enemies to this plantation and doe abuse it," this chapter concludes by trying to come at his question from two different angles. I would hesitate to suggest that playing companies and playwrights were, as Crashaw and co. suggest, systematically opposed to Virginia, however problematic the collapsings of adventurer, *conquistador*, and player were for the Virginia Company. The playing companies and the Virginia Company were, however, both corporations, vying for the disposable income of Londoners. While to us buying entry to a theatrical performance and investing in a company seem like very different activities, in the early modern context these two forms of exchange were not so far apart, as Ben Jonson seems to argue in *Bartholomew Fair*. Moreover, the playhouses were repeatedly associated with smoking: characters smoke on stage; tobacco was sold and consumed in the theaters. Even though Virginia would become heavily associated with tobacco plantations, in the first decades of the seventeenth century tobacco was very much a Spanish-American drug. This chapter closes by drawing analogies between anti-tobacconists and anti-theatricalists: for anti-tobacconists, smokers worshipped a protean, devilish weed and indulged in a treasonous activity by diverting money to Spanish dominion; for anti-theatricalists, the players consorted with the Devil and the papist to bring low the Virginia mission by undermining its transformative agenda. The playhouse, a smoky place if ever there was one, may be said to be predisposed against Virginia, at least in the early years of the colony, because it promoted and celebrated (and also often mocked) the tobacco culture that grew up around it—a culture which revolved around the consumption of a heretically transformative, Spanish commodity.

## "SO GREAT AN UNDERTAKING": PROMOTING VIRGINIA

On April 12, 1609, Don Pedro de Zuñiga, the Spanish Ambassador to England, who was ever watchful on Virginia matters during his seven-year stint at James I's court, as we will see often in this book, wrote to King Philip III of Spain about the gathering momentum of the Virginia Company's religious mission: "[t]he preparations they are making here are the most urgent they know how to make, for they have seen to it that the ministers, in their sermons, stress the importance of filling the world with their religion, and of everyone exerting themselves to give what they have to so great an undertaking."[5]

We may detect a note of condescension here—"the most urgent they know how to make" feels like a dig at England's belatedness in empire-building—but de Zuñiga was genuinely concerned about "the ministers, in their sermons," and in some ways he was right to be. In 1609–10, several prominent churchmen delivered sermons as part of a concerted effort on the Virginia Company's part to rebrand itself as a religious enterprise. On March 24, 1609, Richard Crackanthorpe, chaplain-in-ordinary to James I, delivered a sermon in favor of the colony at Paul's Cross, one of London's few large, open-air venues (outside the theaters), as did the preacher George Benson, a fellow of Queen's College, Oxford, on May 7, and Daniel Price, Chaplain to Henry, Prince of Wales, on May 25.[6] Robert Tynley, Doctor of Divinity and Archdeacon of Ely, delivered two sermons on April 17, the second of which (delivered at St. Mary Spital, Bishopsgate) praised the Virginia colony. Also in April, William Symonds, preacher at St. Savior's and St. Mary Overies in Southwark, delivered a sermon on the 25th at Whitechapel, as did Robert Gray, rector of St. Bennet Sherehog in the Poultry, three days later. Thomas Morton, Dean of Gloucester and later Bishop of Durham, also delivered a sermon in 1609, although the text has not survived. Last, but by no means least, William Crashaw delivered his sermon to the assembled Virginia Company to herald the departure of the colony's new governor, Thomas West, Lord

---

[5] Don Pedro de Zuñiga to Philip III, April 12, 1609, in Phillip L. Barbour (ed.), *The Jamestown Voyages under the First Charter, 1606–1609*, vol. 2 (London: Hakluyt Society, 1969), 259–60.

[6] On the cultural significance of Paul's Cross, see Mary Morrissey, *Politics and the Paul's Cross Sermons, 1558–1642* (Oxford: Oxford University Press, 2011).

de la Warr, in February of the following year. That de Zuñiga's letter was sent before Benson, Price, Tynley, Symonds, and Crashaw made their way to the pulpit indicates that there may have been sermons delivered before April 12, 1609 that have since been lost—only Crackanthorpe's sermon, of the ones that we know about, had been delivered by the time de Zuñiga corresponded with his king.

The pulpit campaign was timed to coincide with the granting of the second Virginia Company charter in May 1609, the departure of the third supply in June 1609, and West's departure, which was eventually pushed back to the spring of 1610 on account of poor weather conditions. It was designed to boost public confidence in an enterprise that had been on the verge of collapse in its early years. The Company suffered from a lack of funding, while the colonists (in the words of historian Edmund S. Morgan) "seem to have made nearly every possible mistake and some that seem almost impossible."[7] From its inception, the colony had been riven with factionalism, its presidency passing from Edward Maria Wingfield (deposed on trumped-up charges of Spanish sympathies) to John Ratcliffe (killed by the Powhatan) to Matthew Scrivener (drowned) to John Smith (maimed in a gunpowder accident) and then to George Percy in quick succession in its first two years. Many adventurers among the small population who had arrived in 1607 were unsuited to the hard graft of settlement (a third were gentlemen unaccustomed both to manual labor and to taking orders). Many were attracted to the dreams of a Mammonian "*novo orbe*" and had little interest in the plantation. Even those more adept colonists fell prone to the harsh conditions and minimal food supplies. New arrivals from the 1608 second supply, consisting of specialized laborers but only twelve out-and-out laborers, plus a further fifty-six gentlemen, burdened rather than aided the colony. Furthermore, relations between the settlers and the Powhatan were tense to say the least, much of the breakdown in relations prompted by English aggression, which was short-sighted in the extreme given the settlers' reliance on trade with Wahunsenacawh, the Powhatan leader, to maintain their meager resources. To cap it all, the third supply, which left London in June 1609 with Virginia's new Deputy Governor Thomas Gates aboard, met with disaster. In August, news reached London that *The Sea Venture*,

---

[7] Edmund S. Morgan, *American Slavery, American Freedom: The Ordeal of Colonial America*, 2nd edition (New York: W. W. Norton, 2003), 72. My account of Virginia's early years is indebted to Morgan's book and to Wesley Frank Craven, *Dissolution of the Virginia Company: The Failure of a Colonial Experiment* (Oxford: Oxford University Press, 1932); Brenner, *Merchants and Revolution*; James Horn, *A Land as God Made It: Jamestown and the Birth of America* (New York: Basic Books, 2005); and Karen Ordahl Kupperman, *The Jamestown Project* (Cambridge, MA: Belnap Press, 2007).

Gates' ship, had been lost in a storm (it wound up shipwrecked on Bermuda), thus depriving the colony of much-needed leadership and even more needed supplies. The pulpit campaigners had their work cut out to account for the colony's disastrous beginning, and no-one more so than William Crashaw, whose sermon, delivered after the loss of *The Sea Venture*, had to buoy an increasingly embattled membership for whom the promise of the second charter was diminishing after "our last fleete was dispersed and sore shaken by a storme."[8]

The sermons attempted to answer Virginia's doom-mongers and nay-sayers by emphasizing the Company's religious mission.[9] To be sure, funding was necessary, and the pulpit campaign was, at least at first, successful in generating funds: as de Zuñiga noted in his letter, "[i]n this way a good sum of money is being collected."[10] The promise of aiding the English economy through colonization was hardly expunged from the pulpit campaign. Crashaw argued that "we shall mightily inrich our nation, strengthen our navie, fortifie our kingdome, and be lesse beholding to other nations."[11] However, from 1609 onwards, religion was front and central to the project, or at least to how the project conceived of itself and presented itself. Crashaw contended that these enrichments were not among "the high and soveraigne ends of this action": instead, the "True ends principall" of the Virginia project were, "respecting the Sauages of that countrie,... the conversion of their soules."[12] Religion had always been part of the Virginia Company agenda—clause III of the first Virginia Company charter of 1606 called for "propagating of Christian Religion"—but the pulpit proselytizing formed part of the greater religious emphasis around the time of the second Company charter in May 1609, which stated (in words that Crashaw's sermon echoed) that "the principal effect, which we can desire or expect of this action, is the conversion and reduction of the people in those parts unto the true worship of God and Christian Religion."[13]

The Company's transformative agenda would not only save the indigenous population. It would also redeem those men (and women, but mainly

[8] Crashaw, *New-Yeeres Gift*, Ev. Little did Crashaw know that worse news was to come, as news of the "starving time" of the winter of 1609–10—the subject of this book's second chapter—did not filter back to London until May 1610.

[9] See John Parker, "Religion and the Virginia Company, 1609–1610," in K. R. Andrews, N. P. Canny, and P. E. H. Hair (eds), *The Westward Enterprise: English Activities in Ireland, the Atlantic, and America* (Detroit, MI: Wayne State University Press, 1979), 245–70.

[10] Barbour, *Jamestown Voyages*, 259.    [11] Crashaw, *New-Yeeres Gift*, K2v.

[12] Crashaw, *New-Yeeres Gift*, Kv.

[13] "Letters Patent to Sir Thomas Gates, Sir George Somers, and Others," in William Walter Hening (ed.), *The Statutes at Large, Being a Collection of All the Laws of Virginia*, vol. 1 (New York: R. and W. and G. Bartow, 1823), 57–66, at 58; "The Second Charter," in Hening, *Statutes at Large*, 80–98, at 97.

men) transported to the colonies and away from the corruptions that England, and specifically London, had to offer. Virginia could lead (according to Tynley) to "the easing of this Land, which euen groaneth vnder the burden of her inhabitants," by (to quote Company alderman Robert Johnson) ridding "our multitudes of such as lie at home, pestering the land with pestilence and penury, and infecting one another with vice and villainie, worse then the plague itself."[14] More than just providing a solution to overpopulation, the promotional pamphlet *A True and Sincere Declaration of the Purpose and Ends of the Plantation begun in Virginia* (1610) argued that, "[B]y transplanting the rancknesse and multitude of increase in our people," the Virginia Company was able to "prouide and build vp for the publike *Honour* and *Safety* of our *gratious King* and his *Estates* . . . some small Rampier of our own," "a Bulwarke of defence, in a place of aduantage, against a stranger enemy," the Spanish.[15] Moreover, because they were part of a new-found mission of national defense, and also because they were implicated in the religious mission too, colonists would (to quote Crashaw) "become new men" and "proue good and worthie instruments and members of a Common-wealth."[16] "The sins of this our nation haue been horrible," and the only way of pacifying "the wrath of our offended Father" and countering the papists who have "sent many men into the West and East Indies to preach Christ" was to settle Virginia as an evangelical, Protestant plantation.[17] That is to say, not only would the native population be saved from their devil-worshipping ways; England would see salvation as well, thanks to its colony full of transformed, productive, pious subjects.

## "THEY PLAY . . . WITH GOD AND RELIGION, AND ALL HOLY THINGS": DENOUNCING THE PLAYERS

It is in this context that we find Virginia Company anti-theatricalism. In his 1612 treatise *The New Life of Virginea*, Robert Johnson complained that "the malitious and looser sort (being accompanied with the licentious

---

[14] Tynley, *Two Learned Sermons, The One, of the Mischeuious Subtiltie, and Barborous Crueltie, the Other of the False Doctrines, and Refined Heresies of the Romish Synagogue* (London: for Thomas Adams, 1609), 68; Robert Johnson, *Nova Britannia* (1609), 19, in Peter Force (ed.), *Tracts and Other Papers* (New York: Peter Smith, 1947).

[15] *A True and Sincere Declaration of the Purpose and Ends of the Plantation Begun in Virginia* (London: for I. Stepneth, 1610), 3. As Karen Ordahl Kupperman points out, "Although planners [from the Virginia Company] were concerned about the response of the Indians on whom they would intrude, their main fear lay in the rivalry with Spain." Kupperman, *Jamestown Project*, 6.

[16] Crashaw, *New-Yeeres Gift*, F.     [17] Crashaw, *New-Yeeres Gift*, K2.

vaine of stage Poets) have whet their tongues with scornfull taunts" against Virginia.[18] Johnson does not explicitly link the "taunts" with religion, but he repeatedly describes the enterprise as divinely ordained. He claims that "manifold difficulties, crosses and disasters, being such as are appointed by the highest providence... [were] an exercise of patience and other ver-tues, ... to make more wise thereby the managers thereof." The "injurious scoffers," among whom numbered the stage poets, failed to understand that the "manifold difficulties" were proof of God's favor rather than its absence.[19]

Other anti-theatricalists are more explicit in linking the players' taunts with religion. In his 1610 sermon Crashaw attacked the plays because they "play... with *God* and *Religion*, and all *holy things*: nothing that is good, excellent, or holy can escape them."[20] The Jamestown prayer asked God to "fortiffe vs against... Papists & players." Spoken by the guard at Jamestown, it also saw print twice in the 1610s: it was appended to the *Lawes Divine, Morall and Martiall* (1612) by William Strachey, while Ralph Hamor's address to his readers in *A True Discourse of the Present Estate of Virginia* (1615) borrowed from it.[21] Crashaw repeated his attack on the players in his introduction to Alexander Whitaker's *Good Newes from Virginia* (1613), in which he denounced "the iests of prophane Players, and other Sycophants, and the flouts and mockes of some" against "the place, Plantation, and persons that are in it" and attacked "the calumnies and slanders... being deuised by the Diuell, and set abroad by idle and base companions,... blowen abroad by Papists, Players and such like, till they have filled the vulgar eares."[22] Daniel Price's denounce-ment of "Scepticall Humorists," who level "lying speeches" which "have vilified the Plantation of Virginia... wherein every Christian ought to set his helping hand" may well have been targeted at Ben Jonson, who earned

---

[18] Robert Johnson, *The New Life of Virginea* (1612), 4–5, in Force, *Tracts and Other Papers*.

[19] Johnson, *New Life of Virginea*, 3–4.      [20] Crashaw, *New-Yeeres Gift*, H4.

[21] Strachey, *For the Colony in Virginea Britannia*, N4; Ralph Hamor, *A True Discourse of the Present Estate of Virginia and the Successe of the Affaires There till the 18 of Iune. 1614* (London: for William Welby, 1615), A4. The nineteenth-century historian Edward Neill argues that "[t]he daily prayer... was probably prepared by Crashaw." However, that the prayer contains many similarities to Hamor's complaint about the players in *A True Discourse of the Present Estate of Virginia* at least opens up the possibility that Hamor penned it (although he might also have borrowed the prayer for his own polemic). Edward D. Neill, *The English Colonization of America during the Seventeenth Century* (London: Strahan and Co., 1871), 50.

[22] William Crashaw, "To the Right Honorable, My Very Good Lord, Raph Lord Ure," in Alexander Whitaker, *Good Newes from Virginia* (London: for William Welby, 1613), A2, C2–C2v.

the epithet "Humorist" during the War of the Theaters in 1600–01; or more generally at writers of Comedies of Humors, among whom numbered Jonson and his *Eastward Ho!* co-authors, George Chapman and John Marston.[23]

Moreover, many of the booksellers who published Virginia-related matter carried no playbooks. William Welby, from whose shop in St. Paul's Churchyard Crashaw's sermon was sold, had no playbooks in his inventory, although his reason is unknown. The cases of Nicholas Bourne and his one-time apprentice John Bellamie are clearer: they outright refused to stock any playbooks whatsoever (even though the former inherited the stock of Cuthbert Burby, which included Robert Greene's *The Historie of Orlando Furioso* and some notable Shakespeare quartos). Recalled Bellamie in 1646, "neither my selfe, nor any of my fellow Servants did sell any Play-books, or other books in that nature; and our not selling these, was by my Masters [Bourne's] owne order and direction."[24] Both Bellamie and Bourne were noted members of London's Puritan community, the former famous for publishing matter on New England puritanism in addition to tracts on Virginia, the latter for the Pan-European, Protestant news network he established with Nathaniel Butter. Virginia Company anti-theatricalism, then, revolved not just around what was articulated in sermons and circulated in print, but around what was refused publication and excluded from certain booksellers' shops—refused, it seems likely, on religious grounds.

---

[23] Daniel Price, *Saul's Position Staid, or the Apprehension, and Examination of Saule* (London: for Matthew Law, 1609), F3. Both John Weever and Richard Brereton use the epithet "Humorist" to describe Jonson, the first in *The Whipping of the Satyre* and the second in *No Whippings, nor Trippings: but a Kinde Friendly Snippinge* (both 1601). On Weever and Brereton, see D. H. Craig (ed.), *Ben Jonson: The Critical Heritage* (London: Routledge, 1990; 2005), 39–42. The *Oxford English Dictionary* gives as its second usage of "Humorist" the definition "A facetious or comical person, a wag; a humorous talker, actor, or writer," and cites Jonson's *Everyman out of His Humour* as the first instance of this usage, which implicates players as well ("To turn an actor and a humorist," IND. 212).

[24] John Bellamie, *A Iustification of the City Remonstrance and Its Vindication* (London: Richard Cotes, 1646), 19. In fact, Bourne did publish one playbook, a translation of Terence's *The Eunuch* (1629), but the play was printed as a Latin grammar—the edition was a facing-page translation. Bourne's opposition to theater may have been predicated as much on his distaste for commercial playhouse drama as on drama as a whole, which many anti-theatricalists insisted could perform a religious and educational role if done in the "proper" manner. Philip Gosson, one of the most famous and oft-quoted anti-theatricalists, was a playwright, while Philip Stubbes structured his *Anatomie of Abuses* as a five-act play. In the Virginian context, we might note that the printed version of William Crashaw's 1610 sermon concludes with a playlet dramatizing England's conversion of the Indians, with all of the dialogue lifted from the Bible.

To some degree the anti-theatricalists' antagonism was at a personal level. Crashaw had some previous form with the players. At Paul's Cross two years earlier, on St. Valentine's Day 1608, he had railed against "The vngodly Playes and Enterludes so rife in this nation" and asked, "what are they but *a bastard of Babylon*, a daughter of error and confusion, a hellish deuice, (the divels owne recreation, to mock at holy things) by him deliuered to the *Heathen*, from them to the *Papists*, and from them to vs?"[25] Crashaw's sermon was provoked by Thomas Middleton's satirical depiction of Puritan practices at two London churches, St. Antholins and St. Mary Overies, in his play *The Puritan, or the Widow of Watling Street*, performed by the notorious Paul's Boys Company (who were also behind *Eastward Ho!*). So damning was Crashaw's attack on Paul's Boys that he has been credited with bringing about the demise of the company.[26] Crashaw's friend, William Symonds was also likely to have been oppositional to the players for personal reasons. He was the object of satire in *The Puritan* through the character of Simon St. Overies, an amalgam of his surname and one of the churches at which he preached.[27] But even if Crashaw and Symonds felt themselves to be attacked personally, religious affront was still crucial, because the attacks, as they saw them, were about their religious beliefs and practices.[28]

We can also understand the Virginia Company's anti-theatricalism as a product of the longstanding antagonism between the church and the playhouse. The players had long served as whipping boys for all manner of social ills; to give you some idea how long, as Lucy Munro points out, Crashaw's 1608 sermon quotes from Saint Ciprian's prohibition against actors from the third century.[29] In the debates that arose at the first outgrowth of the commercial theaters in the 1570s and 1580s, preachers and pamphleteers painted a stark contrast between the work of the church and the work of the theater. Plays, preached John Stockwood at Paul's Cross in 1578, just two years after the opening of The Theatre in

---

[25] William Crashaw, *The Sermon Preached at the Crosse* (London, 1609), 169.

[26] See W. Reavley Gair, *The Children of Paul's: The Story of a Theatre Company* (Cambridge: Cambridge University Press, 1982), esp. chapter 6: "The Triumph of Profit and Puritanism," 160–75; Enno Ruge, "Preaching and Playing at Paul's: The Puritans, *The Puritaine*, and the Closing of Paul's Playhouse," in Beate Müller (ed.), *Censorship and Cultural Regulation in the Modern Age* (Amsterdam: Rodolpi, 2004), 33–61.

[27] Thomas Middleton, *The Puritan or The Puritan Widow or The Widow of Watling Street*, in Taylor and Lavagnino, *Thomas Middleton: The Complete Works*.

[28] More indirectly, Richard Crackanthorpe was a student of John Rainolds, author of the anti-theatrical tract *Th'Overthrow of Stage Playes*, at Queen's College, Oxford. George Benson was also a fellow at Queen's and so would have known John Rainolds, although I have found no proof that he was in sympathy with Rainolds' anti-theatrical sentiment.

[29] Munro, *Children of the Queen's Revels*, 47. See also Jonas Barish's seminal work, *The Anti-Theatrical Prejudice* (Berkeley, CA: University of California Press, 1985).

Shoreditch, were "diuellishe inuentions."[30] One of the key proofs of such
ungodliness in the theater was the fact that until 1603 plays were performed on Sundays and thus rivaled the church as a public gathering
place: complained Stockwood, "Wyll not a fylthye playe, wyth the blast of
a Trumpette, sooner call thyther a thousande, than an houres tolling of a
Bell, bring to the Sermon a hundred?"[31] As Peter Lake and Michael
Questier point out, the anti-theatricalists argued that "the theatre was a
place in which no self-respecting godly person should be seen dead," and
by so doing defined "godly personhood" in opposition to "ungodly
playgoer."[32] The theater was deemed to be engaging in social upheaval:
as Jean Howard argues, players were accused of encouraging physical
mobility and social changeability, because "[p]eople at the theater are
not *where* they should be (i.e. in their parishes, at work or at worship);
consequently, they are not *who* they should be, but are released into a
realm of Protean shapeshifting with enormous destabilizing consequences
for the social order."[33] The theater corrupted its playgoers: for Philip
Stubbes in *The Anatomie of Abuses* (1583) it was the perfect "school ... if
you will learn falsehood, if you will learn cozenage: if you will learn to
deceive: if you will learn to play the hypocrite: to cog, lie and falsify: if you
will learn to jest, laugh, and fleer, to grin, to nod and mow: if you will
learn to play the vice, to swear, tear, and blaspheme, both Heaven and
Earth."[34] According to anti-theatricalists, drama manipulated the human
senses, making the audience believe in what was not there, even reani-
mating the historical dead, and Satan regularly made his victims believe in
what was not there as well; while the papacy was, for its opponents,
predicated both on (to quote Lake and Questier) "the manipulation of
the senses, through sound, spectacle, and gesture" and on the greatest
reanimation act of all, the literal interpretation of the Eucharist.[35] Both
Satan and the papacy reveled in idol worship: drama, meanwhile, had
its roots in pagan prehistory and was, in the words of Stubbes, "practised
by the heathen gentiles and dedicated to the false idols, gods and
goddesses."[36]

---

[30] John Stockwood, *Sermon Preached at Paules Crosse* (London: for George Bishop, 1578), 133.

[31] Stockwood, *Sermon Preached at Paules Crosse*, 23–4.

[32] Peter Lake and Michael Questier, *The Archbishop's Lewd Hat: Protestants, Papists and Players in Post-Reformation England* (New Haven, CT: Yale University Press, 2002), 430.

[33] Jean E. Howard, *The Stage and Social Struggle in Early Modern England* (London; New York: Routledge, 1994), 27.

[34] Philip Stubbes, *The Anatomie of Abuses* (London: Richard Jones, 1583), L4–M.

[35] Lake and Questier, *Archbishop's Lewd Hat*, 447.

[36] Stubbes, *Anatomie of Abuses*, L7.

We might argue therefore that the Virginia Company was already predisposed against the theater. Both the Devil and the papists were already the enemies of Virginia and, given the theater's already-present diabolical and papist affiliations, that the players followed suit was to be expected and anticipated. In a sense, then, whatever the plays said about Virginia, even if not explicitly critical of its religious mission, was implicitly critical of its religious mission, because Virginia was "a holy thing" and players played with holy things—at least according to Virginia Company propaganda. The players may have been simply the most obvious, convenient enemies to pick and place alongside the Devil and the papist.

## "WE SEND OF ALL TRADES TO VIRGINIA, BUT WILL SEND NO PLAYERS": LABORING COLONISTS, IDLE PLAYERS

William Crashaw's complaint against the players goes beyond anti-theatrical convention in revealing fashion. In his answer to the question, "Why are The Players enemies to this plantation and doe abuse it," Crashaw mused as follows:

> First, for that they are so multiplied here, that one cannot liue by another, and they see that wee send of all trades to *Virginea*, but will send no *Players*, which if wee would doe, they that remaine would gaine the more at home. Secondly, as the *diuell* hates vs, because wee purpose not to suffer *Heathens*, and the *Pope* because we haue vowed to tolerate no *Papists*: so doe the *Players*, because wee resolue to suffer no *Idle persons in Virginea*, which course if it were taken in *England*, they know they might turne to new occupations.[37]

The second Virginia Company charter laid out the colony's active prohibition against papists, decreeing that "we should be loath, that any person should be permitted to pass, that we suspected to effect the superstitions of the church of Rome," yet no such language about player prohibition is to be found in the charter or indeed in any of the Company's promotional materials.[38] While Virginia's laws were intended to clamp down on "vnlawfull and prohibited games, . . . excesse of drinking, surfitting and ryot," and while the publication of said laws in 1612 included the Jamestown prayer which features language against the players, there do not seem to have been any legal attempts to suppress theater

---

[37] Crashaw, *New-Yeeres Gift*, H4.
[38] "The Second Charter," in Hening, *Statutes at Large*, 97–8.

in Virginia or exclude its practitioners until the 1660s.[39] As Hugh Rankin puts it, the early settlers were "actors in the more pressing true-life drama of carving homes out of the wilderness and the struggle for survival in hostile surroundings. There was no place for artificial comedy or tragedy."[40]

Crashaw may have overstated Virginia's "no-players policy" but his explanation for the players' enmity was a canny piece of rhetoric in a number of ways. Crashaw reminded his congregation (and subsequently the readers of the printed text) that one of the key justifications of colonization was that it would provide an outlet for England's excess population. These emigrations, under the governance of the departing Lord de la Warr, would "rectifie and reforme many disorders which in this mightie and populous state are scarce possibly to be reformed without euacuation."[41] They would also transform the settlers, "such fellowes, such loose, leud [lewd], licentious, riotous, and disordered men," into productive settlers, "new men, euen as it were cast in a new mould," "worthie instruments" and no longer a moral and financial drain on the nation.[42] Players, by contrast, were left out of this transformative, spiritual economy, because they could only see the colony as a means for social advancement, wealth accumulation, and an escape from the perils of home. In Crashaw's estimation the players stood to gain either by going to Virginia and starting anew or by staying in London and having less competition; that is, they intended to transform their fortunes in Virginia without transforming themselves. The very fact that they wanted to go to Virginia (or stay in London) *as* players, rather than "turne to new professions," was proof of their irreligious approach to colonization.

Furthermore, Crashaw takes the criticism that Virginia's settlers were work-shy and applies it to the players, who were often cast as glorified vagrants, idle themselves and encouraging idleness in others. He countered the public perception that "we send men that cannot liue here, men that are in debt, men of base fashion" by arguing that the bad-mouthing returnees who had spread ill-reports about the colony had expected to "liue for the present, as they liued in *England*," a nation which had become, in

---

[39] Strachey, *For the Colony in Virginea Britannia*, 75. The first dramatic performance in the British colonies did not occur until 1665, of a play entitled *The Bear and the Cub*, performed in a tavern at Pungoteague, Accomack County, Eastern Virginia. The play was something of a cause célèbre: three of the actors were brought to trial accused of public wickedness, although the case was dismissed. See Odai Johnson and William J. Burling (eds), *The Colonial American Stage 1665–1774: A Documentary Calendar* (Cranbury, NJ: Associated University Presses, 2001), 92–4.

[40] Hugh Rankin, *The Theater in Colonial America* (Chapel Hill: University of North Carolina Press, 1960), 1.

[41] Crashaw, *New-Yeeres Gift*, K2v–K3.      [42] Crashaw, *New-Yeeres Gift*, E4–F.

Crashaw's estimation "now *degenerate* . . . by want of exercise of armes and actiuitie, want of trades and labour, by our idlenesse, lazinesse and las-ciuiousnesse."[43] Crashaw, like many in the Virginia Company, contended that these first colonists had been anomalies and that, with the right leadership (i.e. that provided by the departing governor), the colonists would throw off the effeminizing corruption of contemporary London: "were it not good for us if our people were inured to more hardnesse, and brought vp vnder obedience of sharper discipline, and accustomed to lesse daintinesse & tendernesse then heretofore."[44] The "men of base fashion," who were reputed to be among those transported over to the Virginia colony, were the same kinds of people who attended London's fashionable playhouses. Such men spent their money on entertainment and clothing and ran up so much debt that they were forced to flee to new lands. These men were not likely to become "new men," but rather would transport their old selves to the New World. Thankfully for the Company, these earlier colonists had either returned disenchanted from Virginia or perished there. The new stock would adapt to the conditions of the colony and be able to take advantage of the transformative possibilities that it offered.

In Crashaw's account, the players embodied characteristics from which the Virginia Company sought to distance itself. They were crypto-Catholic, whereas Virginia was to be Catholic-free. They were disorderly, whereas Virginia was to be well governed. They were idle, whereas Virginia was to be a hardworking colony. Their exclusion confirmed the seriousness of the transformational project: only people who bought into it, and were willing to give up their prior afflictions, could be considered. While the players turn what is godly into what is base (themselves), the Virginia project will turn what is base (what Crashaw branded London's "*superfluitie*") into what is godly.[45] The ideal adventurer, unlike the player, was open to the right kind of transformation.

## TRANSFORMING "PESTILENCE AND PENURY" TO "HONEST, WISE AND PAINEFULL MEN"? THE THEATERMEME ADVENTURER

What Crashaw tried to establish as abnormal—the malcontent returnees who were "those who live for the present"—came to epitomize the adventurer on stage. Drama's Virginia adventurers, or characters to whom the Virginia adventurer theatermemes are attached, imagine the colony as

---

[43] Crashaw, *New-Yeeres Gift*, E3v, F4–F4v.     [44] Crashaw, *New-Yeeres Gift*, Gv.
[45] Crashaw, *New-Yeeres Gift*, E4v.

an "Indies" teeming with mineral wealth and sexual promise; they wish to travel there to escape their (often self-inflicted) financial hardships at home. There is no talk of conversion: the only interest they have in the native population is the likely adoration they will offer them on their arrival. Nor is there talk of personal, spiritual betterment in the harsh wildernesses of the New World. The only interest they have in self-transformation is into wealthy—or at least solvent—settlers in a lawless, easeful New World.

In part, these adventurer theatermemes can be attributed to the fact that the reputation of the first settlers was hard to live down—most early Virginia tracts had to wrestle with, and often acknowledge, the conduct of some "irregular persons," even as they tried to argue that more recent settlers did not have such failings (and that the first two supplies were not entirely worthless in and of themselves).[46] With news from the colony at close to an all-time low (worse was to come in May 1610, when news of the "starving time" started circulating, as will be discussed in the next chapter), Crashaw was certainly up against it (even if he was preaching to the converted, the assembled members of the Company).

The persistence of adventurer theatermemes may also be attributed to the paradox at the heart of the Virginia Company's transformational logic. Crashaw claims that the colony will work on its settlers as follows:

> considering we finde that the most disordered men that can bee raked vp out of the *superfluitie*, or, if you will, the very *excrements*, of a full and swelling State, if they be remoued out of the fat and feeding ground of their *native countrey*, and from the licentiousnesse and too much libertie of the States where they haue liued, into a more bare and barren soile, as euery countrie is at first, and to a harder course of life, wanting pleasures, and subiect to some pinching miseries, and to a strict forme of gouernement, and seuere discipline, doe often become new men, euen as it were cast in a new mould, and proue good and worthie instruments and members of a Common-wealth.[47]

Evacuating England's waste will ease overpopulation; it will also aid the transformation of its wasters, placing them within an environment where they can reform themselves away from the temptations of home. But how was this transformation supposed to take place? Crashaw saw "[t]he ancient valour and hardnesse of our people" as a model to which the current generation should aspire—a nod to the Tacitean logic underpinning Virginia Company thought.[48] Yet Crashaw's argument about how

---

[46] Johnson, *New Life of Virginea*, 10.        [47] Crashaw, *New-Yeeres Gift*, E4v–F.

[48] "England had taken a back seat to the Iberians and France in efforts to exploit the fabled treasure of America, but the period when the English rage for Tacitus began also saw the first tentative efforts to found a permanent English presence across the Atlantic. In fact

this model might be replicated is vague. His insistence on "a strict forme of gouernement, and seuere discipline" acknowledged that the governance of the colony had been chaotic in its early days. At the end of the sermon he advised de la Warr to "suffer no sinfull, no leaud [lewd], no licentious men, none that liue not vnder the obedience of good lawes."[49] However, after positing the possibility that "disordered men" could be redeemed in Virginia in the middle of the sermon, Crashaw does not return to the notion that the men themselves would be transformed from "excrement" to "new men" in these closing remarks. Governance and discipline are prescribed not for the salvation of the settlers but for the security of the settlement.

Even at the moment of its articulation, the idea that "*superfluitie*" can be transformed by environment is beset with contradictions. According to Crashaw, these "disordered men" will be reformed by "a harder course of life, wanting pleasures, and subiect to some pinching miseries." However, these very same "pinching miseries" had afflicted "the vulgar and viler sort" who had found "but cold entertainment" and then reported "all euill that can be of that countrie"—the "sort," that is, whose reports Crashaw and co. repeatedly had to counter.[50] If this group had not been transformed by the harshness of conditions, what then could guarantee the transformation of England's excrement? Weren't, by Crashaw's own admission, both groups similar in that they were defined by wastefulness and idleness? Neither Crashaw nor anyone in the Virginia Company was able to provide a systematic answer to this question. For example, even though Robert Johnson's *Nova Britannia* lays out a system of settlement and governance (far more so than Crashaw's sermon), he also fails to account for the gap between the justification for settlement based on overpopulation (ridding the land of multitudes "pestering the land with pestilence and penury") and a characterization of desired settlers as "honest, wise and painefull men" of "euery trade and profession."[51]

Crashaw's claim that the environment would order the disorderly is also inconsistent. His argument rebutted the claims of "the vulgar and viler sort" about "the *difficultie of Plantation*, ... the *climate* hot and disagreeing with the state and temper of our bodies."[52] Argued Crashaw and his fellow promoters, Virginia was "farre enough from the *Torrida Zona*, and from

America, both as place and as concept, offered thoughtful Tacitists unique ways of thinking about the problems the nation faced, and posed solutions to those problems." Karen Ordahl Kupperman, "Angells in America," in Phillip Beidler and Gary Taylor (eds), *Writing Race across the Atlantic World: Medieval to Modern* (New York: Palgrave MacMillan, 2005), 27–50, quotation at 37.

[49] Crashaw, *New-Yeeres Gift*, L.   [50] Crashaw, *New-Yeeres Gift*, F2.
[51] Johnson, *Nova Britannia*, 19.   [52] Crashaw, *New-Yeeres Gift*, E.

the distempering heate of the Sunne:... [and] rather of the same temper with the South of *France*, which is so temperate and indifferent, as if our owne were something neerer vnto it, we would be well content with it."[53] The climate would not transform English settlers: "*our brethren in Virginea*, who some of them haue been there many yeeres,...doe not complaine of any alteration, caused by distemper of the Climate."[54] These climate theories—familiar to us thanks to Mary Floyd-Wilson's work on geohumoralism—were deployed to assuage fears that English bodies would degenerate.[55] Virginia's climate was sufficiently similar to England's own to prevent degeneration: Virginia, that is, was like home.[56] However, by adhering to these theories, the Company's advocates also created a paradox. England's climate, characterized by Crashaw as "fat and feeding ground" and by Robert Johnson as "pestilent," had *already* degenerated English bodies—a phenomenon that Londoners could see all around them (at least according to Virginia's promoters) and which had also afflicted the colony in its early years, thanks to the conduct of "the vulgar and viler sort." So, how could the settlers, made up of the "superfluitie" and "excrement" of England, become "new men" in a country that did not alter one's "temper" and was in many ways just like England? Crashaw's belief that hard work and strict governance would be transformative has a significant gap at its center. "We finde" this transformative phenomena to be the case, argues Crashaw, without offering a program by which this transformation would take place. For all the talk of personal redemption, Crashaw and the Company seemed more interested in making the colonists instrumental in the planting and maintenance of the settlement than in altering their temper—something which they stressed Virginia's climate would not do anyway.

As we will see, drama tapped into these contradictions. It undid the Virginia Company's message, not just by suggesting that its pious motives thinly masked materialistic ones, but also by suggesting that its transformational logic folded in on itself. Moreover, the characteristics Crashaw associates with the players were ones that early modern drama attached to the figure of the adventurer. The theatermeme adventurer is Catholic, at least in the sense that his longing to travel to Virginia is borne out of

[53] Crashaw, *New-Yeeres Gift*, E2.    [54] Crashaw, *New-Yeeres Gift*, E2.
[55] Mary Floyd-Wilson, *English Ethnicity and Race in Early Modern Drama* (Cambridge: Cambridge University Press, 2003).
[56] See Karen Ordahl Kupperman, "Fear of Hot Climates in the Anglo-American Colonial Experience," *William and Mary Quarterly*, 41 (1984): 213–40. See also Jean Feerick, *Strangers in Blood: Relocating Race in the Renaissance* (Toronto: University of Toronto Press, 2010), esp. chapter 3, "*Cymbeline* and Virginia's British Climate," and chapter 4, "Passion and Degeneracy in Tragicomic Island Plays," 78–136.

the worship of riches and a desire for sexual conquest. That is, he resembles the Spanish-Catholic *conquistador*, albeit that his desires are frequently unsatisfied because, unlike New Spain, Virginia had little to offer in the way of mineral wealth. He is associated with playing—because he performs the role of the adventurer, when in fact he has nothing substantial to show for himself; because he frequents plays, and/or because he is adept at playing roles, showing himself to be a protean shape-shifter with a penchant for the theatrical. Far from being distinct from the world of the theater, the Virginia adventurer is very much part of its fabric. That is, theater is offered up as an alternative transformational space—one which did not contend that waste could be turned to redemption by magical thinking but contended rather that everything was continually in flux.

## "THAN ALL THE INDIES": THE ADVENTURER AND THE *CONQUISTADOR*

The motives of drama's Virginia adventurers owe a considerable amount to the motives for conquest and colonization associated with New Spain. For the Virginia Company members, this collapsing of adventurer and *conquistador* was problematic. They wanted Virginia to serve the nation by providing it with much-needed commodities and provide an outlet for its excess population, as well as converting its native inhabitants, while at the same time warding off greedy investors who viewed the colony as a get-rich-quick scheme, an imagining based on the fables of Spanish New World wealth. Haunted by what Eric Griffin has called "the specter of Spain," England's promoters were keen to distance themselves from the Spanish, however alluring their success.[57]

To distinguish itself from Spain, the Virginia Company reminded potential supporters about the rumors of mistreatment of Indians that were circulating in England in the wake of Bartholomae de las Casas' *Brevísima Relación de la Destrucción de las Indias* (1552), first published in English as *The Spanish Colonie* in 1583. George Benson, for example, channeled de las Casas when he warned his congregation at Paul's Cross in 1609 that in New Spain there was "a people of the like qualitie (with the naturall inhabitants of Virginia) poore and naked things." There had been so much "crueltie vsed vnto them, that scandall was giuen vnto the name of Christ, the name of Christianity grewe odious vnto them, [and] by reason of that

---

[57] See Griffin, *English Renaissance Drama and the Specter of Spain*.

cruelty they would let it haue no roome in their thoughts."[58] According to the Company's promotional rhetoric, while the Indians of New Spain had been subject to Spanish violence and had as a result grown averse to Christianity, the English would ensure that the Indians of Virginia would not suffer the same fate by placing conversion at the center of their mission. The English, then, would not repeat the Spanish cruelties but would employ more charitable means in the establishment of their empire. As Robert Johnson states in *Nova Britannia*, "our dominion shall be enlarged...not by stormes of raging cruelties (as West India was conuerted) with rapiers point and Musket shot, murdering so many millions of naked Indians, as their stories doe relate, but by faire and louing meanes, suiting to our English natures." Johnson does not name de las Casas, but these "stories" probably emanated from *The Spanish Colonie*.[59]

At the same time the English couldn't help but make comparisons between Spain's successes and their own failures.[60] The Virginia Company repeatedly praised the way that the Spanish had capitalized on the New World discoveries while the English had lollygagged. In *Nova Britannia*, Johnson contrasts "the wisedome of Spaine: whose quick apprehension and speedy addresse, preuented all other Princes: albeit (as you know) their greatness of minde arising together with theire money and meanes, hath turmoiled all Christendome these fourtie yeares and more," with "the blind diffidence of our English natures, which laugh to scorne the name of *Virginia*, and all other new proiects, be they neuer so probable, and will not beleeue till we see the effects."[61] So the story went, Columbus had initially come to the court of Henry VII, "offering to invest his Majestie with the most pretious and richest vaines of the whole earth, never knowne before," but was rejected because of "his poore apparell and simple lookes, and for the noveltie of his proposition": "the Spanish better conceiving then some others, beganne to entertaine and make use of his skill, which within these hundred yeares, hath brought foorth those

[58] For further reading, Benson directed his readers in the published text's margins to "what *Benzo* and *Bartholomeus a Casa* write of." George Benson, *Sermon Preached at Paules Crosse the Seaventh of May, M.DC.IX* (London: for Richard Moore, 1609), 92. Benzo is Girolamo Benzoni, whose *Historia del Mondo Nuovo* (1565) was largely cribbed from de las Casas.

[59] Johnson, *Nova Britannia*, 14. On the influence of de las Casas in England, see William Maltby, *The Black Legend in England: The Development of Anti-Spanish Sentiment, 1558–1660* (Durham, NC: Duke University Press, 1971).

[60] For comparison of the two empires, and how the English were inspired and intimidated by their Spanish forerunners, see J. H. Elliott, *Empires of the Atlantic World: Britain and Spain in America, 1492–1830* (New Haven, CT: Yale University Press, 2006).

[61] Johnson, *Nova Britannia*, 10.

apparent fruits to the world as cannot be hidde."[62] Thus while promoters wanted to distance themselves from Spanish crimes and save the indigenous population, at the same time they wanted the English to emulate the Spanish mission in the New World and make up for their own belatedness.

Part of Virginia's early appeal prior to settlement was that it could prove a northerly counterpart to New Spain's southerly mines. The colony was rumored to be replete with "dripping-pans and . . . chamber-pots [of] pure gold," imaginings heavily indebted to reports of Iberian voyaging (*Eastward Ho!* 3.3.20). The poet and playwright Michael Drayton, an investor in the Virginia Company, promoted the idea that the first settlers would acquire "pearl and gold" effortlessly "Without . . . toyle" in his "Ode to the Virginia Voyage."[63] A letter from several prominent Virginia settlers, including John Smith, dated June 22, 1607, reported enthusiastically to the Company in England about the "gold-showing mountains" which needed to be secured before "that all devouring Spaniard [could] lay his hands upon" them.[64] On August 12, 1607, Sir Walter Cope wrote to Robert Cecil, Lord Salisbury, that "we are falne vpon a land, that promises more, then the Lande of promisse: In steed of mylke we fynde pearle. & gold Inn steede of honye."[65] In 1606–07, then, Virginia adventurers fully expected to find vast quantities of mineral wealth underfoot. After all, the Spanish had found plentiful pearl and gold to the south, so why wouldn't they?

Virginia's promise proved illusory, its "gold-showing mountains" nothing but show. Cope wrote back to Cecil on August 13 with the words "Thys other daye we sent you newes of golde And thys daye, we cannot returne yow so much as Copper."[66] After 1607 promoters of the colony regularly played down the possibilities of mineral wealth in the colonies. Daniel Price, for example, compared Virginia's commodities favorably with their counterparts elsewhere in the world (thus "the Country is not unlike to equalize . . . Tyrus for colours," etc.) in his 1609 sermon, but could not do so with "India for gold" as there was nothing to compare.[67]

---

[62] Johnson, *Nova Britannia*, 9.

[63] Michael Drayton, "On the Virginian Voyage," in J. William Habel (ed.), *The Works of Michael Drayton* (Oxford: Blackwell, 1931), 363–4.

[64] "XIX. The Council in Virginia to the Council in England," in Alexander Brown (ed.), *The Genesis of the United States*, vol. 1 (New York: Houghton Mifflin, 1890), 106–8, at 108.

[65] Sir Walter Cope to Robert Cecil, Lord Salisbury, August 12, 1607, in Barbour, *Jamestown Voyages*, vol. 1, 108.

[66] Sir Walter Cope to Robert Cecil, Lord Salisbury, August 13, 1607, in Barbour, *Jamestown Voyages*, vol. 1, 111.

[67] Daniel Price, *Saul's Prohibition Staid*, F.

Promoters attempted to quell the gold rush that the Virginia Company instigated in its early days and encourage investment from people who supported the religious mission and would be patient about the level and amounts of their return. Crashaw bemoaned those who "make many excuses, and deuise obiections... because they may not haue present profit... [;] tell them of planting a Church, of conuerting 10000. soules to God, they are senselesse as stones."[68] Nevertheless, the dream of a mineral-rich Virginia refused to die. Indeed the Virginia Company frequently kept it alive, tantalizing the possibility of future wealth of India-like proportions, even as it downplayed the immediate possibilities. The second Virginia Company charter (1609, two years after Cope's testing) included provisions for "royal mines of gold and silver, as other minerals."[69] In 1611, William Welby entered at Stationer's Hall "bylls of adventure, with blanckes concerninge the Summes of money disbursed for adventures towards the voyage of Virginia." The bills included stipulations that the adventurers would gain a share "of all such mines and minerals of Gold, Silver and other mettalls or treasure... which shall be obtained or gotten in the said Voyage according to the porcion of money."[70] The Company's promotional machine did not entirely eschew the possibilities of accruing mineral as well as spiritual wealth. The most conspicuous example of this is George Chapman's *The Memorable Masque* in February 1613, which began with a street procession by masquers dressed as Virginian priests and princes clad in luxurious gold-laced costumes. More subtly, but no less tantalizingly, Daniel Price added a proviso in his 1609 sermon that gold in Virginia "is not impossible yet" just moments after acknowledging that the colony had no gold, let alone any of India-like proportions.[71] Thus while some promoters amped up the Company's spiritual concerns, other aspects of its promotional machine kept its commercial promise on the boil, despite all evidence that Virginia was not New Spain Mark II.

Playhouse drama ignored such subtleties and emphasized the supposed financial benefits of colonization. The adventurers of *Eastward Ho!* are allured by the promise that mineral wealth was simply lying around the colony and aim to capitalize on it—a reflection, no doubt, of the gold-rush frenzy before the arrival of the first settlers in 1607. But even after 1607, Virginia was associated with riches. Haddit in Tailor's *The Hog Hath Lost*

[68] Crashaw, *New-Yeeres Gift*, C2.
[69] "The Second Charter," in Hening, Statutes at Large, 89.
[70] "CLXIV. A Bill of Adventure," in Brown, *Genesis of the United States*, vol. 1, 471.
[71] Price, *Saul's Prohibition Staid*, F.

*of His Pearl* (1613) considers his plan to steal away Hog's daughter, Rebecca, and his wealth as going "better forward than the plantation in Virginia." In the same breath, on seeing her father, he proclaims, "here comes half the West-Indies, whose rich mines this night I mean to be ransacking" (3.3.27–9).[72] Haddit collapses Virginia and the West Indies into one—all under the auspices of his twin-fold plan to defeat Hog— rendering both as a space where he can "ransack . . . rich mines." In Massinger's *The City Madam*, Luke throws in his lot with his Virginian Indian guest (actually his brother in disguise), who offers him "wealth and worldly honors" if he will surrender his sister-in-law and nieces: "A mine of gold for a fee / Waits him that undertakes it, and performs it" (5.1.27, 45–6).[73] Massinger's play, written and performed in 1632, goes to show that the vision of a gold-rich, India-like Virginia persisted long after the news that the colony was not mineral rich had reached London.

In addition to these imaginings of a Virginia where "gold is more plentiful than copper," we find the far more prevalent imaginings of "the Indies"—a place teeming with riches beyond one's wildest dreams. This imagery circulates throughout early modern drama, but in particular it is attached to characters who claim that their love for someone is greater than the wealth of the Indies, or that they will not do something for personal gain at someone else's expense for all the wealth of the Indies. Take, for example, Thomas Middleton's *No Wit, No Help Like a Woman* (1611), in which Savourwit describes Grace,

> a sweet young Gentlewoman; but one
> That would not sell her honor for the Indies
> Till a Priest struck the bargain, and then half
> A crown dispatched it. [i.e. the cost of getting married][74]

In Cyril Tourneur's *The Atheist's Tragedy* (also 1611), Castabella's "courage" is valued by D'Amville so highly that, if he possessed it, "The Indies should not buy't out o' my hands."[75] By contrast, Falstaff desires to make Mistress Page and Mistress Ford his "East and West Indies" to whom he will "trade" in Shakespeare's *The Merry Wives of Windsor* (1597) (1.3.61). In *Satiromastix* by Thomas Dekker (1601), the lustful Tucca attempts to

---

[72] Robert Tailor, *The Hog Hath Lost His Pearl*, in Lloyd Edward Kermode (ed.), *Three Renaissance Usury Plays* (Manchester: Manchester University Press, 2009). All citations are to this edition.

[73] Philip Massinger, *The City Madam*, ed. Cyrus Hoy (Lincoln: University of Nebraska Press, 1964). All citations are to this edition.

[74] Thomas Middleton, *No Help/Wit Like a Woman's*, in Taylor and Lavagnino, *Thomas Middleton: The Collected Works*, 1.1.83–6.

[75] Cyril Tourneur, *The Atheist's Tragedy*, in Katherine Eisaman Maus (ed.), *Four Revenge Tragedies* (Oxford: Oxford University Press, 2008), 5.2.195.

seduce Mistress Miniver, his "Gwyniuer," by declaring, "thou shalt bee my West Indyes," and that "none but trim *Tucca* shall discouer thee" (much to her amusement/bemusement).[76] "The Indies," then, stand as an index of virtue: to desire them and prize them above all other things shows a lack of virtue (Falstaff and Tucca); to value people or chastity as worth more shows an abundance of it (Grace and D'Amville).

My point is not so much that theatermemes alluding to Indian mines and Indian gold are automatically about Virginia, but rather that they perpetuate the notion that "the Indies" are a source of vast wealth often associated with Spanish possessions. These are the same kinds of imagining that fueled early Virginia speculation, imaginings that persisted even after the Company rebranded itself as a predominantly religious enterprise from 1609 onwards. Moreover, the theatermemes distinguish between virtuous and iniquitous characters: while the former believe that human relations are above material concerns, the latter believe that everything has a price—even friends, families, and lovers. The first kind of person fits the Virginia Company's ideal adventurer, who looked beyond the promise of Indian riches; the second accords more with the theatermeme adventurer, who is allured by the promise of Indian riches for personal gain. What seem like allusions about Spain could also be taken as slights about the true motives of the Virginia Company: after all, the Virginia Company continually found itself condemning disgruntled former colonists who derogated the settlement because it had not conformed to their get-rich-quick schemes—all the while that the Company fostered deferred gold-rich dreams of its own.

## "WILDE VIRGINIA": THE ADVENTURER, LAW, AND CONSCIENCE

In addition to theatermemes alluding to New World wealth, we also find theatermemes that circulate the idea that the Indies or the Americas were sites of criminality where only the most villainous or most desperate dared venture. In Beaumont and Fletcher's *The Coxcomb* (1608), the villainous Richardo and Valerio desire "to search the earth, / Till we have found two in the shapes of men, / As wicked as our selves." Richardo would then dispatch his friends to the four corners of the world to extend his villainy into Africa, Asia, and Europe, but he would keep America for himself

---

[76] Thomas Dekker, *Satiromastix*, in Fredson Bowers (ed.), *The Dramatic Works of Thomas Dekker* (Cambridge: Cambridge University Press, 1961), vol. I, 3.1.163–6.

(5.2.39–49).[77] In Ford, Dekker, Middleton, and Rowley's *The Spanish Gypsie* (1623), Roderigo is accused of being a hangman, to which he replies that he should be sent "to the West-Indies, [to] buy mee some Office" (4.3.79–80).[78] The logic here seems to be that a hangman would be able to find steady employment in the New World, so dissolute and seditious are the settlers (and also, by extension, so brutal was the colonial regime).[79]

By contrast, nobody of sound mind would want to go to the Indies. In Fletcher's 1616 play *The Mad Lover*, a surgeon, charged with the title character Memnon's request to "cut / My heart out" asks what he is supposed to do after performing this task against his will: "Is there ne're a Cat hole where I may creep through? / Woo'd I were in the *Indies*."[80] We find similar sentiments in Fletcher's *The Little French Lawyer* and Thomas Dekker's *The Noble Spanish Soldier*.[81] "The Indies," then, is the last place on Earth you'd want to go to—only when events at home are so abysmal do they seem like the preferable option.

If we map these theatermemes onto the Virginia adventurer theatermemes we begin to see notable resonances. Characters who express a desire to go to Virginia are often in desperate straits. At the beginning of John Cooke's *Greenes Tu-Quoque, or The City Gallant* (1611), for example, Staines laments to the audience about the parlous financial state in which he finds himself on account of his landlord's exaction of his rents: "Well, I am spent, and this rogue has consumed me; I dare not walke abroad to see my friends, for feare the Serieants should take acquaintance of me: my refuge is *Ireland*, or *Virginia*, necessitie cries out, and I will presently to *Westchester*."[82] As Staines' lines suggest, Virginia will provide an escape from the law, not only because it is far away but also because it is a place (to quote *Eastward Ho!*'s revised quarto) with "no more Law then Conscience" (3.3.39 n). Nathaniel Field's *A Woman Is a Weather-cocke* (1612)

---

[77] John Fletcher, *The Coxcomb*, in Bowers, *The Dramatic Works in the Beaumont and Fletcher Canon*, vol. 1. See also the character of Crispiano in John Webster's *The Devil's Law-Case*, who owns a private West Indian mine and uses the wealth accrued to fund his villainous enterprises. John Webster, *The Devil's Law-Case*, ed. Francis Shirley (Lincoln: University of Nebraska Press, 1971).

[78] John Ford, Thomas Dekker, Thomas Middleton, and William Rowley, *The Spanish Gypsie*, in Taylor and Lavagnino, *Thomas Middleton: The Collected Works*.

[79] See also Anonymous, *The Wasp or the Subject's Precedent*, ed. Julius Walter Lever (Oxford: Malone Society, 1974), 2.3.17–20.

[80] John Fletcher, *The Mad Lover*, in Bowers, *The Dramatic Works in the Beaumont and Fletcher Canon*, vol. 5 (3.2.42–3; 47–8).

[81] See John Fletcher, *The Little French Lawyer*, in Bowers, *The Dramatic Works in the Beaumont and Fletcher Canon*, vol. 9, 3.3.133; Thomas Dekker, *The Noble Spanish Soldier*, in Bowers, *The Dramatic Works of Thomas Dekker*, vol. 4, 5.2.88–91.

[82] John Cooke, *Greenes Tu-Quoque, or the City Gallant* (New York: AMS Press, 1914), B3.

provides a further example of this idea. Scudamore and Bellafront are betrothed but are prevented from marrying by Sir John Worldly, her father. On the day of her wedding to another man, Count Frederick, Scudamore attempts to stop the ceremony. Sir John dismisses the "ydle words . . . t'may be haue past / Twixt Scudmore, and my Daughter heeretofore," and threatens him with the law (2.1.150–1).[83] Scudamore replies,

> There is indeede [law],
> And Conscience too, old *Worldly*, thou hast one;
> But for the other, wilde *Virginia*,
> Blacke *Affricke*, or the shaggy *Scithia*,
> Must send it ouer as a Merchandize,
> Ere thou show any here.   (164–70)

Scudamore acknowledges that Worldly has command of the law ("thou hast one"), but argues that he has no conscience ("the other"), because if he did he would recognize that Scudamore and Bellafront should be wed. Alternatively, Worldly has a conscience ("thou hast one"), but does not apply the law ("the other"), which should recognize Bellafront as Scudamore's betrothed because of their pre-existing verbal contract. In a variation of "when hell freezes over," "wilde *Virginia*" (and "Blacke *Affricke*" and "shaggy *Scithia*") will begin exporting "conscience" before Worldly will ever show any himself; or they will export laws and lawmaking capacities before Worldly follows juridical procedure. These lines can be interpreted to mean either that Virginia is a lawless colony or that it is a colony populated by people who lack any conscience—or, given the ambiguity, both at the same time.

In these plays Virginia is imagined as a place analogous to the Spanish New World. For all that the Virginia Company attempted to distinguish its honorable and holy actions from the cruelties of the gold-lusting *conquistadores*, drama rebuffed such attempts, both by continuing to circulate rumors of Indian "enormities" (extreme wealth, extreme human behavior) and eliding those "enormities" with Virginia. For all that the Company attempted to stress its strong governance and lawfulness—even going so far as to publish its laws for all to see in 1612—drama persisted with the idea that the colony was a place to hide from the law and where the lawless might make hay. Thus, while the ideal adventurer of the Virginia Company was pious and hardworking, the

[83] Nathaniel Field, *A Woman Is a Weather-Cocke*, reprinted in William Peery (ed.), *The Plays of Nathan Field* (Austin: University of Texas Press, 1950). All citations are from this edition.

playhouse version was papist (because he was like the Spanish Catholics) and diabolical (because he was allured by vast wealth and evildoing).

## "LIKE SOME CHEATING BANKROUT": THE ADVENTURER AND THE PLAYER

Just because Virginia adventurers were aligned with the Devil and the papists on stage doesn't mean that they were necessarily villains. Some figures to whom New World adventuring is attached are fools—the *Eastward Ho!* crew in particular.[84] However, the majority of the characters to whom adventurer theatermemes are attached display wiliness and trickery, often manifest through some form of theatricality, which allows them to win the day and gain the riches needed to recover their precarious financial position. In Jonson's *Epicene* (1609), Sir Dauphine Eugenie is threatened with bankruptcy by his uncle Morose, who wishes to disinherit his nephew by marrying the title character and producing an heir. So impoverished will Dauphine be that even moving abroad to seek his fortune in "Constantinople, Ireland, or Virginia" will not "repair" his standing (2.5.97–8).[85] Dauphine, however, thwarts his uncle by having him marry a boy dressed up as a woman. That is, his victory is the result of a theatrical trick which he masterminds, one very apt for the transvestite stage of the early modern period, as of course Epicene would have been played by a boy actor. In *The Hog Hath Lost His Pearl*, Haddit is a "prodigal" (1.1.35) who "hath consumed eight hundred pound a year in as few years as he hath ears on his head" (29–30). His plan to rob Hog of both riches and daughter—which goes "better forward than the Plantation in Virginia" (3.3.27)—involves a theatrical troupe, who are friends of his (as established in the play's first scene), and who pretend to be infernal spirits visiting Hog in a dream. They persuade him to give them his silver so as to "Transform it into gold" and his gold so as to "Metamorphose... [it] / Into pearl" (in fact they are stealing it) (5.1.113; 140–1). The heist succeeds thanks to the involvement of players, who mount a theatrical

---

[84] Other examples of characters foolishly invested in the Americas include Timothy Seathrift in Jasper Mayne's *The City Match*, who at the beginning of the play has returned "from the new world" and later in the play gets drunk and finds himself dressed up as a "strange fish" caught near "the Mouth of the Rio de la Plata." Jasper Mayne, *The City Match*, in Isaac Reed and Octavius Gilchrist (eds), *A Select Collection of Old Plays*, vol. 9 (London: Septimus Prowett, 1825), 245, 273.

[85] Ben Jonson, *Epicene, or the Silent Woman*, in Bevington, Butler, and Donaldson, *Cambridge Edition of the Works of Ben Jonson*, vol. 3. All citations are from this edition.

entertainment devised by Haddit, acting as writer, director, and theatrical impresario.

Other characters adopt disguise themselves. We have already heard Staines lament that his "refuge is *Ireland*, or *Virginia*" in Cooke's *Greene's Tu Quoque*. Staines doesn't end up fleeing London, but instead finds himself demoted to being the servant of his former servant, Bubble, who inherits the estate of Staines' landlord (Bubble's uncle). However, by adopting a range of disguises, including appearing "*like an Italian*," Staines outwits Bubble and gets back the money that was taken from him. He declares his ploy to be to

> vary shapes, and my first shift shall be in sattin:
> *Proteus* propitious be to my disguise,
> And I shall prosper in my enterprise.[86]

In *The Honest Lawyer* by "S. S." (1614), the merchant Vaster fakes his own death on suspicion of his wife's infidelity and takes on "the russet-shape of a plaine-dealing yeoman" so as to test his wife's fidelity.[87] In disguise, he enlists his wife's help in a scam and tries to test her honesty by attempting to seduce her. In so doing, he makes the following demand: "Come, will you vnlocke? I ha'the golden key. If not, Ile to Virginia, like some cheating Bankrout, and leaue my Creditour i'th'suddes."[88] At the end of the play, once his wife has proved that she is faithful to him by refusing his advances while he is disguised, Vaster proclaims himself to be "new borne; / Renc'd from the plague of a suspected horne."[89]

All of these characters to whom adventurer theatermemes are attached are attracted to Virginia because it offers them a way out of their situation. However, none actually voyage to the New World, but rather they all change their fortunes by recourse to quick wit and theatrical creativity. None change their moral complexion, even if their desperate situation is by and large of their own making because of their prodigality. They remain resolutely unconverted, and nowhere close to the "new men" imagined in Crashaw's sermon: even Vaster's claims for self-transformation are hollow, as there is no evidence that his wife has been or ever would be

---

[86] Cooke, *Greene's Tu Quoque*, I3v, D4. In this play and in *Epicene* Ireland and Turkey are imagined as potential locations for people looking to escape the debtors' jail. Yet while the Virginia Company bemoaned the mocking representation of Virginia on stage, none of the backers of the Ulster Plantation (found in 1609) or the Levant Company (founded in 1581) complained—although neither company had as pronounced a religious component to their mission.

[87] S. S., *The Honest Lawyer* (New York: AMS Press, 1914), C3v.

[88] S. S., *Honest Lawyer*, H4v.    [89] S. S., *Honest Lawyer*, K2v.

unfaithful, and the "suspected horne" of cuckoldry is nothing but a figment of his overactive imagination.

## "YOU WOULD E'EN AS GOOD GO TO VIRGINIA": THE ADVENTURER AND THE PLAYGOER IN *BARTHOLOMEW FAIR*

In this light the Virginia Company's anti-theatricalism seems specific to Virginia's early history, even though it was indebted to earlier strains of anti-theatricalism dating back to the first flourishing of the permanent, commercial playhouses as voiced by the likes of Philip Gosson, John Stockwood, and Philip Stubbes. The Company's attempts to market itself as a religious enterprise were repeatedly challenged by the circulation of adventurer theatermemes, which not only undermined all protestations of piety by suggesting materialistic and even diabolical motives for investment and settlement but also represented the adventurer as an amalgam of Spanish *conquistador* and unruly player. Which is as much to say that Crashaw and co.'s assessment of the opposition of the theater to Virginia was not so far wide of the mark; at the very least we can begin to understand why the players were regarded as enemies on a par with the Devil and the papists, both because players were habitually described as such in the anti-theatrical tradition and because drama repeatedly and slyly counterclaimed that the adventurers were player-like themselves.

What is less clear is why drama mocked and flouted the Virginia Company. To be sure, the playhouse was a site through which gossip spread—to quote Shakespeare's *Henry IV, Part Two*, it was rumor's "household" (IND. 22). Virginia was periodically a hot topic in the first decades of the seventeenth century: the first steps towards settlement, the loss of *The Sea Venture*, the starving time, the embassies of the Powhatan, the presence of Native American captives, and the Good Friday attacks of 1622 are all spoken about in playhouse drama, albeit in often oblique ways.[90] These events seem to have reached such notoriety that they attracted the attention of the London rumor mill: promoters routinely had to speak out against such rumors that propagated in the playhouses and throughout the capital and beyond. The playing companies were therefore just doing what they

---

[90] The following suppositions form the basis of much of this book's argument: *The Sea Venture* was an inspiration for *The Tempest*; the starving time inspired *The Sea Voyage* (and, as Chapter 2 argues, *The Roaring Girl*); Powhatan embassies are referenced in Jonson's *Epicene* and *The Staple of News*; Indian captives are alluded to in *Henry VIII*; and the Good Friday attacks inspired *The City Madam*.

usually did, namely articulating and re-circulating the language of the streets and capitalizing on the playhouses' position as nodes in the network of rumor-dissemination. That this occurred at the level of the theatergram and, more frequently, at the level of the theatermeme was itself problematic because, as described in the Introduction to this book, this was where the play communed with its audience in the playhouse—where rumor was most likely to seize the audience's attention and hold power.

However, something more systematic may have been going on vis à vis the playhouse's circulation of adventurer theatermemes and indeed more generally in its evocations of Virginia. In closing this chapter, I wish to posit two rationales for playerly opposition to the Virginia Company. Both concern the relation between the theaters and the marketplace: one revolves around their status as sites vying for Londoners' money, and the other revolves around a commodity—tobacco—which was associated with both playhouses and the New World. Both revolve around the idea that the theater was a better investment than the colony, even if both involved taking a chance on smoky intangibles.

The playing companies were oppositional to the Virginia Company in part because they were rival commercial ventures. As Douglas Bruster reminds us, "the theater was, *a priori*, a market," "a place of business . . . [selling] dramatic literature."[91] Colonial trading companies like the Virginia Company resembled playing companies in their structure, and both were, in a sense, operating in overlapping markets and competing for the disposable income of Londoners. Moreover, both the trading companies and the theater companies asked their publics to invest in imaginary constructs, albeit that the Virginia Company strived to make the public's engagement with the colony real by stressing how home-like it was.

These points of comparison between playing and trading companies are evident most conspicuously in Ben Jonson's *Bartholomew Fair* (1614). Jonson's play parallels London and the New World in a number of scenes.[92] In the Induction the Stage-keeper offers an apology for what the audience is about to experience, because the fair that the play depicts is far removed from the real Bartholomew Fair. The play is "a very conceited scurvy one"; "the poet . . . has not hit the humours, he does not know 'em": "When 't comes to the Fair once, you were e'en as good go to Virginia, for anything there is of Smithfield" (IND. 6–9). Yet what at first seems like a dismissal of the playwright's powers of verisimilitude—so

[91] Douglas Bruster, *Drama and the Market in the Age of Shakespeare* (Cambridge: Cambridge University Press, 1993), 10.

[92] See Rebecca Ann Bach, "The New Atlantic World Transformed on the London Stage," in Bach, *Colonial Transformations*, chapter 3, 113–48.

inaccurate is its representation of the real fair that Virginia would serve as just as good an analogue—proves to be prophetic, as Jonson repeatedly argues that the fair is as strange a new world as the one in which the English had settled seven years earlier. Justice Overdo's crusade against the fair is cast in terms of New World exploration. He sets about discovering the "enormities" of the fair and grandiosely compares his "labours" and "discoveries" to "Columbus, Magellan, or our countryman Drake, of later times" (5.6.26–31). At one point Wasp describes his master Bartholomew Cokes' tenants as "a kind o' civil savages, that will part with their children for rattles, pipes, and knives," and by so doing employs a commonplace notion about American Indians not knowing the true value of things and hence being good to "truck with" (3.4.27–9) (a logic evident also in *Eastward Ho!*). In Wasp's estimation, though, it is the English who do not know the true value of things, rather than the Indians; and most particularly it is Cokes himself who wastes his money on toys, "Fine rattles," "Drums," "Babies," "Little dogs," and "birds for ladies" (3–4). In both examples, English men come to the fair and approach it as a New World experience: Overdo with horror, Cokes with wonder. For both the experience is fraught—Overdo is locked in the stocks; Cokes loses his money and his fiancée. However, the play seems to suggest that these denigrations have little to do with the colonial experience, because, for all that the fair is a "brave new world" of sorts, it is also London, filled with home-grown criminality, drunkenness, tobacco-taking, and economic malpractice. Overdo and Cokes, then, are of a piece with the pseudo-knowledgeable travelers elsewhere in the Jonson canon, such as Sir Politic Would-Be and Lady Politic in *Volpone*, albeit both of the fair adventurers are exploring far closer to home.[93]

Jonson's Induction does more than just parallel London and Virginia: it constructs an analogy between voyaging to and investing in the colony and the experience of playgoing. Towards the end of the play's Induction, the Scrivener and Book-Holder announce the "Articles of Agreement indented between the spectators or hearers at the Hope on the Bankside in the County of Surrey" (IND. 49–50). The "Articles" both mock the audience—not the first or last time that Jonson would take his audience to task for misunderstanding his plays or not appreciating his talent—and also Jonson's own desire to control the reactions of his audience.[94] The

[93] On the "English *Monsieur*" in Jonson's drama and poetry, see Rebecca Ann Bach, "Foreign Travel and Exploration," in Julie Sanders (ed.), *Ben Jonson in Context* (Cambridge: Cambridge University Press, 2010), 263–70.

[94] See Kate McLuskie, "Making and Buying: Ben Jonson and the Commercial Theatre Audience," in Julie Sanders with Kate Chedgzoy and Susan Wiseman (eds), *Refashioning Ben Jonson: Gender, Politics and the Jonsonian Canon* (London: MacMillan, 1998), 134–54.

second article mandates that "every person here [can] have his or their free-will of censure," i.e. that the audience is permitted "to like or dislike" the play, but they should do so only in accordance with the money they have paid "at their own charge" (64–5).[95] The Scrivener announces that whoever pays the highest price can "like or dislike" the play the most:

> It shall be lawful for any man to judge his sixpenn'orth, his twelvepenn'orth, so to his eighteen pence, two shillings, half a crown, to the value of his place—provided his place get not above his wit. And if he pay for half a dozen, he may censure for all of them, too, so that he will undertake that they be silent. He shall put in for censures as they do for lots at the lottery: marry, if he drop but sixpence at the door and will censure a crown's worth, it is thought there is no conscience or justice in that. (66–72)

Anyone censuring above their level payment does so unjustly, according to the Scrivener's logic.

In this passage the Scrivener compares paying to enter the theater and the "free-will of censure" (64) that is permitted with the price of admission to buying into "the lottery." As editors of the play generally agree, "the lottery" alluded to here is the Virginia Company lottery scheme that was launched "for the more effectual advancing of the said plantation" as part of the third charter of the Virginia Company of 1612.[96] The lotteries were heavily publicized (at least eleven Virginia Company tracts were printed to promote them) and proved popular, as for the relatively inexpensive sum of twelve pence an individual might stand a chance of winning 4,500 crowns. De Zuñiga wrote in August 1612 that the Virginia Company "have established a lottery from which they will obtain sixty thousand ducats, and by these means they will dispatch six ships, with as many people as they can get by such pretexts." Two weeks later he wrote that so lucrative was the scheme that "another lottery worth 120.000 ducats" had been granted so that the Company can "send more than two thousand men to that country".[97] Through these lotteries, which were drawn in Smithfield (the location of Bartholomew Fair) and in Southwark (the location of the Hope Theatre, where *Bartholomew Fair* was the inaugural production), the Company raised £8,000 by 1621—almost half of its £17,800 budget. Upon their cessation by parliamentary order in 1621,

---

[95] The *Oxford English Dictionary* gives two now-obsolete meanings for "censure" that date from this period, "A formal judgement or opinion (of an expert, referee, etc.)," and "Judgement; opinion, *esp.* expressed opinion; criticism."

[96] "A Third Charter of K. James I," in Hening, *Statutes at Large*, 98–110, at 108.

[97] Pedro de Zuñiga to Philip III, August 1, 1612, in Brown, *Genesis of the United States*, vol. 2, 572–3; Pedro de Zuñiga to Philip III, August 16, 1612, in Brown, *Genesis of the United States*, vol. 2, 575.

John Smith commented in a Virginia Company meeting that the lotteries had been the "reall and substantiall food, by which Virginia hath been nourished."[98]

Why does the Induction to *Bartholomew Fair* compare venturing to playgoing through the recently instituted lottery scheme? The idea that the cost of entry should accord with the level of censure is, of course, an absurdity that Jonson, for all his oft-expressed desire to micro-manage his audiences, seems to recognize. "Censure" or judgment could not be monitored or mandated by the amount paid for the right of entrance. Playgoers paid to go to the theater to experience something for which the returns could not be calculated: to attempt to regulate "censure" on the basis of the cost of admission was doomed to failure. Conversely, according to the logic of the Scrivener's analogy, to put in "for lots at the lottery" is absurd because, like the theater, there was every chance that there would be no payback on the investment. Virginia Company investors were putting money into the imaginary construct known as Virginia, while playgoers paid to see a theatrical event, which is as much to say that they paid to imagine what was not actually there. To buy lots in the Virginia Company and to pay for entrance at the theater were, in this sense, analogous investments: both playgoing and lot-buying were Ponzi schemes, investments in absences, although only the players were honest enough to acknowledge it.

*Bartholomew Fair* hints at a form of travel-experience offered by the playhouse, one that came into being through a combination of imaginative projection and economic concern. In the debate about the accuracy of *Bartholomew Fair*'s representation of Bartholomew Fair, and the simultaneous discussion of what was expected and allowed of playgoers, Jonson seems to be contending not just that the playhouse provided consumers with the opportunity to imagine travel to far and distant places (or to see familiar places anew), but also that *going* to the playhouse was an experience that involved a financial transaction comparable to that of the Virginia adventurer. Jonson, through his proxies the Stage-keeper, the Scrivener, and the Book-holder, implies that buying into Virginia was a folly because you might as well pay to go the playhouse to experience the world, even if *Bartholomew Fair* gets Bartholomew Fair wrong. To invest in Virginia was to invest willingly in false hope: it was better to invest in the real Hope. *Bartholomew Fair*, then, posits theater as a rival commercial

---

[98] "Captain John Smith Proposes to Compile a History, April 12, 1621," in Edward D. Neill, *History of the Virginia Company of London* (Albany, NY: Joel Munsell, 1869), 210; see also John Ezell, "The Lottery in Colonial Virginia," *William and Mary Quarterly*, 3rd series, 5(2) (1948): 185–200.

enterprise in imaginary travel, granting its audience an experience of the foreign and the strange without ever having to leave the city—indeed, without the audience even having to travel across the river from Bankside to Smithfield.

## "TOBACCONING IS BUT A SMOAKIE PLAY": THE SMOKING STAGE

Whether or not Ben Jonson opposed the Virginia plantation on religious or any other grounds we will never know. Indeed, there is circumstantial evidence to suggest that this was unlikely, given his relationship with his patron, Pembroke, a Virginia Company member. Rather, Jonson seems to have seen satirical opportunities here and elsewhere in his drama (most notably *Eastward Ho!*) to mock the pretensions of Virginia Company advocates. It may not be too much of a stretch to see Bartholomew Cokes as a foolish adventurer, Justice Overdo as a hypocritical reformist, while Zeal of the Land Busy, the firebrand Puritan who travels to the fair to convert its inhabitants and is disgusted by the perceived perversions of the fair's puppet show, may even be a depiction of the likes of William Crashaw. These portraits probably antagonized the Virginia Company, but it seems like a stretch to concur with Crashaw and use them as evidence of an outright assault on the colony.

While Jonson offers grounds for playhouse opposition to the Virginia Company, how symptomatic *Bartholomew Fair* is of other playing companies' or of individual playwright's feelings towards the colony is hard to say. Perhaps the most frequent deployer of Virginia theatergrams and theatermemes was John Fletcher, in whom Gordon McMullan has diagnosed an unease about transoceanic travel and trade, evident in much of his oeuvre.[99] Unlike Jonson, Fletcher's plays are less inclined to employ the adventurer theatermemes to mock the Company. Indeed, as we will see in Chapters 2 and 3, Fletcher's plays dwell both on the harsh realities of colonial life (especially in relation to food shortages) and the limitations of the mission of Indian conversion. Fletcher's unease though need not be taken as strictly oppositional since, like Jonson, his patrons were Virginia Company members.

In one further regard, however, we can delineate playhouse opposition to the Virginia Company, albeit of an inadvertent variety, by thinking

---

[99] See Gordon McMullan, *John Fletcher and the Politics of Unease* (Amherst: University of Massachusetts Press, 1994), esp. chapter 6, "Discovery," 197–256.

about tobacco. Tobacco-taking was frequently associated with playhouses "both common and private," according to Thomas Middleton in *The Black Book* (1604).[100] From the late 1590s onwards, stage conversations about tobacco were common, whether they concerned particular strains, the form, the cost, or the effects of smoking or drinking it (both positive and negative). Tobacco pipes were an oft-used stage property and smoking scenes (where characters smoke, display the effects of smoking, or buy or sell tobacco) are a feature of several plays, including *Bartholomew Fair*, along with Jonson's *Every Man in* and *Every Man out*, Marston's *The Malcontent*, and Chapman's *All Fools* and *Monsieur D'Olive*, to name but a few examples. This ubiquity reflects the emergent coolness of smoking in the last decade of the sixteenth century, a habit oft-associated with London's fashionable crowds and locales (for example, at Paul's Walk, where, in Jonson's *Every Man out of His Humour* (1600), Shift goes to take "an ounce of tobacco hard by here with a gentleman" (3.1.20–1)).[101] But many other tobacco-taking scenes pass unremarkably, without any argument being voiced or any joke being made about tobacco, as if the activity was just part and parcel of everyday London life.

Smoke did not just emanate from the actors on stage. "A Satiricall Epigram upon the Wanton and Excessive Use of Tabacco," printed among the commendatory verse in the front matter to the pro-tobacco tract *Dyets Dry Dinner* (1599), recounts a visit to a theater, where the poet "chaunc'd . . . To spie a Lock-Tabacco Chevalier, / Clowding the loathed ayr with foggie fume / Of Dock-Tabacco, friendly foe to rume."[102] Plays

---

[100] Thomas Middleton, *The Black Book* (1604), in Taylor and Lavagnino, *Thomas Middleton: The Complete Works*, 204–18, at 218. On the interconnections between smoking and dramatic literature, see Jeffrey Knapp, "Divine Tobacco," in *An Empire Nowhere*; Joan Pong Linton, "Gender, Savagery, Tobacco: Marketplaces for Consumption," in *The Romance of the New World: Gender and the Literary Formations of English Colonialism* (Cambridge: Cambridge University Press, 1998), 104–30; Craig Rustici, "The Smoking Girl: Tobacco and the Representation of Mary Frith," *Studies of Philology*, 96(2) (1999): 159–79; Dennis Kezar, "Shakespeare's Addictions," *Critical Inquiry*, 30 (2003): 31–62; Tanya Pollard, "The Pleasures and Perils of Smoking in Early Modern England," in Sander L. Gilman and Zhou Xun (eds), *Smoke: A Global History of Smoking* (London: Reaktion, 2004), 38–45; Sandra Bell, "The Subject of Smoke: Tobacco and Early Modern England," in Helen Ostovich, Mary V. Silcox, and Graham Roebuck (eds), *The Mysterious and the Foreign in Early Modern England* (Andover, DE: University of Delaware Press, 2008), 153–69.

[101] Ben Jonson, *Every Man out of His Humour*, in Bevington, Butler, and Donaldson, *Cambridge Edition of the Works of Ben Jonson*, vol. 1.

[102] Henry Butts, *Dyets Dry Dinner Consisting of Eight Seuerall Courses* (London: for William Wood, 1599), 3. This more gentle mockery is amplified in Joshua Sylvester's lengthy poem-polemic, *Tobacco Battered*, in which tobacco "best becomes a *Stage*, or else a *Stewes*, / Or *Dicing-house*, where All Disorders use." Joshua Sylvester, *Tobacco Battered* (London: Humphrey Lownes, 1615), 87.

frequently commented on the ubiquity of the drug amongst audience members. In the Induction scenes to Jonson's *Cynthia's Revels* (1600) and to Marston's *The Malcontent* (1604), and in the puppet scene in Jonson's *Bartholomew Fair* (1614), we find characters who describe their enjoyment in indulging in it while going to see plays. In the case of the grocers who attend Beaumont's *The Knight of the Burning Pestle* (1607), we hear of their aversion to second-hand audience smoke, one of many indicators that they are not sophisticated playgoers. So co-dependent were the theater and the tobacco seller that *The Actors Remonstrance*, published in 1643 in the wake of the closure of theaters during the Civil War, acknowledged the fate of "The Tobacco men, that used to walk up and downe, selling for a penny pipe, that which was not worth twelve-pence an horse-load"; no longer could these micro-entrepreneurs thrive without the micro-economy of the playhouse, where they could inflate prices considerably, suggesting that pre-closure they were heavily reliant on the theater as their marketplace.[103]

Smoke, then, could be said to be a key part of the experience of playgoing. We might imagine the stage to be perpetually shrouded in smoke, with all theatrical productions visible through a tobacco haze. In this sense, then, the New World consistently enveloped the early modern stage—in the various forms of the weed carried around by the smoker (or "tobacconist"), in the pipes, in the ash particles swirling in the atmosphere or sticking to walls, floors, and clothing.

As strange as it may sound to us now, however, the presence of tobacco (if presence is quite the right word) made playgoing a decidedly non-Virginian, and arguably even anti-Virginian, experience. Tobacco and the Tidewater region would soon become synonymous, but in the first decades of the seventeenth century tobacco was not a Virginian commodity.[104] Although descriptions of Indians smoking tobacco emerge in the early Virginia tracts, it was not until 1612 that John Rolfe planted seeds originating from Trinidad for tobacco cultivation. There are reports of the profundity of tobacco growth in the colony dating from the late 1610s, but it was only after considerable protections were placed on importing tobacco into England in the 1620s that Virginia became known as a

---

[103] Anonymous, *The Actors Remonstrance* (London: for Edward Nickson, 1643). My thanks to Craig Rustici for pointing me to this source.

[104] On the history of tobacco cultivation and consumption in early modern England and beyond, see Jerome E. Brooks, *The Mighty Leaf: Tobacco through the Centuries* (Boston, MA: Little, Brown, 1953); Jerome E. Brooks (ed.), *Tobacco: Its History Illustrated by the Books, Manuscripts, and Engravings in the Library of George Arents Jr.*, 2 vols (New York: Rosenbach Company, 1958); Jordan Goodman, *Tobacco in History: The Cultures of Dependence* (London: Routledge, 1993).

tobacco producer. Indeed, the English appear ignorant of the Virginia tobacco plantations long after the colony started producing its own strain. A pro-tobacconist tract, *An Advice on How to Plant Tobacco in England*, published in 1615, suggests that Virginia has the potential to match its Caribbean counterpart, but does not mention tobacco cultivation in Virginia despite Rolfe's intervention three years earlier.[105] The first explicit stage reference that links Virginia and tobacco comes from the 1630s, in James Shirley's *The Constant Maid* (1636), where a character enquires after the quality of London's tobacco only to be assured that "Virginia tobacco grows here."[106] Given frequent complaints about the quality of Virginia tobacco by, amongst others, Sir Francis Bacon, we might detect a joke here, marking out the "expert" smoker as nothing of the sort.[107]

Rather than helping to develop Virginia's economy, the plant was associated with bolstering the Spanish hold in the New World. To the English tobacco was as much a Spanish as an American commodity, benefiting the Spanish economy while being deleterious to the English economy. Joshua Sylvester, one of the most fervent critics of tobacco, characterized it as "Don Tobacco," a figure who "hath an ampler Raign / Than Don Philippo, the Great King of Spain," in his poem-polemic *Tobacco Battered*.[108] According to *An Advice on How to Plant Tobacco*, "there is paid out of England and Ireland, neere the value of two hundred thousand pounds every yeare for Tobacco," because "when our Englishmen for these seven or eight yeares last part, traded it at *Trinidado*, or in *Orenoque*, that great store of Gold, Silver, Coine, and plate was carried hence, and given to the Spaniard there in exchange:" "This Trade therefore, where the Treasure of this land is vented for smoke, cannot but greatly preiudice the Common-weale."[109] In *A Treatise Concerning the Importation of Tobacco* (MS, 1620), economist Edward Bennett claimed that English smokers had aided Spanish dominion in the Caribbean. Whereas in former times "their people went there more unwillingly, then ours nowe go to Virginia and the Somer Islands...nowe the case is altered" because of the profits that can be made from tobacco plantations.[110] That moneys spent on tobacco seemed to be going into the

---

[105] C.T., *An Advice How to Plant Tobacco in England* (London: for Walter Burre, 1615).

[106] James Shirley, *The Constant Maid*, in William Gifford and Alexander Dyce (eds), *The Dramatic Works and Poems*, vol. 4 (New York: Russell and Russell, 1966), 465.

[107] Francis Bacon criticized "the *Virginian Tobacco*" for being "too *Dull* and *Earthy*." Francis Bacon, *Sylva Sylvarum: Or a Natural Historie in Ten Centuries* (London: for William Lee, 1635), 221.

[108] Sylvester, *Tobacco Battered*, 91.

[109] C.T., *An Advice on How to Plant Tobacco*, A3–A3v.

[110] Edward Bennett, *Treatise Concerning the Importation of Tobacco* (London: MS, 1620), unnumbered pages.

pockets of England's great rivals in the Atlantic world was one reason why (to quote John Deacon, another anti-tobacconist) tobacco was "pestiferous to the publike state."[111]

The "pestiferousness" diagnosed by Deacon and others drew on medical literature detailing the detrimental effects of tobacco on the smoker's body—and by extension to the body politic. Anti-tobacconist literature outlined the effects of tobacco, which we can see represented on stage in the tobacconist theatergram. The tobacconist is a character frequently poor either in wit, in wage, or in both, whose knowledge of tobacco is extensive but whose cultural affectations are frequently undermined by his folly. This behavior is itself attributed to the effects of his smoking habit, which transforms and effeminizes him. Petoune, the designated smoker from Edward Sharpham's *The Fleer* (1607), epitomizes this type.[112] His name derives from *petun*, a Spanish American word for tobacco. He is a spendthrift, bankrupting himself on his expensive tobacco habit. He contends, "I take it now and then fasting for the purification of my wit" (1.4.79–80), but frequently shows himself lacking in any. His smoking habit renders him impotent (signified by his suggestive "empty pipe") and possibly even syphilitic. He also refers to "divine smoke" and a "celestial herb" (85), and asks that his friends "Profane not the Indian plant" (189–90), provoking a rebuke for "mak[ing] tobacco your idol, taking it in a morning before you say your prayers" (237–8). By equating "the Indian plant" with God, Petoune transfers what should be the object of his religious devotion to a substance often associated with Native American religious practices. Anti-tobacconists frequently claimed that smoking "Indianized" the smoker: as Justice Overdo states in *Bartholomew Fair*, "that tawny weed, tobacco" has a "Complexion...like the Indians that vent it" (2.6.23).[113] By becoming Indian-like through smoking, the Tobacconist engages in diabolical practices, because (to quote James I's *Counterblast to Tobacco*, perhaps the most famous of all anti-tobacconist

---

[111] John Deacon, *Tobacco Tortured* (London: Richard Field, 1616), title page.

[112] Edward Sharpham, *The Fleer*, ed. Lucy Munro (London: Nick Hern Books, 2007). All citations are from this edition.

[113] Kristen G. Brookes argues, "Many antitobacconists who participated in the tobacco controversy of the late sixteenth and early seventeenth centuries spoke of tobacco's insinuation into England and English bodies in the racialized language of fair and dark." Kristen G. Brookes, "Inhaling the Alien: Race and Tobacco in Early Modern England," in Barbara Sebek and Stephen Deng (eds), *Global Traffic: Discourses and Practices of Trade in English Literature and Culture from 1550 to 1700* (New York: Palgrave MacMillan, 2008), 157–78, at 160. See also Craig Rustici, "Tobacco, Union, and the Indianized English," in Jonathan Gil Harris (ed.), *Indography: Writing the "Indian" in Early Modern America, Asia, and England* (New York: Palgrave MacMillan, 2012), 117–32.

tracts) the Indians "denie God and adore the Devil."[114] Tobacconists like Petoune are as smokily insubstantial as the commodity to which they are devoted: Petoune's oft-repeated swearing "by tobacco" becomes a token of his willingness to take meaningless oaths, say meaningless things, and perform meaningless actions. But their insubstantiality comes at a cost: in *The Fleer* the cost may only be to Petoune, but to the anti-tobacconist the cost was to the nation at large, and could be measured not just in lost revenues but in lost masculinities.

As the example of Petoune suggests, playhouse drama often used the tobacconist as a theatergram of fun. But the playhouse was a place that sold tobacco, and this tobacco-selling formed part of its self-cultivation as a gathering place for a public of urban sophisticates—people willing to open themselves up to the protean logic of the theater who imbibed the protean weed. Both tobacco and the theater produced a populace who, in the minds of anti-tobacconists, anti-theatricalists, Virginia Company members, and combinations of all three, eschewed the transformative mission of early modern nationhood. For James I in *A Counterblast to Tobacco*, it was the "greatest sinne of all, that you the people of sortes of this Kingdome, who are created and ordeined by God to bestowe both your persons and goods for the maintenance both of the honour and safetie of your King and Common-wealth, should disable your selues in both" by smoking (or "drinking") tobacco.[115] For William Crashaw, people spreading rumors about Virginia showed "the pusillanimitie, the basenesse, the tendernesse and effeminatenesse of our English people: into which our nation is now *degenerate*, from a strong, valiant, hardie, patient and induring people."[116] While Crashaw doesn't name tobacco as among the causes or symptoms of the national malaise, both he and the anti-tobacconists use similar rhetoric to diagnose it. The theater catered to the degenerate crowd, diverting them from the holy, national project of Virginia and turning them instead to idle recreations that perpetuated different kinds of transformative experience—recreations of which smoking was one.

The most persistent trace of the Americas that we find in early modern drama collected around figures who smoked and practically idolized a Spanish-Indian product and whose conduct was detrimental to the person and to the state. A walking advertisement for Virginia this was not, yet this was also the figure in a sense most invested in the Atlantic world. For the Virginia Company, however, they were invested in the wrong part of the

---

[114] James I, *A Counterblaste to Tobacco* (London: Robert Barker, 1604), B2.
[115] James I, *Counterblaste to Tobacco*, C4.
[116] Crashaw, *New-Yeeres Gift*, F4v.

Atlantic world, and in the wrong thing—degenerating rather than regenerating themselves, self-Indianizing rather than converting the Indian, and idling away their time and money drinking tobacco at the playhouse.

*

While the Virginia Company distinguished between the ideal adventurer and the unholy trinity of Devil, papist, and player, plays collapsed the adventurer, Devil, papist, and player into one another. By so doing drama pointed to the significant paradox in the Virginia Company's transformative logic. The Company argued that the colony would transform English settlers from the vent of England into productive subjects, but it had no systematic program to bring this promise into reality. Its propaganda implied that this would come about thanks to a combination of the harsh environment and strict governance; after all, the English had once been a heroic nation according to its mythical past, and could become so again given the right conditions. At the same time it implied that there was no significant difference between the Virginian and the English environment, that English bodies would cope easily with being transplanted, and that life in the colony would not be so different from life at home. Virginia, then, was imagined in two contradictory ways—as a difficult environment habitable only as a result of labor and as a home-like environment to which the English would easily adapt. Playhouse drama latched on to this paradox and denied the transformative possibilities of the colony, instead offering up a different transformative agenda via the protean possibilities of the commercial theater. By so doing it mocked the pretensions of the Virginia Company; but it also began constructing and even celebrating a vision of the New World—a vision that celebrated the transformative excesses of the imaginary Americas in the smoke-filled auditoria of the London playhouses.

# 2

# Plantation and "the Powdered Wife"

## The Roaring Girl, Eastward Ho!, *and* The Sea Voyage

And one amongst the rest did kill his wife, powdered her, and had
eaten part of her before it was known, for which he was executed, as he
well deserved; now whether she was better roasted, boiled or carbona-
do'd, I know not, but of such a dish as powdered wife I never heard of.

John Smith, *The Generall Historie of Virginia,*
*New-England, and the Summer Isles*

... never choose a wife as if you were going to Virginia.

Thomas Dekker and Thomas Middleton, *The Roaring Girl*

Better sleep with a sober cannibal than a drunken Christian.

Herman Melville, *Moby Dick*

## THE CANNIBAL HUSBAND, THE POWDERED WIFE

That cannibalism structured much European colonialist imaginings is a
commonplace notion.[1] From the circulation of Columbus' letter in 1493
the cannibals, the "ferocious consumers of human flesh," came to be
figures employed in colonial discourse to justify colonization.[2] Europeans
needed to quash the cannibal in order to gain access to the riches of the
New World: wrote Columbus in his journal, "on the island of *Carib* there

---

[1] See Peter Hulme, *Colonial Encounters: Europe and the Native Caribbean 1492–1797*
(London: Routledge, 1992); Frank Lestringant, *Cannibals: The Discovery and Representation
of the Cannibal from Columbus to Jules Verne*, trans. Rosemary Morris (Berkeley: University
of California Press, 1997); essays in Francis Barker, Peter Hulme, and Margaret Iverson
(eds), *Cannibalism in the Colonial World* (Cambridge: Cambridge University Press, 1998);
Jeff Berglund, *Cannibal Fictions: American Explorations of Gender, Race, Colonialism and
Sexuality* (Madison: University of Wisconsin Press, 2006), esp. "Introduction," 1–25.
[2] Hulme, *Colonial Encounters*, 84.

was much filigree..., although it will be difficult in *carib* because those people...eat human flesh."[3] Cannibals were the peoples whom the Europeans' native interlocutors feared; hence stories told about them in European travel narratives served to confirm the natives' tremulousness and their likely yielding to their European saviours: "[the cannibals] are ferocious among these other people [the Arawak] who are cowardly to an excessive degree."[4] The cannibal was the marker of human savagery against which Europeans could measure their own civility—as with Edmund Spenser's description of the Irish in *A View of the Present State of Ireland* (1596); or a lack of European civility, as in the case of Jean de Lery's *Histoire d'un voyage faict en la terre du Brésil* (1578) and Montaigne's famous essay "Des Cannibales" (1580).[5] Psychologically, the cannibal trope was a response to what Anne McClintock calls "the fear of being engulfed by the unknown," which was "projected [by colonizers] onto colonized peoples as *their* determination to devour the intruder whole," rather than the colonizers' own transgressive desires and behaviors, "[t]heir unsavory rages, their massacres and rapes, their atrocious rituals of militarized masculinity, [which] sprang not only from their economic lust for spices, silver and gold, but also from the implacable rage of paranoia" experienced in the New World—"a world of terrifying ambiguities."[6] Anthropophagy, reported at the edges of known worlds since Herodotus, served as a useful and convenient way of countering European anxieties and ambivalences about colonization while both demonizing or dismissing the peoples whom they encountered and validating their conquest and oppression, their figurative and actual rape.[7]

We may expect to find the cannibal in English writing about Virginia. And we do, but not as we might expect. In the first decade or so of the

---

[3] "The Journal of Columbus," in Peter Hulme and Neil L. Whitehead (eds), *Wild Majesty: Encounters with Caribs from Columbus to the Present Day* (Oxford: Clarendon Press, 1992), 17–28, at 27.

[4] "The Letter of Columbus," in Hulme and Whitehead, *Wild Majesty*, 9–16, at 15.

[5] On Irish cannibalism in Spenser, see Robert Viking O'Brien, "Cannibalism in Edmund Spenser's *Faerie Queene*, Ireland, and the Americas," in Kristen Guest (ed.), *Eating Their Words: Cannibalism and the Boundaries of Cultural Identity* (Albany: State University of New York Press, 2001), 35–56.

[6] Anne McClintock, *Imperial Leather: Race, Gender and Sexuality in the Colonial Contest* (New York: Routledge, 1995), 28. McClintock's argument echoes William Arens' influential re-examination of cannibalism in the European imaginary, *The Man-Eating Myth: Anthropology and Anthropophagi* (Oxford: Oxford University Press, 1979).

[7] The cannibal trope was not employed solely in this period to understand New World encounters. For a broader analysis, see Maggie Kilgour, *From Communion to Cannibalism: An Anatomy of Metaphors of Incorporation* (Princeton, NJ: Princeton University Press, 1990); Merrall L. Price, *Consuming Passions: The Uses of Cannibalism in Late Medieval and Early Modern Europe* (London: Routledge, 2003).

Virginia colony, the figure of the cannibal was attached to the settler and
not to the native. There are accounts of settlers, ravaged by the winter of
1609–10, otherwise known as the "starving time," who were forced by
ferocious hunger to consume human flesh. Some "fedd on the Corps of
dead men."[8] Others hunted down the more able-bodied and attempted to
kill them for food. An Indian was killed, buried, and then dug up by "the
poorer sort" and "boyled and stewed with roots and herbs."[9] According to
an oft-repeated (and, it must be said, never verified) anecdote, "one man out
of the mysery that he endured, killing his wiefe, powdered her up to eat her,
for wch he was burned" (powdered meaning salted, for preservation).[10]
These reports arrived in London in late spring 1610, and came to be re-
circulated across the city and beyond for over a decade, despite the Virginia
Company's denials that any such acts had taken place.[11]

　　Of particular notoriety was the last of these, the story of the plight of
the cannibal husband and the powdered wife. Every written account of the
starving time concludes with the story, indicating that to their authors this
cannibal act was the most outrageous of the lot (even in accounts which
deny the veracity of the tale). It seems to have been the most repeated and
reproduced of all of the starving time tales, quickly attaining almost
literary status as "The tragicall historie of the man eating of his dead
wife in Virginia."[12] As we'll see, a number of plays written and performed
in the 1610s and 1620s re-imagine the story through a theatermeme about
the lack of wisdom in bringing women as wives to Virginia because, it
seems, male carnal desire is out of control there. The women will be
threatened by rape, which is described in terms of cannibalism. Ben
Jonson, George Chapman, and John Marston's *Eastward Ho!* (1605),

---

　　[8] Quotation from "The Tragical Relation of the Virginia Company, 1624," in Lyon
Gardiner Tyler (ed.), *Narratives of Early Virginia, 1606–1625* (New York: Charles Scribner,
1907), 419–26, at 423.
　　[9] John Smith, *The Generall Historie of Virginia*, in James Horn (ed.), *Capt. John Smith:
Writings with Other Narratives of Roanoke, Jamestown, and the First English Settlement of
America* (Washington, DC: Library of America, 2007), 411.
　　[10] "The Tragical Relation of the Virginia Company, 1624," in Tyler, *Narratives of Early
Virginia*, 423.
　　[11] That cannibalism took place in the winter of 1609–10 has long taken on the
substance of truth, but has only recently been confirmed by the discovery of a young
woman's skull ("Jane"), unveiled at the Smithsonian in May 2013, which shows signs of
being cut up posthumously for the purposes of consumption. On the place of cannibalism
in colonial American historiography, see Rachel B. Herrmann, "The 'Tragicall Historie':
Cannibalism and Abundance in Colonial Jamestown," *William and Mary Quarterly*, 68(1)
(2011): 47–74.
　　[12] It is accorded this soubriquet in *A True Declaration of the Estate of the Colonie in
Virginia*, the first written response to the starving time. *A True Declaration of the Estate of the
Colonie in Virginia, with a Confutation of Such Scandalous Reports as Have Tended to the
Disgrace of So Worthy an Enterprise* (London: for William Barret, 1610), 16.

which pre-dates the powdered wife but anticipates its impact, depicts a Virginia voyage as a lust-fueled enterprise of desperate men intent on devouring the colony, which is embodied by Winifred, the sole woman on the voyage brought along unwillingly to satiate the men's carnal desires. Middleton and Dekker's *The Roaring Girl* (1611) comments on the place of women in the colonial imaginary, castigates the men of the play for their (metaphorical) consumption of female flesh, and also casts doubt on the longevity of a plantation still reeling from its difficult beginnings when it almost came to consume itself. Fletcher and Massinger's *The Sea Voyage* (1622) expands the meme and features both male and female potential cannibals, and conflates recent debates within Virginia Company circles about the appropriate division of "shares" (of plantation land, of women in marriage) with the imagined shares of body parts among hungry (and often lusty) shipwreck survivors.

The figure of the cannibal husband haunted the English colonial imaginary for a number of reasons. It highlighted the dysfunction of colonial governance, which gave rise to the husband's desperation. It confirmed how ill-suited the first supplies of colonists were to the harsh conditions, because the settlers failed to plant, then alienated the Powhatan who refused to trade with them, and as a result were forced to scrabble around to provide for themselves. It suggested that the very environment of Virginia failed to support the inhabitants—indeed, it had transformed settlers into savages capable of acts far more taboo than anything committed by the local inhabitants. After these reports circulated, it became hard to claim that Virginia was an attractive, viable destination for potential settlers and not a place of depravation, depravity, and despair. But perhaps most significantly of all, the cannibal husband and powdered wife troubled the ways in which the husband–wife dyad was imagined as the structural foundation of colonization, which would gain permanence through a process of husbandry and domestication. The cannibal husband threatened to destroy this image of blissful colonial domesticity. The husband was not fulfilling the role of even-tempered colonist, but rather was distempered, unable to control his appetite. If the domicile was not safe from the cannibal predations of colonists, then the whole plantation was doomed—both because women (according to plantation logic) were there to ensure the future of the plantation, tying and rooting male planters to the soil and providing them with the comforts of home, and because the female body was a metaphor for the plantation, which should be mastered by colonial husbandry but certainly not destroyed by it.

The plight of the powdered wife and the cannibal husband continues to have currency in colonial American historiography. However, as we'll see towards the end of the chapter, the connection between English husbands, English wives, and cannibals fell out of circulation shortly after the attacks on the colony in March 1622, and the cannibal trope came to be grafted onto the Indian. That is to say, it wasn't until this point that the cannibal conformed to conventions established in earlier New World writing. At the same time marriage came to serve more prominently as a guarantor of the colony's preservation rather than as a metaphor for its potential, overhasty dissolution. In the accounts of the attacks, written as the governance of the colony transferred from the Virginia Company to the crown in the mid-1620s, "the powdered wife" was re-located to the colony's distant past, both to condemn the inability of the previous leaders to curtail the colonists' intemperance and to promote the idea that, finally, Virginia's time had come.

## VIRGINIA IS FOR LOVERS

Marriage was a recurring structural motif in English imaginings of overseas plantation. Repeatedly, Virginia is gendered female in the Company's promotional matter, "a countrie so faire," its "soyle so rich, fertill, and fruitefull," its "wombe and bowels" waiting to be "open[ed]," its name a "remembrance of that *Virgine Queen* of eternal memory, who was first godmother to that land and Nation."[13] Promoters framed the relationship between England and Virginia as that of husband and wife. In the "epistle dedicatory" to the printed version of his sermon of 1609, William Symonds imagined the union of Virginia and Britain in terms of marriage: Virginia was "a Virgin or Maiden Britain, a comfortable addition to our Great Britain."[14] Similar sentiments are to be found in the work of Samuel Purchas, who asked the readers of *Purchas His Pilgrimes* (1625) to be suitors and "Looke upon Virginia; view her lovely lookes...her...so

---

[13] Quotations taken from *The Proceedings of the English Colony in Virginia*, in Horn, *Capt. John Smith: Writing*, 37–118, at 41; Benson, *A Sermon Preached at Paules Crosse*, D2; *A True and Sincere*, 18; Price, *Saul's Position Staid*, F2v. On the trope of male "colonizer" or "cartographer" and the female land/body in English writing, see Peter Stallybrass, "Patriarchal Territories: The Body Enclosed," in Margaret Ferguson, Maureen Quilligan, and Nancy J. Vickers (eds), *Rewriting the Renaissance: The Discourses of Sexual Difference in Early Modern Europe* (Chicago, IL: University of Chicago Press, 1986), 131–42; Patricia Parker, "Rhetorics of Property: Exploration, Inventory, Blazon," in *Literary Fat Ladies: Rhetoric, Gender, Property* (London and New York: Methuen, 1987), chapter 7, 126–54; and Kristen G. Brookes, "A Feminine 'Writing that Conquers': Elizabethan Encounters with the New World," *Criticism*, 48(2) (2006): 227–62.

[14] William Symonds, *Virginea: A Sermon Preached at Whitechapel* (London: for Eleazar Edgar and William Welby, 1609), "Epistle Dedicatorie."

goodly and well proportioned limmes and members; her Virgin portion nothing empaired... and in all these you shall see, that she is worth wooing and loves of the best Husband."[15] As John Gillies points out, "Such nuptial imagery is typical of Virginian apologists": "The *nomen* bespoke a kind of coy allure which the propagandists were not slow to exploit."[16] Virginia was the bride to be, and England its husband—a slightly more chaste iteration of what McClintock calls "the porno-tropic tradition," whereby foreign lands and their peoples are feminized and eroticized.[17] The relationship between the two became legible to potential investors through this normalizing rhetoric.[18] As a result Virginia itself became less threatening. As Annette Kolodny has argued in the broader American context, "to make the new continent Woman was already to civilize it a bit, casting the stamp of human relations upon what was otherwise unknown and untamed."[19] Promoters, then, were effectively promising that Virginia was *already* a domesticated space and that it would only become more so thanks to its settlers' husbandry (in both senses of the word). With Virginia as wife, that is, England could secure its position at the head of a transatlantic household.

It was not just at the level of rhetoric that the Virginia Company used marriage to domesticate the colony. Marriage was also employed as a tool of social control. Noting that some male planters grew restless and unruly and that some wanted to come home, the Company attempted to encourage marriage to make them stay, settle down, and have children. In 1619 and again in 1621, the Virginia Company planned to transport a total of 190 women to the colony. At a meeting of the Quarter Court on November 21, 1621, the intention was announced to send

---

[15] Samuel Purchas, *A Discourse on Virginia* (1625), in *Hakluytus Posthumus, or Purchas His Pilgrimes*, vol. 9 (Glasgow: MacLehose, 1906), 242.

[16] John Gillies, "Shakespeare's Virginian Masque," *English Literary History*, 53(4) (1986): 673–707, at 677.

[17] McClintock, *Imperial Leather*, 22. On the English gendering of Virginia and of Guiana, see Louis Montrose, "The Work of Gender in the Discourse of Discovery," *Representations*, 33(Winter) (1991): 1–41.

[18] Other promoters framed the relationship between Virginia and England in terms of parenthood. Thus in the playlet that concludes William Crashaw's *A New-Yeeres Gift* England (quoting the psalms) addresses Virginia, "Come children, hearken vnto me: I will teach you the feare of the Lord"; and Alexander Whitaker, accounting for Virginia's troubled beginning, compares it to "an Infant, which hath been afflicted from his birth with some greiuous sicknes, that many times no hope of life hath remained, and yet it liueth still." While the parent–child dynamic is different from the husband–wife dyad in many ways, we might also understand such rhetoric as positing the Virginia–England relationship in domestic terms. Crashaw, *New-Yeeres Gift*, L3; Whitaker, *Good Newes from Virginia*, 22.

[19] Annette Kolodny, *The Lay of the Land: Metaphor as Experience and History in American Life and Letters* (Chapel Hill: University of North Carolina Press, 1984), 9.

Mayds to Virginia to be made Wyues, wch the Planters there did verie much desire by the want of whome haue sprang the greatest hinderances of the increase of the Plantaĉon, in that most of them esteeming Virginia not as a place of Habitaĉon but onely of a short soiourninge haue applied themselues and their labors wholly to raisinge of the present profit and vtterly neglected not only staple Com̄odities but euen the verie necessities of mans life.[20]

The Company believed that it could "tye and roote the Planters myndes to Virginia by the bonds of wives and children"—children who would stay in the colony and continue its growth and development.[21] Through this new policy, the Company would not only "relieve the disconsolate mindes of our people ther," but also enable the colony to transform itself from trading outpost to permanent settlement.[22]

The Company also seems to have employed marriage as a way of structuring life in the colony, and sometimes brokering peace in it, even before they announced their policy of sending "woemen, Mayds young and vncorrupt to make wifes to the Inhabitn̄ts" in 1619.[23] In a letter from Don Pedro de Zuñiga to Philip III dated September 22, 1612, the ambassador notes "a determination to marrie some of ye people that goe thether with the Virginians," a policy instituted because "the Plantation doth rather diminish then increase." De Zuñiga claimed that his spy "telleth me there are fortie or fiftie persons alreadie married there and other English intermingled with them."[24] The only known example of intermarriage is the famous one between John Rolfe and Pocahontas, but there were likely to have been other English–Native American unions of one kind or another. Governor Thomas Dale proposed marriage to one of Pocahontas' sisters in order to solidify relations between the English and the Powhatan, only to be rebuffed by Wahunsenacawh, who (according to Ralph Hamor) saw that it was "not a brotherly part of your King, to desire to bereaue me of two of my children at once."[25] In addition, archaeologists have estimated that up to forty native women lived in Jamestown in its early years, and have surmised that some of these women lived with men, so de Zuñiga's figures may not

---

[20] Kingsbury, *Records of the Virginia Company*, vol. 1, at 566.

[21] "A Coppie of the Subscription for Maydes," which was discovered amongst the Ferrar Papers at Magdalene College, Cambridge, and dated July 1621. Reprinted in David R. Ransome, "Wives for Virginia, 1621," in *William and Mary Quarterly*, 3rd series, 48(1) (1991): 3–18, at 7.

[22] "A Coppie of the Subscription for Maydes," in Ransome, "Wives for Virginia."

[23] Kingsbury, *Records of the Virginia Company*, vol. 1, at 256.

[24] Don Pedro de Zuñiga to Philip III, September 22, 1612, in Brown, *Genesis of the United States*, vol. 2, 632–3.

[25] Hamor, *True Discourse*, 44.

be far off.[26] About these relationships the Virginia Company said nothing: only William Symonds commented, declaring at Whitechapel that the colonists must "keep themselves to themselves... [and] may not marry nor give in marriage to the heathen, that are uncircumsized," but this is a rare instance of the topic being discussed (and indeed, Symonds doesn't mention whether marrying a "circumcised" or converted Indian was prohibited as well).[27] Rolfe wrote to Dale that he did not know what "should provoke me to be in love with one, whose education hath byn rude, her manners barbarous, her generation Cursed, and so discrepant in all nutriture from my selfe," and agonized over the fact that biblical mixed marriages did not provide him with favorable precedents (especially those detailed in the Book of Nehemiah, which Symonds had drawn upon in his sermon five years earlier).[28] Yet, as we know, Rolfe's fear that his desire for Pocahontas would be frowned upon in Jamestown and in England could not have been further from the truth, as the Virginia Company milked the Rolfe–Pocahontas union for all it was worth. The fact that the Company does not seem to have defended itself from rumors of sexual impropriety (either consensual or non-consensual) need not mean that it was unconcerned by this behavior—under martial law it was decreed, "No man shall ravish or force any woman, maid or Indian, or other, upon pain of death."[29] But its silence may also have been a form of tacit approval, as long as sexual relations did not threaten the status quo. After all, interrelationships could secure relations between settlers and native inhabitants; they may also answer "the wants of the comforts" experienced by the male planters, "without which God saw that Man could not live contendedlie noe not in Paradize"—at least in the short term, while the settlement was being established.[30]

The long-term gender imbalance of the colony, however, was something that greatly concerned the colonial authorities. Alliances like the one predicated on the Rolfe–Pocahontas match could not be entirely trusted: for all the talk of Wahunsenacawh submitting himself to the English crown, it was clear to observers that he very much had his own agenda, regardless of the provenance of his son-in-law (as his refusal to let Dale

---

[26] See William Kelso, J. Eric Deetz, Seth Mallios, and Beverley Straube, *Jamestown Rediscovery*, vol. 8 (Richmond: Association for the Preservation of Virginia Antiquities, 2001), 41–7.

[27] Symonds, *Virginea*, 30.

[28] John Rolfe, "Copy of John Rolfe's Letter to Sir Thomas Dale Regarding His Marriage to Pocahontas," in Philip Barbour, *Pocahontas and Her World* (Boston, MA: Houghton Mifflin, 1970), 249.

[29] Strachey, *For the Colony in Virginea Britannia*, 11.

[30] "A Coppie of the Subscription for Maydes," in Ransome, "Wives for Virginia, 1621," at 7–8.

into his family suggested). In addition, there were rumors that English women had come "out of Bridewell but of soe bad choyse as made the Colony afraide to desire any others," and now lived in the colony as prostitutes—rumors which we find circulated in plays like *Bartholomew Fair* and *The City Madam*.[31] The Company repeatedly stressed that the women whom it transported in 1619 and 1621 were of good reputation and attempted to address the potentially unseemly nature of their policy: these were "younge, handsome, and honestly educated Maides ... being such as were specially recomended vnto the Companie for their good bringing vp by their parents or friends of good worth." What's more, they were to be "disposed in marriage to the most honest and industrious Planters."[32] Correcting the gender imbalance would lend the colony an air of respectability that its reputation notably lacked.

The population imbalance came also to be understood as one of the main causes of the starving time. In his essay "Of Plantations," Sir Francis Bacon, a member of the Virginia Company, advised colonists to "plant with women" only "[w]hen the plantation grows to strength," which is to say when it could provide for itself "and not be ever pieced from without."[33] While Bacon doesn't mention Virginia directly, he was reflecting on the starving time. His essay places repeated emphasis on the necessity for "victuals": Bacon cautions against idlers who "spend victuals, and be weary quickly"; encourages Planters to "consider what victual or esculent things there are, which grow speedily, and within the year"; and argues, "The victual in plantations ought to be expended almost as in a besieged town." The supply and control of food, that is, trumps any other consideration in his timeline for plantation—it determines population ("Cram not in people, by sending too fast company after company; but rather harken how they waste, and send supplies proportionably"), location (avoid seas and river, "marish and unwholesome grounds"), and even security (the savages should often be sent "over to the country that plants, that they may see a better condition than their own, and commend it when they return").[34] For Bacon, it is only after the food supply is established that women could be included in the colony: only then, it seems, could it be guaranteed that there would be sufficient victuals to go around, so that "the plantation may spread into generations" and ensure

---

[31] Quoted by Ransome, "Wives for Virginia," at 5.

[32] Kingsbury, *Records of the Virginia Company*, vol. 1, at 566.

[33] Francis Bacon, "Of Plantations," in Brian Vickers (ed.), *Francis Bacon: The Major Works*, revised edition (Oxford: Oxford University Press, 2002), 407–9, at 409.

[34] Bacon, "Of Plantations," at 408–9.

that its male planters would not (to borrow from *King Lear*) make their "generation messes" (1.1.117).[35]

Bacon's insistence on the timely addition of women reminds us that temperance was a key component in early colonial English thought. As Kasey Evans has articulated, temperance "allows English writers to distinguish their colonial endeavors from those of the vainglorious Spanish; their purportedly evangelical aims represent the temperate subjugation of worldly appetites to loftier spiritual aims." Temperance as understood as the ethical management of time also helped the English to explain away their imperial belatedness: "while the heedless Spanish rush in, despoiling the landscape in their insatiable lust for gold, the English will gradually, temperately, accrue wealth through settlement and plantation."[36] Temperance also defined the ideal colonizer. As argued in *A True Declaration of the Estate of the Colonie in Virginia*, "the Climate is wholesome and temperate, agreeing with the constitutions of our men."[37] The seeming contradictions of the starving time, the pairing of "a temperate climate, and distempered bodies," could be explained away by blaming some among the first settlers for bringing their distemper, their "sluggish idleness," with them from England.[38] Subsequent settlers, already inclined to temperance, would find that the climate suited them (although, as argued in Chapter 1, there was frequently a disjuncture between how potential settlers were imagined on one side of the Atlantic—as "excrement"—and then on the other—"new men"). As Michael Schoenfeldt points out, temperance was understood as "the classical virtue by which appetite is made subject to discipline"—appetite understood both in terms of food and in terms of sexual desire.[39] In Virginia, then, settlers could maintain a temperate constitution both by virtue of living in "a temperate climate" but also by following a bodily regimen, which would be enabled through proper planting and harvesting. As a result they would be able to perform their roles as colonial husbands—a role that involved planting the colony and producing heirs who would carry the colony forward.

[35] Bacon, "Of Plantations," at 409.

[36] Kasey Evans, "Temperate Revenge: Religion, Profit, and Retaliation in 1622 Jamestown," *Texas Studies in Literature and Language*, 54(1) (2012): 155–88, at 161. For a useful, brief history of temperance, see Evans, "Temperate Revenge," 159–62, and Evans, *Colonial Virtue: The Mobility of Temperance in Renaissance England* (Toronto: University of Toronto Press, 2012), esp. chapter 1, "Temperance's Renaissance Transformations," 14–59.

[37] *True Declaration*, 12.      [38] *True Declaration*, 14, 19.

[39] Michael C. Schoenfeldt, *Bodies and Selves in Early Modern England: Physiology and Inwardness in Spenser, Shakespeare, Herbert, and Milton* (Cambridge: Cambridge University Press, 1999), 33.

The winter of 1609–10, then, was attributed to distemper, caused in part by the constitutions of the settlers and by the untimely presence of women. Bacon's essay appeared in print in 1625, at a time when tales of Virginia's cannibalism were much in circulation again (in official Virginia Company documents, which Bacon would have seen, and in first-hand reports by John Smith, George Percy, and William Strachey). Implicit to his model is the idea that Virginia did not have its food supply sufficiently established prior to the arrival of women in the colony. The winter of 1609–10 had been made worse by the fact that the planters were not ready to adopt the mantle of colonial husband. For colonial advocates, women were vital to the colony because they settled the minds of the male colonists and because they ensured that the colony "spread into generations." As Patricia Akhimie has argued, huswifery (domestic and reproductive labor) was deemed crucial for the success of a colony, even though frequently, as here, its importance was underplayed or effaced in much colonial rhetoric.[40] Added too soon, however, and women were more mouths to feed. For Bacon, colonial temperance could only be achieved once the diet of the colony was sufficiently established: with the addition of wives, after the act of proper planting, this temperance could be continued into perpetuity. While he doesn't say as much, we might interpret his reading of the starving time, and of the plight of the powdered wife in particular, as the result of untimely, distempered planting, a marriage in haste, with women being in the wrong place at the wrong time.

The tale of the cannibal husband and the powdered wife tapped into anxieties about what it meant to plant with tempered households.[41] As Patricia Seed has argued, the English announced their possession of American territory through building a house, erecting a boundary, and planting a garden, symbolic acts which inscribed *meum* and *teum* onto the landscape and distinguished English colonist from Indian savage.[42] The cannibal husband dissolved these boundaries: far worse than any Indian, he was already inside the colony, his unruly appetite ready to consume everything, even in the seemingly safe space of the home. He proved that, rather than give rise to a colony of good husbands, Virginia was a place of distempered English savages. Rather than behaving as ideal husbands, the "new men" imagined by William Crashaw, the male settlers displayed

---

[40] Patricia Akhimie, "Travel, Drama, and Domesticity: Colonial Huswifery in John Fletcher and Philip Massinger's *The Sea Voyage*," *Early Modern Travel Writing*, special issue of *Studies in Travel Writing*, 13(2) (June 2009): 153–66.

[41] John Smith, *Generall Historie of Virginia*, in Horn, *Capt. John Smith: Writings*, 411.

[42] See Seed, *Ceremonies of Possession*.

aber das Ingeweyd behalten die Weiber/siedens/vnd in der Brühe machen sie
einen Brey/Mingau genañt/den trincken sie vnd die Kinder/das Ingeweid es-
sen sie/essen auch das Fleisch vmb das Haupt her/das Hirn in dem Haupt/die

Zungen/vnd was sie sonst daran geniessen können/essen die Jungen. Wenn das
alles geschehen ist/so gehet denn ein jeder widerumb heym/vnd nemen jr theil mit
sich. Der jenige so diesen getödtet hat/gibt sich noch einen Namen. Vñ der König
der Hütten kratzet jn mit einem Wilden thiers Zan oben an die Arme. Wenn es
recht geheylet ist/so sihet man die Masen/das ist die Ehre darfür. Denn muß er
denselbigen tag still ligen in einem Netz/geben jhm ein kleins Flitschbögl in mit einem Pfeil/darmit er die zeit vertreibt/scheusset in Wachs/Geschicht darum/daß
jn die Arm nicht vngewiß werden von dem Schrecken deß todtschlagens. Diß
alles hab ich gesehen vnd bin darbey gewesen. Sie können auch bey keiner gesatz-
ten zahl.

N iiij

**Fig. 2.1.** Hans Staden, Ceremonies by which the the Tuppin Ikins kill their
enemies and eat them, from Theodor de Bry, *America Part III*, Frankfurt 1593.
Courtesy of the John Carter Brown Library at Brown University.

traits associated with the worst of the natives—traits that were themselves gendered feminine, the result of excessive and unruly appetites, as is evident in countless evocations of the cannibal trope in which either cannibal acts are carried out by women or by men whose behavior is feminized (see for example Figure 2.1, an engraving depicting Tupinamba women and children eating the bowels and head of a male ritual offering, from Theodor de Bry's *America Part III*). To invoke the plight of the powdered wife was to tap into anxieties about Virginia's union with England, by positing the idea of a colony/home on the verge of self-annihilation as a result of distempered masculinities and the untimely consumption of female flesh.

## THE "TRAGICALL HISTORIE" IN PRINT AND ON STAGE

In a report circulated in the publication *A Briefe Declaration of the Plantation of Virginia duringe the First Twelve Yeares* (1624), the anecdote about the powdered wife is staged as an intimate bedroom scene: "[O]ne amonge the rest slue his wife as she slept in his bosome, cutt her in peeces, powdered her & fedd upon her till he had clean devoured all parts saveing her heade, & was for soe barbarouse a fact and cruelty justly executed."[43] More morbidly and disturbingly, in a report written in the 1620s but not printed until the 1930s, George Percy includes the detail that the woman was pregnant: "This was most Lamentable That one of our Colony murdered his wife Ripped the childe out of her womb and threw it into the River and after chopped the Mother in pieces and salted her for his food. The same not being discovered before he had eaten Part thereof."[44] For all these inconsistencies (and likely embellishments), common themes remain here. In both accounts the appetites of the colonists are unruly: bedroom intimacy descends into a cannibal feast; a child is sacrificed in the attempt to provide future nourishment. The powdered wife, then, serves almost as a parody of the proper form of plantation as promoted by Bacon and other colonial advocates. Her meat is preserved

---

[43] *A Breife Declaration of the Plantation of Virginia duringe the first Twelve Yeares, when Sir Thomas Smith was Governor of the Companie, & downe to this present tyme. By the Ancient Planters nowe remaining alive in Virginia*, reprinted in *Colonial Records of Virginia* (1894; reprinted Baltimore, MD: Genealogical Publishing, 1973), 69–81 at 71.

[44] Mark Nicholls (ed.), "George Percy's 'Trewe Relacyon': A Primary Source for the Jamestown Settlement," *Virginia Magazine of History and Biography*, 113(3) (2005): 212–75, at 249.

by being salted, creating a future food supply, but once her body is consumed there is nothing to replace it with and no way for the plantation to "spread into generations."

Appetite is front and central also to the account written closest to the events of the starving time, the colony's publication *A True Declaration of the Estate of the Colonie of Virginia* (1610). The pamphlet was written to discredit the disgruntled former colonists who had fled back to London in May 1610 aboard a stolen ship, *The Swallow*, having taken an oath "to agree all in one report to discredit the Land, to deplore the famine, and to protest that this their comming away, proceeded from desparate necessitie." The rumors that they brought with them and persisted in "roar[ing] out" included "The tragicall historie of the man eating of his dead wife in Virginia." Using the testimony of Thomas Gates (Virginia's deputy governor, who arrived in May 1610), the pamphlet describes the events as follows:

> There was one of the Company who mortally hated his Wife, and therefore secretly killed her, then cut her in pieces and hid her in divers parts of his House: when the woman was missing, the man suspected, his House searched, and parts of her mangled bodie were discovered, to excuse himselfe he said that his Wife died, that he hid her to satisfie his hunger, and that hee fed daily upon her. Upon this, his House was againe searched, where they found a good quantitie of Meale, Oat-meale, Beanes and Pease. He thereupon was arraigned, confessed the Murder, and was burned for his horrible villainy.[45]

Gates' refutation places the blame on a particular "one of the Company," thus isolating him, while the detection of this crime was thanks to the efforts of "the rest" of the Company. As a result the "one" is transformed into an aberration rather than a symptom. Gates' stressing that the man's "villainy" was detected because he had a "good quantitie" of food underscores the idea that, contrary to the claims that the colony was beset with famine, there was food available in the colony. The husband's motive ("desparate necessitie") was undermined by the fact that he had supplies in his house (in perhaps a first, the husband uses cannibalism as part of his defense against charges of uxoricide). The Virginian appetite, according to Gates, was not unruly, even if the appetite of one particular Virginian had been.

Subsequent Virginia Company tracts bypassed details of the events: states one, "It were vild to say what we endured," while another refers to

---

[45] *True Declaration*, 16.

"monstrous sinnes."[46] Others flat out ignored them.[47] However, Gates' refutation, and the coyness or denials of other reports, clearly did not have the desired effect, and the rumors about cannibalism continued to be "roared" out. The anecdote was revived in various print and manuscript sources in the 1620s, but it was also clearly in circulation in other media. The soubriquet given to the tale in 1610, "tragicall historie," suggests that the rumor had attained some kind of balladistic status, a story sung through the streets of London to some popular tune, or the status of drama, to be performed in one of the London theaters.

The speed at which the story spread—indeed, the speed at which it was given a title—can be attributed to the fact that many of its main elements were already part of popular cultural representation. Cannibals are often invoked in early modern drama as the figure at the edge of the map, inhabiting (to quote Othello's famous speech to the Venetian senate) "antres deep and deserts idle" (*Othello*, 1.3.139). They are frequently imagined as threats to women in particular—think of Caliban, whose name is one letter and a small rearrangement away from cannibal, who once threatened to "violate" Miranda in *The Tempest* (1.2.350). Yet for all their strangeness, cannibals are often invoked as figures disturbingly close to home. Othello has "thick-lips" and "gross clasps" (1.1.66, 127) which threaten to envelop Desdemona—a conflation of the trope of dark-skinned foreign man as cannibal and as rapist—and he wants to "chop her into messes [i.e. food]" (4.1.190) on discovering her (purported) infidelity. However, he was "oft invited" into Brabanzio's household (1.3.127), and he ends up killing Desdemona in perhaps the most domestic space of all, the bedchamber. Lear famously will have "the barbarous Scythian" ("Maneaters," according to Herodotus) and "he who makes his generation messes / To gorge his appetite" "as well neighbored" to his

---

[46] *The Proceedings of the English Colonie in Virginia* (1612), in Horn, *Capt. John Smith: Writings*, 115; Whitaker, *Good Newes from Virginia*, 22. In a perhaps inadvertent slippage, Whitaker describes "the famine [of 1609–10], which had by that time deuoured the most of our countrimen heere, [and] would haue consumed the rest" (23).

[47] For example, *The Lost Flocke Triumphant*, a poem by one of the survivors of *The Sea Venture* wreck, alludes only to how the "English-men [have been] opprest with greife / and discontent in mind"; while a single-page bulletin from 1611 celebrating the belated arrival of Thomas Gates and Thomas Dale the year before and advertising for competent, skilled laborers, alludes only to "manifold impediments known to the world." A later bulletin heralding the return of Dale in 1617 offers assurance "of the good estate of that colony" and the "great plentie and increase of Corne, Cattell, Goates, Swine, and such other prouisions, necessary for the life and sustenance of man." Perhaps understandably, given its purpose was to attract settlers, it does not mention the poor state of the colony—which came about through great dearth—seven years earlier. Robert Rich, *The Lost Flocke Triumphant* (London: for John Wright, 1610), B; *By the Counsell of Virginia* (London: for William Welby, 1611); *By His Maiesties Councell for Virginia* (London: Thomas Snodham, 1617).

"bosom" as his youngest daughter (*Lear*, 1.1.116–19).[48] Cannibals, as imagined in early modern drama, are a threat not just at the frontier but also in the household. If, like Lear, you find yourself preferring the company of cannibals, then something must be profoundly wrong with your home life.[49]

That "the tragicall historie" caught the imagination should not therefore be surprising. In a sense it was a story that had already been told even before 1610—a story in which a cannibal is invited through the threshold or, more horrifyingly, found to have already passed through the threshold, whether invited or not, and was already lying in wait, in plain sight. In the colonial context, however, it was especially horrifying, confirming the very worst fears about the English in the New World. It wasn't so much that the English were encountering cannibals beyond the edges of the known—although this is where explorers' accounts and cartographers tended to place them. Rather, it was that the English were discovering themselves.

## "SACRIFICE FOR A PROSPEROUS VOYAGE": CARNAL DESIRE AND GLOBAL COMPASSING IN *EASTWARD HO!*

Jonson, Chapman, and Marston's *Eastward Ho!* (1605) may predate the settlement of Virginia by two years, and the powdered wife by five, but suggests that rape and cannibalism were already conflated terms in circulation in the run-up to the departure of the first supply. It also anticipates the image of the Virginia adventurer *avant la lettre*, a construction enabling later rumors about the "desparate necessitie" of the starving time. As discussed in Chapter 1, Flash, Seagull, Scapethrift, and Spendall wish to travel to Virginia because of the parlous state of their finances and because they have heard about the riches on offer over there. The voyage also resembles a form of sex tourism: in his suggestive borrowing from Sir Walter Raleigh's *Discoverie of Guiana* (1595) and its claim that "*Guiana* is a Countrey that hath yet her Maydenhead," Seagull declares that "Virginia

---

[48] Robert Strassler (ed.), *The Landmark Herodotus: The Histories* (London: Quercus, 2007), 326.

[49] On Shakespeare and his contemporaries' use of cannibal imagery, see Stephen Orgel, "Shakespeare and the Cannibals," in Marjorie B. Garber (ed.), *Cannibals, Witches, and Divorce: Estranging the Renaissance* (Baltimore, MD: Johns Hopkins University Press, 1987), 40–66; Raymond J. Rice, "Cannibalism and the Act of Revenge in Tudor-Stuart Drama," *SEL Studies in English Literature 1500–1900*, 44(2) (Spring 2004): 297–316.

longs till we share the rest of her maidenhead" (3.3.11).[50] Recalling one of
the theories behind the disappearance of the Roanoke colony, Seagull
describes how the English who are already there "have married with the
Indians and make 'em bring forth as beautiful faces as any we have in
England, and therefore the Indians are so in love with 'em that all the
treasure they have, they lay at their feet" (14–16). The welcoming native
women, with whom the previous colonists intermarried, have given rise to
a new race of beatific English, who continue to hold sway over the native
population.

Even though the voyagers expect a warm reception from the Indians
and from the mixed-raced descendants of the settlers, they also include in
their party Winifred, wife of the villainous usurer, Security. Winifred's
presence in the scene where the voyagers discuss their plans has not been
discussed or even acknowledged by critics of the play.[51] Smuggled aboard
by the adventurers in part to anger her husband, Winifred is the object of
desire for the crew, and the end of act 3, scene 3 features them dancing
around her as a form of ritual in preparation for their departure. Her
presence in the party underscores the crew's ill-suitedness for a transoceanic voyage—women on ships were deemed to be bad omens, hence
only the inexperienced sailor would have a woman on board (in *The Sea
Voyage*, for example, the Master shows his adeptness as a sailor *through* his
disapproval of the presence of a woman on board his ship (*The Sea Voyage*,
1.1.65–9)).[52] But Winifred's presence on board also testifies to further
associations between women, voyaging, plantation, and male cannibalism.
The dance of *Eastward Ho!*'s adventurers around the captive Winifred,

[50]  Sir Walter Raleigh, *Discovery of the Large, Rich, and Beautiful Empire of Guiana, by Sir
W. Raleigh: With a Relation of the Great and Golden City of Manoa (which the Spaniards call
El Dorado), etc. Performed in the Year 1595*. The Hakluyt Society, First Series, vol. 3
(Farnham; Burlington: Ashgate, 2010), 115.

[51]  While *Eastward Ho!* has received some critical attention for its imagining of travel and
its envisioning of a cosmopolitan city, outside of the work of Rebecca Ann Bach and Joseph
Sigalas the significance of Virginia has been subject to very little analysis. See Bach, *Colonial
Transformations*, esp. 116–27; Joseph Sigalas, "Sailing against the Tide: Resistance to Pre-
Colonial Constructs and Euphoria in *Eastward Ho!*," *Renaissance Papers* (1994): 85–94. On
*Eastward Ho!*'s cosmopolitanism, see Jean E. Howard, "Credit, Incarceration, and Per-
formance: Staging London's Debtors' Prisons," in *Theater of a City*, 68–113; and Howard,
"Bettrice's Monkey: Staging Exotica in Early Modern London Comedy," in Jyotsna Singh
(ed.), *A Companion to the Global Renaissance* (Oxford: Blackwell, 2009), 326–39; on
*Eastward Ho!*, travel and genre, see Anne-Julia Zwierlein, "Shipwrecks in the City: Commercial Risk as Romance in Early Modern City Comedy," in Dieter Mehl, Angela Stock,
and Anne-Julia Zwierlein (eds), *Plotting Early Modern London: New Essays on Jacobean City
Comedy* (Aldershot: Ashgate, 2004), 75–94.

[52]  John Fletcher and Philip Massinger, *The Sea Voyage*, in Anthony Parr (ed.), *Three
Renaissance Travel Plays* (Manchester: Manchester University Press, 1995). All citations are
to this edition.

who will, in Sir Petronel Flash's suggestive phrase, "bear us company all our voyage" (48–9), performs the equation of female bodies and feminized landscape. As the world was "compassed" by Sir Francis Drake (119), so she is "encompassed" by the crew—Security addresses her as the "lady . . . encompassed there" (132). Winifred's body, then, serves as an embodiment of the colony they mean to conquer. In Jonson, Chapman, and Marston's play, then, Raleigh's optimistic deployment of the land–body figuration is twisted into its latent other potential—that Virginia does not long "till we share the rest of her maidenhead" but is fated to be raped by drunken and debauched English voyagers.

*Eastward Ho!*, however, goes beyond signifying Winifred's body as a Virginia substitute. The threat to Winifred is not just posed as an act of rape, but also as an act of absolute consumption in a cannibal sacrifice. We learn that the adventurers intend to spend their last night in London prior to the voyage "aboard Sir Francis Drake's ship" (119). Their "new ceremony at the beginning of our voyage" (114–15), imagined as the establishment of a ritual which "will be followed of all future adventurers" (115–16), revolves around orgiastic eating and drinking that takes on a cannibalistic flavor. "[W]e will do sacrifice for a prosperous voyage," Flash declares, to "some good spirits of the water" that haunt the *Golden Hind*, who will look favorably on "all that honour her memory" (120–2). Their "sacrifice," initially it seems of the "supper" to be brought aboard Drake's vessel, also seems to encompass Winifred (118). She is to be the figurative sacrifice to placate the spirits, the virgin who will be "shared" by all of the crew aboard the ship, and also cut into shares, just as Virginia will "share with us her maidenhead." Winifred is also conflated with the vessel on which they will sup: Flash describes the "desert ribs of her" (121–2), which the spirits haunt, a reference superficially to the hull of the *Hind*, but which also suggests Winifred's impending rape. Her "desert ribs," evoking her exposed body, also recalls descriptions of the hollowed rib cages of the cannibal feasts. At the same time they fold back into the association between Winifred and the "desert" lands where Flash and his fellow voyagers are hoping to "live freely" (29). Flash's imagery suggests both that the sacrifice aboard the *Golden Hind* and that the sacrifice of Winifred's "desert ribs" through cannibal-rape will lead to an auspicious trip—a pagan honoring of the ghosts performed by English adventurers en route to the colony.

In the following scenes we find that the adventurers' plans run aground, as it were, and their cannibal desires are not fulfilled. Their dance around Winifred occurs before they have even encountered the propitious ghosts of the *Golden Hind*: the would-be colonists are so intemperate that they begin their rituals before the allotted time and not in the place designated for them. The impotence of these imaginings is revealed two scenes later, when the vessel runs aground at Cuckold's Haven—a location most immediately appropriate for Security, husband to Winifred, but which also seems to apply more generally to all of the crew, whose attempts at the virile conquest of Virginia become undone, their ship unmanned. However, in the scene that precedes the setting sail and shipwreck, Jonson, Chapman, and Marston graft together a variety of significations through the body of Winifred—she is virgin sacrifice, the virgin landscape, the object of desire, the figure-to-be-raped, the cannibal victim. Her presence in the play also serves to bring out the latent characteristics of the adventurers, whose Virginia voyage is not only one of self-interest, but one which also has the potential to transform them into monstrous, hypersexual cannibals. Indeed, the play seems to suggest that this transformation is more of an unveiling, as these tendencies seem very much present in English adventurers before their encounter with Virginia, as a set of thoughts and practices that they will import with them from London into the colony rather than ones that they will absorb from their encounters.

## "NEVER CHOOSE A WIFE AS IF YOU WERE GOING TO VIRGINIA": *THE ROARING GIRL*

*Eastward Ho!* may have anticipated "The tragicall historie of the man eating of his dead wife in Virginia," but *The Roaring Girl* capitalized on it. In the play Sebastian, the romantic hero, makes a show of attempting to woo Moll, in full knowledge that his father will disapprove of the match and instead allow him to marry his true love, Mary (who is deemed beneath Sebastian's station). Moll rebuffs Sebastian's advances, warning him to think more carefully before proposing marriage to someone he barely knows: "Think upon this in cold blood, sir; you make as much haste as if you were a-going upon a sturgeon voyage. Take deliberation, sir, never choose a wife as if you were going to Virginia" (4.70–3).[53] These lines are open to multiple interpretations—indeed, the play's recent editors seem to have little consensus. Moll could mean that Sebastian should not marry as if he is voyaging to somewhere with uncertain prospects. Moll, then, becomes a Virginia-like figure, in the sense that she is a bad investment—a contrast to Winifred's Virginia-like body in

---

[53] Thomas Middleton and Thomas Dekker, *The Roaring Girl*, in Taylor and Lavagnino, *Thomas Middleton: The Collected Works*. All citations are from this edition.

*Eastward Ho!*, and a marker of the difference between the desirability of Virginia in the English imaginary before and after settlement in 1607.[54] She could mean that Sebastian is marrying with all the haste of someone who is about to put to sea, where either on the sea or in the colony coming by a wife would be hard, since (to quote Elizabeth Cook) in Virginia "there would be no chance of finding a wife once there, [hence] one must take one from home."[55] What Sebastian fails to realize, according to Moll, is that he is not about to embark on a long voyage—he has more time to choose a wife than he seems to think.

Moll's lines could mean the exact opposite, however. It may not be that there are no women in the colony, but rather that there are plenty. Moll's maxim, then, could be read as bawdy. She may be thinking of the relations between English men and Indian women, about which Don Pedro de Zuñiga wrote in his letter to Philip III in September 1612. She may also be commenting on the reputation of English women who had already voyaged to the colony and turned (it was rumored) to prostitution, an association we find elsewhere in early modern drama. In Jonson's *Bartholomew Fair* (1614), two gentlewomen, Dame Overdo and Mrs Littlewit, take on the appearance of prostitutes, having been subjected to a make-over by the bawd, Alice: there may here be a suggestion that anyone who goes to the Virginia-like Fair (or the Fair-like Virginia) will turn to prostitution. The association can also be found in Philip Massinger's *The City Madam* (1632), where the title character and her daughters, horrified on hearing about their impending transportation to the colony, complain that "Strumpets and bawds, / For the abomination of their life, / [are] Spew'd out of their own country" and are "shipp'd thither" (5.1.106–10). We may also detect a note of satire in John Smith's account of cannibalism in Virginia in *The Generall Historie*: his description of "such a dish as powdered wife" evokes debates about women's use of cosmetics (powdering meaning both make-up and salting for preservation), such that Smith's grisly imagining of the fate of the victim may also have been a satirical swipe at the reputed professions of the women of the colony.[56] The word

---

[54] Coppélia Kahn glosses the line in this way in Taylor and Lavagnino, *Thomas Middleton: The Collected Works*, 742 n. 71–2.

[55] Thomas Middleton and Thomas Dekker, *The Roaring Girl*, second edition, ed. Elizabeth Cook (London: Methuen, 1997), 44 n. 67.

[56] The *Oxford English Dictionary* cites Jonson's *Epicene* (1609; pub. 1616) as the first usage of "powder" in relation to cosmetics (def. 4. a). On cosmetics and misogyny, see Frances E. Dolan, "Taking the Pencil out of God's Hand: Art, Nature, and the Face-Painting Debate in Early Modern England," *PMLA*, 10(2) (1993): 229–30; Shirley Nelson Garner, "'Let Her Paint an Inch Thick:' Painted Ladies in Renaissance Drama and Society," *Renaissance Drama*, 20 (1989): 123–39; Annette Drew-Bear, *Painted Faces on the Renaissance Stage: The Moral Significance of Face-Painting Conventions* (Lewisburg,

"dish," too, has erotic connotations—just think of Cleopatra as Antony's "Egyptian dish" in *Antony and Cleopatra* (2.6.123). Moll's lines, then, may serve as a warning that there are plenty more fish in the sea, and that Sebastian should enjoy his youth rather than marry in haste.

Moll's lines also express sympathy for any woman pursued by hot-headed males. One scene after her encounter with Sebastian, Moll meets with Laxton on what he wrongly assumes to be a sexual assignation. Moll, however, is repulsed by his approach, and castigates his behavior as a "good fisherman" (5.101). Women who fall for the likes of Laxton are "Distressed needlewomen and trade-fallen wives, / Fish that must needs bite, or themselves be bitten" (95–6), "hungry things" who are "took / With a worm fastened on a golden hook. / Those are the lecher's food, his prey" (97–9). Moll's lines not only serve as evidence of her female solidarity; they also suggest that the plight of the powdered wife lies beneath her warning to Sebastian one scene earlier. Laxton's (and Sebastian's) "angling" is equated with a form of cannibalism. These men ruin women by dangling the hook and then consuming them, as a fisherman does fish.

Moll's terms seem not only to suggest that such a hasty marriage would be bad for Sebastian, but also that it would be bad for his wife, whoever she may be: the wife, once consumed, will be of no further use, precisely because there are plenty more sturgeon in the sea and there are plenty more women in Virginia. The language that surrounds the maxim has cannibalistic overtones. She rejects Sebastian's advances by saying that she has "the head now of myself" and dismisses marriage as "but a chopping and changing, where a maiden loses one head, and has a worse i'th'place" (4.45–7). While the primary meaning here revolves around a loss of virginity, in Moll's language lies the grisly reminder of a dismembered, married woman whose "head" was literally lost on a Virginia voyage—all that remained of the powdered wife, herself "chopped and changed," was her head. The colony is an unsuitable place for a wife—because there is no food there, but also because of the danger that wives will become food to hungry, hot-blooded males.

In Moll's rebuttal of Sebastian (and her subsequent stand against Laxton), and in subsequent iterations of her aphorism in other plays, we can hear a trace of the experiences of women who were transported to Virginia in its early years. Through the complex chain of associations that

PA: Bucknell University Press; London: Associated University Presses, 1994); and Farah Kareem-Cooper, *Cosmetics in Shakespearean and Renaissance Drama* (Edinburgh: Edinburgh University Press, 2006). My thanks to Shereen Inayatulla for pointing out this connection.

link the female body to the model of plantation, we can also hear parodied the whole prospect of the colony as a venture with a future. Its continuation was predicated on the figurative reproductive capacities of the land and on the actual reproductive capacities of its inhabitants, both of which proved problematic, given the lack of planting and the lack of women in the colony. It is in the female body, then, that the hopes of the plantation resided: yet the female body was also the site of much anxiety—without women, the plantation would falter; without plantation, the women were in danger of falling prey to male carnal desire. Moll's advice to Sebastian, and the encircling language of dismemberment and consumption, disseminates the idea that Virginia's time was distinctly out of joint, by preserving the story of the powdered wife, remembering the plight of women in the colony, and predicting the woes that would befall any wife embarking on an all-too-hasty Virginian marriage.

## "WHY DID YE NOT . . . SPARE THE WOMAN TO BEGET MORE FOOD ON?": CONSUMING THE COLONY IN *THE SEA VOYAGE*

Thomas Middleton utilized the analogy of marrying in too much haste being akin to far-reaching travel in his later play, *Women Beware Women* (1621). At the beginning of the play Livia stalls the overhasty marriage of her niece Isabella to the idiotic Ward, saying "Tis fit, I'faith, she should have one sight of him, / And stop upon't, and not be joined in haste / As if they went to stock a new-found land" (1.2.59–61).[57] Middleton's return to the meme ten years after *The Roaring Girl* may be testament to its longevity, but we should note a slight change in emphasis. Livia alludes not just to bringing a wife to Virginia in an overhasty manner but to the purpose of the marriage, "to stock a new-found land." Middleton here may have been drawing on a line in a play from earlier in his career, but he may also have been alluding to the transporting of wives to Virginia in 1619 and 1621. By the late 1610s, that is, the Virginia Company had deemed it an appropriate time to "plant with women."

John Fletcher drew on the theatermeme that women voyaging to Virginia was a bad idea in three plays. In his *The Loyal Subject* (1618), the title character Archas, a general, is forced to send his two daughters Honora and Viola to the court to appease his master the Duke, who suspects him of encouraging the army to mutiny. The Duke's court is characterized as

---

[57] Thomas Middleton, *Women Beware Women*, in Taylor and Lavagnino, *Thomas Middleton: The Collected Works*.

corrupt, but Archas hopes that by seeing such corruption the court will act as "vertue's school" for his daughters, because it will expose them to sins which they will subsequently be better able to avoid (3.3.53).[58] Honora accepts her fate: "I will to court most willingly, most fondly. / And if there be such stirring things amongst 'em, / Such travellers into Virginia, / As fame reports, if they can win me, take me" (67–70). Honora links "travellers into Virginia" to courtiers "with stirring things amongst 'em." By so doing, she casts herself as "Virginia," mapping the colony onto her body which she fears will be violated by courtiers just as the colony had been by "travellers." Thus she suggests that those who travel to Virginia are sexual predators, and that Virginia itself is, as its name suggests, virgin terrain that has been "taken." Honora's figurative language also collapses rape and cannibalism in the ensuing dialogue. She envisions welcoming the hungry courtiers to look on her and her sister, who will "feed so, and be fat" (72)—their lusty gaze transformed into rabid carnality.

In another Fletcher play, *The Noble Gentleman* (first performed in 1606 by the King's Men at the Globe, revised and revived at Blackfriars in the 1620s), the vain gentleman of the title, Monsieur Marine, who has pretensions to courtly status, attempts to encourage his male cousin to accompany him to the court with his wife. His cousin is not impressed: "Sir I had rather send her to Virginia / To help to propagate the English nation" (90–1).[59] As in *The Loyal Subject*, the court is characterized as a place of sexual decadence: it is clear that among the things that allure Marine to the court is "the wealth of Nature, the faire dames, / Beauties" (76–7). His cousin, however, believes that Virginia is a more suitable place for a woman than the court—his wife would be far safer from male predation over there. Again, Fletcher collapses the threat of rape and the threat of cannibalism. The language used to describe the court takes on gustatory connotations subsequently when Marine praises court life: "Cozen, how savours this? Is it not sweet / And very great, tasts it not of Nobleness?" (101–2). His cousin, who is disgusted by the taste of court life, admits that his "pallat is too dull and lazy" (103–4). Thus in both plays Fletcher condemns court life as corrupt and cannibalistic and its female inhabitants threatened by intemperate male appetites—so much so that in the case of *The Noble Gentleman* Virginia itself seems a preferable place for women, despite its notoriety.

[58] Francis Beaumont and John Fletcher, *The Loyal Subject*, in Fredson Bowers (ed.), *The Dramatic Works in the Beaumont and Fletcher Canon*, vol. 5 (Cambridge: Cambridge University Press, 1992). All citations are to this edition.

[59] Fletcher, *The Noble Gentleman* in Bowers, *The Dramatic Works in the Beaumont and Fletcher Canon*, vol. 3. All citations are to this edition.

The most sustained example of the theatermeme in the Fletcher canon—indeed, to be found anywhere in early modern drama—is his collaboration with Philip Massinger, *The Sea Voyage* (licensed June 22, 1622). The play is set on two neighboring islands. The first is barren. On it live two Portuguese men, Sebastian and Nicusa, shipwrecked and separated from the rest of their family, which had set to sea after their plantations were ransacked by the French several years prior to the events of the play. To this island come a crew of Frenchmen, and one French woman, Aminta, who has been captured by Albert, a pirate, because of his rivalry with her brother, Raymond—a rivalry which originated with the opposition of their fathers, Frenchmen who fell out after ousting the Portuguese way back when. Sebastian and Nicusa, realizing that many of the French are greedy, distract them with the promise of riches and flee the island on their boat, leaving them to starve. The second island, by contrast, is fecund. It was once inhabited by an Amazon colony, and is now by Sebastian's wife, Rosellia, his daughter Clarinda, and three waiting women. Halfway through the play the inhabitants of the islands meet, thanks to Albert, who swims across the channel; however, the meeting does not go well, as Rosellia recognizes that Albert's father was one of the men who forced her family from their plantation homes and led to their separation at sea. She decides to put the French to death in an elaborate, sacrificial ritual, which, as we'll see, has a cannibalistic flavor to it. Their execution is averted only when Sebastian and Nicusa return and reveal their true identities, at which point Rosellia's rage relents, and the reunited families return home in what, as we'll see, seems like a markedly over-hasty manner.

Although the play was performed twelve years after *The Swallow*'s returnees "roared out the tragicall historie of the man eating of his dead wife in *Virginia*," it is clear that Fletcher and Massinger remembered the story, and that they expected their audience at Blackfriars to do so as well. In act 3, scene 1, four Frenchmen, shipwrecked and starving, plot to kill Aminta, "And then divide her, every man his share" (3.1.112). When Aminta protests, "Are ye not Christians," one of the Frenchmen, "*an usuring merchant*" named Lamure, responds, "Why, do not Christians eat women?" (140–1), a question which suggests (according to Anthony Parr) that "The gallants seem to have been listening to the renegades who deserted the Jamestown colony in 1609–10."[60] To justify their cannibalism, Lamure and Morillat,

[60] Fletcher and Massinger, *The Sea Voyage*, 176, n. Critics have tended to agree with Parr that *The Sea Voyage*, rather than *The Tempest*, is the closest extant play we have to be set in the Atlantic context—its drawing on French and Portuguese Atlantic colonial history often being held up as evidence. For Atlantic readings of the play, see Gordon McMullan, *The*

"*a shallow-brained gentlemen*," remember "Stories—/ Of such restoring meats" where cannibal acts have "allowed for excellent" (the noun governed by "excellent" is absent, but presumably the apostrophized word here is "health," a reference to medicinal cannibalism).[61] These "stories" include "Husbands [that] devoured their wives (they are their chattel)" and "a schoolmaster that in a time of famine / Powdered up all his scholars" (98–100). In a similar vein, the Surgeon states "we shall want salt," to which Franville, "*a vainglorious gallant*," replies "Tush, she needs no powdering" (104–5).

These exchanges point to how desperate the would-be cannibals are and serve as reminders of how starved their Virginia corollaries were. References to salt and powdering, while primarily alluding to Aminta's physical attractiveness (she does not need cosmetics), also underscore how shortsighted these would-be cannibals are. She doesn't require "powdering" because they don't intend to leave any part of her remaining for future meals, but rather they intend to consume her here and now in one "dainty meal" (124). These men display no settler mentality, a lack evident throughout the play and which recalled the oft-heard complaint that the early Virginia settlers were too "dainty" and ill-suited for the hard graft of plantation. Moreover, the Frenchmen's attempt to consume Aminta has sexual overtones, recalling the sexualization of the story of the powdered wife in its subsequent iterations and the ways in which rape seems to undergird Moll's proverb about marriage and Virginia. The Master, rushing onto the stage in response to Aminta's cries, interprets their circling of her as an attempted rape ("They would have ravished her" (146)). The fact that the four men zero in on Aminta's "hinder parts" (133)

*Politics of Unease*, esp. 235–54; Claire Jowitt, "'Her flesh Must Serve You': Gender, Commerce and the New World in Fletcher's and Massinger's *The Sea Voyage* and Massinger's *The City Madam*," *Parergon*, 18(3) (2001): 97–113; Heidi Hutner, "*The Tempest*, *The Sea Voyage* and the Pocahontas Myth," in *Colonial Women: Race and Culture in Stuart Drama* (Oxford: Oxford University Press, 2001), 21–44; Julie Sutherland, "'What Beast Is This Lies Wallowing in His Gore?': The Indignity of Man and the Animal Nature of Love in *The Sea Voyage*," *Modern Language Review*, 107(1) (2012): 88–107. However, this view has been challenged recently by Jean Feerick, Michael Neill, and Gitanjali Shahani, who argue that Fletcher and Massinger engage in "the obfuscation of geography" on a par with Shakespeare in *The Tempest* and that their play's "island logic" engaged as much with East India Company matters as with the New World. See Neill, "'Material Flames'"; Jean Feerick, *Strangers in Blood*, (quotation at 115); Gitanjali Shahani, "Of 'Barren Islands' and 'Cursèd Gold': Worth, Value, and Manhood in *The Sea Voyage*," *Journal for Early Modern Cultural Studies*, 12(3) (2012): 5–27 (quotation at 5, borrowing from Roland Greene, "Island Logic," in Peter Hulme and William H. Sherman (eds), The Tempest *and Its Travels* (Philadelphia: University of Pennsylvania Press, 2000), 138–45, at 140).

61 See Louise Noble, "Chapter 3: Flesh Economies in Foreign Worlds: *The Unfortunate Traveller* and *The Sea Voyage*," in *Medicinal Cannibalism in Early Modern English Literature and Culture* (New York: Palgrave MacMillan, 2011), 59–88.

explains the Master's mistake. It also points to the slippage of the men's "appetite" between food and sex, a slippage which we hear voiced once more a few lines later when the shipwrecked crew encounter the female inhabitants of the neighboring island, and the four would-be cannibals desire "eringoes ... Potatoes, or cantharides" (211–12)—all foods and all aphrodisiacs.

The play also implies that by eating Aminta the four Frenchmen will consume the colony itself. Upon rushing to Aminta's rescue, Tibalt reprimands them not so much for their cannibal instincts but because they did not "Begin with one another handsomely" (155). According to Tibalt, they should "spare the woman to beget more food on" (156). Here, for the first time in the play, the new arrivals on the barren island imagine it as a space that they might occupy for a time rather than a place from which they will soon escape—perhaps understandably, because there seems to be no way off the island. In this imagining, Tibalt warps Bacon's model, stressing the importance of women to the perpetuation of the colony, not to beget more colonists but rather to beget "more food." Whether Tibalt is collapsing Aminta's future children and the labor that they will subsequently perform in planting, or whether he means that these children will serve as food, is unclear. Given the poverty of the island's soil ("The earth ... / Let's nothing shoot but poisoned weeds" (1.3.136–7)), we could be forgiven for thinking that Tibalt is here anticipating Jonathan Swift's solution to Irish poverty in *A Modest Proposal*. The division and sharing out of Aminta is untimely (they should "begin" with eating themselves and "spare" her) because it is through her body that the future of plantation holds: without her body, nothing will grow, including a new supply of foodstuffs that may result from having more and better suited planters or a new supply of "brawns and ... buttocks" to store and consume later (3.1.158). For the island plantation's perpetuation it needs division and sharing out, even of human meat if nothing else will grow; but the divisions and sharing are not to be undertaken yet, without order or governance, and not in the intemperate manner proposed by the four hungry Frenchmen.

While the Frenchmen are comic distractions, their cannibal appetites are echoed by the main plot of the play, which is catalyzed by the destruction of Portuguese plantations several years before the events of *The Sea Voyage*, leading to the separation of Sebastian, Rosellia, and Clarinda and the antagonism between Raymond and Albert. The fathers of Raymond and Albert forced "the industrious Portugals / From their plantations in the happy islands" (5.2.87–8). The displanting of the Portuguese was "lawless rapine" (92) through which the fathers "reaped the harvest which their labours sowed" (93), an image that literally refers to the destruction of the Portuguese crops so as to force them out by starving them, but which metaphorically suggests that the French consumed the plantation's food supply and/or that they raped the plantation's women. The latter sense seems to undergird Raymond's memory of their fathers who "for spoil ever forgot compassion / To women" (110–1), and Rosellia's statement that "We are they / That groaned beneath your fathers' wrongs" (5.4.20–1). These associations have been carried through into the next generation by Albert's "rape" of Aminta following the outbreak of hostilities amongst the French, albeit that he does not seem to have sexually assaulted her. The war between the fathers—each of whom suspected the other of letting the Portuguese escape with their wealth—led to the bloodying of "swords... / With innocent gore" (5.2.103–4). These sacrifices anticipate Rosellia's "horrid rites" (5.4.9), the "innocent gore" connoting less blood shed by the warring factions (if so, then why "innocent"?) than by sacrificial lambs. Like Rosellia's "rites," which aim to placate the ghosts of the dead but instead instate a bloody and short end to all, the shedding of "innocent gore" only serves to bloody "their wretched selves" (5.2.104). While the fathers do not consume the bodies of the fallen innocents, their sacrificial acts fail to placate the spirits, and the violence continues into the next, and potentially last, generation.

Despite its turn towards revenge tragedy, *The Sea Voyage* concludes with forgiveness, and nobody is eaten. As such, the play follows through with Prospero's logic in *The Tempest*, a play to which *The Sea Voyage* is considerably indebted.[62] Forgiveness is a greater virtue than vengeance, a faith which ends the cycles of violence that have plagued the Portuguese and French families through multiple marriages of the younger characters and the reunion of Sebastian and Rosellia. But the conclusion barely defuses either the play's lurch into tragic possibility at Rosellia's altar, or its backward look at "The Tragicall Historie of the man eating of his dead wife." Instead, at this moment of reconciliation the play remembers its earlier fascination with fleshly consumption. Moreover, its anagnorosis is laden both with cannibalistic and with incestuous overtones. The connection between cannibalism and incest is not, of course, Fletcher and Massinger's invention. As Anthony J. Lewis argues, the connection became "familiar to readers and audiences in the seventeenth century as a time-honored indication of evil."[63] For Lewis, *Pericles* is a key literary example, while for Minaz Jooma "[i]ncest is ... established as familial cannibalism"

[62] See Rita Banerjee, "Gold, Land, and Labor: Ideologies of Colonization and Rewriting *The Tempest* in 1622," *Studies in Philology*, 110(2) (2013): 291–317.

[63] Anthony J. Lewis, "'I Feed on Mother's Flesh': Incest and Eating in *Pericles*," *Essays in Literature*, 15(2) (1988): 147–63, at 149.

in Milton's imagining of Satan-Sin-Death and Adam and Eve in *Paradise Lost*.[64] Such connections are not limited to early modern European culture: in *The Naked Man*, Claude Lévi-Strauss articulates the connection in the mythos of South and North American indigenous cultures (in variations of the "lewd grandmother" myth), coining the suggestive description of familial cannibalism as "alimentary incest."[65]

These "drive wishes" for "alimentary incest" seem not far beneath the surface of the last moments of *The Sea Voyage*, which draw subtly and strangely from the literary lineage that Lewis and Jooma trace.[66] When Sebastian sees his daughter, he repeats the conceit that we've seen elsewhere in romance, recognizing the wife in the daughter—a moment often accompanied with incestuous longing. Having compared Rosellia to a "ruined building" (75), Sebastian describes his daughter "a perfect model of thyself / As thou wert when thy choice first made thee mine" (78–9). He then proceeds with a carving up of his own, describing how Rosellia's "cheeks and front [forehead] ... had equal pureness / Of natural white and red, and as much ravishing, / Which by fair order and succession / I see descended on her" (80–4). "Ravishing" may simply be glossed here as "attractive," but the transference of the epithet from mother to daughter by the father is troubling—especially so when we consider that, when rescuing Aminta from the would-be cannibals, the Master proclaimed, "They would have ravished her" (3.1.146). When Sebastian repeats the term, and finds within his daughter what has been lost to his wife, we may detect a longing that echoes that of the cannibalistic adventurers.

The play concludes with a hurried re-distribution of bodies, immediately following a reunion of ravishing, and potentially to be ravished (sexually, cannibalistically), bodies. Sebastian's blazon-esque carving up of his wife and daughter, and his description of his daughter as ravishing, re-voices the play's continued conflation of rape and cannibalism that the

---

[64] Minaz Jooma, "The Alimentary Structures of Incest in *Paradise Lost*," *English Literary History*, 63(1) (1996): 25–43, at 29.

[65] Claude Lévi-Strauss, *Mythologiques: Volume 4: The Naked Man*, trans. John and Doreen Weightman (Chicago, IL: University of Chicago Press, 1981), 174.

[66] Sigmund Freud listed cannibalism and incest as among the "drive wishes" in *The Future of an Illusion*, ed. Todd Dufresne and trans. Gregory C. Richter (Peterborough, ON: Broadview, 2012), 77. In *Totem and Taboo*, Freud describes a son who kills and consumes his father as the result of incestuous desire for the same woman (Freud doesn't articulate whether or not this is the mother), a set of drive wishes against which a culture must police itself through the figure of the totem. Sigmund Freud, *Totem and Taboo: Resemblances between the Mental Lives of Savages and Neurotics*, trans. James Strachey (London: Routledge, 1950, reprinted 2001), 164–70.

reuniting of the families has not resolved, and that only a return home—to "our several homes" (5.4.112)—will resolve.

## "WE HAVE SHARES, AND DEEP ONES": ANATOMIZING THE COLONIAL BODY POLITIC

The cannibal scene of *The Sea Voyage* and its echo in the closing moments of the play, then, testifies to the longevity of the "tragicall historie." But the play also attends to how the plight of the powdered wife had gained new significance in the 1620s. By remembering the early accounts of the starving time, Fletcher and Massinger invoke more recent strains of Virginia Company policy and practice, designed both to correct the gender imbalance of the colony and to determine exactly what kind of settlement it was. *The Sea Voyage* is invested in recent Virginia Company controversies about shares, a word that recurs throughout the play, tying together ideas of land, investment, and the body, and pointing to the divisions undergirding the colony—divisions which would eventually bring about the Company's demise (and very nearly the colony with it). The play is invested also in the transportation of wives, a practice begun a few years before the play's first performance, and focuses on the unin- tended consequences of a mixed colony not only for the men-folk but also for the women, whose appetites (for revenge and for sexual gratification) take on a distinctly cannibalistic turn.

Shares—of various types—had been a topic of consternation ever since the colony's inception.[67] The distribution of resources in Virginia (of land, of food, of munitions) was a point of controversy in the colony's early days, as various planters fought over land rights and the rights of governance in ways that saw multiple changes in leadership. In the wake of the starving time, renewed effort was put in to maintaining the public store, and new planters were indentured to the Company for seven years before acquiring their freedom, in order to make sure that there were sufficient provisions for the colony as a whole. In the late 1610s and early 1620s, disputes about land reached new immediacy. There had always been disputes surrounding the two different kinds of planters, those who had paid their own way to get there (the private planter) and those later planters who had been subsidized by the Virginia Company (the public planter). Broadly speaking, the two classes related to the Company quite

---

[67] On the issue of shares and the discourse of public and private planting, see Morgan, *American Slavery, American Freedom*, esp. chapter 5, "The Persistent Vision," 92–107, and chapter 6, "Boom," 108–30.

differently: while the private planters believed that their shares of land were their own, that they had paid for the right to plant and that that right was inviolable, the public planters owed much more to their colonial masters, as through their servitude to the Company for seven years they earned their right to freedom. The private planters did not take kindly to government centralization. As the years went by, to their numbers were added former public planters, who by the late 1610s, had earned their freedom after serving their time laboring on Company property, and thought that their debt to the public good had been served. Private planters, whether among those who had paid their way or who had served their time, repeatedly articulated reservations, and sometimes opposition, to the Company's vision of what their "shares" meant: to them, their shares were their own (a freedom that is anticipated by *Eastward Ho!*), while to the Company's hierarchy their shares formed part of an overall body politic, instated precisely so that another starving time could be prevented.

After the near collapse of the colony in its early years because of poor food management, the Company was keen to stress the idea that the planters should work together to ensure that there was sufficient food, security, governance, and law and order to provide a coherent structure for the colony and ensure its survival and longevity. Many planters were not disposed to these encouragements, increasingly so as more and more planters became independent from centralized control. The disputes brought with them ugly reminders of the starving time, as year-on-year reports about potential shortages in the colony arose—even if never with the severity of 1609–10, then at least with a glimmer of that disaster. In 1617 Samuel Argall, the Governor, bought 600 bushes of corn from the Powhatan for the relief of the colony.[68] In 1619, Argall's replacement, George Yeardley, found the colony's food supplies worryingly low and wrote to Sir Edwin Sandys that "our chiefest care must be for Corne."[69] As Edmund S. Morgan sums up, "If, then, the colony's failure to grow food arose from its communal organization of production, the failure was not overcome by the switch to private enterprise."[70] The issue of shares, then, conflated contentious issues of land, food, and (self-)governance.

The word "share" recurs throughout *The Sea Voyage*. In act 1, scene 3, the French gallants bicker over who should get what portion of the gold that Sebastian and Nicusa present to them to distract them. Lamure declares, "We have shares, and deep ones," in reference to the moneys they have put into the expedition "To buy new lands and lordships in new

[68] Morgan, *American Slavery, American Freedom*, 83.
[69] Kingsbury, *Records of the Virginia Company*, vol. 3, 120.
[70] Morgan, *American Slavery, American Freedom*, 83.

countries," so as to argue that he is justified in claiming a larger portion of the treasure. Franville uses the word a few lines later, inviting "All that will share / With us, assist us" (1.3.172–3), an invitation that descends into a frantic free-for-all. The hungry resort for private gain, under the guise of claiming one's rightful share, brings calamity, as Sebastian and Nicusa use the confusion to escape on their ship, leaving the crew without any sustenance. Their claim of shares in this scene anticipates the cannibalistic claims on their shares of Aminta's body—"divide her, every man her share" (3.1.112): the claiming of private shares at the cost of the public good—failing to "spare the woman to beget more food on" (156)—will bring about the demise of the colony. What happens to the plantation as a result of the selfishness of the private shareholder is almost meted out on the body of Aminta.

That shares in adventuring and the sharing of Aminta's body are aligned is significant in the context of the Virginia Company's marriage policy. As discussed earlier in the chapter, marrying off the planters would, it was believed, be an incentive for them to stay in Virginia. However, even though transporting wives redressed the gender imbalance of the colony a little, not all planters became husbands. The wives were intended for what the Company called "the most honest and industrious Planters," which it defined as being those who could afford to pay the 150 lb. of tobacco, the set price to acquire one of the women.[71] There was disquiet among the poorer planters, who couldn't afford such an outlay and were left to suffer alone. Thomas Niccolls wrote in 1623,

> Women are necessary members for the Colonye, but poore men are neu the
> nearer for them they are so well sould . . . I am sure for all these women yor
> poore Tenants that haue nothing dye miserable through nastines & many
> dep[ar]te the World in their own dung for want of help in their sicknes
> Wherefore for preuention I could wish women might be sent out to serue the
> Company for that purpose for certayne yeares whether they marry or no.[72]

Despite their status as shareholders in the Virginia colony, by virtue of their tenancy, "poore men" like Niccolls were not able to enjoy any shares in wives. The arbitrariness of the divisions of shares in spouses is echoed in *The Sea Voyage*, although the playwrights take the perspective of the women, who find themselves distributed as potential mates for the men, in some cases against their will. Faced with an undesirable match with the Master, Crocale bemoans that she has "A poor old man allotted to my

[71] Ransome, "Wives for Virginia," 6.
[72] Kingsbury, *Records of the Virginia Company*, 4, 231–2.

share!" (3.1.297)—a reaction perhaps shared by the women who were transported to Virginia and given away to older planters.[73]

## AMAZONS, CANNIBALS, AMAZON-CANNIBALS

Critics have tended to focus on the Amazon-ness of *The Sea Voyage*'s Portuguese women—understandably so, given the fact that the island that they were shipwrecked on was occupied by Amazons, whose example they have been trying follow ever since.[74] Less focus has been placed on their cannibalism. In the closing scene, Albert and Raymond are to be put to death. Rosellia's "horrid rites" (5.4.9), "a sacrifice to vengeance" (4.2.15) in "remembrance of that dear man" (13) (she doesn't know that Sebastian is alive), are not as overtly cannibalistic as the four Frenchmen's attempts to quench their appetite by eating Aminta, but there are numerous cannibal undertones. Decked out like a "priest" in "full trim of cruelty" to answer "the wrath / Of the incensèd powers" (5.4.9, 6; 3.1.401–2), Rosellia would have called to mind the Aztecs, whose rites were described as concluding with the consumption of the sacrificial victim: José de Acosta's *Historia natural y moral de las Indias* (published in English as *The Natural and Moral History of the West Indies* in 1590) reported how the victims, "being thus slaine, and their bodies cast downe, their masters, or such as had taken them, went to take them vp, and carried them away: then having divided them amongst them, they did eate them, celebrating their feast and solemnitie."[75] The scene also recalls the earlier cannibal attempt on Aminta, as Rosellia's command to Albert and Raymond to "prepare your throats" echoes Morillat's command to the surgeon to "cut [Aminta's] throat." Moreover, the "dreadful sounds" that greet Raymond and Albert at the altar are described as "Infernal music / Fit for a bloody feast" by Aminta (5.4.2–3).

Rosellia's "horrid rites" carry with them a short-sightedness similar to that displayed by the Frenchmen. Rather than adopt a policy of intermarriage, even in the manner of Amazonian mating, where the women will

[73] We have no first-hand accounts by women who were transported to Virginia. David Ransome speculates that many lost their lives as a result of the attacks on the colony in March, 1622. Ransome, "Wives for Virginia," 17–18.

[74] Michael Hattaway, "Seeing Things: Amazons and Cannibals," in Maquerlot and Willems (eds), *Travel and Drama in Shakespeare's Time*, 179–92; see also Hutner, "*The Tempest*, *The Sea Voyage* and the Pocahontas Myth"; Sutherland, "'What Beast Is This Lies Wallowing in His Gore?'"

[75] José de Acosta, *The Naturall and Morall Historie of the East and West Indies*, trans. Edward Grimestone (London: for Edward Blount and William Aspley, 1604), 385.

"choose a husband, and enjoy his company / A month" in order to "prove fruitful," Rosellia orders the women of her colony to "Use 'em with all austerity" in the run up to their execution (2.2.237–9; 4.2.1). By executing them, and (metaphorically at least) feasting on them in their "horrid rites," she forecloses on the possibility of any future plantation. While Sebastian and the other ousted Portuguese settlers will be remembered in the sacrifice, all that this act of vengeance will achieve is a future imagined by her daughter earlier in the play: "Should all women use this obstinate / Abstinence you would force upon us, in / A few years the whole world would be peopled / Only with beasts" (2.2.207–10). Clarinda's complaint here, that by excluding men the women will ensure that they are the last generation to inhabit the island, is to be enacted by Rosellia. The cannibalistic undertones of her act emphasize the doom to which she is consigning herself and her "commonwealth / Which in ourselves begun" but which "with us must end" (17–18). In remembering the dead, Rosellia forgets the living.

Rosellia's "resolve, thus shaped like Amazons, / To end our lives" (5.4.44–5) is not shared by the other members of the female commonwealth. Although they first enter the play as archetypal Amazons, "*armed with bows and quivers*" (2.2.1SD), it is soon clear that their Amazon resolve is lacking. On failing to hunt down a stag, Crocale is immediately reminded that "this place yields / Not fauns nor satyrs, or more lustful men" (14–15), moving from rural deities associated with lustfulness to human men who are even more in heat. Hippolita complains that he would "rather be the chase" (35), and Crocale also confesses "imagination helps me sometimes, / And all that's left for us to feed on; / We might starve else!" (41–3). As elsewhere in the play, erotic desire is crossed with the language of food: sexual abstinence is equated with starvation, while appetite is both a hunger for food and for sexual satisfaction. We find the tessellation of unruly appetites later in the play, when the women, who have only five days to try to mate with their male captives before their execution, try to force-feed them. Juletta and Crocale attempt to persuade Tibalt and the Master to eat in order to regain their strength and potency, but they refuse, stating that they will not "serve your uses." Women's "greedy appetites are never satisfied" and they would as soon "famish me as founder me" (4.3.44–5). The sailors would rather "eat one another like good fellows" (50) than succumb to the women's "sordid impudence" (69). The women are cast as cannibalistic, because they will consume the men's vitality through excessive "use." The men's only viable response is to consume themselves.

Cannibalism is repeatedly gendered a feminine act throughout *The Sea Voyage*. The four Frenchmen resort to cannibalism because they are not

**Fig. 2.2.** Jan van der Straet, called Stradanus, *Discovery of America: Vespucci Landing in America*, ca. 1587–89. The Metropolitan Museum of Art (<http://www.metmuseum.org>). Gift of the Estate of James Hazen Hyde, 1959.

"manly to their sufferance" (4.2.53), an impotence underscored later when their willingness to have sex with their captors and "get a world of children" cannot be realized because "They are weak, abject things" (4.3.105, 110). This gendering is consistent with descriptions of cannibalism elsewhere in early modern culture. As Figure 2.1 shows, cannibalism was a practice often associated with the female indigenous population. In Figure 2.2, the famous engraving by Johannes Stradanus of America being discovered by Amerigus Vespucci depicts female natives enjoying a cannibal feast in the background. Richard Eden's translation of Sebastian Münster's *A Treatyse of the Newe India* (1553) describes how, during the third Vespucci voyage, a young *conquistador* was slain by a woman, who then "cut him in pieces even in the sight of the Spaniardes, shewinge them the pieces, and rosting them at a greate fyre."[76] What's more, Amazons and cannibals were often associated with one another. In Herodotus, both hail from Scythia, the famed outpost of barbarity. In Columbus' letter, the *carib*/cannibals live in close proximity to, and "have intercourse with the

---

[76] Sebastian Münster, *A Treatyse of the Newe India*, trans. Richard Eden (1553), reprinted in Edward Arber (ed.), *The First Three English Books on America* (London: Archibald Constable, 1895), 3–42, at 39.

women of Matinino," a group who are Amazonian in all but name: "there is not a man" on the island, wrote Columbus; "These women engage in no feminine occupation, but use bows and arrows of cane, like those already mentioned, and they arm and protect themselves with plates of copper, of which they have so much."[77]

Amazons and cannibals then, had long been associated with one another: Massinger and Fletcher's linking of these two types draws on this prehistory. But just as *The Sea Voyage* remembers more recent cannibal stories in English colonial history, so does it tap into anxieties about women's intemperance in Virginia. As we have seen, the reputation of the women transported to the colony in its early years was low (they were "out of Bridewell"). In 1619, the same year that the marriage policy was instituted, the Assembly of the House of Burgesses called for more punitive measures against "skandalous offenses, as suspicions of whordomes, dishonest company keeping with weomen and suche like."[78] In the same assembly, the Burgesses agreed upon a prohibition that "No maide or woman servant, either now resident in the Colonie or hereafter to come, shall contract herselfe in marriage without either the consente of her parents, or of her Mr or Mris, or of the magistrate and minister of the place both together" (punishment could also be meted out to whatever minister contracted the match).[79] Such measures were designed to keep control of the colonists by forbidding matches between maids and servants and their social superiors (such as the planters) or their social inferiors (the laborers), so as to keep their bodies first for the necessary labors within the household until such a time that an appropriate match could be found.

Moreover, there was concern about how much the women in the colony would consume. The records of the Virginia Company routinely emphasized that the women would come with supplies and apparel. Nevertheless, the colonists expressed unhappiness: "Wee haue taken as greate care as possible wee colde ([***] wthowt any p[ro]visione at all) for the well disposing of the maides sent in t[*he Marmaduke*] and the Warwick, and could wishe that the next Supplie of m[aides] may bringe some smale p[ro]visione w^th them for [***] vntill they may bee convenientlie disposed of."[80] Colonist Thomas Niccolls complained, "For all that I can find that the multitude of women doe is nothing but to deuoure the food of the land without doing any dayes deed whereby any benefitt may arise

[77] "The Letter of Columbus," in Hulme and Whitehead, *Wild Majesty*, 15.

[78] *Proceedings of the Virginia Assembly 1619*, in Tyler, *Narratives of Early Virginia*, 245–78, at 272.

[79] Tyler, *Proceedings of the Virginia Assembly*, 272.

[80] Kingsbury, *Records of the Virginia Company*, vol. 3, 583.

either to ye Company or Countrey."[81] The Virginia Company, then, attempted to control women's bodies, by regulating into whose households they were permitted, and by regulating their "appetites" to insure that their own temperance did not slip. In Rosellia's Amazons, on the verge of sacrificing and consuming the male colonists, *The Sea Voyage* puts on show the nightmare of what could happen if these appetites were not adequately tempered.

## THE INDIAN CANNIBAL, THE COLONIAL HUSBAND

*The Sea Voyage* may be the culmination of the powdered wife's dramatic afterlife, but around the time of the first performances of the play we find her plight being re-voiced in printed matter. *A True Declaration*, published in November 1610, was the account closest to the events, and the story was circulated orally, but the story was not recorded in writing again until the 1620s. Accounts appear in 1623–24 Virginia Assembly records; in John Smith's *Generall Historie of Virginia* in 1624 and then later in the same year in George Percy's *A Trewe Relacyon*; and in William Strachey's *A True Reportory*, incorporated into Samuel Purchas' compendium, *Purchas His Pilgrimes*, in 1625 (although Strachey wrote his account closer to the events). The proliferation of these reports in the early 1620s reflects anxieties that a second starving time was on the horizon, as more colonists (including more women) arrived without what were deemed to be the necessary qualities needed to survive. But, as Rachel Herrmann has argued, the proliferation also reflects the positions of their authors.[82] In the years in which the Virginia Company was falling apart, some of its most prominent members wished to position themselves in such a way that absolved themselves of any blame for the Company's shortcomings while pointing fingers at others. Smith's account was an attempt to establish positively his role as an early settler—the starving time began as soon as his presidency ended and he was on his way back to England—and lay the blame for the horrors at the feet of those he left behind. Percy, whom Smith attacks in *The Generall Historie*, wrote his account in part to correct Smith's "many falseties and malcyous detractyons."[83]

While these accounts are very different—from the details of the cannibal acts, to the tone in which they are composed—they all agree on one

[81] Kingsbury, *Records of the Virginia Company*, vol. 4, 232.
[82] Herrmann, "The 'Tragicall Historie.'"
[83] Nicholls, "George Percy's 'Trewe Relacyon,'" 242.

thing: that these horrors were in the past, and that with better management they would never happen again. The Assembly placed the events "In those 12 yeeres of *Sr Tho: Smith* his government"—consigned, that is, to a prior period of rule (Smyth having been replaced as Treasurer by Sir Edwin Sandys in 1619).[84] John Smith's account can be found in his *Generall Historie*, its chapters on the Virginia colony designed to allow readers to "easily understand and answer to their question, how it came to passe there was no better speed and successe in those proceedings," i.e. to understand what happened, rather than what *was* happening.[85] Percy's *Trewe Relacyon* places the early plight of Virginia settlers within a recent historical continuum of "the diversety of miseries mutenies and famishmentts w[hi]ch have attended upon discoveries and plantacyons in theis our moderne Tymes."[86] Virginia, that is, became historicized: the powdered wife was a reminder of its savage past, rather than an index of its doubtful future.

"The diversety of miseries" presumably was Percy's allusion to the 1622 attacks on the colony. The attacks precipitated the demise of the Virginia Company, but in some ways they were the making of the colony. In promotional matter the attacks outed the colony's real cannibals—the Powhatan, who had been neighbored to the colonist's bosom, oft-invited for food and religious instruction, but who now were no better than Lear's barbarous Scythian in their attempt to chop the settlers into messes. That is to say, in the wake of Opechancanough's attacks on the settlement in 1622, the cannibal began to become associated less with the English settlers—although tales of their disorderliness continued to circulate— and more with the Indians.

A number of the reports of the attacks drew on cannibal imagery to describe the actions of the Powhatan. Christopher Brooke's *Poem on the Late Massacre in Virginia* (1622) describes the "Hoast of Hells black brood, / Wolves, Tygars, Tyrants, that have suckt the blood / Of Christian soules." Brooke addresses God and describes how "Those Diuelish hands haue layd vpon thine Altar; / Made tuneless iarrs in musique of their peaces."[87] Addressing the now-dead Captain William Powell, whose "*Head*... / They parted from the rest, as proud to bring / A *Trophee* of such Honor to their *King*," Brooke states that "here [the Powhatan] stinted

[84] "The Tragical Relation of the Virginia Company," in Tyler, *Narratives of Early Virginia*, 422. In fact, the starving time predated Thomas Smyth's treasurership; the report was likely composed to slam the former treasurer.

[85] Smith, *Generall Historie of Virginia*, 302.

[86] Nicholls, "George Percy's 'Trewe Relacyon,'" 242.

[87] Christopher Brooke, "A Poem on the Late Massacre in Virginia" (1623), reprinted in *The Virginia Magazine of History and Biography*, 72(3) (1964): 259–92, at 276.

not." The death of Powell was only a "taste" to "feed their bloody thirst": "these *Cupps* of Gore / Do but incense their appetites to more." Brooke then imagines scenes of rampage, "A whole Townes-life-blood in a generall Flame," which concludes in a cannibal orgy of "Quaffing the life-blood of dear Christian Soules."[88] Brooke daubs his account with cannibal gore, employing cannibalistic imagery to heighten the cruelty of the Indians.

The Company account of the attacks, *A Declaration of the State of the Colonie and Affaires in Virginia* (1622), does not record any instances of cannibalism, but even so it shares some of Brooke's shock value. Its author Edward Waterhouse dwells on the Indians' desecration of the bodies of the dead settlers: "they fell after againe vpon the dead, making as well as they could, a fresh murder, defacing, dragging, and mangling the dead carkasses into many pieces, and carrying some parts away in derision, with base and bruitish triumph."[89] This parade of the dead may not be cannibalistic, for all its horrors, but the description of the death of George Thorpe gets closer. Waterhouse refuses to go into details about what happened to Thorpe's body: the "viperous brood did . . . not onely murder him, but with such spight and scorne abused his dead corps as is unfitting to be heard with civill eares."[90] Waterhouse earlier in his account doesn't stint on gory details, and a few lines later he conveys the gruesome execution of Captain Powell: the refusal to describe the death of Thorpe, but the hint at the "uncivil" treatment of his body, suggests that whatever happened was worse than the "defacing, dragging, and mangling" meted out on Powell. We could of course insert all manner of crimes exacted on Thorpe, but cannibalism certainly seems to be one such possibility.[91]

John Smith, who folded Waterhouse's account into his *Generall Historie of Virginia*, also employs cannibalism imagery. After the attacks, Smith praised the resolve of the Council and Company in continuing to send ships and settlers, so as "to leape out of this labyrinth of melancholy."[92] The labyrinth, of course, recalls the story of Theseus and the Minotaur, half-man/half-bull to whom virgin sacrifices were fed. The

---

[88] Brooke, "Poem on the Late Massacre," 282.

[89] Edward Waterhouse, *A Declaration of the State of the Colonie and Affaires in Virginia* (London: for Robert Mylbourne, 1622), 14.

[90] Waterhouse, *A Declaration of the State of the Colonie*, 17.

[91] Waterhouse's description uncannily echoes (almost certainly unintentionally) the description of the Welsh Women in Shakespeare's *Henry IV Part I*, whose placement of dead English soldiers' penises in the corpses' mouths is left undescribed by the Earl of Westmoreland ("Upon whose dead corpse there was such misuse, / Such beastly shameless transformation, / By those Welshwomen done as may not be / Without much shame retold or spoken of" (1.1.43–46)).

[92] Smith, *Generall Historie of Virginia*, 491. The Council was the upper house in the colonial legislature.

Virginian labyrinth may here be a metaphysical one, but to Smith it captured perfectly the state that the Council and Colony found itself in—prone to monstrous half-human creatures intent on devouring the settlers.[93]

Smith's *Generall Historie* also rewrites the saga of Virginia by inserting cannibalism into early America's primal scene, his salvation at the hands of Pocahontas. In his account of his captivity in *The Generall Historie*, Smith describes his treatment at the hands of Wahunsenacawh, who continually gave Smith meat, "which made him thinke they would fat him to eate him."[94] The earlier account of Smith's captivity, published in 1608, contains no mention of Smith's fears that he was going to be eaten. Indeed, accounts written prior to 1622 fail to mention any anxiety that the Powhatan wanted to eat the English settlers. Instead, cannibalism is mentioned only to dismiss it: for example, Edward Maria Wingfield, the colony's first president, made it clear that the early colonists "found them no Cannyballs," while Percy, in his earlier *Observations Gathered out of a Discourse of the Plantation* (dated 1606) clearly separates the people "called by the names of Canibals, that will eate mans fleshe," whom he encountered in the West Indies, from the native Virginians, who although described as performing barbaric acts (sun-worshiping being chief among them) did not resort to cannibal acts.[95] Promotional matter printed and circulated in London sometimes dwelled on Indian eating habits, but did not suggest that cannibalism was practiced among them. Instead, the prevailing image in propaganda was of an innocent people: contended Alexander Whitaker, "Murther is a capitall crime scarce heard of among them."[96] Rather, the native Virginians were at the mercy of the Devil and had to be freed, in the words of Robert Johnson, "from the deuourer" (rather than being "deuourers" themselves).[97] Even writing drawn from first-hand observation, which tended to be more likely to

---

[93] On the significance of the labyrinth in colonialist discourse, see Joan Pong Linton, "*The Tempest*, 'Rape,' the Art and Smart of Colonial Husbandry," in *Romance of the New World*, 155–84.

[94] Smith, *Generall Historie of Virginia*, 318.

[95] George Percy, "Observations Gathered out of a Discourse of the Plantation of the Southerne Colonie in Virginia by the English, 1606," reprinted in Horn, *Capt. John Smith: Writings*, 920–34, at 921.

[96] Whitaker, *Good Newes from Virginia*, 27.

[97] Johnson, *Nova Britannia*, 27. The closest references I have found linking the Powhatan and cannibalism in early promotional matter are in Robert Gray's *Good Speede to Virginia* (1609), which claims that "in Virginia the people...worship the diuell, offer their young children in sacrifice to him" (a borrowing from Spanish accounts); and in *A True Declaration*, Wahunsenacawh is described as a "greedy Vulture," in reference to the ambush of Capt. Ratcliff in 1609. Robert Gray, *Good Speed to Virginia* (London: for William Welby, 1609), C2v; *True Declaration*, 41.

describe the Powhatan's more violent practices (Wahunsenacawh was "very terrible and tyrannous in punishing such as offend him"), noted, matter-of-factly, that in warfare "the *Werowances*, women, and children they put not to death but keepe them Captiues" (a practice which this particular observer, John Smith, experienced in person).[98] However, after 1622, the Indian-cannibal association became more prevalent. By re-writing himself as a potential cannibal victim in *The Generall Historie*, Smith not only cemented the Pocahontas mythos, but also anticipated the cannibal acts of the 1622 attacks within the frame of his own narrative, by suggesting that the Indians were always trying to consume the English and would succeed if only they were given the chance (which they hadn't been thanks to Pocahontas' intervention in 1608 but which they had been in 1622).

As the cannibal became Indian, so the English husband became normalized as a figure for the ideal planter—no longer the figure who could not fend for himself and as a result had to eat his wife, but rather a figure who could provide for his family, provide for the plantation, and provide for the colony as a whole. The wife, in turn, became no longer the victim of male predation but rather an active agent in the establishment of the colonial home (and, by extension, of plantation life). Accounts of the 1622 attacks reclaimed marriage as proof that the colony would get back on track. The ballad "Good Newes from Virginia, sent from James his Towne this present Moneth of March 1623 by a Gentleman in that Country" concludes by praising Governor Wyatt's wife, "that woman worth renown," as a great exemplar to the rest of the colony: "The wife unto our Gouernour, did safely here ariue: / With many gallants following her, whom God preserue aliue. / What man would stay when Ladies gay, both hues and fortunes leaues: / To taste what we haue truely sowne, truth neuer man deceaues."[99] Brooke's "On the Late Massacre" praised a previous governor, Lord de la Warr (whose arrival in 1610 saved Jamestown), admitting that "His endear'd Lady"—his late wife—had been "underpriz'd" in her lifetime, but granting him instead a new wife, Virginia, whose "Armes enfold his Bones."[100]

After the 1622 massacre the spectre of cannibalism arose again, but this time haunting the representation of an Indian population desirous to feed its long-suppressed, bloody thoughts. Cannibalism, it was true, had been part of its early settler past, but those times were gone, and a new

---

[98] John Smith, *A Map of Virginia* (Oxford: for Joseph Barnes, 1612), 36, 26.

[99] Anonymous, *Good Newes from Virginia* (1623), reprinted in *William and Mary Quarterly*, 3rd series, 5(3) (1948): 351–8, at 357–8.

[100] Brooke, *Poem on the Late Massacre*, 289.

cannibal threat had presented itself. The solution, as far as the Virginia Council was concerned, was an extirpation—a weeding, a rooting out—removing those who would consume the colony. The settlers, through a combination of marriage among one another—thanks to a slightly more equal balance of men to women—and violence directed towards those outside, would order their colony by casting out the cannibal—a figure who had earlier in Virginia's history been found among its company, but now could be found only among the enemy. As a result, the powdered wife was preserved as an artifact of the past, an anecdotal reminder of the calamitous mismanagement of certain individuals but no longer a figure for the colony's overhasty and intemperate settlement.

## "CANNIBAL-CHRISTIANS"

The London stage was far from complicit with the Virginia Company, as complaints by William Crashaw et al. attest. However, just as the Company's rhetoric took advantage of the 1622 attacks to transfer the cannibal epithet from settler to native, so did drama post-1622. While the drama of the previous decades articulated the image of the male colonist as carnally desirous of both the fleshly and the fleshy through a seemingly innocuous theatermeme doubting the wisdom of women travelling to Virginia—articulations indebted to "The tragicall historie of the man eating of his dead wife in Virginia" and directly countering the official line of the Virginia Company—in drama post-1622 the cannibal, where specified, is indigenous to the colonial space. And, having been repeated in a range of drama before Opechancanough's rebellion, "never marry as if you were going to Virginia" does not seem to have been uttered in the drama that followed.

In Massinger's *The City Madam*, a play which draws heavily on the 1622 attacks (as Chapter 4 will argue in more detail), Virginian Indians (actually Englishmen in disguise) attempt to transport the title character and her daughters across the Atlantic to sacrifice them to the Devil. The cannibalistic underpinnings of this act are revealed when Luke, their accomplice and the city madam's brother-in-law, assures them that the women will be carried over in a "dry fat" (5.1.129)—a barrel used to transport dried foodstuff on sea voyages—should they refuse to travel willingly. A minor plot-strand in Jonson's *The Staple of News* (1626), a play mostly concerned with the emergence of news culture in 1620s London, revolves around Lickfinger's enterprise to sail to America to found "a colony of cooks / To be set ashore o'the coast of America / For the conversion of the cannibals, / And making them good-eating

Christians" (3.2.155–8).[101] *The Sea Voyage*, that is, is something of a watershed moment. Licensed for the stage and first performed in the same year as the attacks but prior to news of them crossing the Atlantic, the play seems to have been the last one haunted by the memory of the powdered wife.

That said, as I argue here by way of conclusion to this chapter, even in episodes where Indians are associated with cannibalism, the specter of the English cannibal is not entirely exorcised. The outward conformity in these two plays to the Virginia Company's grafting of the Indian and the Cannibal is undermined by a number of factors. In *The City Madam*, the plan to transport the women as if they were food is Luke's, not the Indians'. He projects the image of a cannibalistic Virginia, no doubt encouraged by talk of ritual sacrifice that will profit him. His image of Virginia says more about his own cannibalistic desires (he is "surfeit here in all abundance" (5.3.31)) than it does about Virginia—a motif consist-ent with the rest of the play, where characters' descriptions of Virginia reveal as much about themselves as they do about the place itself (which none of them ever visit). Throughout the play, that is, Massinger uses Virginia as an index of the various characters' moral standing, and Luke, the most reprehensible of all, is arguably the character who displays the most cannibalistic tendencies.

Lickfinger's "conversion of the cannibals" off "the coast of America" with "spit-and-pan divinity" (3.2.166) in *The Staple of News* at first seems squarely focused on Indian conversion. However, there is perhaps more ambiguity than first appears. In *The Cambridge Edition*, the play's editor Joseph Loewenstein amends the Second Folio's "good, eating Christians" to "good-eating Christians," to indicate that thanks to Lickfinger's mission the cannibals will be "properly dieted" (158 n.). Loewenstein is surely correct that this is the primary meaning in this passage. However, emend-ing the comma undoes the possibility that "good, eating Christians" can mean either that the cannibals will be converted to Christianity and thus will no longer have a predilection for human flesh (and perhaps there is a reference to the "correct" consumption at communion, i.e. the Protestant interpretation of transubstantiation); or, in direct contrast, the cannibals will be good *because* they eat Christians—that is, the cooks.[102] Far from a

---

[101] Ben Jonson, *The Staple of News*, in Bevington et al., *The Cambridge Edition of the Works of Ben Jonson*, vol. 6.
[102] As Loewenstein mentions, a "strained argument" could be made for reading these lines from F2 as "the colony of cooks might be imagined as themselves serving as meals for the cannibals, who, having eaten the good colonists, assimilate their values by mere digestion." F3 has no comma at all. While I agree the reading is not the primary one (and not what the speaker Nathaniel intends), given the date of the play it does not seem

successful act of colonial conversion, this reading suggests that Lickfinger's "spit-and-pan divinity" will flounder, and that rather than adopting civility the cannibals will devour the very symbol of it, an act of cannibalism that may well have recalled the 1622 attacks and the ensuing cannibal rhetoric that we witnessed earlier in this chapter.

What's more, Lickfinger's cannibals may not be entirely native. We assume that the cannibals who are being converted thanks to Lickfinger's introduction of a better diet are indigenous and, again, this seems likely to be the primary meaning. However, Lickfinger himself describes the mission as follows:

> In one six months, and by plain cookery,
> No magic to't, but old Japhet's physic
> (The father of the European arts)
> To make such sauces for the savages
> And cook their meats with those enticing steams
> As it would make our cannibal-Christians
> Forbear the mutual eating one another,
> Which they do do more cunningly than the wild
> Anthropophagi that snatch only strangers,
> Like my old patron's dog there.    (171–80)

"Our cannibal-Christians" most likely means English or European cannibals. Lickfinger here suggests that so great will be the colony of cook's "sauces" and "meats with those enticing steams" that it would convert "our predatory fellow Christians in Europe" (176 n.), who are in his estimation all the more cunning than "the wild / Anthrophagi" because they "snatch" (and then eat) their own rather than "strangers." Much of the news of *The Staple of News* emanates from the news networks that developed in the Thirty Years' War (Lickfinger is the sole factor with any "news from the Indies" (153)).[103] A European context for these lines has considerable valence, given that Lickfinger's lines owe more than a little to the logic of de Lery and Montaigne. In *Histoire d'un voyage faict en la terre*

---

impossible (nor, for that matter, does this reading depend on the placement of the comma). Loewenstein may be right that consuming the cooks will civilize the cannibals; consuming the cooks may also underscore the futility of conversion, something much discussed and feared in the wake of the 1622 attacks. *The Staple of News*, n. 158.

[103] See Alan B. Farmer, "Play-Reading, News-Reading, and Ben Jonson's *The Staple of News*," in Marta Straznicky (ed.), *The Book of the Play: Playwrights, Stationers, and Readers in Early Modern England* (Amherst: University of Massachusetts Press, 2006), 127–58; and more generally on Jonson's engagement with print culture and nascent journalism, Julie Sanders, "Print, Popular Culture, Consumption and Commodification in *The Staple of News*," in Julie Sanders with Kate Chedgzoy and Susan Wiseman (eds), *Refashioning Ben Jonson: Gender, Politics and the Jonsonian Canon* (London: MacMillan, 1998), 183–207.

*du Brésil* Jean de Léry compared the Tupinamba of Brazil to the Catholics who victimized the Huguenots in France, and concluded that, however cruel "the anthropophagous," their behavior was more civil than that of Europeans, because "there are some here in our midst even worse and more detestable than those who, as we have seen, attack only enemy nations, while the ones over here have plunged into the blood of their kinsmen, neighbors, and compatriots": "one need not go beyond one's own country, nor as far as America, to see such monstrous and prodigious things."[104] Montaigne famously concurred in "Of the Cannibals" (1580), questioning who was the true savage, the European or the cannibal, and arguing, "there is more barbarism in eating men alive than to feed upon them being dead."[105] But even post-1622, "our cannibal-Christians" who eat their own rather than "strangers" may well have recalled another group of "cannibal-Christians," those in Jamestown who could not "forbear the mutual eating one another" and, in the case of the cannibal husband, "cunningly" attempted to conceal the fact.

\*

Both *The City Madam* and *The Staple of News* argue for the futility of conversion by suggesting that America was filled with unrepentant cannibals who refused to hear the word of God and instead went about eating Christian colonists. And both plays do not fully let go of the idea that cannibalism in the New World was in fact an Old World phenomenon—a European import, as it were—even though the party line of most Virginia Company propaganda suggested quite the opposite. Many other plays written and performed between 1576 and 1642 allude to Indians without alleging their man-eating ways, before and after the 1622 attacks. But many theatermemes that revolved around the Indian indicated that they could not be converted at all, that they would stick to their heathenish practices, and that they would refuse or ignore all attempts at civilizing them.

Before the establishment of Jamestown, Indians are referenced in terms of their worship of the sun—as in Shakespeare's *All's Well that Ends Well* (1605), when Helena describes her emotions as "Indian-like," because "Religious in mine error, I adore / The Sun, that looks upon his worshipper, / But knows of him no more" (1.3.188–91)—or in terms of their slavish devotion to their Spanish masters—as in Marlowe's *Doctor Faustus*, when Valdes compares the devotion of the spirits to magicians to

---

[104] Jean de Léry, *A History of a Voyage to the Land of Brazil* (1578), trans. Janet Whatley (Berkeley: University of California Press, 1992), 133.

[105] Michel de Montaigne, "Of the Cannibals," in Stephen Greenblatt and Peter G. Platt (eds), *Shakespeare's Montaigne: The Florio Translation of* The Essays*: A Selection*, trans. John Florio (New York: New York Review of Books, 2014), 56–71, at 64.

"Indian Moores [who] obey their Spanish Lords" (1.1.115).[106] However, there is little reference to any cannibalistic behavior on their part. While we find more nuanced imaginings of the Indian in drama post-1607, the idea that Indians could be transformed at all into "good, eating Christians" seems to be either debunked—in *The City Madam* the Virginians who come to London as converts reveal themselves to be devil-worshippers— or even more readily ignored. The "Indian" signifies a sun-worshipping, Spanish devotee for many decades after the English Protestant mission was in process, with plays written and performed after 1607 and even up to the 1640s continuing to peddle the image of the Indian unswayed by Protestantism. In Henry Glapthorne's *The Tragedy of Albertus Wallenstein* (1639), the German Emperor laments that the people "all looke / On [Wallenstein], as superstitious Indians on the Sunne, / With adoration."[107] In Glapthorne's *The Ladies Privilege* (1640), Doria describes Chrisea as a woman whose eyes brandish "beames, whose purity dispence, / Light more immaculate then the gorgeous east, / Weares when the prostrate *Indian* does adore / Its rising brightnesse."[108] Glapthorne's plays were written and performed late in the reign of Charles I, yet still they insist on Indians maintaining their own beliefs rather than having been converted to Christianity.

Glapthorne's Indians are not cannibals: what came to be elided in colonialist discourse is less readily apparent in the contemporary drama. But while the Indian remained a static symbol in the drama, despite the multiple transformations of the meaning of the term in the seventeenth century (not to mention before and after), the colonist, who was supposed to be "made a man" by the experience of colonization (an experience predicated in part on conversion of the Indian), became frequently unmade. As this chapter has argued, he was transformed into a cannibal. As Chapter 3 argues, he was transformed also into a peculiarly English form of barbarity predicated by the very sight of the Indian body on display.

---

[106] Christopher Marlowe, *Doctor Faustus A-Text*, in David Bevington and Eric Rasmussen (eds), *Christopher Marlowe: Doctor Faustus and Other Plays* (Oxford: Oxford University Press, 1995), 137–84.

[107] Henry Glapthorne, *The Tragedy of Albertus Wallenstein* (London: for George Hutton, 1639), Dv.

[108] Henry Glapthorne, *The Lady's Privilege* (London: for Francis Constable, 1640), H2.

# PART II

# INDIANS AND LONDONERS

# 3

## The Dead Indian

*Virginians in* The Memorable Masque,
"The Triumph of Time, " Henry VIII,
*and* The Tempest *of 1613*

[This] strannge man & his Bote...was such a wonder vnto th[e]
whole City, & to the rest of the Realm that heard of yt, as seemed
neuer to have happened the like great matter to any mans knowledge.

> Michael Lok on Inuit captive from the first
> Frobisher voyage, 1576

This Newport brought a lad who they say is the son of an emperor of
those lands and they have coached him that when he sees the King
he is not to take off his hat, and other things of this sort, so that
I have been amused by the way they honour him, for I hold it for
surer that he must be a very ordinary person.

> de Zuñiga to Philip III, June 26, 1608, on Namontack

There would this monster make a man.

> Trinculo on Caliban, *The Tempest*, 1611/13

### VIRGINIA ON DISPLAY

On March 16, 1606, less than a month before the first charter of the
Virginia Company was ratified by James I, Don Pedro de Zuñiga informed
Philip III about the progress of an English settlement in the New World.
He advised his King that a recent voyage had "brought 14 or 15 months
ago about ten natives, that they might learn English and they have kept
some here [in London] and others in the country, teaching and training
them to say how good that country is for people to go there and inhabit it."[1]

---

[1] Don Pedro de Zuñiga to Philip III, March 16, 1606 in Brown, *Genesis of the United
States*, 45–6.

These "ten natives," likely the Abenaki (five of whom we know the names of: Sassacomoit, Maneddo, Skicowaros, Amoret, and Tahanedo) captured in Mawooshen (New England) and brought to England by George Way-mouth in 1605, were not the first to cross the Atlantic to England, nor the first to be put on public display.[2] But what is noteworthy here is that, from the inception of the Virginia Company—indeed, one year before the founding of Jamestown—Native Americans were being deployed as pitchmen, to speak on its behalf to encourage investment in and migra-tion to the nascent colony.

As de Zuñiga pointed out to his king, this was a potentially powerful marketing strategy. Native Americans had long been media sensations. As far back as the reign of Henry VII, a group of inhabitants of "the new found ilands" returned with Sebastian Cabot to be paraded around in London.[3] More recently, the Inuit (Kalicho, Arnaq, and Nutaaq, plus the captive described by Michael Lok in this chapter's epigraph, whose name was not recorded), brought back by Martin Frobisher from north-eastern Canada in 1576 and 1577, were heralded as marvels. Arrivals under the Virginia Company auspices also seem to have created a stir. A group of "Virginian" canoeists demonstrated their talents on the Thames on September 2, 1603 (although their impact was lessened by the fact that they put on their show in a period of plague).[4] Nomentack, a kinsman of Wahunsenacawh, became sufficiently well known to merit an allusion in Jonson's *Epicene* (1609), as one of the preoccupations of John Daw, who "draw[s] maps of persons...of Nomentack, when he was here" (5.1.17–19). Pocahontas' embassy to England in 1616 was paid for by the Virginia Company, which saw her as a promotional opportunity to generate enthusiasm for the colony. Jonson's *The Staple of News* recalls the visit of "The blessed / Pocahontas," the "great king's daughter of Virginia," evidence that her stay in London continued to be remembered ten years on, even though characters in the play disagree

[2] On the Native Americans who visited or were captured and taken to the British Isles, see Alden T. Vaughan, *Transatlantic Encounters: American Indians in Britain, 1500–1776* (Cambridge: Cambridge University Press, 2006); and Sir Sidney Lee, "The American Indian in Elizabethan England," in *Elizabethan and Other Essays* (Oxford: Clarendon, 1929), 263–301. On the practice of Native American display in Europe, see Steven Mullaney, "The New World on Display: European Pageantry and the Ritual Incorporation of the Americas," in Rachel Doggett, Monique Hulvey, and Julie Ainsworth (eds), *New World of Wonder: European Images of America* (Washington, DC: Folger Shakespeare Library, 1993), 105–13.

[3] Raphael Holinshed, *Holinshed's Chronicles of England, Scotland, and Ireland*, vol. 3 (London 1808), 528.

[4] See D. B. Quinn, "'Virginians' on the Thames in 1603," *Terrae Incognitae* 2(1970): 7–14. The exact provenance of these "Virginians" has never been established.

over their memory of whether or not she "came forth of a tavern" (2.5.121–3; 2 INT. 34).[5]

Promenaded and displayed Indians were also revenue generators. John Smith described how Epenow, one of five captives brought back from Capawack (Martha's Vineyard) by Captain Edward Harlow in 1611, was "shewed up and downe London for money as a wonder."[6] That money changed hands when he was displayed across the city suggests that there may have been an admission charge, as is evident also in Trinculo's famous recollection of the "dead Indian" who once caught the English imagination in *The Tempest* (2.2.31), and in the lesser known example of the "fish taken in the Indies" in the Plate River, displayed for money for the edification of London's curiosity market, in Jasper Mayne's *The City Match*.[7] Smith's description, however, can be interpreted in a different way: Epenow was put on display with the purpose of getting "money," that is, of encouraging investment in the Virginia Company. Eiakintomino and Matahan, who were in London in and around 1615, were employed to do just that. They were depicted on a broadside, *A Declaration for the Certaine Time of Drawing the Great Standing Lottery*, praying for Londoners to invest in the worthy cause with the promise of prizes: "Bring *Light*, and *Sight*, to Vs yet / Leade *Vs*, by *Doctrine* and *Behauoiur*, blinde / Into one Sion, to one SAVIOVR" (Figure 3.1).[8] Appealing to Christian charity, the two Virginians called upon the English to help them achieve salvation.

The promenaded and displayed Indian also reminded observers of the centrality of conversion to the Virginia Company mission—"the principall scope of this business," as Chapter 1 has discussed.[9] Having actual Native Americans voice this desire made the message more immediate. As Daniel Price observed in his sermon of 1609, "The *Virginian* desireth it," and by bringing over and training Native American advocates, the Virginia Company could give that desire expression.[10] What's more, they could remind potential adventurers that Virginia was not about self-interest but rather that there was a wider, holy mission. Not only would converting Virginians be doing God's work, argued the Company in its pamphlet *A True and*

---

[5] Pocahontas attended Jonson's *The Vision of Delight* in January 1617. See Karen Robertson, "Pocahontas at the Masque," *Signs: Journal of Women in Culture and Society*, 21(3) (1996): 551–83.

[6] Smith, *Generall Historie of Virginia*, 593. On Epenow, see Vaughan, *Transatlantic Encounters*, 65–7.

[7] Mayne, *The City Match*, 273.

[8] *A Declaration for the Certaine Time of Drawing the Great Standing Lottery*, in *Three Proclamations Concerning the Lottery in Virginia, 1613–1621* (Providence, RI: John Carter Brown Library, 1907).

[9] Quotation from Robert Tynley, *Two Learned Sermons*, 67–8.

[10] Daniel Price, *Saul's Prohibition Staide*, F2v.

# A Declaration for the certaine time of dravving the great ſtanding Lottery.

*Once, in one State, as of one Stem, / Moore Strangers from ISRAELVM, / Asiúw, were You; till Others Vine / Sought, and brought You to That Caſe.*

1125 li.    500    500

*Deere Sweames none, he Tax as blinde; / Being Light and Sight, to P¹ yet blinde / Leade P², by Doctrine and Behaviour, / Into one Sun, to One SAVIOVR.*

It is apparent to the world, by how many former publications the manifested our intents to haue drawne out the great ſtanding Lotterie long before this day: which not falling out as we our ſelues deſired, and others expected, whoſe moneyes are already aduentured therein, we thought good therefore for auoiding of vnjuſt and ſiniſter conſtructions, to reſolue the doubts of all in differenly minded, in three ſpecial points for their better ſatiſfaction.

The firſt is, for as much as the aduentures came in ſo ſlackly with ſuch poore and barren receits of moneys at the Lotterie houſe for this twelue moneth paſt, that without too much preiudice to our ſelues and the aduenturers in leſſening the blankes & prizes, we found no meanes nor ability to proceed in any competent proportion, but of neceſſity are driuen to the honourable Lords by petition. Who out of their Noble care and diſpoſition to further that publike plantation of Virginia, haue recommended their letters to the Counties, Cities and good Townes in England, which we hope by ſending in their voluntarie Aduentures, will ſufficiently make that ſupply of helpe, which otherwiſe we ſhould not in any reaſonable time haue effected.

The ſecond point for ſatisfaction to all honeſt and well affected minds, is, that notwithſtanding this our meanes of Lottery anſwered not our hopes, yet haue we not failed in that Chriſtian care of the Colony in Virginia, to whom wee haue lately made two ſundry ſupplies of men and proviſions, where wee doubt not but they are all in health, and in ſo good a way with corne and cattell to ſubſiſt of themſelues, that were they now but a while ſupplied with more hands and materials. We ſhould the ſooner reſolue vpon a diuiſion of the Countrey by lot, and to leſſen the generall charge, by leauing each ſeuerall tribe or family to huſband and manure his owne.

The third and laſt is our conſtant reſolution, that ſeeing our credits are now ſo farre engaged to the honourable Lords, & to the whole State for the drawing and accompliſhment of this great ſtanding Lotterie, which we intend ſhall be our laſt of all ſtanding Lotteries for this plantation, that our time fixed and determined for accompliſhing thereof, ſhall be if God permit, without longer delay, the 26. of June next being in Trinitie tearme, deſiring all ſuch as haue vndertaken with bookes to ſolicite their friends, and all ſuch as intende the proſperity of that worthie plantation, that they will not withhold their monies till the laſt weeke or moneth, be reſpited, leſt the be vnwillingly forced to proportion a leſſe value and number of our blankes and prizes which hereafter followſ.

And whoſoever vnder one name or poſie ſhall ad-

### VVelcomes.
| | |
|---|---|
| To him that firſt ſhall bee drawne out with a Blanke | 100. Crownes. |
| To the ſecond | 50. Crownes. |
| To the third | 25. Crownes. |
| To him that euery day during the drawing of this Lottery ſhall bee firſt drawne out with a Blanke | 10. Crownes. |

### Prizes.
| | |
|---|---|
| 1. Great Prize of | 4500 Crownes. |
| 2. Great Prizes, each of | 2000 Crownes. |
| 4. Great Prizes, each of | 1000 Crownes. |
| 6. Great Prizes, each of | 500. Crownes. |
| 10. Prizes, each of | 300. Crownes. |
| 10. Prizes, each of | 200. Crownes. |
| 100. Prizes, each of | 100. Crownes. |
| 100. Prizes, each of | 50. Crownes. |
| 400. Prizes, each of | 20 Crownes. |
| 1000. Prizes, each of | 10. Crownes. |
| 1000. Prizes, each of | 8. Crownes. |
| 1000. Prizes, each of | 6. Crownes. |
| 4000. Prizes, each of | 4. Crownes. |
| 1000. Prizes, each of | 3. Crownes. |
| 10000. Prizes, each of | 2. Crownes. |

### Rewards.
| | |
|---|---|
| To him that ſhall bee laſt drawne out with a Blanke | 25. Crownes. |
| To him that putteth in the greateſt number of Lots vnder one name or Poſie | 400. Crownes. |
| To him that putteth in the ſecond greateſt number | 300. Crownes. |
| To him that putteth in the third greateſt number | 200. Crownes. |
| To him that putteth in the fourth greateſt number | 100. Crownes. |

If diuers bee of equall number, then theſe Rewards are to be diuided proportionally.

### Addition of new Rewards.
| | |
|---|---|
| The Blanke that ſhall bee drawne out next before the Greateſt Prize, ſhall | 25. Crownes. |
| The Blanke that ſhall bee drawne out next after the ſaid Great Prize, ſhall haue | 25. Crownes. |
| The Blankes that ſhall bee drawne out immediately before the 3. next Greateſt Prizes, ſhall haue each of them | 20. Crownes. |
| The ſeuerall Blankes next after them ſhall haue alſo each of them | 20. Crownes. |
| The ſeuerall blanks next before the foure Great Prizes, ſhall haue each of them | 15. Crownes. |
| The ſeuerall Blankes next after them ſhall haue alſo each of them | 15. Crownes. |
| The ſeuerall Blankes next before the ſix Great Prizes, ſhall haue each of them | 10. Crownes. |
| The ſeuerall Blankes next after them ſhall haue each of them | 10. Crownes. |

venture twelue pounds ten ſhillings or vpward, if he pleaſe to leaue & remit his Prizes and Rewards, bee they more or leſſe, the Lottery being drawne out, hee ſhall haue a bill of Aduenture to Virginia, for the like ſum he aduentured: & ſhall be free of that Company, & haue his part in Lands, & all other profits hereafter ariſing thence, according to his aduenture of twelue pounds ten ſhillings or vpward.

Whoſoever is beſinde both the payment of any ſum of money, promiſed heretofore to be aduentured to Virginia, if hee aduenture in this Lotterie the double of that ſum, & make payment thereof in ready money to Sir Thomas Smith Knight, Treaſurer for Virginia, he ſhall be diſcharged of the foreſaid ſumme ſo promiſed to haue been aduentured to Virginia, and of all actions and damages therefrom ariſing, and haue alſo the benefit of all Prizes and Rewards whatſoever in this Lottery, but by reaſon of the like ſum which he ſhall bring in, and yet notwithſtanding, if after the Lottery drawne, he liſt to remit at his ſaid Prizes and Rewards, he ſhall haue a bill of aduenture to Virginia for the ſaid entire ſumme according to the laſt preceding Article.

And if vpon too much delay of the Aduenturers to furniſh this Lottery, we bee driuen to draw the ſame before it be full, the we purpoſe to ſhorten both blankes and prizes in an equall proportion, according to that number they ſhall come ſhort, bee it more or leſſe, that neither the Aduenturers may bee defrauded, nor our ſelues as in the former, any way wronged.

The Prizes, welcomes, & Rewards ſhall be paid in ready Money, Plate, or other goods reaſonably rated. If any diſlike of the ſaid plate or other goods, he ſhall haue ready money for the ſame, abating onely a tenth part: Except in ſmall Prizes of tenne Crownes or vnder, wherein nothing ſhall be abated them.

The money for Aduentures is to be paid to Sir Thomas Smith Knight, Treaſurer for Virginia, at his houſe in Philpot lane: or to ſuch officers as ſhall be appointed to attend for that purpoſe at the Lottery houſe: or to ſuch other as ſhall elſewhere, for the eaſe of the Countrey be authoriſed, vnder the Seale of the Company, for receipt thereof.

The Prizes, welcomes & Rewards being drawne, they ſhall be paid by the Treaſurer for Virginia, without delay, whenſoever they ſhall be demanded.

And for the better expedition to make our ſum compleat, as well to haſten the drawing of our Lottery, as chiefly to inable the ſooner to make good ſupplies to the Colonie in Virginia: Whoſoever, vnder one name or poſie ſhall bring in ready money three pounds, either to the Lottery houſe, or to any Colleans, the ſame party receiuing their money, for euery three pounds ſo receiu'd ſhall tender them preſently a ſiluer ſpoone of 5. ſhillings 3. pece price, or 6. ſhillings 8. pece in money.

Imprinted at London by Felix Kyngſton, for William Welby, the 22. of Februarie. 1615.

**Fig. 3.1.** *A Declaration for the Certaine Time of Drawing the Great Standing Lottery*, 1615. Courtesy of the Society of Antiquaries of London.

*Sincere Declaration of the Purpose and Ends of the Plantation Begun in Virginia* (1610): conversion would "add our myte to the treasury of Heauen, that as we pray for the comming of the kingdome of glory, so to expresse in our actions, the same desire, if God haue pleased, to vse so weak instruments, to the ripening & consummation thereof."[11] The Protestant mission in Virginia, that is, was a key component of the war between Protestantism and Catholicism, and the successful completion of said mission would guarantee God's favor and confirm England's place among the elect.

The promenaded and displayed Indians reminded the English that it was possible to live and thrive in the New World. Virginia may have been initially sold as a land of opportunity, but the first years of Jamestown seemed to offer evidence to the contrary. As William Crashaw complained in his sermon in 1610, "the Countrie is ill reported of by them that haue been there," and even though he and others protested that "it is not true, in all, not in the greater or better part," the news had spread and taken hold in English public consciousness.[12] Native American advocates were taught English so that they could speak against the ill reports of the country; indeed, even if they had no English, their healthy bodies could speak for them, articulating that, far from being barren and ill-suited for planting, the land could sustain people who lived there with ease. That the majority of visitors were male is significant. Virginia Company propaganda regularly propounded the idea that English and American climates were similar, and English and Native American bodies comparable—to quote the 1615 lottery broadside, both were "Once in a State, as of one Stem."[13] The Company promoted these ideas about the proximity of English and Indian bodies to counter suggestions that settlers' bodies would degenerate in Virginia. Crashaw argued that the climate was perfectly suitable for the English because "a Virginean, that was with vs here in *England*" had "skinne . . . so farre from a *Moores* or East or West *Indians*, that it was little more blacke or tawnie, then one of ours would be if he should goe naked in the South of *England*."[14] By observing Epenow and the other Virginian "specimens," Londoners could see how the masculine body could thrive across the Atlantic, and imagine how their own bodies might cope with conditions that had previously been described as hostile and enervating.[15]

---

[11] *True and Sincere Declaration*, 2–3.     [12] Crashaw, *New-Yeeres Gift*, F2.
[13] *Declaration for the Certaine Time of Drawing the Great Standing Lottery.*
[14] Crashaw, *New-Yeeres Gift*, E2.
[15] On English constructions of bodily differentiation in the New World, see Joyce E. Chaplin, *Subject Matter: Technology, the Body, and Science on the Anglo-American Frontier, 1500–1676* (Cambridge, MA: Harvard University Press, 2001); and Kupperman, "Fear of Hot Climates in the Anglo-American Colonial Experience."

The campaign found its apotheosis in George Chapman and Inigo Jones' *The Memorable Masque*, a cross-London spectacular mounted for the wedding of Princess Elizabeth Stuart to the Elector Palatine in 1613. The conceit of *The Memorable Masque* (which began on London's streets and culminated in a masque proper at Whitehall) revolved around a troupe of Virginian princes and priests who arrive in England, convert to Christianity, and express their love for James I, his daughter, and his son-in-law. By so doing they heralded a golden age for the English on both sides of the Atlantic. Their display of Virginian masculinity transcended the divisions between Indian and Englishman, presenting an idealized, transatlantic masculine form in service to the English crown. Their presence in London made Virginia seem closer to home, something that was emphasized even further by the procession of Virginians along the streets of London to the royal palace.

However, the Virginia Company message seems to have been often scrambled. In part this is evident in the confused responses to *The Memorable Masque*, which seems to have been a misunderstood spectacle (even by its authors). These scramblings are particularly evident in a series of plays that followed in *The Memorable Masque*'s wake and were performed in 1613: Fletcher and Field's *Four Plays, or Moral Interludes, in One*, Shakespeare and Fletcher's *Henry VIII, or All Is True*, and Shakespeare's *The Tempest*, which was revived at court as part of the wedding celebrations and quite possibly revised for the occasion. All three voice the theatermeme of the displayed Indian. In them the Indian is indifferent to Christianity, rather than being the embodiment of the colony's well-being; and Londoners seem to be little convinced by, or even interested in, the Protestant mission, and are more taken with, even aroused by, dead Indians, painted fish, or "the strange Indian with the great tool" (5.3.32). In the last of these examples, from *Henry VIII*, a porter remembers how once one Indian's phallic "tool" elicited "a fry of fornication" (33–4) in the assembled crowds. That this memory arises at a christening is itself significant: the crowds at Westminster should be gathered in solemn respect for a sacred rite (the christening of Princess Elizabeth, the future Elizabeth I), but instead they have been whipped up into a frenzy, and the crowds which once gathered to see the Indian, which should also be contemplating religious matters (namely the conversion of the Indians), experienced a similar erotic charge. The Porter's remembrance counters Trinculo's claim that in England "any strange beast will make a man" (*The Tempest* 2.2.2–89) as the strange Indian unmakes men into an amorphous, feminized mass. In a sense, then, we move here from the Indian sublime—a sense of transcendent contemplation brought on by the presence of an Indian begging the English to "come over and help us," to quote the seal of the Massachusetts Bay Company—to the Indian grotesque—that is, to a prodigiously endowed, displaced body whose presence precipitates societal collapse: as the Porter predicts, "here will be father, godfather, and all together" (*Henry VIII* 5.3.35–6). *Henry VIII* suggests that the practice of Indian display made the English estranged from themselves and turned them to barbarities to which even the Indians would not succumb—and that these transformations were not solely occurring amongst those transplanted to the colony but amongst the populace who remained at home.

We will return to the great-tooled strange Indian later on to trace how the practice of Indian display signifies elsewhere in *Henry VIII*, and we will return also to Trinculo's encounter with Caliban and his memory of England's sensational "dead Indian" craze. This chapter, however, takes as its starting point the procession of Virginian priests and princes (actually English masquers and musicians) through the streets of London at the beginning of Chapman's *The Memorable Masque*. The masque has often been interpreted as a Virginia Company puff-piece (and with good reason: it was funded by Virginia Company members in the Inns of Court), but by reading it in the context of the practice of Indian display we can unstitch its unease and discordance, as it tries to wrestle with the complex signification of the bodies of its sublime Virginian masquers and its grotesque anti-masquers. This unease becomes even more evident when we compare *The Memorable Masque* with *Four Plays, or Moral Interludes, in One*, in which a troupe of sunburned Indians sing and dance wildly. Whereas Chapman and Jones' Virginians willingly submit themselves to Christianity, Fletcher and Field's Indians remain unconverted, a fact which has consequences for the play's colonizer-figure, Anthropos, and which by extension serves as a commentary on the Virginia Company, whose pious message in Fletcher and Field's play sounds like nothing more than empty cant.

*Four Plays* and *Henry VIII* borrow extensively from *The Memorable Masque*, using the topicality of the most elaborate display of Indians yet to re-inscribe a vision of Virginia that oscillates between the masque-like vision of Indian sublimity to the anti-masquing of the Indian grotesque. They both bring out the latent complexity of *The Memorable Masque*, in particular its own struggles with dividing out the various signifying energies of the Virginian bodies it puts on display. They help us also to revisit *The Tempest*, a play that takes on a different topicality in its re-performance at court in 1613, on the same bill of entertainment as *The Memorable Masque*. In its 1613 context, *The Tempest*'s remembrance of a display of dead Indians recalls the fake Indians of the masque; it also casts new, and distinctly ambivalent, light on the play's marriage masque, mounted by Prospero for Miranda and his soon-to-be son-in-law,

Ferdinand, which echoes many of the themes of *The Memorable Masque*, not least its proclamation of a New World golden age and its employment of Plutus, the god of riches.

## "OUR BRITON PHOEBUS": VIRGINIA AND *THE MEMORABLE MASQUE*

*The Memorable Masque* began with a procession of Virginian priests and princes—in fact musicians "attired like Virginians" and masquers "in Indian habits, all of a resemblance"—from Chancery Lane "to *White Hall*, in as royall a manner as euer gallants did to the Court of *England*." Courtesy of Inigo Jones' lavish designs (Figure 3.2), the "chiefe Masquers" costumes were

> richly embroidered, with golden Sunns and about euery Sunne, ran a traile of gold, imitating Indian worke: their bases of the same stuffe and work, but betwixt every pane of embroidery, went a row of white Estridge feathers, mingled with sprigs of golde plate; under their breasts, they woare bawdricks of golde... Ruffes of feathers with pearle and siluer. On their heads high sprig'd-feathers, compast in Coronets, like the Virginian Princes they presented. Betwixt euery set of feathers, and about their browes, in the vnderpart of their Coronets, shin'd Sunnes of golde plate, sprinkled with pearle; from whence sprung rayes of the like plate, that mixing with the motion of the feathers, shew'd exceedingly delightfull and gracious. Their legges were adorn'd, with close long white silke-stockings: curiously embroidered with golde to the Midde-legge. (48–60)[16]

Gold, silver, pearl, feathers: so stunning was the procession that the usually underwhelmed James encouraged the masquers to make "one [more] turn about the yard" when they arrived at the royal palace (124).

Upon their entrance into Whitehall, the conceit of the masque began to reveal itself. After the anti-masque portion was complete, the Virginians emerged out of a rock, which was positioned center stage, having been summoned by a song calling the Earth to "Ope... thy womb of gold." (488). This display of opulence, however, came with an important qualification. The Virginians were summoned to the court, along with their god Pluto, by Honour, "To do due homage to the sacred nuptials" (468) and to offer themselves up as converts, turning away from "superstitious worship of these Suns" to "Christian piety" and "heaven's true light" (569, 573, 575). The display of Virginians celebrated the marriage of the virgin

---

[16] George Chapman, *The Memorable Masque*, in David Lindley (ed.), *Court Masques: Jacobean and Caroline Entertainments 1605–1640* (Oxford: Oxford University Press, 1995), 74–91. All subsequent line references are to this edition.

**Fig. 3.2.** An Indian Torchbearer from *The Memorable Masque*, designed by Inigo Jones, 1613. © Devonshire Collection, Chatsworth. Reproduced by Permission of Chatsworth Settlement Trustees.

Elizabeth, it celebrated the union of Virginia and England under James I, "our Briton Phoebus" (572), and it propagated an image of a gold-rich New World, whose inhabitants, once converted, would help the English attain "the blessings of the golden age" (624). It also reminded observers that the golden age evolved not solely from mineral plunder—that was a Spanish approach to the New World—but only could begin once the Virginians were incorporated into James' kingdom and into God's. As a result, the pursuit of wealth in the New World could be classified an honorable, blessed enterprise.

*The Memorable Masque*, often disregarded as little more than propaganda, is far more complex than may first appear.[17] As a number of critics have contended, Stuart masques were not the simple, self-congratulatory affairs they were once thought to be, but were, to appropriate Martin Butler's formulation, "courtly negotiations" of power, place, policy, and prestige, often directed at the monarch and sometimes implicitly critical of him.[18] *The Memorable Masque* is no different. Chapman's masque was performed before various and competing constituents—court factions divided in their loyalties and in their opinions about Jacobean foreign policy, and the London crowds made up of various interest groups—and Chapman was keenly aware of the need to balance the masque's appeal.[19] As Patricia Crouch has deftly observed, his masque displays "a formal and

---

[17] On *The Memorable Masque* as puff-piece, see Jack E. Reese, "Unity in Chapman's *Masque of the Middle Temple and Lincoln's Inn*," *Studies in English Literature, 1500–1900*, 4 (2) (1964): 291–305; D. J. Gordon, "Chapman's *Memorable Masque*," in Stephen Orgel (ed.), *The Renaissance Imagination* (Berkeley: University of California Press, 1975), 194–202; Graham Parry, "The Politics of the Jacobean Masque," in J. R. Mulryne and Margaret Shewring (eds), *Theatre and Government under the Early Stuarts* (Cambridge: Cambridge University Press, 1993), 87–117.

[18] Martin Butler, "Courtly Negotiations," in David Bevington and Peter Holbrook (eds), *The Politics of the Stuart Court Masque* (Cambridge: Cambridge University Press, 1998), 20–40. The most influential interpretation of the Stuart masque, Stephen Orgel's *The Illusion of Power*, which theorizes the relationship between spectators, performers, and patrons, has been expanded upon by a number of critics who suggest that the form was not just "an expression of the royal mind" and that the relationship between masque and king was not the only relationship at stake. Stephen Orgel, *The Illusion of Power: The Political Theater in the English Renaissance* (Berkeley: University of California Press, 1975), quotation at 43. See also Martin Butler, "The Invention of Britain and the Early Stuart Masque," in Malcolm Smuts (ed.), *The Stuart Court and Europe: Essays in Politics and Political Culture* (Cambridge: Cambridge University Press, 1996), 65–85; essays in Bevington and Holbrook, *The Politics of the Stuart Court Masque*; Martin Butler, "Reform or Reverence? The Politics of the Caroline Masque," in J. R. Mulryne and Margaret Shewring (eds), *Theatre and Government under the Early Stuarts* (Cambridge: Cambridge University Press, 1993), 118–56.

[19] See David Lindley, "Courtly Play: The Politics of Chapman's *The Memorable Masque*," in Eveline Cruickshanks (ed.), *The Stuart Courts* (Stroud: Sutton Press, 2000), 42–58.

thematic intricacy, and multivocalism" that stems from the fact that Chapman conceived of the masque in relation to its different "sites of patronage" (the street and in the court), which experienced the different "major sections of the entertainment—procession, anti-masque, masque, epithalamium"—in divergent ways.[20]

This intricacy is evident in the masque proper, which balances the competing visions of Virginia, and more broadly of English foreign policy, held at court on one side by the faction that had until recently surrounded Henry, Prince of Wales, and on the other by the king.[21] The masque owed a significant debt to the recently deceased Prince Henry, who, as unofficial "Patron of the Virginia Plantation," had showed considerable interest in the emerging Virginia colony: he backed George Waymouth's voyage to Virginia of 1605; Sir Thomas Dale, one of the colony's founders, was one of his former servants; Robert Tyndall sent a manuscript map of Virginia directly to him in 1607; and Henrico College, Henricopolis, Fort Henry, and Cape Henry were named after him. *The Memorable Masque* was designed at least in part to promote the aims of the Virginia Company's most celebrated supporter, aims which extended beyond the nascent colony and into the European theater of war.[22]

However, it is notable how *The Memorable Masque* submits to James' approach to foreign policy even as it encourages a more active involvement in geopolitical matters on both sides of the Atlantic. The conversion of the Virginians, the transformative act that dominates the masque proper, happens in James' presence—a common enough trope in masques, in which the monarch incorporates outsiders into the polity, but one which gains especial relevance with the divided court of 1613. The "troop of the noblest Virginians" (306) and "*the Phoebades* (or Priests of the sun)" (485), who have arrived in England with Plutus, god of riches, to commend the royal wedding, sing a "superstitious hymn" in honor of their deity, the

---

[20] Patricia Crouch, "Patronage and Competing Visions of Virginia in George Chapman's *The Memorable Masque* (1613)," *English Literary Renaissance*, 40(3) (2010): 393–426, at 394–5.

[21] Graham Parry goes so far as to suggest that this was "very much the Prince's masque," and that its appeal to Virginian and Guianan venturing (and by extension its evocation of the now-captive Sir Walter Raleigh) and its covert message of greater state intervention in Europe and the New World "cannot have been very pleasing to the king." Parry, "Politics of the Jacobean Masque," 105.

[22] As Parry suggests, "Chapman, by linking the Palatine marriage with Virginia, was in effect trying to draw the Elector Frederick (and behind him the German princes of the Protestant Union) into an anti-Spanish grouping." Parry, "Politics of the Jacobean Masque," 104. On the broader politics of all of the masques staged for the Palatinate wedding, see Kevin Curran, *Marriage, Performance, and Politics at the Jacobean Court* (Farnham and Burlington, VT: Ashgate, 2009), esp. chapter 3, "Competing Fictions and Fictional Authority at the Palatinate Wedding Celebrations," 89–128.

"Sun" (520). In response, Eunomia, the goddess of Law, exhorts the "Virgin Knights" to "turn the events / To this our Briton Phoebus, whose bright sky, / Enlightened with a Christian Piety, / Is never subject to black Errors night, / And hath already offered heaven's true light, / To your dark region; which acknowledge now. / Descend, and to him all your homage vow" (571–7). The Virginian Indians, then, are converts to Protestantism and also to the English cause in Virginia, willingly giving up their superstitions. But more specifically they are converted to James. As D. J. Gordon points out, "[i]t is a reconciliation rather than a violent conversion," thus more in keeping with the tenor of Jacobean foreign policy than with Henrician hawkishness.[23] While the sun/son worshipped at the masque's conclusion no doubt recalled the late Prince Henry, in whose name these acts of devotion (the marriage of Elizabeth and Frederick, and the union of England to Virginia under the auspices of James I) were silently solemnized, and while the sun was Frederick, who (in the eyes of Henry's faction) could unite Protestants across Europe through marrying James' daughter, Phoebus was James above all others, sitting at the end of the banqueting hall in the prime seat. The masque harped on themes dear to the late Prince of Wales' heart, yet at its conclusion it promoted not only the Christian duty of the English to convert the natives of the New World, but also James I's role in that process—not as a military Caesar but as a benevolent, loving vassal of God.

The masque's "competing visions of Virginia" also extend to the procession that preceded it. As Crouch notes, the procession "was calculated to promote on the grandest possible scale the colonial propaganda of the Virginia Company."[24] By putting Virginians on display, walking "up and down London" like Epenow the previous year, Chapman was tapping into an emerging tradition of Virginians speaking (or being made to speak, or being seen to speak) on behalf of the colony and its work so as to encourage investment. The yoking of Virginia and Virginians with gold may seem surprising given the lack of mineral wealth in the colony, confirmed by the traces of fool's gold brought back by Captain Christopher Newport in 1607, but the costume design also promoted the third

---

[23] D. J. Gordon, "Chapman's *Memorable Masque*," 200. Chapman's "De Guinam" also called for "Conquest without bloud" and imagines in Guiana a place "Where . . . / A world of Sauadges fall tame before them." Such appeals to pacifism are complicated however by his appeal to Elizabeth to "let thy soueraigne Empire be encreast, / And with *Iberian Neptune* part the stake." No such anti-Spanish appeals are apparent in *The Memorable Masque*, perhaps because there was an Iberian presence in the banqueting house in the form of the Spanish ambassador. George Chapman, "De Guiana, Carmen Epicum," in Lawrence Kemys, *A Relation of the Second Voyage to Guiana* (London: Thomas Dawson, 1596), Av–A4.

[24] Crouch, "Patronage and Competing Visions," 399.

Virginia Company charter, Article XVI of which decreed that "for the more effectual advancing of the said plantation" the treasurer and Company could "set forth, erect, and publish, one or more lottery or lotteries to have continuance, and to endure and be held, for the space of one whole year."[25] Thus observers of the procession were reminded that, for a relatively small outlay of twelve pence, it was possible to win vast sums. Moreover, they were reminded that they were contributors to the Company's religious mission, "the establishing of the Gospell, and the honour of our king and country."[26] They may accrue personal profit by investing in the lottery, but they could be sure that they would accrue spiritual profit in the process—for themselves, for the Indians, and for the English nation.

Of course, by cladding the Virginians in gold and silver, the masque was in danger of pandering to certain prospective interests from whom the Company had hitherto wished to divorce itself, namely the gold-hungry desperadoes we've seen play out in theatermemes in Chapter 1. But another aspect of the procession seems designed to counteract this appeal through a juxtaposition of figures that appeared at its head. We learn from Chapman's account that "all the performers and their assistants . . . thus set forth":

> Fifty gentlemen, richly attired and as gallantly mounted, with footmen particularly attending, made the noble vanguard of these nuptial forces. Next (a fit distance observed between them) marked a mock-masque of baboons, attired like fantastical travellers in Neapolitan suits and great ruffs, all horsed with asses and dwarf palfreys, with yellow foot-clothes, and casting cockle-demois about, in courtesy, by way of largesse; torches borne on either hand of them, lighting their state as ridiculously as the rest nobly. (31–7)

As Crouch argues, these baboon-travelers "could be seen to mock the purportedly gallant adventurers of the Virginia Company."[27] The baboon-travelers resemble the adventurers of *Eastward Ho!* and could, as Crouch argues, be said to critique the Company as a whole for empty promises of economic largesse.[28] However, Chapman attempts to counteract this reading by sandwiching the baboons between the fifty gentlemen and the Virginian priests and princes. The procession operates on the logic of the masque and anti-masque, juxtaposing the sublime with the grotesque. The gentlemen are followed by the baboons, just as the Virginian priests and princes are followed by their torchbearers and their Moorish slaves, whose "more stravagant" costumes are designed to offset "The humble

---

[25] "A Third Charter of K. James I," in Hening, *Statutes at Large*, 108.
[26] *Declaration for the Certaine Time of Drawing the Great Standing Lottery.*
[27] Crouch, "Patronage and Competing Visions," 403.
[28] For this interpretation of *Eastward Ho!*'s primate, see Howard, "Bettrice's Monkey."

variety" of the masquers' costumes (in the masque proper, the torchbearers perform an anti-masque (75–7)). Although the baboons appear
directly before the Virginians, they are contrasted with them and offset by
them—a passage of bodies symbolizing the disorder that needs to be
overcome for the Virginian promise to be fulfilled.

We don't know who comprised the "fifty gentlemen"—maybe they
were Virginia Company affiliates, perhaps even members—but even if we
dismiss this as speculation, we might think of these figures standing in for
the ideal kind of Virginia Company adventurer: gentlemanly and noble,
an appropriate vanguard for the "nuptial forces" not only because they
begin the finery that it is to follow in the figures of the Virginians but also
because they are at "a fit distance" from the "mock-masque of baboons."
Through the placement of bodies and the repetition of gestures and design
motifs, the grotesquery of the "fantasticall travellers" is offset by the
nobility both of the vanguard and the real "nuptial forces" whom they
herald. The placement of the gentlemen, the baboons, the Virginians, and
their torchbearers offer an interpretive frame for the Virginian bodies on
display, contrasting the right and wrong way to approach the riches
offered by the New World.

## "ANTICKE SUITES," "ALTOGETHER ESTRANGEFUL AND INDIAN-LIKE": MISREMEMBERING *THE MEMORABLE MASQUE*

Although the masque was something of a triumph, arguably the pinnacle
event of the year's festivities, its message does not seem to have been easily
heard. Prolific letter writer John Chamberlain witnessed the procession,
informing Dudley Carleton that the masquers "made such a gallant and
glorious shew that yt is highly recommended" and Ralph Winwood that
they "gave great contentment... with theyre gracefull coming on horse-
back, as in all the rest of theyre apt invention, apparel, fashion, and
specially their excellent dauncing." However, though Chamberlain was
allured by the magnificence of the display, he found no room to interpret
what he saw. He singled out the "dousen little boyes, dresst like babones
that served for an antimask... [who] performed yt exceedingly well when
they came to yt," but he did not mention to either Carleton or Winwood
that the masquers were attired as Virginians.[29] He was bedazzled by the

---

[29] Letters quoted in Stephen Orgel and Roy Strong, *Inigo Jones: The Theatre of the Stuart Court*, vol. 1 (Berkeley: University of California Press, 1973), 255.

finery and then by the boys' comic stylings, not by the message behind them. Chamberlain's letters show him to be repeatedly interested in the colony and an astute observer of its goings-on. Here, however, he seems to have missed the point of the Virginia procession.

Chamberlain was not alone. The pamphlet *The Mariage of Prince Fredericke and the Kings Daughter, the Lady Elizabeth, vpon Shrouesunday Last*, an account of the wedding celebrations published twice in 1613, recounts how "[t]he Gentleman of the Innes of Court, in the best and rarest manner they could deuise, prepared Maskes and Reuells in the Court" that began with the procession "to *White Hall*, in as royall a manner as euer gallants did to the Court of *England*." The account praises the masquers' attire of "cloth and tissue, most glorious shining," and marvels at how each masquer had "a Blackamore Page attending on horse backe, with torch light burning in their hands." Nowhere does the account mention that the masquers are Virginians—indeed, its author seems confused as to what these figures represent, saying that the masquers wear "most strange Anticke sutes," an indication that the distinctions that Chapman and Jones were trying to make were not registering.[30]

Even Chapman himself doesn't sound too sure about what exactly Jones' creations looked like. After his lengthy description of the masquers' attire, he proclaims them "altogether estrangefull, and Indian-like" (62). The primary meaning of "estrangefull" is probably "wondrous" or "amazing," but the word carries with it a sense of incomprehension—a sense that the Virginians were strange, unknown, and, perhaps, unknowable. This sense is partially cancelled by Chapman's assertion that the figures are "Indian"—indeed, he uses the word "Indian" to describe their "habits" and "garb" and assures the readers that they were dressed "like those of their country" (46). However, his addition of "like" after the word "Indian" destabilizes this certainty, because even though the word suggests similarities between the appearance of masquers and "real" Indians, it also distances the representation from the real thing. The representations are not Indian in so far as they are masquers—but they are not Indian in so far as their appearance only approximates "Indian-likeness."

Chapman's uncertainty about the Virginians that his entertainment purports to represent is reflected elsewhere in the masque. The gold details on Inigo Jones' costume designs had little correlation with Virginian clothing. Indeed, by 1613 it had become clear that Virginia was not mineral-rich, let alone gold-laden, and, as D. J. Gordon has suggested, the masque seems to transfer ideas about Guiana (in particular Walter

---

[30] *The Mariage of Prince Fredericke and the Kings Daughter, the Lady Elizabeth, vpon Shrouesunday Last* (London: for W. Wright, 1613), B3–B3v.

Raleigh's fantasy of El Dorado) onto Virginia.[31] Chapman's assertion that
the "high sprigged feathers, compassed in coronets" worn by the masquers
were "like the Virginian Priests they presented" (53–5) is inaccurate
(Virginian Indians did not wear feather-crowns, but instead seem to
have favored single feathers extending from the hair). This information
was available to Jones through Cesare Vecellio's *Habiti Antichi et Moderni*
(1598), the source book for many of his costumes. His *Memorable Masque*
designs resemble the "Indo Africano" in Vecellio (Figure 3.3), but the
book's depictions of the inhabitants of Virginia—based heavily on Theodor de Bry's engravings of John White's watercolors from Thomas Harriot's *Brief and True Report of the Newfoundland of Virginia* (1590)
(Figure 3.4)—do not appear to have influenced him.[32] The African origin
of Jones' costumes is underscored by the presence of Moors "attired like
Indian slaves" who accompanied each of the masquers (72). Jones may
also have been inspired by a masque performed on January 1, 1604, the
first performed at James I's court, which featured "certain Indian and
China knights" who wore "loose robes of crimsen satin embroidered with
gold and bordered with silver laces, dublets and bases of cloth of siluer;
buskins, swords and hatts alike and in theyr hats ech of them had an
Indian bird for a fether with some jewels."[33] Chapman's description of the
"turbans, stuck with several coloured feathers" in the text of *The Memorable Masque* (44–5) suggests that the design for the Indians' headwear was
different to and more spectacular than those of 1604—"several coloured
feathers" as opposed to a single "fether with some jewels"—but, regardless,
the "turban" was headwear usually associated with Turks or Persians.[34]
The Indians of *The Memorable Masque*, although named "Virginian," are
amalgams of peoples from both hemispheres.

[31]  See Gordon, "Chapman's *Memorable Masque.*"
[32]  Cesare Vecellio, *Habiti Antichi et Moderni di Tutto Mondo* (Venice: Giovanni
Bernardo Sessa, 1598), 472–7.
[33]  The text of this masque does not survive, but Sir Dudley Carleton recorded what
few details we have in a letter to John Chamberlain dated January 15, 1604. See
E. K. Chambers, *The Elizabethan Stage*, vol. 3 (Oxford: Clarendon Press, 1923), 279–80.
[34]  The term "turban" is applied by the English to the national costume of a variety of
peoples, but not, it seems, to peoples of the Americas. The majority of references to turbans
in this period seem to associate them with Turks: thus, for example, in his lexicon *World of
Words* John Florio defined "Turbant" as "a wreathed round attire of white linnen, as all the
Turkes weare on their head. It is iust like a top or gig that children play withall turned
vpside downe." Susan Castillo explains that the costume choice was accurate, as "turbans
were actually worn by the Cherokees, one of the Five Civilized Tribes," but this would seem
to have been entirely inadvertent, since the English had limited contact with the Cherokee
until the mid-seventeenth century. John Florio, *World of Words* (London: for Edward
Blount, 1598), 436; Susan Castillo, *Performing America: Colonial Encounters in New World
Writing, 1500–1786* (London: Routledge, 2006), 148.

**Fig. 3.3.** "Indo Africano," from Cesare Vecellio, *Habiti Antichi et Moderni*, 1590. Courtesy of the Huntington Library, San Marino, California.

# A weroan or great Lorde of Virginia. III.

He Princes of Virginia are attyred in suche manner as is expressed in this figure. They weare the haire of their heades long and bynde opp the ende of the same in a knot vnder thier eares. Yet they cutt the topp of their heades from the forehead to the nape of the necke in manner of a cokscombe, stirkinge a faier loge pecher of some berd att the Beginninge of the creste vppun their foreheads, and another short one on bothe seides about their eares. They hange at their eares ether thicke pearles, or somwhat els, as the clawe of some great birde, as cometh in to their fansye. Moreouer They ether pownes, or paynt their forehead, cheeks, chynne, bodye, armes, and leggs, yet in another forte then the inhabitantz of Florida. They weare a chaine about their necks of pearles or beades of copper, wich they muche estee me, and ther of wear they also braselets ohn their armes. Vnder their brests about their bellyes appeir certayne spotts, whear they vse to lett them selues bloode, when they are sicke. They hange before the the skinne of some beaste verye feinelye dresset in suche sorte, that the tayle hangeth downe behynde. They carye a quiuer made of small rushes holding their bowe readie bent in on hand, and an arrowe in the other, radie to defend themselues. In this manner they goe to warr, or tho their solemne feasts and banquetts. They take muche pleasure in huntinge of deer wher of theris great store in the contrye, for yt is fruitfull, pleasant, and full of Goodly woods. Yt hathe also store of riuers full of diuers sorts of fishe. When they go to battel they paynt their bodyes in the most terible manner that thei can deuise.

**Fig. 3.4.** A Weroan or Great Lorde of Virginia, from Thomas Harriot, *A Brief and True Report of the New Found Land of Virginia*, 1590. Courtesy of the John Carter Brown Library at Brown University.

The idea of the Indian, therefore, could elicit recognition—Chapman must have expected the phrase "Indian-like" to conjure some image. But it was at the same time "estrangeful," as it was an ill-defined composite of tropes that straddled the Atlantic and beyond. Indians are both entirely alien ("altogether estrangeful") and possess recognizable qualities that are associated with Indianness ("Indian-like"). Chapman's oxymoron destabilizes how "Indian" these figures are, or rather what *kind* of Indians they are.

## "INNOCENT PEOPLE / NOT KNOWING YET": THE INDIANS OF "THE TRIUMPH OF TIME"

What may have been a failure of signification for many of those gathered on the streets of London does not however seem to have been lost on Fletcher, Field, and Shakespeare. Indeed, these playwrights seem to latch on to the complexities of Chapman and Jones' undertaking—its signifying malfunction—and rewrite its scenes of opulence, conversion, and Indian display in light of a more skeptical outlook towards the Virginia project.

Fletcher and Field's *Four Plays, or Moral Interludes, in One* held up a mirror to the Whitehall celebrations—indeed, the fact that the Lady Elizabeth's Men (named for the newlywed princess) were probably the company who performed it makes the homage all the more pointed.[35] The conceit of the play revolves around a troupe of actors who present, as the title suggests, four plays to celebrate the "sacred union" of the "brave King of *Portugal, Emanuel*" and "his worthie mate Isabella, the King of Castiles Daughter" (IND. 46–54).[36] The gaps between playlets are punctuated by commentary from the newly married couple, who note the lesson that each playlet has taught them. The fourth and final playlet, "The Triumph of Time," shows to Emanuel and Isabella the "weaknesse" in rulers who make themselves prone to becoming "master'd by abuses" such as greed, desire, ostentation, and excessive materialism (4.INT.2–3).

It is in the middle of "The Triumph of Time" that we encounter Plutus and "*a troop of Indians singing and dancing wildly about him, and bowing to*

---

[35] *Four Plays, or Moral Interludes, in One* has not been precisely dated. Fredson Bowers narrows the field to 1612–15 on the basis of the careers and whereabouts of the two authors. I follow Gordon McMullan in his conjecture of a date of 1613 because of the close affinity between "The Triumph of Time" and *The Memorable Masque*. See McMullan, *John Fletcher and the Politics of Unease*, 105.

[36] John Fletcher and Nathaniel Field, *Four Plays, or Moral Interludes, in One*, in Bowers, *The Dramatic Works in the Beaumont and Fletcher Canon*, vol. 8. All subsequent citations are referenced parenthetically.

*him*" (4.3.SD). The plot of the playlet centers on the plight of Anthropos, who is lured by his false friends Desire and Vain Delight into wasting his money on fripperies. As a result he is forced to accompany Poverty "to purge [his] pleasures" (4.1.102). He calls upon Jupiter for assistance, and Jupiter urges Plutus and Time to release him from Poverty, Humility, and Simplicity. Plutus and Time take Anthropos to a rock, which is revealed to be "A glorious mine of metal" (4.4.38). The false friends flock back to Anthropos in disguise, hoping that his newly discovered wealth will line their coffers, but Jupiter unmasks them and forces them to become part of Time's Triumph, thus ensuring that "Their memories [will] be here forgot for ever" (4.4.57). To ensure that Anthropos "never more . . . shalt . . . feel want," Jupiter makes him "Live in that rock of gold" (the mine) (4.4.64). The abuses (represented by false friends), which the watching monarchs conclude rulers must master, are defeated, and Anthropos can forever live in peace and limitless wealth.

"The Triumph of Time" echoes *The Memorable Masque* in several ways. At the conclusion of both Anthropos and James are assured success and riches. The scenic design for "The Triumph of Time," with its prominently positioned mountain of gold center stage, seems likely to have been inspired by Jones' scenery, which included "*an artificial rock* . . . [which] *grew by degrees up into a gold colour, and was run quite through with veins of gold*" (*Memorable Masque*, 129–34). Like *The Memorable Masque*, "The Triumph of Time" features a troop of Indians. In "The Triumph of Time," the character of Jupiter describes them as "sunburnt Indians," which perhaps indicates that the players wore some kind of blackface. The costumes may have been inspired by the designs of Inigo Jones for *The Memorable Masque*: Colin Gibson has argued that Massinger's *The City Madam* may have borrowed costuming from *Tempe Restord* in 1632, and it is not inconceivable that there was a similar arrangement in 1613.[37] Some audience members may have recognized these figures from the publicity campaigns in the first years of the Virginia Company, while some would have witnessed the lavish procession, perhaps even the masque itself, which accompanied the wedding of Princess Elizabeth earlier in the year. Finally, Plutus plays a prominent role in "The Triumph of Time," and, just as in *The Memorable Masque*, he is far from the crippled, blind figure of Aristophanes' *Plutus*.

However, while many of the constituent parts are the same, there are significant differences between the play and the masque's treatment of their Indian figures. In the *Memorable Masque*, the Virginians' realignment of

---

[37] See Colin Gibson, "Introduction to *The City Madam*," in Colin Gibson (ed.), *The Plays and Poems of Philip Massinger*, vol. 4 (Oxford: Clarendon, 1976), 5.

allegiance from sun to king seems intended to justify the English proclaiming not just territorial but spiritual dominion over Virginia. The Virginians' turn away from sun-worship is a declaration of the godliness of crown-sponsored colonial pursuit. The wealth that Plutus offers the English is therefore justified because James, as the anointed servant of God upon the English throne, is the approved beneficiary. This form of wealth accumulation is contrasted favorably with that promoted by Capriccio, the "Man of Wit," whom the Plutus of *The Memorable Masque* rejects as "an attendant for reward" rather than for honor (423). The bellows that Capriccio wears on his head signify both that he can "puff up with glory all those that affect me" (370–1); i.e. he is an avid promoter of people whose pay he is in, and that he is a "religion-forger" (334), whose puritanical outbursts against the sins of wealth mask a thirst for riches and a desire to "blow up the settled governments of kingdoms" (335–6). Capriccio, the masque suggests, is not a justified beneficiary of Virginian wealth precisely because of his abject materialism and his bankrupt religiosity.

In contrast, in "The Triumph of Time" no native conversion takes place. Instead, the Indians persist in worshipping Plutus, albeit that "They know [him] not, nor hurt [him] not, yet hug [him]" (4.2.21–2). Jupiter describes the Indians as "idly" adoring the god of riches—they are "inno-cent people / Not knowing yet what power and weight he carries" (18–19). The Indians' reverence resembles not the Virginian worship of Kiwasa (whom European observers did not associate with the accumula-tion of wealth), but rather Nahua worship of Quetzalcoatl in Mexico. José de Acosta, describing Quetzalcoatl as "the god of marchandise, being to this day greatly given to trafficke" (inaccurately, as it happens, as Quet-zalcoatl was the sky god and creator god), recorded that the god's idol was made from "golde, silver, jewells, very rich feathers, and habites of divers colour, . . . and they worshipt it, for that hee enriched whome hee pleased, as *Memnon* and *Plutus*."[38] In contrast to the Nahua, however, the Indians of "The Triumph of Time" do not worship Plutus for reasons of self-enrichment. They adore Plutus "idly"—that is, "as an idol" and "emp-tily"—because they do not know "yet" his "power and weight." When Time approaches Plutus to get him to help Anthropos, he asks whether there is "some fool . . . some *Midas* / That to no purpose I must choke with riches," but it does not appear that he has choked the Indians who worship him in "innocence" (24–5). However, Jupiter's "yet" suggests a future

---

[38] De Acosta, *Naturall and Morall Historie*, 354.

Indian conversion to worship Plutus' "power and weight" rather than to the Christian god.

The Plutus of "The Triumph of Time" is not converted either. The god of riches, who was usually associated with (in poet John Davies' phrase) "th'infernall deepes" of the underworld, was also often linked with the New World, primarily in relation to the Spanish mines, underpinning the oft-rehearsed and derogatory link between the Spanish Americas and excessive, almost diabolical, wealth (as described in Chapter 1).[39] In Edward Daunce's *A Briefe Discourse of the Spanish State* (1590), Plutus is declared "the Hesperian [i.e. western] god," who allows New Spain to abound "with fruitfull fields and rich mines."[40] Plutus, then, rules over the mines of the New World; Plutus rules over the underworld; hence Plutus is another name for the Devil, tempting and corrupting people with the promise of (new) worldly wealth—a false idol.

In *The Memorable Masque* Plutus is co-opted by the English and, while he helps persuade the Virginians to turn their worship to the court and not to the sun, he is not depicted as their or anyone else's false god. Indeed, Plutus' status as an idol is mollified in the masque by the fact that before the masque begins he has been converted to the goddess Honour's cause. To follow Plutus in the *Memorable Masque* is itself honorable, because by so doing one maintains obeisance to the crown and to God. However, Fletcher and Field's Plutus is a Protean shape-shifter, who when needed can "change my figure" either to one "goodly and full of glory" when "I willingly befriend a creature" or to one "old, and decrepit" if "I am compell'd" (4.3.16–17). In comparison to his *Memorable Masque* incarnation, Plutus transforms *himself*—he is not a convert, his advocacy of wealth has not been colored as honorable, and he changes himself for his own benefit. And an unconverted Plutus was, to all intents and purposes, the Devil.

That Fletcher and Field's re-imagining of *The Memorable Masque* omits both of its conversion narratives may seem a marginal concern as, after all, the main figure in the playlet does undergo a lasting transformation: Anthropos turns away from the vanity of "Desire" and "Vain Delight" to work at the "glorious mine of metal" with "hook and mattock" (4.4.38–45). The primary target of critique in this play seems to be James' court, which famously indulged in "Desire" and "Vain Delight," ruining itself, as Anthropos himself does, "on clothes, and Coaches, / Perfumes, and

---

[39] John Davies, *Microcosmos: The Discovery of the Little World* (Oxford: for Joseph Barnes, 1603), 250.

[40] Edward Daunce, *A Briefe Discourse of the Spanish State* (London: for Richard Field, 1590), 32.

powder'd pates," on "an endlesse troop of Tailors, / Mercers, Embroiderers, Feathermakers, Fumers" (4.1.21–30). Chapman and Jones' masque was an example of this waste: as Tucker Orbison calculates, £2,255. 8s. 11d. was spent on the masque, a figure that caused the Venetian ambassador, one of the audience members, to write, "the expenses have been so great that, in spite of their being rich, they will feel it for some time."[41] The play's framing device of the wedding of Emanuel and Isabel comments not only indirectly on the wedding of Elizabeth and Frederick, but also directly on James, boldly announcing in the opening exchanges that it "will censure not onely the King in the Play here, that reigns his two hours; but the King himself [i.e. James], that is to rule his life time" (IND. 64–6). By rejecting vanity, Anthropos seems to be being rewarded—in a way that James I, whose court embraced vanity, may not.

But there is another way of reading Anthropos' acquisition of a "glorious mine" that is less than glorious. Anthropos' new (world) wealth may be acquired by hard work and the rejection of a certain kind of materialism, but that it is achieved without any form of conversion of the natives is significant when we consider his fate at the end of the playlet. His industry and his rejection of his *faux-amis* may be rewarded with the goldmine, but Jupiter's declaration that Anthropos' conversion to industriousness allows him to "Live in that rock of gold, and still enjoy it" seems in many ways menacing (4.4.64). The meaning here is somewhat obscure, but, since Anthropos has already been awarded custody of Plutus' mine after promising to be industrious, it is unlikely that Jupiter is restating Anthropos' ownership. Given that Anthropos is not accorded an exit in the stage directions, presumably he leaves the stage by being encased *in* the mine— Jupiter's words would certainly seem to indicate this. This does not indicate a triumphant transformation away from "vain delight," but rather an excessive, Midas-like greed—and this is, after all, Plutus' mine that Anthropos is commanded to live in. Without any conversion of the Indians, or of Plutus, Anthropos is entrapped in a mountain of gold. Significantly, in *The Memorable Masque*, Capriccio makes his first appearance by cracking out of a rock (Plutus' mine). Anthropos makes the same journey as Capriccio but in reverse—that is, into the mine, or into the depths of hell.

As we've seen, promoters of colonization strove hard to dispel the notion that adventurers only saw in Virginia its lucrative possibilities, and they advanced the idea that the mission was not simply about accumulation but was one of spirituality and communion, with the plight

---

[41] See Crouch, "Patronage and Competing Vision," 398 (figures from Orbison quoted here).

of the native inhabitants at its core. As Chapter 1 has described, one of the main reasons for the Virginia Company's disgust with the players was their insistence that anybody interested in colonial endeavor was a rogue, as it deflected from its major raison d'etre. Fletcher and Field's refusal to rehearse the centrality of the Indians to Virginia Company propaganda, their focus on the importance of Anthropos' conversion, and his eventual subterranean encasement highlights key differences between the *modus operandi* of the *The Memorable Masque* and *Four Plays*. In *Four Plays* Plutus' Indians are imagined as sun-worshipping heathens resolutely unaffected by the advance of English Protestantism. While these Indians' actions may seem innocent enough, their unconvertedness serves to dismiss the religious protestations of the Virginia Company as a mask and expose its money-grabbing and diabolical tendencies beneath.

## "AND TOMORROW THEY MADE BRITAIN / INDIA": *HENRY VIII*, THE CLOTH OF GOLD, "THE STRANGE INDIAN"

In contrast to *Four Plays, or Moral Interludes, in One*, the Indians of Shakespeare and Fletcher's collaboration *Henry VIII or All Is True* do not appear on stage. The play was in the King's Men's repertoire by June 29, 1613 (the day that the first Globe Theatre burnt down, during one of its early outdoor performances), but may have been performed at Blackfriars earlier in the year as part of the company's winter season.[42] It has often been noted as one of the most visually spectacular plays in the Shakespeare canon, with crowd scenes and trial scenes, a masque of shepherds at Cardinal Wolsey's banquet, royal coronation and christening processions, and Katherine of Aragon's dream sequence. Indeed, as John D. Cox argues, the play seems to be modeled on the logic of the Jonsonian masque, following a pattern of anti-masque and masque in order to validate the reign of its titular monarch and that of the residing monarch at the time of its first performance.[43]

In act 5, scene 3, a porter describes the massed crowds who have gathered at the christening of Princess Elizabeth (the future Elizabeth I) and have been whipped up into a frenzy of excitement. He asks his man, "Is this Moorfields to muster in? Or have we some strange Indian with the

---

[42] See Gordon McMullan, "Introduction," in Gordon McMullan (ed.), *Henry VIII or All Is True* (London: Thomson Learning, 2000), 9–15.

[43] John D. Cox, "*Henry VIII* and the Masque," *English Literary History*, 15 (1978): 390–409.

great tool come to court, the women so besiege us? Bless me, what a fry of fornication is at door! On my Christian conscience, this one Christening will beget a thousand: here will be father, godfather, and all together" (5.3.31–6). That is to say, the Porter wishes that such "a multitude" had gathered at Moorfields, open land outside the city walls that would be better suited for a large gathering, since the last occasion that he can remember such numbers was at the arrival of an Indian at court, whose presence caused London's womenfolk to crowd the royal palace.

As Gordon McMullan points out, act 5, scene 3 of *Henry VIII* is often cut from performance, and plot-wise it is arguably expendable, a diversion from the act 5 storylines revolving around Archbishop Thomas Cranmer's ascendancy and the birth of Princess Elizabeth. The Indian reference seems like little more than a throwaway joke in a throwaway scene. I agree with McMullan, however, that "the scene has . . . a significant symbolic, as well as practical function," a function that for McMullan expresses the play's engagement with time and truth, concepts key to and much contested in the Henrician Reformation of the 1530s and in the early years of James I's reign, particularly in the wake of Prince Henry's death and the Palatinate marriage.[44] The scene is also crucial in terms of its evocation of Virginia. The "strange Indian with the great tool," a figure recalling both the first flourishing of England's transatlantic engagement and more recent developments under the auspices of the Virginia Company, forms the penultimate link in a chain of signification which stretches back to the play's opening scene, which records the Field of the Cloth of Gold, the lavishly celebrated accord between England and France; back to the middle of the play, with the coronation of Anne Boleyn, heralded by one observer as "all the Indies . . . / And more, and richer" (4.1.45–6); and looks forward to the end, with the birth and christening of Elizabeth, described prophetically by Archbishop Thomas Cranmer as "the maiden phoenix" whose reign will be followed by "another heir" (James I) who will "make new nations" (5.4.52). These moments of the play chart the movement of English history from its Catholic past, dominated by Cardinal Wolsey and exemplified by the meaningless ritual display of the Field of the Cloth of Gold, through the royal divorce and subsequent marriage of Anne and Henry, the event that marked England's break from Rome, to an imagined future where Elizabeth and then James fulfill the promise of the English Reformation—a future which was the audience's recent past.

These moments also recall a more recent event, the royal wedding of Elizabeth and Frederick and, more particularly, *The Memorable Masque*'s

---

[44] McMullan, "Introduction," 144–7, quotation at 144.

procession through the streets of London. All of the "Indian" scenes in *Henry VIII* involve procession and display, and all evoke "Indian" wealth and riches. When placed in relation to one another, these scenes form something of a critique of *The Memorable Masque*—of its opulence and cost; of its positioning as Virginia Company propaganda. In turn, the Indian scenes express ambivalence about the project of the Virginia Company, exposing the fault lines within its heady rhetoric, especially as regards the place of the Indian and Indianness, and covertly question its truth claims, its history, and its future. *Henry VIII* shares some of its ambivalence with *Four Plays*; yet, as we will see, the resolution to the ambivalence moves beyond the image of mankind entrapped in a mountain of gold in "The Triumph of Time" to an image of "every man . . . / Under his own vine" (5.4.34)—a vision of England's imperialist future under Elizabeth and James, where the Protestant supersedes the Catholic, the space of the plantation supersedes the space of the goldmine, and the Indian both enables these conquests yet is ultimately relegated to the past. This "making" is contingent and temporary, and in danger of being un-made at any point. *Henry VIII* looks back to the birth of English Protestantism to question the success of that moment in time, and it looks forward to the state of English Protestantism in the reign of James I, expressing doubt that the providential vision espoused by Archbishop Cranmer has come to pass or ever can come to pass. This is a vision in which Virginia and Virginians should stand as markers of England's centrality to God's plan but in which they also mark the possibility of England's degeneration and collapse.[45]

Within the first few lines of *Henry VIII* we find an image of "India" employed to describe an event that occurs offstage, so as to conjure a vision of vast and shining riches plucked from Indian mines. In the play's first scene the Duke of Norfolk offers the following description of the Field of the Cloth Gold, nominally to the soon-to-be disgraced Buckingham and his son-in-law, Lord Abergavenny, but also to the play's audience:

> Then you lost
> The view of earthly glory. Men might say
> Till this time pomp was single, but now married

[45] On *Henry VIII*, historiography, and futurity, see Ivo Kamps, *Historiography and Ideology in Stuart Drama* (Cambridge: Cambridge University Press, 1996), especially chapter 4, "Shakespeare, Fletcher, and the Question of History," 91–139; and Thomas Healey, "History and Judgment in *Henry VIII*," in Jennifer Richards and James Knowles (eds), *Shakespeare's Late Plays: New Readings* (Edinburgh: Edinburgh University Press, 1999), 158–75.

To one above itself. Each following day
Became the next day's master, till the last
Made former wonders its. Today the French,
All clinquant, all in gold, like heathen gods,
Shone down the English; and, to-morrow, they
Made Britain India. Every man that stood
Showed like a mine. Their dwarfish pages were
As cherubims, all gilt. The madams too,
Not used to toil, did almost sweat to bear
The pride upon them, that their very labour
Was to them as a painting. Now this masque
Was cried incomparable; and th'ensuing night
Made it a fool and beggar. The two kings,
Equal in lustre, were now best, now worst,
As presence did present them: him in eye,
Still him in praise, and, being present both
'Twas said they saw but one, and no discerner
Durst wag his tongue in censure. When these suns—
For so they phrase 'em—by their heralds challenged
The noble spirits to arms, they did perform
Beyond thought's compass—that former fabulous story,
Being now seen possible enough, got credit
That Bevis was believed. (1.1.13–38)

Henry VIII's reign of course did see a famously gold-laden meeting of the French and English monarchies in 1520; Shakespeare and Fletcher's main source, Holinshed, provides an extensive description of the event, of the gold-lined clothing worn by both sides, and of the general sumptuousness of proceedings. However, so celebrated an occasion as the wedding of Elizabeth and Frederick, and so vivid an event as the procession that began *The Memorable Masque*, makes it likely that Norfolk's description of the Field of the Cloth of Gold recalled the much more recent procession through London by mock-Virginian princes. The Field of the Cloth of Gold is described as a "masque" (1.1.26); the Field of the Cloth of Gold bears witnesses to the conjoining of two dynasties, just as *The Memorable Masque* was performed as part of festivities celebrating the merger of the House of Stuart with the German princes. Visually, *The Memorable Masque* was a spectacle beyond compare—indeed, Chapman's description keeps upping the ante, with each new costume superseding what came before in terms of splendor; while for Norfolk, each day trumps the day before. Most importantly for our purposes, gold dominated both processions: like the "Virginians," the French appeared "all in gold like heathen gods"; the following day, the English matched them, making "Britain India," and were accompanied by "dwarfish pages . . . / As cherubim's, all gilt" (18–23). In response to the speech quoted above, Buckingham exclaims, "O, you go far" (i.e. you are getting carried away), and this indeed seems like an apt summation (38). Norfolk constantly reaches for the right words to convey what he has seen, describing "the earthly glory" through a range of ever expanding comparatives that culminate in the assertion that fables are "now seen possible enough" (37).

Yet as an encomium to English "Indianness," Norfolk's testimony is not quite what it seems. As Julia Gaspar points out, it is "an artful piece of time-release poetry." What starts as "a panegyric of the court . . . reveals more and more skepticism, disgust and ridicule the more often we read it."[46] While the scene begins in the key of admiration, once Norfolk reveals the identity of the man behind the "masque," the corrupt and lavish Cardinal Wolsey, the attitude towards the Field of the Cloth of Gold shifts too. Buckingham describes the spectacles surrounding the Cloth of Gold as "fierce vanities," and berates Wolsey for "this French going-out, [which] he took upon him, / Without the privity o'th'King" (54, 73–4). That Buckingham is antagonistic towards the Field of the Cloth of Gold is understandable given his antagonism towards Wolsey— as Norfolk warns, "The state takes notice of the private difference / Betwixt you and the Cardinal" (100–1). But both of his companions are similarly disposed, even if they keep their counsel rather than voice their contempt (Buckingham's outspokenness comes back to haunt him in act 2 when he is executed for treason at Wolsey's behest). Abergavenny describes how his three "Kinsmen" have "By this [the Field of the Cloth of Gold] so sickened their estates that never / They shall abound as formerly" (80–2), i.e. that Wolsey has paid for the spectacle by forcing the gentry to pay for it. Having praised the grandeur of what he has seen in France, Norfolk agrees with Buckingham that "this vanity" did nothing more than "minister communication of / A most poor issue" (85–7) (i.e. that the discussions between the French and the English will yield little future amity), and concedes the point that "The peace between the French and us not values / That cost that did conclude it" (88–9)—the cost of putting on the Field of the Cloth of Gold celebrations, which was felt by people like Abergavenny's kinsmen. Indeed, Norfolk subsequently reveals that "France hath flawed the league" even though the memory of the accord between the two nations is still "fresh" (95, 3). Norfolk's seeming *volte face* forces us to revisit what seems on the face of it to be an enthusiastically delivered report. Thus, in the course of the play's first

---

[46] Julia Gaspar, "The Reformation Plays on the Public Stage," in J. R. Mulryne and Margaret Shewring (eds), *Theatre and Government under the Early Stuarts* (Cambridge: Cambridge University Press, 1993), 190–216, at 208.

scene, the perspective on the Field of the Cloth of Gold shifts from the admiration articulated breathlessly by Norfolk to condemnation evinced not just by Buckingham but by Norfolk and Abergavenny about the machinations of Wolsey and about the masque-like spectacle's political efficacy, economic wastefulness, and symbolic vacuity.[47]

What does this condemnation of Wolsey's memorable "masque" of 1520 have to do with Chapman's *Memorable Masque* of 1613? Wolsey elsewhere in the play shows a taste for masquing extravagance. His home life at York Place consists of parties and masques, including one staged at the end of act 1 where Henry meets Anne Boleyn for the first time. His downfall is the result not only of attempting to obstruct the marriage of Anne and Henry but also because of the "worldly wealth I have drawn together / For mine own ends" (3.2.211–12). The symbolic weight of *The Memorable Masque* begins to diminish when viewed through the lens of its surrogate scene in *Henry VIII*. Rather than a glorious celebration of the uniting of France and England, Wolsey's "masque" bankrupts the latter and exposes the treachery of the former. While we could see this tension as casting doubt on the marriage union being celebrated by *The Memorable Masque*, this seems unlikely. The target seems to be more specific, directed at the emptiness of *The Memorable Masque* and the Wolsey-esque wastefulness of its Virginia Company backers.

Moreover, Norfolk's panegyric casts doubt about the project of conversion that underpins so much Virginia Company rhetoric. Even though Norfolk marvels at the wealth on display from both nations, his description is also embedded with skepticism and even distaste. Of the French he says they are "all in gold like heathen gods" (1.1.19). On its own this statement could be taken as redolent of anti-French, even anti-Catholic sentiment, but Norfolk's following description of the English suggests equivalence between the two nations: while the French "Shone down the English" (i.e., outshone them in terms of their appearance) on the first day, the English matched the French on the following day—the day "they / Made Britain India" (21–2). Not only do the English resemble the French in this instance but also, more damagingly, both have taken on a heathenish, Indian-like visage, which presents both a "view of earthly glory" (14) and of idolatry. That the English matched the French at their own game has the effect then of undoing English sovereignty (or here, in a pointed anachronism, British sovereignty—"Britain" having gained new currency following James I's accession in 1603). Whereas

---

[47] On the multiple meanings of Norfolk's "admiration," see Lee Bliss, "The Wheel of Fortune and the Maiden Phoenix in Shakespeare's *King Henry the Eighth*," *English Literary History*, 42 (1975): 1–25.

*The Memorable Masque* stresses the conversion of the Virginians to Protestantism and the English cause, here the English are "Indian-like,"
"made" or transformed into "India" rather than the other way around.
Wolsey, then, stands as a figure for the Virginia Company—draining
resources for an empty spectacle that promised riches and delivered none.

The parallels between the Porter's memory of the "strange Indian" and
*The Memorable Masque* are perhaps less obviously apparent than Norfolk's
"India" and *The Memorable Masque*, although the "tool" in question may
allude to the "cane darts of the finest gold" carried by the Virginian Princes
or the "rod of gold" held by Phemis, the herald of Eunomia (Phemis is not
a Virginian, but his costume was similarly bedecked with "gold stuff")
(*Memorable Masque*, 63, 100–1). However, the relationship between the
Porter's Indian and *The Memorable Masque* may become more apparent
when we consider how both seem to draw on the practice of taking
Indians to England and parading them around the court and the city.
The Porter's recollection of the Indian may look back on the "three men
taken in the new found ilands" by Sebastian Cabot in 1498, and who
"were brought vnto" Henry VII's court in 1502, "clothed in beast skins,
and eat[ing] raw flesh, but spake such a language as no man could
understand them." The men were still to be found "in the kings court at
Westminster two yeares after," although they were now "clothed like
Englishmen, and could not be discerned from Englishmen."[48] Three
decades separate Elizabeth's birth and the arrival of the three men at her
grandfather's court, but if this is the event that the Porter remembers, then
it is testament to how sensational their visit was. While first recorded by
Robert Fabian in his *Chronicle of London* early in Henry VIII's reign, the
story of the three men was still in circulation in the late 1500s and early
1600s: Fabian's account was repeated in *Henry VIII*'s chief source, Raphael Holinshed's *Chronicles* (1587), in John Stow's *The Chronicles of
London* (1580), in Richard Hakluyt's *Divers Voyages Touching the Discoverie of America* (1592), and in the two editions of Hakluyt's *The
Principal Navigations* (1589 and 1599–1600).

Even if the Porter has sufficient memory capacity to recall the fuss that
resulted from the arrival of the three Newfoundlanders in the early
sixteenth century, Fletcher and Shakespeare's audience would have
recalled more recent visitors (or captives) from the Virginia and Newfoundland voyages. Epenow has often been held up as the most likely
inspiration for the Porter's Indian. He was celebrated by massed crowds in
London. Both John Smith and Ferdinand Gorges, who housed Epenow in

---

[48] Holinshed, *Holinshed's Chronicles*, vol. 3, 528.

Plymouth, admired his bearing: Smith described him as "of no lesse courage and authoritie, then of wit, strength, and proportion," and "of so great a stature," and Gorges commended him as a "goodly man of a brave aspect, stout and sober in his demeanor."[49] While both admired his character, they also, quite evidently, admired his body, a sense that perhaps carries over into the Porter's sexual joke about the "great tool" that so allured the crowds.

The spectacle of the Indian and Norfolk's panegyric differ in a number of ways. For Norfolk the Field of the Cloth of Gold was ordered—"Order gave each thing view" (1.1.44)—whereas the Porter recalls a previous example of mob chaos to describe the behavior of the "multitude" (5.3.64). The make-up of each procession differs along the lines of social status and gender: the Field of the Cloth of Gold is a procession of courtly male figures, whereas later in the play we are presented with its obverse, an uncontrolled and uncontrollable rabble of feminized figures. The two events, and the recollection of the two events, diverge in terms of their symbolic weight: the Field of the Cloth of Gold, which should mark the amity of the French and the English, does no such thing, whereas the "strange Indian" marks a symbolic register that exceeds what the official-dom wishes to mark, so that (in the words of Ian Munro), "the christening of an infant girl, the future 'Virgin Queen,' is sacrilegiously transformed into an erotic freakshow."[50]

But we might also detect consonance between the two testimonies. If the "clinquant" displays of the French and the English "made" both nations heathen and Indian, and if the orderliness of the procession is unmade by the transformation of these bodies, then "the strange Indian with the great tool" is implicated in another act of transformation, of the English public into a carnivalesque mass whose actions refuse the policing efforts of the Porter and his man. We can glean little about this Indian from the Porter's speech, but what we can say is this: his great tool suggests not only his sexual potency but also his value in terms of labor (his great tool may even connote mining); his status as "strange" suggests that he has not been incorporated into the English polity—he is on display as a wonder (like Cabot's Newfoundlanders) rather than appearing indistin-guishable from the English in all but speech (like Cabot's Newfoundland-ers after two years). Whether or not the Indian has been converted is unclear; but his effect on the English public is certainly transformative. As

---

[49] Smith, *Generall Historie of Virginia*, 593; Sir Ferdinando Gorges, *A Briefe Narration of the Originall Undertakings . . . of New England* (London: for N. Brooke, 1658), 13–15.

[50] Ian Munro, *The Figure of the Crowd in Early Modern England: The City and Its Double* (New York: Palgrave MacMillan, 2005), 100.

with Norfolk's description of the Field of the Cloth of Gold, the masses are implicated in a different kind of muddled, even threatening future, as their excited frenzy at the birth of Elizabeth (and at the Indian) is "a fry of fornication" (5.3.33) of incestuous-sounding couplings that will result in "father, godfather, and all together" (36). Rather than being the direct opposite of the Field of the Cloth of Gold, then, the crowds described in act 5, scene 3 refract the earlier scene, bringing out what is latent within it and pushing its illogic to the limit point. Again the Indian is implicated: here his tool operates as the object of desire that transforms the crowd and brings out the indigenous savagery within, just as the "clinquant" display transforms Britain into a heathenish "India."

## "AND MAKE NEW NATIONS": MASQUE, ANTI-MASQUE, BRITAIN'S VIRGINIAN FUTURE

Thus far, the skepticism inherent to *Henry VIII*'s evocations of India and Indians seems of a piece with "The Triumph of Time." Both suggest that the allure of the New World to the English revolved around Indian wealth, that this desire contradicted the protestations of pious motives, and both question the piety of the conversion narrative at the heart of *The Memorable Masque* by invoking the English-"made" Indian and an unconverted Indian who is valued for his body and for his labor—labor which enables the acquisition of wealth and resources— but who is not offered the prospect of salvation through conversion. Yet *Henry VIII* offers not just critique but also resolves some of its ambivalence through its projections onto the child Elizabeth and the yet-to-be-born James. Its resolution moves through the hawkish rhetoric of Prince Henry's faction, the pious cant of the Virginia Company, and the conciliatory emphasis of *The Memorable Masque*, staging an immanent critique of all three modes of discourse that were circulating, overlapping, and transmutating in the period that saw the death of Henry Stuart and the marriage of Elizabeth Stuart. It does so in two stages, through the marriage of Henry and Anne Boleyn in act 4 and in the final scene of the play, where Thomas Cranmer delivers his prophesy about Elizabeth and James.

In act 4, scene 1 we see the coronation of Anne, and the Gentlemen who act as chorus in the London streets describe the procession and those who take part in it. When the second gentleman sees the new queen, he expresses the following: "Heaven bless thee! / Thou hast the sweetest face I ever looked on. / Sir, as I have a soul, she is an angel. / Our King has the Indies in his arms, / And more, and richer, when he strains that lady. /

I cannot blame his conscience" (4.1.42–7). Anne here is "the Indies," straddling both east and west and embodying riches even greater than that. As with Norfolk's panegyric of act 1, the gentleman's praise seems to undo itself even in the moment of its utterance. Anne is praised as angelic; yet the gentleman stumbles into recalling the reason behind the coronation—Henry's desire for Anne—that has caused this alteration in his conscience (the royal divorce, the split with Rome). This ambivalence is matched elsewhere in the scene, when the third gentleman describes being "stifled / With the mere rankness of their joy" in Westminster Abbey (58–9), a phrase that recalls Hamlet's disgust at the rankness of his mother's marital bed (*Hamlet* 3.4.81–4) even as it stresses the excitement of the crowd at the coronation. The crowds at Westminster also express something of the frenzy of the crowd in act 5. Those "people" that "Had the full view of" Anne let out "a noise / As the shrouds make at sea in a stiff tempest, / As loud and to as many tunes" (70–3), a cacophony that suggests both joyous expression and uncontrolled, even threatening, upsurge. There is also something of the carnivalesque in this scene, too, with "Great bellied women" shaking "the press" of people to get a better view (76–9).

Yet for all that Anne-as-Indies recalls the previous iteration of "India" in Calais and looks forward to the crowds swarming "the strange Indian" in London, this moment seems to me of a different register, pointing not backwards to a confused recollection of a moment in time whose meaning is unfixed but rather to a future end point whose symbolism has, somewhat paradoxically, already achieved fixity. Anne is "all the Indies," enveloped in Henry's embrace, and under the "strain" of sexual intercourse Henry will have his desires met. However, the result of this "strain" will be Elizabeth I, the child whose birth and christening will form the climax of the play: Henry will be able to have "in his arms" something "more" and "richer" than Anne at this moment in time "when" he and Anne have consummated their marriage and produced an heir. While Anne is associated with the negative aspects of the Indies—embodying a symbolic implicated with corruption, wastefulness, sexual incontinence, and effeminized passion—she is also implicated in the Indies that is more than the Indies, Elizabeth I, who in turn will turn England into an Indies that is more than an Indies, rather than transform England into a corrupted, wasteful, incontinent, and effeminate nation (one that belongs to a pre-Reformation past).

This trajectory reaches its culmination in the last scene of the play, when Elizabeth in her christening gown is presented as part of another procession. Cranmer, who is charged with conducting the christening, delivers a lengthy prophecy about the "royal infant":

> Though in her cradle, yet now promises
> Upon his land a thousand thousand blessings,
> Which time shall bring to ripeness.
>
> . . .
>
> She shall be loved and feared. Her own shall bless her;
> Her foes shake like a field of beaten corn,
> And hang their heads with sorrow. Good grows with her.
> In her days, every man shall eat in safety
> Under his own vine what he plants, and sing
> The merry songs of peace to all his neighbours. (5.4.17–35)

Cranmer's prophesy of a future golden age of English history eschews "clinquant" imagery, replacing it with the georgic language of plantation. Elizabeth will bring England to "ripeness"; every man will live by what he plants; England's foes will "shake like a field of beaten corn."

This vision of a "plantational" peace within Elizabeth's kingdom will be further sustained through her successor, or, in Cramner's prophecy, her reincarnation: "Peace, plenty, love, truth, terror, / That were the servants to this chosen infant, / Shall then be his, and like a vine grow to him" (47–9). Moreover, his reign will bear witness to an expansion of this image, with the plantation of England moving beyond its own borders: "Wherever the bright sun of heaven shall shine, / His honour and the greatness of his name / Shall be, and make new nations. He shall flourish, / And, like a mountain cedar, reach his branches / To all the plains about him. Our children's children / Shall see this and bless heaven" (50–5). The combination of cedar and sun stands as an image of Christian, monarchic plantation, whereby the "cedar tree/sun king" James I is planted in foreign "plains," and the rays from his "sun" shine all across the world.

These lines recall the closing moments of *The Memorable Masque*, which contains the promise of "the blessings of the golden age" (624), its penultimate song promising that, when "Mine and thine were then unused, / All things common, nought abused, / Freely earth her fruitage bearing," then "the golden world was made" (618–22). But there is a crucial difference between the prophecies. Cranmer's imagining of a new world has no gold in it. In contrast to the other imaginings of empire and expansion, the promise here is of plenty without materiality. This is the land of milk and honey and not the dawning of a golden age. Moreover, even though the promise of "new nations" is heralded by the birth of the Virgin queen, who has already been declared "all the Indies, and more, and richer" by the gentlemen who observe the coronation of her mother, the prophecy is Indian-free. The new nations that are imagined are subdued with little to no resistance, defeated by being "shaken" like the corn or subdued through "merry songs"—perhaps similar to those sung at court earlier in the year for *The Memorable Masque*, but sung by the English to their neighbors rather than by their neighbors to the English. The songs are devoid of the promise and allure of "un-doing"/"un-making" Indian wealth, which is replaced by the promise of a wealth that is "more, richer."

Nevertheless, Cranmer's prophecy is more ambivalent than this triumphalism suggests. "Thou speakst wonders," declares King Henry, endorsing Cranmer's claims: his archbishop has "made me now a man" with his prophecy, an act of creation that repeats Norfolk's verb usage (*"made* Britain India") of the first scene (not to mention Trinculo's imagining of how "There [in England] would this monster make a man"). While Britain was unmade by being too closely Indian at the Field of the Cloth of Gold, here Henry's masculinity is affirmed by producing "This happy child" before whose birth "Never ... did I get anything" (62–4). But King Henry's declaration of wonderment also contains an echo of Buckingham's skepticism in the very first scene: in "Thou speakst wonders" we might here also hear a trace of the phrase, "O you go far," as both are responses to seemingly excessive, time-bending accounts of what has been and what will be to come. I do not here mean to say that Henry is skeptical, because undoubtedly his positive re-making through the birth of Elizabeth and the prophesy of Cranmer seems to place him as the first begetter of the new life of England. Rather, the play itself offers up a skeptical conclusion even amidst the glorious prognostications. In part, this is because the audience of 1613 knew that the flourishing predicted by Cranmer had only partly been realized—the marriage of Elizabeth and Frederick may have promised a greater role for the English on the world stage, but James was reluctant to seize this opportunity, and the "new nations" founded in his reign amounted only to a Virginia colony that he had chartered but had little governance over. In part this was because the figure to whom the prophecy is presented is sidelined. Henry is not part of the vision but merely its auditor, perhaps a moment that recalls the passing of his namesake, the late prince, who was also effectively an onlooker to England's progress or lack therein. That Henry is "made ... man" by his daughter—despite the fact that historically we know he was desperate for a son—makes him occupy a curiously feminized position, something which the play has continually pushed by highlighting and dramatizing Henry's intemperance.[51]

[51] See Gordon McMullan, "'Thou Hast Made Me Now a Man': Reforming Man(ner) liness in *Henry VIII*," in Jennifer Richards and James Knowles (eds), *Shakespeare's Late Plays: New Readings* (Edinburgh: Edinburgh University Press, 1999), 40–56.

The play also looks askance at Cranmer's prophecy, even as it voices it, through the juxtaposition of the final scene with the scene that precedes it, act 5, scene 3, and the "strange Indian with the great tool." The Porter asks whether the crowds gathered for the christening "take the court for Parish garden" (5.3.1–2), a location that would have resonated with the play's first audiences, since Parish or Paris garden was used for bear-baiting and was situated on Bankside, in the vicinity of the Globe and across the water from Blackfriars. The Porter also labels the disruptive element in the crowd "the youths that thunder at a playhouse and fight for bitten apples" (57–8). The Lord Chamberlain, who enters the scene to question the conduct of the "porters, / These lazy knaves" (66–7), describes the mob (with heavy sarcasm) as "Your faithful friends o'th'suburbs" (69), a reference both to the growth of London (fourfold between Henry VIII's reign and James I's) and also to the position of the outdoor theaters outside the jurisdiction of the City of London.[52] These anachronisms all denote the exuberance and uncontrollability of the crowd, to which can be added the Indian, who is recalled to emphasize these energies all the more. The strange Indian with the great tool, that is, excites the London masses in a manner akin to bear-baiting and theater-going, spectacles that occur at the margins of the city but which threaten to spill over into it.

The scene that follows, which features the arrival of the newly chris-tened Elizabeth, the prophetic Cranmer, and the new-made man, Henry VIII, contains none of these energies, all of which are alluded to (and possibly heard either by deliberate sound effects or—when performed at the Globe—by the acoustic traffic of the world elsewhere) but which do not break out onstage. Instead, we have the procession of royalty and aristocracy, a fitting and decorous conclusion to the play. As such, the relationship between scene 3 and scene 4 is like the relationship between anti-masque and masque proper: the comic grotesquery of the first scene is then redeemed by Cranmer's stately prophecy. But the temptation to cut act 5, scene 3 owes something perhaps to the discomfort that it brings; whereas in the typical masque structure the anti-masque energies are dispelled through some form of transformative act (as in *The Memorable Masque*), here the anti-masque energies persist. There is no transformative act, as the Porter and his Man do not dispel the crowds in any obvious manner. The last we hear of them is their threats to the offstage crowd: to a "great fellow" the Man asks "Stand close up, or I'll make your head ache" (84–5); to another wearing "chamblet" the Porter issues the command to

---

[52] Ironically, of course, Shakespeare and Fletcher's theater company had come under the patronage of other lord chamberlains, Henry Carey, 1st Baron Hunsdon, and his son George, prior to the accession of James I.

"get up o'th'rail" (86). While these commands are successful in some respect—they "Make way there for the Princess" (84) sufficiently for act 5, scene 4 to happen—they do not remove the crowds, who presumably persist at the fringes of the play. The "great fellow," whose designation recalls "the great tool" of the "strange Indian," may or may not move aside, and the Porter's Man may or may not make his head ache. Indeed, since the Porter's crowds have been equated with those that "thunder at a playhouse," they are already and always there, in the audiences at Blackfriars or particularly at the Globe.

The anti-masque and masque that close *Henry VIII*, a play riddled with spectacle and procession, may follow one after the other but it is not entirely clear that one re-configures the other. Act 5, scene 3, with its comic and violent energies, which is personified offstage by the massing crowds, by theater, by the Indian grotesque, and act 5, scene 4, with its decorum, which is personified onstage by the calm procession, prophetic words, and the Indian sublime (through the "more, richer" Elizabeth), combine to form a complex set of associations that implicate the Indian and India as matter both in the lavish masque of spiritual apotheosis and the chaotic anti-masque of temporal collapse. It is telling I feel that the play does not resolve with the prophecy of Cranmer, but rather returns to the theatrical milieu of the present day: the epilogue begins, "'Tis ten to one that this play can never please / All that are here" (Epilogue, 1–2), a strangely downbeat admission following so much surface triumphalism in the scene that precedes it.

## REMEMBERING THE DEAD INDIAN, FORGETTING *THE MEMORABLE MASQUE*

In act 2, acene 2 of *The Tempest*, Trinculo, separated from the rest of Alonso's shipwrecked crew, encounters the prostrate, be-gaberdined, and fishy-odored Caliban, and makes him out to be a monstrous inhabitant of the island. The encounter triggers in Trinculo a memory of a visit to England.

> Were I in England now, as once I was, and had but this fish painted, not a holiday fool there but would give a piece of silver. There would this monster make a man. Any strange beast there would make a man. When they will not give a doit to relieve a lame beggar, they will lay out ten to see a dead Indian.
> (2.2.26–31)

In the middle of Shakespeare's famous romance we find a scene of something close to Jonsonian London comedy. The "painted fish" that

Trinculo proclaims would easily lure the fool into parting with his money is of a piece with Jonson's depiction of the vogue for the monstrous in *Bartholomew Fair*, where Toby Haggis is waylaid by "the man with the monsters." So keen is he to encounter "strange beasts" that he forgets and forgoes his more basic nutritional needs at Ursla's pig stall (3.1.9).[53] The "painted fish" also mocks the gullibility of London's curiosity market, as Trinculo would "paint" the fish, either to exaggerate or entirely construct its strange, beastly nature: Jasper Mayne's *The City Match* plays with the same ideas (almost certainly drawing on the Caliban-be-gaberdined episode) when Timothy Seathrift is dressed up as a talking fish caught in the River Plate and displayed to an eager public. The dead Indian, of course, recalls the transportation of Indians to England, a practice which, as we have seen, was much in evidence at this time. Given the fact that (to the best of our knowledge) the Native Americans who came over to England in the seventeenth century (Nomentack, Epenow) survived the journey, the immediate reference may be to the Inuit carried over to England and displayed at Elizabeth I's court—yet one further connection this play seems to have with the Newfoundland voyages of the late 1570s, as Edward M. Test has argued.[54] Moreover, the sense that Trinculo has that in England "there would a monster make a man" suggests how lucrative the monster market was, how it could transform "the man with the monsters" into a wealthy, much-connected theatrical impresario. Within seconds of encountering the "strange fish" Trinculo is already dreaming of the pieces of silver that will come his way; later in the scene Stephano will dream of his advancement at court if he can carry back the Caliban-Trinculo hybrid; and at the play's end Antonio believes that the "plain fish" Caliban is "no doubt marketable" (5.1.269). Monsters make men because monsters make money.

*The Tempest*'s transatlantic contexts have, of course, been argued for and against, with the topicality of the Virginia colony and in particular of the wreck of *The Sea Venture* on Bermuda being central to the debates.[55]

---

[53] On the popularity of the monstrous, and the relationship between the theater and the fair, see Mark Thornton Burnett, *Constructing "Monsters" in Shakespearean Drama and Early Modern Culture* (New York: Palgrave MacMillan, 2002), esp. chapter 5, "'Were I in England Now': Localizing Monsters in *The Tempest*," 125–53.

[54] Edward M. Test, "*The Tempest* and the Newfoundland Cod Fishery," in Barbara Sebek and Stephen Deng (eds), *Global Traffic: Discourses and Practices of Trade in English Literature and Culture from 1550 to 1700* (New York: Palgrave MacMillan, 2008), 201–20.

[55] A complete bibliography of scholarship about the relationship between America and *The Tempest* would last several pages (or much scrolling): see David McInnis, "Shakespeare and the Atlantic World," in Trevor Burnard (ed.), *Oxford Bibliographies in Atlantic History* (New York: Oxford University Press, 2014, at <http://www.oxfordbibliographies.com>). Among the most influential readings are Paul Brown, "'This Thing of Darkness

Less accounted for in criticism that pieces through the play's topicality is its 1613 "re-performance."[56] The play's audience at Whitehall in the spring of 1613 (we don't know the precise date, but the festivities at court lasted from February until May) would have encountered further layers of meaning to this speech of Trinculo, indeed further layers of meaning to the whole play, in large part because of the altered topicality of "dead Indians."[57] The dead Indian, whose presence encourages people to part with money that could be used instead for charitable causes ("to relieve a lame beggar"), seems to contrast unfavorably with living, speaking, converted Indians, figures utilized with fresh vigor after the granting of the third Virginia Company charter in 1612 and its renewed affirmation of the central place of the spiritual plight of the Virginian to the plantation's work—"for the propagation of christian religion, and reclaiming of people barbarous to civility and humanity."[58] The dead Indian gawped at by the masses may have recalled, somewhat bathetically, the

I Acknowledge Mine': *The Tempest* and the Discourse of Colonialism," in Jonathan Dollimore and Alan Sinfield (eds), *Political Shakespeare: New Essays in Cultural Materialism* (Manchester: Manchester University Press, 1985), 48–71; Hulme, *Colonial Encounters*; Greenblatt, "Learning to Curse"; Gillies, "Shakespeare's Virginian Masque"; Alden T. Vaughan, "Shakespeare's Indian: The Americanization of Caliban," *Shakespeare Quarterly*, 39(2) (1988): 137–53; Deborah Willis, "Shakespeare's *Tempest* and the Discourse of Colonialism," *Studies in English Literature*, 29(2) (1989): 227–89; Paul A. Cefalu, "Rethinking the Discourse of Colonialism in Economic Terms: Shakespeare's *The Tempest*, Captain John Smith's Virginia Narratives, and the English Response to Vagrancy," *Shakespeare Studies*, 28 (2000): 85–119.

[56] I am influenced here by Lois Potter's tracing of the differing topicalities of various performances of *The Two Noble Kinsmen*, and her implicit argument for the ways in which drama signifies differently in different contexts (even if the text itself remains unchanged). Lois Potter, "Topicality or Politics?: *The Two Noble Kinsmen*, 1613–34," in Gordon McMullan and Jonathan Hope (eds), *The Politics of Tragicomedy: Shakespeare and After* (London: Routledge, 1992), 77–91. I borrow the term "re-performance" from Clare McManus, "*Epicene* in Edinburgh (1672): City Comedy beyond the London Stage," in Robert Henke and Eric Nicholson (eds), *Transnational Exchange in Early Modern Theater* (Aldershot: Ashgate, 2008), 181–96, at 182. See also Lucy Munro, "Marlowe on the Caroline Stage," *Shakespeare Bulletin*, 27(1) (2009): 39–50.

[57] Criticism that has focused on the 1613 context of *The Tempest* has done so usually to argue that the play was revised for performance as part of the wedding celebrations. Tristan Marshall is one exception: he compares *The Tempest* to *The Memorable Masque*, but does so to debunk critical insistence on the Virginian contexts of the former: "the masque illustrates how an advertisement for overseas expansion *could* look, and makes *The Tempest* criticism aiming at finding in it a support for colonialism look very weakly founded indeed." Marshall does not consider the 1613 contexts for the play—nor for that matter the possibility that *The Tempest* was not performed as an advertisement for overseas expansion. By contrast, John Gillies notes the contiguities between *The Tempest* and *The Memorable Masque*, but does not account for the differences in context between 1611 and 1613. Tristan Marshall, "*The Tempest* and British Imperium in 1611," *Historical Journal*, 41(2) (1998): 375–400, at 399; and Gillies, "Shakespeare's Virginia Masque."

[58] "A Third Charter of K. James I," in Hening, *Statutes at Large*, 98.

recently dead Henry, Prince of Wales, the "Patron of the Virginia Plantation," whose loss loomed heavily over the marriage proceedings—
Ferdinand's presumed drowning and miraculous survival would have carried
extra weight in this context. Even the wedding celebrations themselves
come to be overshadowed in this context: performed in 1613, the play's
sole reference to England imagines a whole nation transfixed not by a
marvelous display of royal pageantry and power but rather by a "dead
Indian," whose display leads to a moral and economic meltdown.

To look at it another way, perhaps the memory of the "dead Indian"
remembered the events of 1613. After all, all the audiences at Whitehall
and along the streets of London had witnessed was a parade of "dead
Indians," in so far as none of the Virginia princes and priests were actually
Virginia princes and priests, but impersonations of them. What's more,
they were bad impersonations, in "anticke suits," "altogether estrangeful
and Indian-like." They were "dead," therefore, in the sense that their
signification failed. Trinculo's "dead Indian" of 1613, like the "sunburnt"
Indians of "The Triumph of Time" and "the strange Indian with the great
tool" of *Henry VIII*, exposed the fetishistic tremble of the crowd towards
the New World at the expense of a serious engagement with the purposes
and ends of colonization, namely the transformation of the "dead
Indian"—that is, one who thanks to living in superstition under the
power of the Devil cannot be alive—into a living one reborn as a child
of Christ. Indeed, such is the lack of charity that the dead Indian inspires
that the English will happily pay tenfold more to see it than they would
ever give to a beggar in need of charity. *The Tempest* at the wedding,
therefore, seems to expose the hollow rhetoric of conversion at the heart of
the Virginia mission in its invocation of a dead Indian in a throwaway
moment which nevertheless renders the whole rich pageant highly insubstantial, turning a symbol of charity into a symbol of crass commercialism,
un-Christian behavior, financial folly, and hysterical hyper-sexuality. *Pace*
Trinculo, but when we read *The Tempest* of 1613, and place it alongside
these other plays and reinvigorate its topicality in that year, we begin to see
ways in which the monster unmakes the man even in the making of him.

*The Tempest* of 1613's rewriting of *The Memorable Masque* is also
evident in the marriage masque in act 4 of *The Tempest*. Indeed, this
scene has often been thought of as specifically written for the wedding,
and at first glance we can see why this argument has a ring of truth to it.[59]
The masque of Ceres and Juno echoes closely the tenor of other marriage

---

[59]  Henry David Gray was the first to put forward the idea that the wedding masque was
added in honor of the Palatinate wedding. Henry David Gray, "Some Indications that *The
Tempest* Was Revised," *Studies in Philology*, 18(2) (1921): 129–40.

masques, including *The Memorable Masque*: it maps the couple onto a classical precedent, wishes them well in their future together, and blesses the progeny that are to come. But whereas the subject matter of *The Memorable Masque* is upbeat, the choice of subject matter in *The Tempest* seems much more ambivalent. *The Memorable Masque*, performed on the night following the wedding, concludes with an epithalamium blessing the consummation of the match ("So in the Bridegroom's sweet embrace the Bride / All varied joys tastes in their naked pride" (29–30)) and the offspring of the marriage ("There is a seed by thee now to be sown, / In whose fruit England shall see all her glories shown / At all parts perfect" (53–5)).[60] *The Tempest*'s masque, by contrast, is really a masque of chastity designed to quell any untimely "varied joys." "Be more abstemious," warns Prospero, "or else good nigh your vow," to which Ferdinand agrees compliance: "The white cold virgin snow upon my heart / Abates the ardour of my liver" (4.1.53–6). Moreover, while ostensibly a blessing bequeathed by Juno to "this twain, that they may prosperous be / And honoured in their issue" (104–5), the masque's recapitulation of the story of Proserpina against whom (according to Ceres) Venus and Cupid "did plot / The means that dusky Dis" kidnapped (or raped) her, gives it its dark undertone (88–9). Dusky Dis is another name for Pluto/Plutus, whose incarnation in *The Memorable Masque* is remembered here: yet this Dis is not the bright-eyed convert of Eunomia and co-converter of Virginia princes and priests, but more akin to his *Four Plays* incarnation, the demonic underworld king who snatched away Proserpina. Dis/Plutus recalls Tunis, husband to Claribel, who is imagined by Sebastian and Antonio to be "Ten leagues beyond man's life," with the underworld recast as North Africa (2.1.243). Dis/Plutus has close kinship here with Caliban, a "thing of darkness" (5.1.268) no less and of African heritage (Sycorax is from Algiers), whose suit to Miranda was similarly unhappy both to her and to her parent.

The masque of Ceres and Juno tries to dispel the threat inherent to the Proserpina story, as Iris convinces Ceres that Venus and Cupid's attempt to perform "Some wanton charm upon this man and maid" has been in "vain" (4.1.95–7). But the attempt to dispel the story is itself in vain and the allusion to "Dusky Dis" carries over into the rest of the masque. The blessings that follow marry the marriage bed to the agrarian landscape, as

[60] George Chapman, "A Hymn to Hymen: For the Most Time—Fitted Nuptials of Our Thrice Gracious Princess Elizabeth," in Thomas Marc Parrott (ed.), *The Plays and Poems of George Chapman*, vol. 1 (London: Routledge, 1914), 458–60. Line numbers are cited parenthetically. David Lindley does not include the epithalamium in his edition, *Court Masques*, nor does he account for its absence, presumably because it is unlikely that the poem was performed as part of the masque.

the "Long continuance, and increasing" wished for by Juno in her blessing segues into Ceres' blessing of plenty (107): "Earth's increase, foison plenty, / Barns and garners never empty, / Vines and clustering bunches growing, / Plants with goodly burthen bowing; / Spring come to you at the farthest, / In the very end of harvest. / Scarcity and want shall shun you; / Ceres' blessing so is on you" (110–17). The association between "increasing" (Miranda's anticipated pregnancy, and the increasing of the royal family into new generations) and the "Earth's increase" collapses the female body and the land together. This collapsing between female body and land we have seen play out in the discussion of the plantation and the powdered wife in Chapter 2, but in 1613, at a Virginia-themed marriage, would have acquired further resonance, as the virgin bride is implicated in a metaphorical patterning with the Virginian soil. The language of Ceres' blessing recalls Gonzalo's earlier paradisiacal imagining of his "plantation of the isle" in act 2 (2.1.143), a space similarly fertile and abundant, where the only labor it seems is the gathering in of the harvest that will "come to you."[61] But like Gonzalo's dream of a golden age, this promise is offset to the future: it is not that these things happen from hereon in; "foison plenty" will have to wait, Spring is not now but "at the farthest / In the very end of harvest." The promise of "earth's increase" has to wait until the return home: in contrast to the hymn to Elizabeth that closes *The Memorable Masque*, which confidently sings "a rapture to all nuptial ears," perhaps in part because it was sung the night *after* the wedding, Miranda's proper "plantation," while a consummation devoutly to be wished, cannot happen here.

Maybe it cannot happen anywhere, at least in the ordered way imagined by Ceres' tempered rhyming. As Prospero acknowledges when faced with Ferdinand's rapturous wonder that this is paradise and that he wants to remain in this space forever, the images that he is seeing are fake. We are "such stuff as dreams are made on," and it is only in "sleep" that we find, to borrow from another Shakespeare play, "the undiscovered country" (156–7; *Hamlet* 3.1.81). Ceres' invocation of "Earth's increase" recalls both Dusky Dis, whose rape of Proserpina gave birth to the seasonal change that Ceres is in fact celebrating (the transition between spring and harvest, the months of dearth that follow). "Earth's increase" recalls Caliban, "Thou earth, thou" (1.2.305), whose own attempt at forcing "increase" by raping Miranda threatened to lead to a very different and far less tempered "harvest." The tension here is unresolved: Dis, in whom is figured the earth, Tunis, and Caliban, is the demonic foe, but also the

---

[61] See Jonathan Gil Harris, *Marvelous Repossessions: The Tempest, Globalization, and the Waking Dream of Paradise* (Vancouver: Ronsdale Press, 2012).

agent of plantation and increase. The voyage out and the encounter with the new, with its dreams of expansion, abundance, increase, and paradise brings back with it not just the brave new worlds but anxious old ones, where acts of "supplanting" are a constant threat to the order of things and the inherent lack of "foison" is ever on the horizon: this "brave new world" is "new to thee," Prospero says, perhaps with sympathy to the trials that await his daughter, perhaps sardonically as she has yet to fully understand the price of wonder (5.1.186–7). The masque of Ceres and Juno, then, both speaks the dream of future plantation but offsets that dream, as if to say, not yet, and also, maybe, never. It is a "vision" constituted of "baseless fabric" (4.1.151), the same such "stuff" as the theatrical production itself: the green plot of the masque and the green grass ("How lush and lusty the grass looks! how green!" (2.1.53–4)) which engenders Gonzalo's imagining when he sets foot on the island are parts of a stage set. All else has "melted into air, into thin air"; everything that we "inherit...shall dissolve / And, like this insubstantial pageant faded, / Leave not a rack behind" (4.1.150–6).

It is fitting that Prospero's famous deconstruction of theatrical effect comes so soon after he breaks off the marriage masque, following on from his own memory lapse about Caliban, Trinculo, and Stephano drunkenly stumbling towards his cell with thoughts of murder and rape on their minds. Critics have explained Prospero's forgetting as an indication of the joy that he feels able to experience at the prospect of his daughter's union or as a marker of Prospero's infirmity in his advancing years, but the reason why Prospero remembers at this specific point midway through a masque is less clear.[62] The masque itself has clearly not finished ("no more!" (142)), but the point of breaking off is the dance of the nymphs and reapers, a sequence that would have recalled any number of masques, including *The Memorable Masque*. Yet while dance is ordered (the nymphs are "temperate," the reapers "*properly habited*," the dance "*graceful*" (132; 138SD)), it carries within it a chaotic possibility of the anti-masque. These are weary "sunburned sicklemen" who have come to "Make holiday" and encounter the nymphs "In country footing" (134–8). The sicklemen's holidaying recalls the holiday fools that Trinculo thinks will be fooled by the "painted fish." Their sunburn, an external marker of their outdoor lives, carries with it a class distinction. Unlike the pale-faced courtier, these sicklemen work with their hands, or rather with tools in their hands, to reap and sow, in a manner similar to Caliban's own labor (albeit his work is more menial—carrying stuff rather than chopping it down).

[62] See A. Lynne Magnusson, "Interruption in *The Tempest*," *Shakespeare Quarterly*, 37(1) (1986): 52–65.

It has been argued that Caliban and his "confederacy" return to Prospero's mind at this point in lieu of an anti-masque, a claim that seems compelling given how masque-like the play is.[63] Yet I don't think this quite accounts for how the masque of Ceres and Juno functions at this point in the play. The sicklemen are already unleashing anti-masque energies, because of their close alignment with Caliban. Their phallic sickles, their sunburned visages, and their participation in a dance of fertility recall Caliban's attempted violation of Miranda. They also recall the figure of dusky Dis, and his incarnation in *The Memorable Masque* as Plutus; and whereas the latter is the convert to the Christian cause, dusky Dis is the dark-skinned demon who rapes Proserpina. But this collapsing of energies, where the masquing dance of nymphs and reapers contains within it the echo of disorder and chaos, recalls the failure of signification of the Virginians of *The Memorable Masque*: while Chapman and Jones' figures, like the sicklemen, should stand for sanctioned fertility, they become conflated with their opposite; indeed, in the construction of their representation this conflation seems always already present. It is Prospero, after all, who is the author of the masque of Ceres and Juno. It is he whose memory is triggered by encountering the sicklemen and nymphs. And it is he who gives us our anti-masque in his response to his recollection: the stage directions in the Folio tell us that, "*towards the end* [of the dance] *PROSPERO starts suddenly, and speaks; after which, to a strange, hollow, and confused noise, they heavily vanish*" (138SD). This disruption, sound-tracked by "*strange, hollow, and confused noise*" (142SD), transforms the scene into one of disorder, and Prospero is its progenitor. That is, the anti-masque to the masque is born of the masque itself, not distinct from it, and collapses the one into the other—just as *The Memorable Masque* failed to separate its masque and anti-masque elements on the streets of London and articulate to its observers both the distinction between baboonish-adventurer and ideal adventurer and the meaning of its Virginian trappings, a failure observed in the recollections of its spectators and subsequently memorialized in the drama that followed in its wake.

*

Even though only eighteen months apart, the two known early perform-ances (both at court) of *The Tempest* take on very different topicalities. The 1611 *Tempest* mediates between hope and terror, certainty and uncertainty, and conforms more to the generic frame of one of its main inspirations, the shipwreck of *The Sea Venture* in 1609, reported in 1610's

---

[63] See David Bevington, "*The Tempest* and the Jacobean Court Masque," in Bevington and Holbrook, *The Politics of the Stuart Court Masque*, 218–43.

*A True Declaration of the Estate of the Colonie of Virginia* as a "tragicall Comædie."[64] While the discord on the island and the attempted usurpation of Alonso and Prospero mirror the discord on Bermuda as reported in *A True Declaration* and in more detail in William Strachey's *True Repertory*, the discord is eased and eventually subsumed by Prospero's triumph and forgiveness. The dream at the heart of Gonzalo's speech, while still a dream, is a motivational one: nobody would have left *The Tempest* of 1611 wanting to be Sebastian, Antonio, or Caliban.

Read as a response to a range of events in London in early 1613, the whole of *The Tempest* takes on an unexpectedly pessimistic air. The 1613 *Tempest* seems more like a Jonsonian satire (ironically, given its indebtedness to Jonsonian masque), not only because of the scorn it seems to pour on the project of plantation and its adventurers (like Jonson does in *Eastward Ho!* and elsewhere) but more so because of the scorn it seems to pour on contemporary English (and especially urban) tendencies toward outlandish and meaningless display, toward self-deception or loose morality, and to poor financial management—all of which critiques apply to the Virginia Company. *The Tempest* of 1613 rewrites the central conceits of Chapman and Jones' masque and its awkward reception, and exposes the incoherence and self-interest at the heart of the rhetoric of conversion by using the very same strategy of Virginian pageantry and display. The Indian is dead, which is to say that he has ceased to function in the way that its invokers intended, and has become matter divorced from meaning, a stage effect promoting not spiritual growth but barbarous decay.

The 1611 *Tempest*, with its occasional affiliation with the official record of the Virginia Company, seems almost recuperative in its tragicomedy—ironically at a moment when the Company's stock, in all senses of the word, was low following the disaster of the starving time and the loss of *The Sea Venture*. The 1613 *Tempest*, mounted when the colony had been righted, had been granted a new charter, and had articulated its mission, seems almost condemnatory. The Virginia Company failed to animate the dead Indian, or to convince the observers of the masque (observers who seem to have included John Fletcher, Nathaniel Field, and William Shakespeare) that this animation was ever much more than an "insubstantial pageant faded."

---

[64] A *True Declaration of the Estate of the Colonie in Virginia*, 11.

# 4

## "He would not goe naked like the *Indians*, but cloathed just as one of our selves"

### *Indian Disguise in* The Historie of Orlando Furioso, The Fatal Marriage, *and* The City Madam

Truth is a Native, naked Beauty; but
Lying Inventions are but Indian Paints.

> Roger Williams, *A Key into the Languages of America*, 1643

to go naked is the best disguise.

> William Congreve, *The Double Dealer*, 1694

### "IN BASE OR INDIAN SHAPE"

No Native American characters appear in early modern playhouse drama. "The Triumph of Time," the last of the *Four Plays, or Moral Interludes, in One* discussed in Chapter 3, features a brief sequence of dancing Indians, but the conceit of Fletcher and Field's portmanteau play is that it is a series of staged entertainments put on for the newlywed King and Queen of Portugal. Hence the Indians of "The Triumph of Time," like the Virginian priests and princes of Chapman and Jones' *The Memorable Masque*, are *staged* Indians—in this case, Portuguese courtiers taking part in a masque and donning an Indian costume. Otherwise, perhaps the closest early modern drama got to staging a Native American character was *The Tempest*'s Caliban—which is as much to say, it didn't get very far at all.

However, there are a handful of plays from the era which employ the theatergram of the European male who dresses up and disguises himself as an Indian. In Robert Greene's loose adaptation of Lodovico Ariosto's *Orlando Furioso* (1591), Orlando enters "disguisd in base or Indian shape" with a black scarf covering his face, in order to defeat the army of his mortal enemy and reconcile with his betrothed (5.2.1384).[1] In the anonymous *The Fatal Marriage, or, the Second Lucretia* (date unknown), Iaspero, a lowly courtier, dresses up as "some virginia straunger / or remoted Indian falne vpon these Coasts," a disguise that seems to involve a blackening cosmetic, so as to sneak into his beloved Laura's home undetected by her father, the Duke of Piacenza (11.96–7).[2] In *The City Madam* by Philip Massinger (1632), the merchant Sir John Frugal and his friends Sir Maurice Lacy and Mr Plenty disguise themselves as "Indians / Lately sent . . . from Virginia" (what constitutes the disguise in this case is not at all clear) who have arrived in London to be "Assisted by the aids of our divines, / To make 'em Christians" (3.3.76–7), so as to administer "physic" (2.3.3) to Frugal's overly materialistic wife and daughter and expose the corruption of his prodigal brother.

This chapter argues that, because what Indians wore, or did not wear, and what they could be made to wear and what this might signify were key issues of contention both in the Atlantic colonies and in London, the fact that Orlando, Iaspero, Sir John, Lacy, and Plenty (along with the Portuguese courtiers of *Four Plays*) dress up as Indians in the only plays in the period to feature Indians is significant. Drawing on work by critics and theorists of "racial cross-dressing," this chapter pieces together the signifying functions of these Indian disguises.[3] It analyzes the ways in which

---

[1] Robert Greene, *The Historie of Orlando Furioso, One of the Twelve Pieres of France*, in J. Churlton Collins (ed.), *The Plays and Poems of Robert Greene*, vol. 1 (Oxford: Clarendon Press, 1905). Text references to *Orlando Furioso* are to act, scene, and line number of this edition. Here Ariosto's poem is referred to as *Orlando Furioso*, while Greene's play is *The Historie of Orlando Furioso*.

[2] S. Brigid Younghughes, Harold Jenkins, and F. P. Wilson (eds), *The Fatal Marriage, or the Second Lucretia* (Oxford: Malone Society, 1958). Text references to *The Fatal Marriage* are to the scene and line numbers of this edition.

[3] The term "racial cross-dressing" was coined by Eric Lott in the context of nineteenth- and twentieth-century blackface performance in the United States. See Eric Lott, "White Like Me: Racial Cross-Dressing and the Construction of American Whiteness," in Amy Kaplan and Donald E. Pease (eds), *Cultures of United States Imperialism* (Durham, NC: Duke University Press, 1993), 474–95. The term has been applied to late medieval drama by Robert Clark and Claire Sponsler, an appropriation that has influenced critics working in medieval and early modern race studies. See Robert L. A. Clark and Claire Sponsler, "Othered Bodies: Racial Cross-Dressing in the *Mistere de la Sainte Hostie* and the Croxton *Play of the Sacrament*," *Journal of Early Modern and Medieval Studies*, 29(1) (1999): 61–87. On blackface in performance in Shakespeare's era, see Virginia Mason Vaughan, *Performing Blackness on English Stages, 1500–1800* (Cambridge: Cambridge University Press, 2005); and Ian Smith, "Othello's Black Handkerchief," *Shakespeare Quarterly*, 64(1) (2013): 1–25; and on blackface in Shakespearean drama after Shakespeare's era, see Celia Daileader, *Racism, Misogyny, and the Othello Myth: Inter-Racial Couples from Shakespeare to Spike Lee* (Cambridge: Cambridge University Press, 2005), Ayanna Thompson (ed.), *Colorblind Shakespeare: New Perspectives on Race and Performance* (London: Routledge, 2006), and

*The Historie of Orlando Furioso*, *The Fatal Marriage*, and *The City Madam* reflect and refract the emerging discourses of cultural and racial difference as they circulated in London and in England's North American colonies— discourses that attempted to establish correlations between the English and the Indian in terms of their civility and savagery, states of being for which clothing was an index.

While the three plays employ Indian disguise, they do so in very different ways. By charting these differences in the donning and doffing of Indian disguise, and by placing each play in its immediate context (1590s for *The Historie of Orlando Furioso*, likely the 1620s for *The Fatal Marriage*, the 1630s for *The City Madam*), this chapter examines how attitudes changed towards the relationship between Indians and colonists from the late Elizabethan period (when Virginia was just a name on the map) to the Caroline era (when it had been established and was integrated into London's daily life). In *The Historie of Orlando Furioso*, the titular hero's wearing of an Indian disguise to defeat his enemies draws on the Hispanophobia of post-Armada London. It draws on the belief (or really the hope) that indigenous Americans would rise up against Spanish oppression, as a result of which labors the English would gain access to the fabled New World riches. Greene also employs Indian disguise to symbolize the return of Orlando's wits—his recovery from titular "furi- oso." The connection between Indianness and sanity is reversed in *The Fatal Marriage*, in which Iaspero's posing as a "virginia straunger" seems to result in a temporary loss of his own identity. This loss mirrors closely the fears about the effects of contact with Indian fashions in London and with Indians in the colony—which is resolved in *The Fatal Marriage* only once whatever material that constitutes his disguise is removed.

The last of the three plays, Massinger's *The City Madam*, uses Indian disguise to satirize the depravity—or the savagery—of London's inhabit- ants and, as such, could be said to be of a piece with many of the other plays in this study that use Virginia and the New World as a lens through which to mock certain London types. Indeed, as Matthew Steggle and Julie Sanders, among others, have argued, the drama of the 1630s was particularly invested in "place realism"—that is, with the topographies and characteristics of rapidly changing London suburbs and emerging towns like Westminster and Covent Garden.[4] As such, the play also conforms to

Scott L. Newstock and Ayanna Thompson (eds), *Weyward MacBeth: Intersections of Race and Performance* (New York: Palgrave Macmillan, 2009).

[4] Matthew Steggle, "Placing Caroline Politics on the Professional Comic Stage," in Ian Atherton and Julie Sanders (eds), *The 1630s: Interdisciplinary Essays on Culture and Politics in the Caroline Era* (Manchester: Manchester University Press, 2006), 154–70; Matthew

Martin Butler's re-reading of commercial plays of the personal rule as complex, questioning, and often critical responses to the politics of the day—a necessary and influential counter to the Whiggish dictums of prior historiographies which dismissed 1630s drama as royalist apologia and decadent escapism—and to subsequent interpretations, which have broadened our understanding of the Caroline era as not simply a "prelude to an interruption."[5] What makes *The City Madam* strikingly different, not only from the two Indian disguise plays that precede it but from all of the plays that have been discussed thus far in this book, is its imagining of Virginia as a site of possible transformation: if all of our other plays refuse the terms of transformation professed in Virginia Company propaganda by positing the colony as a haven for bankrupts and cannibal husbands, *The City Madam* by contrast imagines a Virginia where Luke, the chief antagonist, can be shipped off to the colony to redeem himself. This transformation (of colony and colonist) occurs in the play, however, only once the indigenous population (as materialized through the disguise) has been removed, leaving the space now empty for English plantation.

## "THE PROSTHESES OF RACE," ALTERITY AS DISGUISE, "PRESENTED NAKEDNESS"

What constituted the Indian disguise is hard to ascertain fully, but what links these dramatic representations of staged Indianness is that they involved darkening the skin or creating the illusion of darkened skin. Whatever was "soild ouer" the faces and bodies of the actors in *The Fatal Marriage* and (possibly) *The City Madam* may have been burned cork or

---

Steggle, *Richard Brome: Place and Politics on the Caroline Stage* (Manchester: Manchester University Press, 2004); Julie Sanders, *The Cultural Geography of Early Modern Drama, 1620–1650* (Cambridge: Cambridge University Press, 2011); see also Jean E. Howard, *Theater of a City*, esp. chapter 4, "Ballrooms and Academies: Producing the Cosmopolitan Body in West End London," 162–208; Zucker, *The Places of Wit*, esp. chapter 3, "Covent Garden: Town Culture and the Location of Wit," 102–43; and Denys Van Renen, "A 'Birthright into a New World': Representing the Town on Brome's Stage," *Comparative Drama*, 45(2) (2011): 35–63.

[5] Adam Zucker and Alan B. Farmer, "Introduction," in Adam Zucker and Alan B. Farmer (eds), *Localizing Caroline Drama: Politics and Economics of the Early Modern English Stage, 1625–1642* (New York: Palgrave MacMillan, 2006), 1–15, at 1; Martin Butler, *Theatre and Crisis 1632–1642* (Cambridge: Cambridge University Press, 1987). See also Julie Sanders, *Caroline Drama: The Plays of Massinger, Ford, Shirley, and Brome* (Plymouth: Northcote House Press, 1999); Kathleen E. McLuskie, "Politics and Aesthetic Pleasure in 1630s Theater," in Zucker and Farmer, *Localizing Caroline Drama*, 43–68; Jessica Dyson, *Staging Authority in Caroline England: Prerogative, Law and Order in Drama, 1625–1642* (Farnham: Ashgate, 2013).

soot, which was also used for Moorish characters, or maybe something akin to the "ointment, / Made and laid on" the gypsy characters by Johann Wolfgang Rumler, the king's apothecary, in Jonson and Jones' masque *The Gypsies Metamorphosed* (Epilogue 9–10).[6] Rumler's gypsies are described as "tawny," a term defined in the *Oxford English Dictionary* as a "composite colour, consisting of brown with a preponderance of yellow or orange," and it was a color often used to describe Native American pigmentation.[7] However, it was sometimes used interchangeably with the word "black": for example, in *The Fatal Marriage* Iaspero's face is described as both "tawny" and "black" (19.78); and, famously, in Shakespeare's *Antony and Cleopatra*, Cleopatra both has a "tawny front" (1.1.6) and is "with Phoebus amorous pinches black" (1.5.28). In addition to using blackening or darkening effects, some of these plays blur distinctions between Indians and other categories of difference—a reminder that the "Indian" was a composite figure in the English imaginary.[8] In particular, the Indian plays invite comparison between, and even conflate, African-Moorish and Indian blackness. Iaspero is described as a "moore" even though he is a "virginia straunger" (19.21). Orlando is called a "moore" when in his "Indian shape" (5.1.1245), and, although Moors were not consistently understood as black-skinned, he is also described as a country "swain" (5.2.1297), which might imply that he has a darker complexion as a result of laboring outside in the sun (like the sunburnt sicklemen of Prospero's marriage masque, discussed in Chapter 3). Although no color is assigned to Orlando's "*scarfe*," it was perhaps made from the same kind of cloth as the "Mores lymes" listed among Philip Henslowe's "Enventary of the Clownes Sewtes and Hermetes sewtes."[9]

Europeans disguising themselves as Indians are not included in critical discussions of racial cross-dressing, but there are ways in which such analyses can be applied to the Indian disguise plays, given their employment of forms of blackface. As Dympna Callaghan writes, "As the primary histrionic signification of racial otherness in Renaissance court and public theatre, blackface concealed under the sign of negritude a host of ethnicities ranging from Eskimo to Guinean... On Shakespeare's stage,

[6] Ben Jonson, *The Gypsies Metamorphosed (Windsor)*, in Bevington et al., *The Cambridge Edition of the Works of Ben Jonson*, vol. 5. On Rumler's innovations, see Andrea R. Stevens, "'Assisted by a Barber': The Court Apothecary, Special Effects and *The Gypsies Metamorphosed*," *Theatre Notebook*, 61(1) (2007): 2–11.

[7] *Oxford English Dictionary*, 2nd edn, s. v. "tawny".

[8] As Rebecca Ann Bach has argued, there emerged in court masques and civic pageants the figure of "the undifferentiated Indian," which combined "an undifferentiated East with an undifferentiated West." Bach, *Colonial Transformations*, 149.

[9] Philip Henslowe, *Henslowe's Diary*, 2nd edn, ed. R. A. Foakes (Cambridge: Cambridge University Press, 2002), 317–18.

blackness marked sheer difference."[10] According to Ian Smith, the blacked-up actor's performance highlighted the ironic distance between the black body adopted and the white body beneath. It also called attention to "the intractable series of negative 'devil' stereotypes that require no further knowledge beyond the skin, no decoding of the chromodermal signifier."[11] Callaghan's and Smith's theorizations of blackface would suggest that regardless of what the actors wore on their faces and their bodies to create the illusion of Indianness, their racial otherness operated in the same way as other black characters of the late sixteenth and early seventeenth centuries, which is to say that any ethnic difference is subsumed under the totalizing, albeit contested, sign of blackness.

Both Callaghan and Smith's ideas are foundational to my argument here. But it must be said that, even though the staging of Indian blackness is analogous to the staging of African blackness in many ways, there are at least four points of complication that could be missed if we link them too readily. First, both Callaghan and Smith address what it means for a white actor to dress up as a black African character, but neither critic addresses the trope of *characters* dressing up as racial others—that is, they consider the racial cross-dressing of the actor onstage but not of the character in the world of the play. While the actor playing Othello is always an actor blacked up, for all that there are references to what lies underneath, Sir John, Lacy, Plenty, Orlando, and Iaspero remove their racial prostheses to reveal their bodies (and hence the bodies of the actors who play them).[12] After all, rather like Chekhov's gun in act 1, there is no point in having a character wearing a disguise at the beginning of a play if it isn't removed by the end of the play. The employment of this form of racial cross-dressing (what we might call "alterity as disguise") operates in multiple ways. On the one hand it amplifies the ironic distancing between the body of the actor and the blackness that it takes on. Any threat that these racialized

---

[10] Callaghan, *Shakespeare without Women*, 78–9.

[11] Ian Smith, "White Skin, Black Masks: Racial Cross-Dressing on the Early Modern Stage," *Renaissance Drama*, 32 (2003): 33–67, at 34–5.

[12] I follow Smith in his use of the term "prosthesis" because of the uncertainty about what the actors wore. Calling a skin-coat (such as that worn by the masquers in *Tempe Restord*) an item of clothing when it is designed to signify the absence of clothing seems confusing and counterproductive. Prosthesis can mean clothing but is not limited to clothing. I also employ the term prosthesis in this chapter because of the way that the term has been employed in theory and criticism. Here I follow Will Fisher's usage of the term as referring to items that "are both integral to the subject's sense of identity or self, and at the same time resolutely detachable or 'auxiliary.'" Will Fisher, *Materializing Gender in Early Modern English Literature and Culture* (Cambridge: Cambridge University Press, 2006), 26.

bodies may pose is nullified by their sheer insubstantiality as bodies; even though in these plays the Indian figures are disruptive, their disruption is transitory and illusory, as is their presence. On the other hand, disguise *both* covers *and* reveals at one and the same time; that is, while it can preserve the distance between the supplemental body or bodily prostheses and the body beneath it can also collapse this distance. As Philip Deloria has argued in *Playing Indian*, his account of "the persistent tradition in American culture" of white Americans adopting American Indian dress, disguise "can have extraordinary transformative qualities ... [and] readily calls the notion of fixed identity into question," but "at the same time, however, wearing a mask also makes one self-conscious of a *real* 'me' underneath."[13] All three plays trade on the relationship between the guise adopted and the identity beneath: in *The Historie of Orlando Furioso* and *The Fatal Marriage* the disguise seems to transform the wearer (in the former the transformative is restorative; in the latter degenerative); but at the conclusion of all three plays the disguise adopted is discarded and revealed to be ultimately disposable.

Second, the idea that blackness marks "sheer difference" is complicated by the oft-repeated connection between English bodies and Indian bodies. The John White and Theodor de Bry images of Roanoke (printed as the appendix to Thomas Harriot's *A Brief and True Report of the New Found Land of Virginia* (1590)), compared the inhabitants of Secota and Pomeiooc to other notable savages from history, the ancient Britons. White and de Bry suggested that settlers in Roanoke would not be met with resistance, and that the task of civilizing the natives would not be arduous, as they were already halfway civil and halfway clothed: indeed, they lacked the barbarism of earlier Britons. As Chapter 3 argues, Virginia Company propaganda regularly propounded the idea that English and American climates were similar and English and Native American bodies comparable. To quote the 1615 broadside, both were "Once in a State, as of one Stem."[14] Observers in the colony described how, like the English, Virginians were born "indifferent white."[15] Thus, Indian blackness was understood not as a distinct state but as part of a continuum that encompassed both Indian and English bodies, and by extension Indian and English identities. The complex comparative element of bodily coloration, through which it is not clear who is the damned and who is the

---

[13] Philip Deloria, *Playing Indian* (New Haven, CT: Yale University Press, 1998), 7.

[14] *A Declaration for the Certaine Time of Drawing the Great Standing Lottery.*

[15] Quoted from William Strachey, *The Historie of Travell into Virginia Britania*, ed. Louis B. Wright and Virginia Freund (London: Hakluyt Society, 1953), 70.

saved, and who is the savage and who is the civilized, can be found in all of the Indian disguise plays.

Third, the employment of alterity as disguise draws attention to the items of apparel by which transformation is achieved, prostheses such as darkening cosmetics or masks and arm/chest pieces, hairpieces, head-dresses, and clothing. As many critics and historians have contended, items of apparel (from clothing to other forms of prostheses) were consti-tutive of identity in the period. In their influential study *Renaissance Clothing and the Materials of Memory*, Ann Jones and Peter Stallybrass argue that "clothes inscribe[d] themselves upon a person who [came] into being through that inscription": fashion certified social position and, as it were, fashioned the wearer.[16] Early colonial propaganda applied this logic when it advocated that clothing the Indians as English would lead them to civility, confirm their conversion to Christianity, and corral them into service against England's enemy, the Spanish (who were invested in converting the Indians to their side). Something like this notion is evident in the use of disguise in *The Historie of Orlando Furioso*, not just in the disguise worn by the title character but also in the "Indian palmer" disguise (that is, converted Indians) worn by two other characters in the play. But if clothing could be put on as well as taken off, was a clothed Indian really converted? Could an Indian use clothing for the purposes of disguise? These anxieties are never far from the surface of colonial dis-course, which insisted that Indians could be clothed in Christian civility, despite evidence to the contrary, and even though this belief was tested and faltered, in particular in the wake of attacks that decimated the Virginia plantations in 1622. These concerns are particularly evident in *The City Madam*, in which prospective converts reveal their true diabolical natures.

Finally, the signifying function of Indian disguise becomes even more complicated by the fact that Indians were culturally coded as naked. Indeed, while English explorers and observers were fascinated by Native American skin color and interpreted it in a variety of ways, they seem just as in thrall of, and confused by, their nakedness, if not more so. Mission-aries, settlers, promoters, and commentators circulated the notion of Indian nakedness: as Karen Kupperman argues, "everyone 'knew' that savages are naked," and it was "a staple of European assumption."[17]

---

[16] Ann Rosalind Jones and Peter Stallybrass, *Renaissance Clothing and the Materials of Memory* (Cambridge: Cambridge University Press, 2001), 2. See also Will Fisher, *Materi-alizing Gender*; and Amanda Bailey, *Flaunting: Style and the Subversive Male Body in Renaissance England* (Toronto: University of Toronto Press, 2007).

[17] Karen Ordahl Kupperman, *Indians and English: Facing off in Early America* (Ithaca, NY: Cornell University Press, 2000), 49.

"Naked" does not mean nude, and in the sixteenth and seventeenth centuries the word had a range of connotations. To be sure, sometimes the word meant "unclothed"—presumably this is how Othello uses the word when he asks whether it is possible to be "naked in bed, Iago, and not mean harm" (*Othello*, 4.1.5). The *Oxford English Dictionary* lists "the absence of normal clothing" among its definitions: thus Edgar in *King Lear* describes both his "presented nakedness" as the vagrant Poor Tom and how he "Blankets his loins" (2.3.10–11).[18] Edgar's disguise works because he is naked in the sense that he wears rags, and hence clothing not befitting his social rank as the son of the Duke of Gloucester, and is not naked in the sense that he wears nothing at all. In the case of reports about Indians, often the term "naked" is accompanied by descriptions of physical appearance that include items of what we would perhaps consider attire, such as animal skins and furs, as well as tattoos, dyeing, and hairstyles. Nakedness also connoted placelessness; the word "naked" was often used to describe vagrants and beggars, as it is with Edgar, and when Lear recalls "Poor naked wretches, whereso'er you are, / That bide the pelting of this pitiless storm," and wonders "How shall your houseless heads and unfed sides, / Your looped and windowed raggedness, defend you / From seasons such as these?" (3.4.27–33). In the North American context, Indians were said to be naked either in the sense that they were nomadic and hence did not have permanent residences or in the sense that their dwellings did not accord with the normative English home. "Naked" might be used to mean "unarmed": thus Hamlet reports that he is "set naked on your kingdom" in his letter to Claudius (*Hamlet*, 4.7.42–3). The term "naked Indian" appears in books on armor and military technology, when authors compare the technologically advanced European nations to the "primitive" Indians who lacked body armor (hence they were naked). Nakedness was also associated with innocence, as when Henry V threatens the citizens of Harfleur that their "naked infants" will be "spitted upon pikes" (*Henry V*, 3.3.115). This association can be seen throughout writing about Indian nakedness, as it was often taken as a sign that the inhabitants of the Americas lived a quasi-Edenic existence and had not yet been taught to have shame in their lack of clothing.[19]

All of which begs the question: what does it mean to disguise oneself as a naked person? What does the naked disguise hide, and what does it reveal? Whatever the actors and characters wore, they would have been interpreted not just as dark-skinned but as naked, too, which is to say as placeless, unarmed or with limited military technology, innocent (or at least

[18] *Oxford English Dictionary*, 2nd edn, s. v. "naked."
[19] On Indian nakedness, see Kupperman, *Indians and English*, 48–55.

potentially innocent), and/or without "normal clothing" (by the standards of Tudor and Stuart England), or perhaps even entirely "unclothed." These plays force the question: what does it mean for characters to disguise themselves as naked Indians? What does dressing up, or undressing, as a naked Indian reveal? These questions take on greater force when we consider that the only extant plays from this period that represent Indians are those that feature Europeans who enter "as Indians." Commentators and observers regularly compared Indian and English behavioral patterns and appearances, and they used the Indian as a yardstick against which the civility (or lack therein) of their own countrymen and women could be measured (something we will see play out in *The Historie of Orlando Furioso* and *The Fatal Marriage*). The Indian was savage, but then so were the English; the Indian was heathen, but then so were many English (either Catholic or Protestant, depending on the writer's denomination); like their English forebears, Indians colored and darkened their skin; Indians were simple people, but in many ways this was preferable to the ostentation of many English who wore outlandish clothing—something which will form part of the critique of *The City Madam*.

## ORLANDO'S FURIOSO IN *L'ABITO ARABESCO*

Unsurprisingly for a play that condenses the forty-two cantos of Lodovico Ariosto's *Orlando Furioso* (1516/1532) into less than 1,500 lines, Robert Greene's *The Historie of Orlando Furioso, One of the Twelve Peers of France* deviates extensively from its source. Like the poem, the play depicts the attempts of its eponymous hero to woo the fair Angelica and the madness that engulfs him when his love is thwarted. Yet many of *Orlando Furioso*'s cast of heroes and heroines are dropped from *The Historie*, and those that remain are altered, so that, for example, Angelica is not a cunning Cathayan but rather the prized virginal daughter of Marsilius, here Emperor of Africa rather than King of Spain; Rodamant is King of Cuba, Mandricard King of Mexico, Brandimart "King of the Isles." The plot differs substantially: the battle between Christian Europe and Pagan Africa and Spain is largely excised; instead, the catalyst for conflict is the love contest for the hand of Angelica, fought between Orlando and sundry royals. In the play, Sacripant (here chief antagonist) drives Orlando to madness, convincing him that Angelica and Medor are having an affair by hanging romantic roundelays about the wood (in Ariosto the relationship between Angelica and Medoro is real). In the closing scenes, Orlando, restored to full mental health by the sorceress Melissa, disguises himself and defeats first Sacripant and then his fellow Peers in a tournament, before revealing his identity, marrying Angelica, becoming heir to the African throne, and returning to France laden with "the glorious wealth / That is transported by the Westerne bounds" (5.2.41–2) (in Ariosto, he is saved thanks to Astolfo's lunar mission to recover his wits and, once cured, desires Angelica no more).

Many of these changes have been documented already in the play's critical history.[20] Indeed, comparative work has been surpassed in discussions of the play only by critics attempting to piece together its complex textual history, but otherwise the play has been largely ignored.[21] But the change that interests me most here—a change that has barely been addressed in Greene scholarship—is how *Orlando Furioso*'s Orlando dresses as a black-attired pagan during his descent into insanity, while in *The Historie* he disguises himself as a Moor and/or an Indian after his recovery by wearing a black scarf over his face. The scarf re-visions the chromatic schema of the rest of the play. A form of racial cross-dressing, it cashes in on Hispanophobic propaganda circulating in London in the late 1580s/early 1590s, in particular the idea that Indians and Moors could be recruited as fifth columnists in order to subvert, even overturn, the Spanish Empire in the New World and in the Old. The multiple transformations of Orlando—from sane to mad to sane again, and from romance hero, valuing chivalric codes and courtly love over worldly riches, to accumulative imperialist, valuing plundered wealth and bombastic verse—are signified, perhaps even enabled, by the adoption and subsequent removal of his Moorish-Indian black matter.

---

[20] On Greene and Ariosto, see Charles Lemmi, "The Sources of Greene's *Orlando Furioso*," *Modern Language Notes*, 31(7) (1916): 440–1; and Morris Robert Morrison, "Greene's Use of Ariosto in *Orlando Furioso*," *Modern Language Notes*, 49(7) (1934): 449–51. Both Lemmi and Morrison show that the plot of *The Historie of Orlando Furioso* closely resembles the Ginevra-Ariodonte story of Canto V. More recently, Miranda Johnson-Haddad has traced the place of Ariosto in Elizabeth I's court, an account that includes a brief but useful account of Greene's play. "Englishing Ariosto: *Orlando Furioso* at the Court of Elizabeth I," *Comparative Literature Studies*, 31(4) (1994): 323–50, esp. 331.

[21] On Greene's text, and in particular the importance of the Alleyn part, see W. W. Greg, *Two Elizabethan Stage Abridgements: The Battle of Alcazar and Orlando Furioso* (London: Malone Society, 1922); and Michael Warren, "Greene's *Orlando*: W. W. Greg's Furioso," in Laurie E. Maguire and Thomas L. Berger (eds), *Textual Formations and Reformations* (Newark: University of Delaware Press, 1998), 67–91. Kirk Melnikoff and Edward Gieskes' collection devoted to Robert Greene lists only two essays in its bibliography on *The Historie*, both of which are really essays about the play's influence on Shakespeare. See Kirk Melnikoff and Edward Gieskes (eds), *Writing Robert Greene: Essays on England's First Notorious Professional Writer* (Basingstoke: Ashgate, 2008), 219. Only James Stone has written on the play, taking it on its own merits (such as they are) and placing it in its immediate context (for Stone, its context is Islamic–Christian relations). See James Stone, "From Lunacy to Faith: Orlando's Own Private India in Robert Greene's *Orlando Furioso*," in Jonathan Gil Harris (ed.), *Indography: Writing the "Indian" in Early Modern America, Asia, and England* (New York: Palgrave MacMillan, 2012), 169–81.

In his first appearance in Ariosto's *Orlando Furioso* in Canto VIII, Orlando is so wracked with desire for Angelica that he forgets both his duties to Charlemagne and his sense of self. To escape the besieged Paris, "His coate of armes, of colour white and red, / He left behind," favouring instead a surcoat of "cypresse blacke . . . / With colour sad, his sorrow to expresse," thus leaving him "disguisd in sad and mourning hue" (VIII, 76).[22] Outer blackness is the visual expression of love melancholy elsewhere in the poem, but here Orlando is cross-dressed too, as he wears arms previously won in battle against the pagan Almonte so that he can wander incognito, "where the kings of Affricke and of Spaine / Did ly in field encampt with all their traine" (IX, 2), to enquire of Angelica's whereabouts. In "*l'abito arabesco*," he passes as a pagan soldier, "As though that bred in Tripoly he had beene" (IX, 5).[23] Orlando's black, pagan exterior, then, marks the diminution of his mental state, not just in terms of his melancholy, but also in terms of his willingness to betray Charlemagne and effectively side with Islam over Christianity, all for the sake of a pagan princess.

This episode is the first of many in which Ariosto charts sartorially the state of Orlando's sanity. When Orlando finally succumbs to madness he "scatters all his armor in the field": "No ragge about his bodie he doth beare / As might from cold or might from shame him shield" (XXIII, 106). When Orlando regains his sanity, he does not wear Almonte's black armor, but instead armor "old and rustie, / [which] He caused to be scowrd and furbusht new" (XL, 57). Finally, in his showdown with Gradasso, he eschews armor and wears instead a coat depicting "High Babels towre with lightning striking it downe" (XLI, 30). Thus Orlando passes through various clothing extremes (the surcoat of the pagan enemy; no clothing at all), which accord with his declining mental state, and ends the poem in simple attire, ornamented only with a symbol of God striking down pagan worship from the Book of Genesis, an emblem marking the renewal of his sanity and his conviction to fight the forces of Islam.

Greene also invokes the relationship between clothing and mental faculty in *The Historie of Orlando Furioso*. Early in the play, Orlando defeats Rodamant and takes his "*coate*" or "case," a moment which echoes Orlando's seizure of Almonte's arms (1.3.418SD, 419). He presumably wears this surcoat when he goes mad (which occurs in the next scene in which we see him), although here Rodamant's coat is not black, nor is he

---

[22] Robin McNulty (ed.), *Ludovico Ariosto's Orlando Furioso, Translated into English Heroical Verse by Sir John Harington, 1591* (Oxford: Clarendon, 1972). All references are to this edition.
[23] Lodovico Ariosto, *Orlando Furioso*, ed. Lanfranco Caretti (Torino: Einaudi Tascabili, 1991). All references are to this edition.

defined as a pagan—he is the King of Cuba. Greene represents Orlando's madness differently—he doesn't tear off his clothes—but it is represented through multiple costume changes. As Miranda Johnson-Haddad suggests, "one indication of his insanity is that he assumes different identities and the costumes that go with it": in the space of less than 400 lines, Orlando appears as "mightie Hercules" (2.1.710), *"attired like a madman"* (3.1.787SD), the leader of an impromptu peasant army (with *"a Drum...,* *with spits and dripping pans* (3.2.881SD)), and *"like a poet"* (4.2.1074SD).[24] As in Ariosto's poem, when Orlando recovers his senses, he also adopts the humble attire of "a simple swaine" (5.2.1298), appearing as "a cuntry seruile swayne, / Homely attird" (Alleyn MS, 1229–30).

Greene adopts "tropes of blackness" similar to Ariosto's. For much of *The Historie*, blackness is associated with the diabolic and the irrational, whereas fairness is associated with purity, chastity, and goodness. The play's palate moves from fairness and light (frequently associated with the sun, and embodied by Orlando and particularly Angelica) to blackness and darkness (associated with hell and—along with the moon—madness or "lunacy"), a chromatic transition through which Greene charts the mental degradation of his title character. Moreover, in the topsy-turvy world of Orlando's insanity, the meaning of fairness is transformed to its opposite. Upon finding the roundelays detailing Angelica's lust for Medor, which Sacripant has littered through the wood, Orlando imagines how the "Base female sex, [was] sprung from blacke Ates loynes" (2.1.674). Angelica's fairness is here transformed into the demonic offspring of the black goddess of delusion. Only once Orlando recovers his senses, and the world is restored to rights, is Angelica's fairness re-defined and even amplified: she is now "faire *saint* Angelica," because of her sufferance and her willingness to forgive those who have wronged her (5.2.1399; emphasis added).

Yet in the play's closing moments Greene diverges from Ariosto's representation of madness and sanity, blackness and dress. While Orlando in *Orlando Furioso* adopts black attire at the beginning of the poem, Greene's Orlando wears it at the end, once he has been restored. In order to rectify the dire situation that he finds himself in, Orlando disguises himself and takes to battle, in the manner of all good romance heroes. The scarf, most likely made from black, dyed cloth, makes Orlando appear outwardly as a "base born moore" (5.1.1246), as a "slauishe Indian mercenary" (Alleyn MS, 1342), and(/or) "in base or Indian shape" (5.2.1384).[25] The scarf

---

[24] Johnson-Haddad, "Englishing Ariosto," 331.

[25] Orlando is described as "Follower of fond conceited Phaeton" (5.2.1348), an allusion to the heliotropic explanation of the origins of blackness, indicating that he is taken as black-skinned by the other characters.

serves a practical function, hiding Orlando's identity, first from Sacripant, whom he goes on to kill in single combat, and then from his fellow
French Peers and his soon-to-be father-in-law, Marsilius, whom he
prevents from executing Angelica for her presumed infidelity. Dressing
up as a pagan enables Orlando to regain his standing—the defeat of
Sacripant and the rescue of Angelica leads Marsilius to declare that "Her
and my Crowne I freely will bestow / Vpon Orlando" (5.2.1429–30),
fulfilling a promise made when they were betrothed at the beginning of
the play. And it marks the restitution of Orlando's mental state: prior to
this transformation he "was troubled with a lunacie" (1395), but after its
adoption and subsequent removal he is "settled in his sense" (1408).
Thus to adopt blackness serves more as a sign of the restoration of
Orlando's mental acuity and his re-establishment as peer of France and
of husband to Angelica, rather than as a harbinger of his ensuing mental
diminution.

Orlando's blackface then does not conform to the *charivari* traditions of
black impersonation, as described by Michael Bristol, nor to the traditions
of black buffoonery that Robert Hornback diagnoses in the figure of the
"butt, laughed at because he was mentally deficient (whether ignorant,
dull-witted, or mad) and often physically different as well (for example,
'hunchbacked,' dwarfish, lame, deformed, ugly, or blackfaced)."[26] But
while Orlando's black Moor or Indian is interpreted as "base" and
"simple" by those who see him, and while Moors are associated with
savagery and cannibalism earlier in the play (by Orlando himself; he
describes voyaging through the lands of "savage Mores and Anthropagei"
(1.1.111)), in act 5 Orlando is no longer wild, nor a figure of ridicule:
when Orlando appears in blackface, his senses are restored. Greene's
Orlando conforms to some of the traits of the "natural fool" before he
takes on the scarf disguise. Indeed, folly could be said to characterize the
action of the middle section of the play, as romance gives way to burlesque
comedy (complete with cross-dressing, mock battles, and clownish squab-
bling). Moreover, Orlando's demeanor recalls another medieval figure, the
wild man, whose characteristics inform later European constructions of

[26] Robert Hornback, "The Folly of Racism: Enslaving Blackface and the 'Natural' Fool
Tradition," *Medieval and Renaissance Drama in England*, 20 (2007): 46–84, at 47; see also
Michael D. Bristol, "Race and the Comedy of Abjection," in *Big-Time Shakespeare* (Lon-
don: Routledge, 1996), 140–61. Ariosto's Orlando could be said at one point to conform to
Hornback's formulation, when he covers himself in mud and resembles inhabitants of the
Nile delta and the Garamanths of southern Libya: "Se fosse nato all'aprica Siene, / O dove
Ammone il Garamante cole, / O presso ai monti onde il gran Nilo spiccia, / Non dovrebbe
la carne aver più arsiccia" (Ariosto, *Orlando Furioso*, XXIX, 59).

racial difference (for example, American Indians).[27] Significantly, these scenes occur before Orlando's adoption of Indian shape.

Here, then, blackface acts as a pivot for Orlando's mental state, signifying his transition from wildness to civility. His description as a follower of Phaeton (5.2.1348) suggests that he worships the sun, which comes to be associated again with Angelica, whose fairness is re-inscribed following his intervention in battle. The adoption of blackface symbolizes then the passing of Orlando's black interiority—his madness, his melancholy—to his exterior, a move that then allows him to discard his blackness and restore himself.

Orlando's blackface also purges the darkness and turbulence from the rest of the play. As a result of actions taken while in this disguise, Sacripant ("thou devil in the shape of man" (5.1.1271)) and his army are massacred. The bloodthirsty rage of the peers and Marsilius is abated, as Orlando's blackface stands in relief to their actions. Marsilius, yielding to minimal suggestion of his daughter's infidelity, elects to "burie fathers name and loue" towards his daughter (4.1.1064)—committing the name to darkness, as it were—and permits the peers to "with furie persecute" her for wronging Orlando (4.1.1067), rage which nearly results in Angelica being consumed "in flames of fire" (5.21311). Anger throughout the play is associated with the furies, demonic agents, who are deemed responsible for Orlando's own plight: when he is restored to his senses by a sorceress, he asks "what furie hath inchanted me" (4.2.1190), to which the sorceress replies, "A furie sure, worse than Megara was, / That reft her sonne from trustie Pilades" (1191–2). The example of parental madness, and its cost towards children, echoes Marsilius' own willingness to sacrifice his daughter and unleash "furie."[28] Orlando's adoption of a shade that hitherto has been associated with madness comes to purge the fury that has afflicted these other characters as well as that which afflicted him.

## "THOSE MOST AFFLICTED INDIANS": ORLANDO AS INSURGENT

The confusing designation of Orlando's "shape" as Moor and/or Indian could be attributed to the indeterminacy and interchangeability of these

---

[27] On the Indian and the Wild Man, see Alden T. Vaughan, "Early English Paradigms for New World Natives," in *Roots of American Racism: Essays on the Colonial Experience* (Oxford: Oxford University Press, 1995), 34–54.

[28] The Megara-Pilades myth is Greene's invention. Megara was Hercules' wife, slaughtered by him during his temporary insanity, while Pilades was Orestes' friend, and hence no stranger to madness.

terms in early modern culture, and the fact that the romance genre is not known for its verisimilitude. The play is nominally set in "Africa," but "India" is also used. The action seems to take place in generic woods, plains, castles, and courts, and the various peoples of the play are often conflated. Here Greene follows his source, as Moor, Turk, Indian, and pagan are used interchangeably in Ariosto, and he may also have been thinking of Spenser's *The Faerie Queene*, which borrows from the romance tradition of placing the land of faerie in the east.[29] What's more, "Moor" and "Indian" are notoriously baggy descriptors and were often undifferentiated. Greene's post-Armada pamphlet *The Spanish Masquerado* (1589) features an episode in which "a company of naked *Moores*," are attacked by *conquistadores* in New Spain, but as the narrative continues they are described as "*Indians*... hunted with dogs, some to be torne with horses, some to haue their handes cut off, and so many sundry Massaquers as greeueth any good minde to report."[30]

However, even if the action takes place in the vague geographies of romance, Greene's place-name markers carry significance, especially when *The Historie of Orlando Furioso* is compared to *Orlando Furioso*. Ariosto's world is expansive, to be sure, but while the New World features in Andronica's Hapsburg prophesies in Canto XV, it escapes the geography of its immediate world. Even when Astolfo circumnavigates the globe on the Hippogriff in Canto X, the Americas are not on his flight path. Greene expands the poem's world to include New World locales. There are kings of Cuba and of Mexico. The Sultan of Egypt describes how his journey to witness "the matchlesse beauty of Angelica / ... Forst [him] to crosse and cut th'atlanticke Seas, / To ouersearch the fearefull Ocean"—a rather circuitous route given that Egypt is *in* Africa (1.1.22–6). The first usage of the word "India" occurs when the French peers arrive in "the rich and wealthie Indian clime" (4.1.996). Oger's description of their journey thither incorporates "the watrie Occident," which suggests that, like the Sultan, they took a somewhat roundabout voyage via the Atlantic rather than across the Mediterranean (997).

If the play's geographical coordinates expand into the Atlantic littoral, so too does Orlando's Moorish-"Indian shape," which in many ways resembles the figure of the American Indian, as conjured up in sixteenth-century European debates by, among others, Jean de Lery and Michel de Montaigne about the relationship between civility and barbarism (see

---

[29] See Marion Hollings, "Spenser's 'Men of Inde': Mythologizing the Indian through the Genealogy of Faeries," in Jonathan Gil Harris (ed.), *Indography: Writing the "Indian" in Early Modern America, Asia, and England* (New York: Palgrave MacMillan, 2012), 151–68.
[30] Robert Greene, *The Spanish Masquerado* (London: for Thomas Cadman, 1589), Ev.

Chapter 2). If understood within this context, Orlando's Moorish-Indian shape shows him as more civilized than his previous incarnation as an enraged wild man, and more so than Sacripant, Marsilius, and the peers of France, who, despite seeming civil, commit (or nearly commit) savage acts.

Placing an Atlantic lens on *The Historie* also allows us to unstitch its persistent strain of anti-Spanish sentiment. As Eric Griffin points out, there was an "outpouring of printed materials from the 1590s that treated Iberian themes [which] suggests that, far from declining, England's anxieties about the Spanish threat *increased* substantially after the Armada crisis."[31] *The Historie* is one such example, although its Hispanophobic temper is less immediate. In the play's opening scene, Brandimart makes the play's only conspicuous anti-Spanish statement, recounting how the "Spaniard... mand with mighty Fleetes, / Came to subdue my Ilands to their King" and how said king "rebated [them] from his coast / And sent them home ballast with little wealth" (1.1.83–8). This scene also contains digs against Spanish imperialism in the New World, particularly in the wooing speeches of Rodamant and Mandricard, who fixate on Cuban and Mexican riches so as to wow Angelica, and are subsequently defeated by the more humble Orlando (both Cuba and Mexico were, of course, under Spanish dominion when *The Historie* was performed).

*The Historie*'s Hispanophobia is evident also through the be-scarfed Orlando, whose actions and appearance recall Bartolomé de las Casas' *Brevísima Relación de la Destrucción de Las Indias* and its English translation *The Spanish Colonie*. Richard Hakluyt's *Discourse on Western Planting* (1584) cribbed from *The Spanish Colonie* to report the "many and...monstrous...Spanish cruelties, suche straunge slaughters and murders..., which haue bene most vngodly perpetrated in the west Indies."[32] In Hakluyt's *Principal Navigations*, an account by Walter Raleigh alludes to a volume by "*Bartholomew de las Casas*, ... translated into *English* and many other languages, intituled *The Spanish Cruelties*" (a telling misnaming).[33] The *Brevísima Relación* also reached the stage, in fleeting allusions to Spanish mines and Indian-Moorish slaves (for example in *Doctor Faustus*) and also quite possibly in fuller form in the

---

[31] Griffin, *English Renaissance Drama and the Specter of Spain*, 29.
[32] Richard Hakluyt, *Discourse of Western Planting*, ed. D. B. Quinn and A. M. Quinn (London: Hakluyt Society, 1993), 53–5.
[33] Walter Raleigh, "The Last Fight of the Revenge," in Richard Hakluyt (ed.), *The Principal Navigations, Voyages, Traffiques, and Discoveries of the English Nation*, vol. 7 (Edinburgh: E. and G. Goldsmid, 1888), 93–105, at 104.

now-lost plays, *The New World's Tragedy* (1595) and *The Conquest of the West Indies* (1601).[34]

Greene was well aware of de las Casas: he lifted his description in *The Spanish Masquerado* of the naked Indians/Moors being savaged by *conquistadores* from *The Spanish Colonie*. In *The Historie* he taps into the oft-expressed desire that Indians (or, as they are sometimes described, Indian Moors) could be brought over to the English side against the Spanish. Orlando may seem to have little in common with the Indians as described in *The Spanish Colonie*, who were "very simple without sutteltie, or craft, without malice, . . . very desirous of peace making, and peacefull, . . . by no meanes desirous of revengement."[35] However, Hakluyt highlights "somme fewe" examples of those who have stood up against the Spanish "out of that mightie masse and huge heap of massacres" listed by de las Casas.[36] These examples allowed his readers to "consider what cause the small remainder of those moste afflicted Indians haue to revolte from the obedience of the Spaniardes and to shake of[f] from their shoulders the moste intolerable and insupportable yoke of Spaine, which in many places they haue already begonne to doo of them selues withoute the helpe of any Prynce."[37]

English projectors like Hakluyt hoped that the peoples oppressed by the Spanish could be induced to rise up against them—insurgencies which

---

[34] Anthony Parr suggests that *The New World's Tragedy* may have been about Roanoke. My suspicion is that it was about Spanish atrocities in its New World empire, as the play's performance dates coincide with a number of other anti-Spanish plays, including Robert Greene's *The Historie of Orlando Furioso*. *The Conquest of the West Indies* may have been about Sir Francis Drake's exploits in Nombre de Dios or about Spanish *conquistadores*, and again have capitalized on post-Armada Hispanophobia. Anthony Parr, "Introduction," in *Three Renaissance Travel Plays* (Manchester: Manchester University Press, 1995), 3. See also entries on *The New World's Tragedy* and *The Conquest of the West Indies* in The Lost Plays Database, at http://www.lostplays.org/index.php/New_World%27s_Tragedy,_The & and <http://www.lostplays.org/index.php/Conquest_of_the_West_Indies,_The>.

[35] Bartolomé de las Casas, *The Spanish Colonie*, trans. M. M. S. (London: for William Brome, 1583), A.

[36] These "somme fewe" included the Cimarrón or Maroon, freed African slaves in Panama, who aided Sir Francis Drake in his assault on Nombre de Dios in 1572. This was possibly dramatized in 1601's *The Conquest of the West Indies*; it was staged in Davenant's *The History of Sir Francis Drake* in 1658. Orlando's black scarf may also have drawn on the Cimarrón–English alliance and the idea of the English liberator in the New World.

[37] Hakluyt, *Discourse of Western Planting*, 55. This desire for insurgency was also applied to Spanish Moors: according to Ambassador Charles Cornwallis (writing in 1607), Moors who had remained in Spain following the *Reconquista* of 1492 had grown in power and wealth, and it would be "to the greate peryll of the Spanyarde, were that people assisted by the fforce of anye fforraigne prince of power." Charles Cornwallis, *Discourse of the State of Spain, Written by My Lord about the Beginning of this Yeare 1607*, BL MS Cotton, Vespasian C X, ff 1–35r, at 10r–v. I am indebted to András Kiséry for alerting me to this reference.

could stem the flow of wealth into Spanish coffers and even displant them from the New World altogether. This fantasy may explain the strange, brief appearance of *The Historie*'s first "Indians," who resemble the converted Indian idealized in much colonialist writing of the late sixteenth and early seventeenth centuries. Marsilius and Mandricard enter as "Indian Palmers" when they encounter the peers of France, who have arrived to avenge Orlando (4.1.1008). The Indian palmers are trusted instantly by the peers, who inquire about "the state of Matchles India" and ask them to "resolue our hidden doubts" within moments of making their acquaintance (4.1.1023, 1009). This trust can be put down to their appearance as pilgrims. Yet the fact that they are dressed as Indian palmers, and not just as "garden-variety" pilgrims, is significant: their "simple weeds" (1033) suggest that they are converted Indians. The Indian palmers, although strangers to the French peers, act as Christian allies to European invaders. The peers interpret from their appearance that they will act in this way—they do not hesitate to seek their counsel. Marsilius and Mandricard embody, or materialize, the colonialist fantasy in which Indians could be converted and co-opted that we see disseminated in much English colonialist propaganda.

Orlando also embodies this desire, but more forcefully, acting not as an intelligencer for Europeans but as a combatant. "Withoute the helpe of any Prynce" he shakes off a "moste intolerable and insupportable yoke." He enacts the hopes placed in indigenous resistance, by ousting an invading army and seizing the royal crown of a foreign nation, before returning to Europe with his booty.

## "TRANSPORTED BY THE WESTERNE BOUNDS": ORLANDO'S NEW WORLD ORDER

Although wearing black cloth (sometimes fashioned into masks, gloves, or leggings) was only one way of signifying racial transformation in early modern drama, Eldred Jones suggests that the scarf was an alternative to using stage make-up, as "a quick discovery may have made this method inconvenient" and so the "unrealistic device [of the scarf] was resorted to because it was more easily shed than paint."[38] Edward Alleyn, the first Orlando, would not have had time to apply make-up or even "Mores

---

[38] Eldred Jones, *Othello's Countrymen: The African in English Renaissance Drama* (Oxford: Oxford University Press, 1965), 121–2. Andrea Stevens finds "no evidence for the use of blackface paint as a disguise device" earlier than 1621. See Stevens, "Mastering Masques of Blackness," 402.

lymes" (there are five lines of dialogue, plus some fighting, between Orlando's exit and his re-entry as the Indian-Moor), but he would have had time to put on a mask or wrap a scarf around his face. But the choice of scarf was not just a matter of convenience. It may have brought to mind the medical practice of wrapping cloth, or kerchiefs, around the head (often after applying a poultice). Shakespeare alludes to the practice in *Othello*, when Desdemona attempts to mop Othello's brow, and in *Julius Caesar*, when Caius Ligarius declares his fitness to act as a conspirator, despite recent health issues, by dramatically removing his headscarf with the words "I here discard my sickness" (2.1.320). Moreover, if scarf and handkerchief are understood to be broadly synonymous, then Orlando's scarf could be seen as a key prop of what Norbert Elias famously dubbed "the civilizing process."[39] It is fitting, therefore, that Orlando wears a scarf when his health and his civility have returned.

The scarf is also emblematic of how the play gauges characters' relative moral worth through their relationship to material goods, in a manner analogous to the trope of someone being worth more than the Indies which was discussed in Chapter 1. At the beginning of the play, the rival suitors pitch their suitability to be Angelica's husband by describing their vast stores of wealth. The Sultan begins his wooing by alluding to "The fairest flowre that glories Affrica," a phrase which initially seems to refer to the "fair Angelica," but instead describes his nation, Egypt, which he proudly boasts "is mine" (1.1.16–20). Rodamant describes Cuba as "a Region so inricht," within whose "bowels" could be found "Millions of Gold" (41–3). Mandricard describes his voyage from Mexico aboard a "Spanish Barke, / Such as transported Iason to the fleece," thus equating Angelica to the Golden Fleece (63–4). These attempts are contrasted to Orlando, the romance hero, whose desire to see Angelica makes him venture from his own country, even though France is "deerer [to him] than pearle / Or mynes of gold" (105–6). Orlando prizes Angelica above the riches of his homeland and, implicitly, above the riches proffered by his wealthier rivals. His voyages through the lands of "The sauage Mores and Anthropagei" (1.1.111), and the distance and the dangers that he has had to overcome, are more significant than his being transported in fancily adorned ships.

Orlando's eventual success could be seen as the continuation of this mentality. He uses the disguise to pose as a lowly common soldier, and as a result he defeats his enemies and saves his love. However, Orlando's position seems to be contradicted in the play's closing speech. Upon

[39] Norbert Elias, *The Civilizing Process: Sociogenetic and Psychogenetic Investigations*, revised edition, trans. Edmund Jephcott (Oxford: Blackwell, 2000).

being bequeathed the African crown, Orlando's language shifts, and begins to echo that of his vanquished rivals:

> Meane while weele richly rigge vp all our Fleete
> More braue than was that gallant Grecian keele
> That brought away the Colchyan fleece of gold:
> Our sailes of sendall spread into the winde;
> Our ropes and tacklings all of finest silke,
> Fetcht from the natiue loomes of laboring wormes,
> The pride of Barbarie, and the glorious welth
> That is transported by the Westerne bounds;
> Our stems cut out of gleming Iuorie;
> Our planks and sides framde out of Cypresse wood,
>
> . . .
>
> So rich shall be the rubbish of our barkes,
> Tane here for ballas to the ports of France,
> That Charles him selfe shall wonder at the sight.
> Thus, lordings, when our bankettings be done,
> And Orlando espowsed to Angelica,
> Weele furrow through the mouing Ocean,
> And cherely frolicke with great Charlemaine. (5.2.1435–57)

Orlando's speech agglomerates and magnifies the sentiments expressed by his rival suitors earlier. The wealth which is literally stitched into the fabric of the ships that form his fleet (superior to the *Argo*) hails from the eastern Mediterranean and the Middle East (the cypress), Africa (ivory and Barbary silks), and from the Americas ("transported by the Westerne bounds").[40] Orlando's allusion to Phoebus Apollo echoes the Sultan's description of Egypt's, rather than Angelica's, beauty, which "Phoebus dares not dash with showres" (1.1.17). The off-hand dismissal of such wealth—as "rubbish" and "ballas"—and the accompanying sense of luxuriant abandon ("cherely frolicke") echoes the rival suitors' tone in the first scene. Whereas Orlando earlier seems to dismiss wealth as a marker of true love, here he dismisses it as useful for "wonder" that can then be tossed overboard. The effortless, processional calm that Orlando imagines for their return voyage (with a little help from Neptune) contrasts sharply with Orlando's journey in the other direction, which was fraught with dangers.

That the shift in Orlando's attitude towards material goods occurs subsequent to his donning of a Moorish-Indian shape seems more than coincidence, and points to a further possible interpretation of the property

---

[40] The Alleyn MS is even more explicit: Orlando lays claims to "What welth within the clime of Africa, / What plesure longst the costes of mexico" (1432.7–8).

that appears to mark his transformation. As Ian Smith has argued in terms of early modern blackface performance, the "prosthetics of race" used to transform actors into Africans "makes visible their radical objectification as they are materially constituted as cloth or paint on white skin." This objectification links these dramatic representations to the ailing English cloth trade, in which dyed and fixed black cloth was circulated and sold, by which process "a view of Africans as material prosthetic devices" came to emerge, laying "the foundation . . . for a still more finely tuned grasp of the emerging need in early modern England for bodies as material in the production of wealth within the slave markets and plantations outside of England."[41] Greene's Orlando is not African, but Smith's overall point seems applicable here: Orlando's adoption of Moorish Indian "shape" allows him to appropriate real Indians and Moors (or Indian Moors), whose labor lies behind the acquisition of riches that adorn the returning French ships, but who have no place in the world of the play. The Indian-Moorish presence is ephemeral and insubstantial, bound up in a property that can be detached from the body. Orlando, the French peer, is heralded as Emperor of Africa-India after he discards his Indian-Moorish shape, a disguise which has given him passage and enabled his mental restoration, which has saved his beloved from execution and thus preserved the possibility of perpetuating an Orlando lineage in Africa-India, and which has enabled the gathering, and even conspicuous consumption, of the wealth of his new kingdom(s).

In Greene's *The Historie of Orlando Furioso* we can perceive a layer of violent appropriation, through which surface benevolence towards native peoples (in contrast to the Spanish cruelties) masks imperial self-interest, via the appropriation of their labor and the discardability of their bodies. The base Indian-Moorish shape forwards Orlando's agenda; once it serves its purpose, it can be removed, replaced, forgotten.

## "THE TAWNY THAT SOILED OVER HIS FACE": IASPERO, "VIRGINIA STRAUNGER"

Later in this chapter we will see how the detachability of Indian disguise serves to comment on English–Indian relations in Massinger's *The City Madam* in the context of 1620s and 1630s London and Virginia. For the moment, however, I want to trace how adopting an Indian disguise serves as an index for savagery and the loss of self in the subplot to *The Fatal*

---

[41] Smith, "White Skin, Black Masks," at 41–2.

*Marriage*—a play that has little critical history beyond conjectures about its likely date of composition and performance.[42] At the beginning of *The Fatal Marriage* Iaspero, son of the Marshal, has fallen in love with Laura, the daughter of the Duke of Piacenza. The couple are denied access to each other because of the difference in rank—both Marshal and Duke are in agreement about the inappropriateness of the match—so they hatch a plan to dress Iaspero up as "some virginia straunger / or remoted Indian falne vpon these Coasts" (11.96–7). Iaspero not only dresses "like an Indian" but speaks like one too, if in a nonsense dialect (11.95SD). Laura offers to take in the "virginia straunger" and "make him of my traine" so that "he may in time / perfect another language [i.e. English]" (11.119–20). Her deception is discovered when she is overheard giving Iaspero her "heart" and "constant hand," and the pair are arrested, but everybody is convinced by the disguise and believes that Laura's lover is "an Indian slave" (17. 44, 52). The Duke sentences them all to "perish since all guilty are" (60); and they are led "to the block" to be beheaded (81). Iaspero only survives decapitation because the clown, who has been left in charge of the execution, fails to complete the job—unsurprisingly, he proves to be an incompetent axe wielder. Iaspero's disguise comes off, revealing that the Indian is an "impostor" after all (19.120).[43] As a result, the Duke relents, believing that "nothing can separate yo[r] hearts" and tells the lovers to "long liue, still loue, and may the blest heauens guide you" (131–3).

As with *The Historie of Orlando Furioso*, Iaspero's choice of disguise reflects the savagery that is to be found elsewhere. The Duke, for example, decides to kill his own children, declaring in a Lear-like frenzy that he is "noe more a ffather that name's lost" and is now "a tyrant / that feedes

---

[42] Andrew Duxfield posits that the play was originally written prior to 1600 but subsequently revised in the 1620s—the former date because of allusions to the Duke of Parma (who died in 1592) and "That horse that runs upon the top of Paul's," an allusion to Thomas Dekker's pamphlet, *The Dead Term*; the latter date because of allusions to French galoshes (popular in the 1620s). I would add that the inclusion of the "Virginia straunger" plot also points to a 1620s composition date (or revision). While the threat of the Virginian in the household is explored more fully in *The City Madam*, its inclusion in *The Fatal Marriage* seems likely to be a reference to the 1622 attacks on the Virginia plantation. Andrew Duxfield, "Introduction," *The Fatal Marriage*, at <http://extra.shu.ac.uk/emls/iemls/renplays/fatalintro.htm>; and Andrew Duxfield, "'That Horse that Runnes Vpon the Toppe of Powles': Middleton, Dekker and the Anonymous *The Fatal Marriage*," *Notes and Queries*, 54(3) (2007): 264–5.

[43] It is not entirely clear what happens at the moment of execution. The clown's exclamation "why then haue at it" and Iaspero's "oh" implies some contact, as does the Marshal's statement "the Indian's sounded" (19.112–14). But the blow is clearly not decisive, as the Duke tells the Marshal to "helpe to recouer him to perish by the law / for such his sentence was" (19.115–16), and Iaspero speaks afterwards, apparently unharmed.

vpon the entralles of his owne / nay worse, a turke an infidel" (85, 89–90). His actions recall Marsilius, who will burn Angelica at the stake for her (alleged) indiscretion. His description of himself as one who "feedes vpon the entralles of his own" associates his behavior with cannibalism— indeed, he is worse than cannibals because they feed "vpon the entralles of" their enemies and not their "own." Iaspero may look like an Indian, or (in the Duke's words) "worse then the ffuries offspring," but it is the Duke who acts like a savage, offering up his own children for death and (metaphorically) feasting upon them (17. 52). His encounter with an Indian, and the revelation of the Indian's identity, cures him of his fury.

However, even though Indian disguise in both *The Historie of Orlando Furioso* and *The Fatal Marriage* serves as an index for the savage behaviors of the other characters, in a Montaigne-esque critique of western European-Christian hypocrisy, we can also begin to see shifts in attitudes towards Indians and towards Europeans who wore Indian attire between the composition dates of the two plays. For Orlando, the adoption of Indian shape is wholly positive, but for Iaspero it is negative. This shift may have something to do with the greater integration of Indian "fashions" in London, and because of fears that these integrations were having a detrimental effect on the physical and mental health of the populace, which began being voiced in London in the first decade of the seventeenth century. They can also be detected in Virginia itself, especially through the figure of "the white Indian," that is, the colonist whose close proximity to the Indian makes him "turn heathen." Unlike Orlando, who comes to find himself through adopting his Indian shape, Iaspero's decision to dress up as an Indian endangers him. He is sentenced to death while dressed as and mistaken for a Virginian. But also his choice of disguise threatens his sense of self, not only making everyone else in the play fail to see who he is beneath "the tawny" that "soils" his face but seemingly making him unable to articulate his own identity until "the tawny" is accidentally removed.

As many critics and historians have noted, the Stuart era was dominated by what Aileen Ribeiro has wittily dubbed "sartorial Esperanto," when the fashionable elite wore Dutch slops, Spanish stops, Polish boots, "the French standing coller," "the *Danish* sléeue," and "the *Switzers* blistred Cod-péece," many of these items together as part of an ensemble.[44] From the early 1600s onwards we can add to this list a variety of fashions inspired by the Americas. Furs and skins were significant products in

[44] Aileen Ribeiro, *Fashion and Fiction: Dress in Art and Literature in Stuart England* (New Haven, CT: Yale University Press, 2005), 165; quotations taken from Thomas Dekker, *The Gull's Horn-Book* (London: for R.S., 1609), 6. See also Bailey, *Flaunting*.

transatlantic trade both in the colonies and in Europe. Hairstyles took their cue from across the Atlantic. The lovelock—a strand of pleated hair hanging to one side of the forehead—became popular in the late sixteenth century and was associated with Virginians. Portraits of Robert Devereux, the Earl of Essex, and Henry Wriostheley, the Earl of Southampton, show them sporting this style, as does a painting of Sir Thomas Hanmer by Cornelius Johnson from 1631 (Figure 4.1). In his epigram "In Ciprium"

**Fig. 4.1.** Cornelius Johnson, *Sir Thomas Hanmer*, 1631. Courtesy of the Amgueddfa Cymru/National Museum of Wales.

Sir John Davies links the lovelock with other New World fashions and mocks the affectations of the youth who pursue "the newest fashion" and "take Tobacco, and doth weare a locke."[45] As Davies' epigram reminds us, perhaps the most famous Indian affectation was smoking—albeit that Virginia only began producing and exporting tobacco in large quantities to England in the late 1610s, as discussed in Chapter 1.

In common with most foreign fashion imports these styles were met with scorn from certain sectors of the populace. At the heart of the concerns expressed about Indian fashion was the confusion as to why, in the words of James I, the English might be moved "to imitate the barbarous and beastly maners of the wilde, godlesse, and slauish *Indians*."[46] The target of the King's condemnation was tobacco, about the effects of which multiple tracts both for and against were composed and published in the early seventeenth century, as we've seen in Chapter 1, but even something so seemingly slight as the sporting of a different hairstyle gave rise to passionate reactions. Samuel Purchas expressed his disgust with the lovelock when recounting his conversation with Uttama-tomakkin, Pocahontas' kinsman, who explained that "the Virginians weare these sinister locks" with "a long blacke lock on the left side, hanging downe neere to the foote" in deference to their god Okeus. Purchas was horrified that the "faire vnlovely generation of the *love-locke*" had been "borrowed from these Saluages": "Christians [were] imitating Saluages" who were in turn imitating Okeus, whom Purchas believed to be the Devil leading the Virginians (and now the English) astray.[47] William Prynne took the idea of Indian imitation one stage further. In 1628 he published *The Vnlovelinesse of Lovelockes ... Prooving: the Wearing, and Nourishing of a Locke, or Loue-Locke, to be Altogether Vnseemely, and Vnlawfull vnto Christians*, in which he wondered why the English, "who professe our selues Christians ... turne such prodigious, and incarnate Deuils, as to imitate the very Deuill himselfe, in this his guise and portraiture, which wee haue so seriously renounced in our very first initiation, and admittance into the Church of Christ."[48] To Prynne the wearing of the lovelock was not only a symbol of the transformation of England from a Christian to a godless society but also the very article through which this transformation occurred. Prynne's contention that the

---

[45] Sir John Davies, *Epigrammes and Elegies* (Middleborough, 1599), B4.

[46] James I, *Counterblaste to Tobacco*, Bv.

[47] Samuel Purchas, *Purchas His Pilgrimage*, vol. 4 (London: for Henry Fetherstone, 1617), 954.

[48] William Prynne, *The Vnlovelinesse of Love-Lockes ... Prooving: The Wearing, and Nourishing of a Locke, or Loue-Locke, to Be a Altogether Vnseemely, and Vnlawfull vnto Christians* (London, 1628), 4.

wearers of lovelocks "turne such prodigious, and incarnate Deuils" implies that for him at least the wearing of fashions associated with Indians might also make the wearer "turn Indian."

Prynne should not be taken as a reliable cultural barometer, but his sense that the English could "turn Indian" through imitation was not without precedent. As Jones and Stallybrass have famously argued, fashion certified social position and, as it were, fashioned the wearer, but could also undo that sense of identity, precisely because "clothes are detachable, . . . they can move from body to body. That is precisely their danger and their value: they are bearers of identity, ritual, and social memory, even as they confuse social categories."[49] Will Fisher argues that Prynne's pamphlet on love-locks taps into contemporary notions that gender was materialized through certain prostheses, including hair: "it becomes evident that Prynne's hyperbole lies in suggesting that a change in hair length *in and of itself* could move an individual from one sexual category to the other, not in suggesting that such a transformation was possible in the first place or that a change in hair length might help instantiate it."[50] As Jones and Stallybrass put it, "[i]f one was permeated by what one wore," then wearing foreign clothing meant "that one was permeated by the material forms of heresy."[51] According to this logic, then, the wearer of Indian fashion was transformed into a heathen savage. Rather than serving as the pious model for Indian conversion, London's fashionistas were being transformed themselves, and not for the better.

## "TURNING HEATHEN": IASPERO AS "WHITE INDIAN"

While William Prynne agonized over the transformational properties of Indian fashions in London, English colonizers perceived the possibilities of what would happen to colonists who dressed like and adopted the habits of the indigenous population. A handful of settlers across North America willingly became what James Axtell has dubbed "white Indians," either for their own protection or because they felt that life with the Native Americans was far preferable to life among their own.[52] During the

---

[49] Jones and Stallybrass, *Renaissance Clothing*, 5.
[50] Fisher, *Materializing Gender*, 135. The italics are Fisher's.
[51] Jones and Stallybrass, *Renaissance Clothing*, 59.
[52] The term "white Indian" was coined by James Axtell in *The Invasion Within: The Contest of Cultures in Colonial North America* (Oxford: Oxford University Press, 1985), 302–27; see also Alden T. Vaughan and Daniel Richter, "Crossing the Cultural Divide: Indians and New Englanders, 1605–1763," in Vaughan, *Roots of American Racism*, 213–52.

colony's period of martial law, 1611–18, anyone "Running vnto the enemy, or intending, and plotting to runne albeit preuented," or "any one taken prisoner by the enemy, hauing meanes to escape, & not returning to the Colony againe" could expect severe sanctions: "No man or woman, (vpon paine of death) shall runne away from the Colonie, to Powhathan, or any sauage Weroance else whatsoeuer."[53] Making an example of runaways would, in George Percy's phrase, "terrefy the reste for attempteinge the Lyke."[54] The authorities regarded people who consorted with the Powhatan as undermining the colony and threatening its survival, in some cases with good reason. John Smith's *The Proceedings of the English Colony in Virginia*, a compendium of accounts by fellow colonists printed along with Smith's own *Map of Virginia* in 1612, records the treachery of a group of "Dutchmen" (in fact Poles and Germans), some among whom came "disguised Salvage like" to convey "powder, shot, swords, and tooles" to the Powhatan despite the fact that this was strictly prohibited by the colonial authorities.[55]

Colonists who spent time with native tribes as envoys or spies were accused of turning Indian. These accusations were directed at English boys who were employed to infiltrate Native American tribes (hence they had to dress in native garb) in order to provide intelligence for the English colonists and to intervene as negotiators when relations broke down. The boys were often mistrusted precisely because of their proximity to native families: if they could provide intelligence about the Indians, could they not do the same *for* the Indians? In 1619 Henry Spelman, an English boy who had lived with and dressed as a Powhatan Indian, was charged with conspiring with Opechancanough because of an overheard comment made about the current Governor of Virginia, Sir Francis Wyatt. Spelman was threatened with the death penalty but was eventually convicted of bringing the government of the colony into disrepute. While Spelman's life was spared, he was still not to be trusted: according to the account of the trial written by John Pory, Secretary of Virginia, he was "one that had in him more of the Savage then of the Christian" and showed no "remorse for his offense, nor yet any thankfulness to the Assembly for theire sofavourable censure."[56] Spelman's accuser, Robert Poole, who had also lived with the Powhatan and acted as an interpreter, was likewise

---

[53] Strachey, *For the Colony in Virginea Britannia*, 42, 14.
[54] Nicholls, "George Percy's 'Trewe Realcyon,'" 261–2.
[55] John Smith, *The Proceedings of the English Colony in Virginia*, in Horn, *Capt. John Smith: Writings*, 97.
[56] John Pory, Report of the First Meeting of the Virginia Assembly, July 30 to August 4, 1619, in Kingsbury, *Records of the Virginia Company*, vol. 3, 175.

thought of as untrustworthy: according to John Rolfe, Poole had "turned heathen."[57]

The anxiety about runaways and "white Indians" revolved around fears that those working in the name of the civilizing mission were in danger of becoming de-civilized themselves. Ralph Hamor recalled meeting with William Parker, who had "almost three yeeres before that time [been] surprised, as he was at worke neere Fort Henrie." His time with the Powhatan had radically altered him, as he had "growen so like both in complexion and habite to the Indians, that I onely knew him by his tongue to be an Englishman."[58] Hamor's confusion might have stemmed from the fact that many observers concurred that the Indians were, like the English, born white-skinned, after which their mothers dyed and adorned them. In *A Map of Virginia* (1612) John Smith observes that "the naturall Inhabitants of Virginia" were "of a colour browne when they are of any age, but they are borne white."[59] In *A Historie of Travell in Virginea Britania* (1612) William Strachey, basing his observations on Smith who had lived "sometyme amongst" the Powhatan, states that the Indians were "from the woumb indifferent white."[60] So if the white Indian wore Indian attire, and changed their "complexion" through dyeing, then the Englishman and the Indian might prove to be indistinguishable. In the sonnet "To the Right Honorable, the Lords of the Councell of Virginea" that begins *For The Colony in Virginea Britannia, Lawes Diuine, Morall, Martiall*, Strachey writes, "where white Christians turne in maners Mores / You wash Mores white with sacred Christ[ian] bloud." Strachey praises the Lords of the Virginia Council for their godly work in converting the native peoples—with the Moors standing in for the Indians. Strachey's praise for the Council persisting with its religious mission in the colony where other "white Christians turne in maners Mores" may be a reference to English Christians who ran away to live with the Indians or who adopted Indian habits (perhaps even body painting).[61]

Dressing up in Indian attire permeated the wearers of Indian attire, who found it difficult to re-assimilate when they returned to the English. As Ann Little notes, "[w]hen redeemed captives returned to their Euro-American communities, they often performed a similarly transformative stripping and re-dressing... [because] [m]any captives reported feeling very self-conscious about their appearance upon leaving Indian captivity

[57] John Rolfe to Edwin Sandys, January 1620, in Kingsbury, *Records of the Virginia Company*, vol. 3, 245.
[58] Hamor, *True Discourse of the Present Estate of Virginia*, 44.
[59] John Smith, *A Map of Virginia*, in Horn, *Capt. John Smith: Writings*, 282.
[60] Strachey, *Historie of Travell into Virginia Britania*, 70.
[61] Strachey, *For The Colony in Virginea Britannia*, A.

and were eager to re-establish their identities as English people through their clothing."[62] But these acts of re-clothing were not always completed easily. As Karen Kupperman notes, redeemed captives "wanted to save their long hair after it was cut off; or they were uncomfortable wearing European clothes . . . Some part of themselves was embodied in those alien forms, and it was not to be given up by a simple act of divestiture."[63] Many cultural cross-dressers returned to the prostheses associated with their capture, a phenomenon we might understand as a kind of sartorial Stockholm Syndrome.

The anxieties about dressing Indian explains in part why the Duke and the Marshal do not recognize Iaspero—like William Parker, he blends all to easily into his Virginian identity. It also helps us understand why Iaspero doesn't simply tell them who he is. Of course, there is no guarantee that by revealing himself Iaspero will be let off the hook. Iaspero is supposed to have been "dispatch'd for banishmt" (11.73). He might fear that the Duke, who in another of the play's plot lines has already expressed his desire to execute his own son Lodowick for disguising himself so as to continue a prohibited liaison, might feel the same way about him. However, when the Duke catches Laura and Iaspero-as-Indian together, he proclaims that Iaspero, "tho most vnworthy, hee had better bene" than the Indian and that "of too illes" he is "the least" (17. 53–4). Iaspero says nothing in response as he is carted off to execution. Given the Duke's more favorable words towards him, it seems strange that he doesn't choose this moment to confess who he is.

It is possible to trace through Iaspero's few utterances while dressed as an Indian—a disguise that nobody can see through—a sense that his disguise is pressing on his sense of self, which recalls the crisis of identity experienced by some English colonists forced to undergo cultural cross-dressing. He refers to himself as a "prodigious Monster" (19.30). He does so in part to maintain the fiction that he is an Indian. The phrase also (from a thematic point of view) highlights the monstrousness of the Duke. But given the fact that the Duke just expressed his preference for Iaspero over the Indian, it seems strange that he refers to himself as such. Surely this would be the ideal moment to reveal his identity? It is almost as if he has forgotten that he is not the persona that he has adopted.

When Iaspero is about to be executed he states that his "teares are not my own" (9). This separation of self from bodily act suggests some form of

---

[62] Ann M. Little, " 'Shoot that Rogue, for He Hath an Englishman's Coat on!': Cultural Cross-Dressing on the New England Frontier, 1620–1760," *New England Quarterly*, 74(2) (2001): 238–73 at 257–8.

[63] Kupperman, *Jamestown Project*, 108.

disconnect between his emotional and physical states. Whose tears are they if they are not "my owne"? If Iaspero is speaking as an Indian (and his address to Laura as "royall mrs" indicates a certain formality that they do not have when they are alone together) then this statement means that the tears shed do not belong to the Indian but to Iaspero beneath the disguise. If Iaspero is speaking as himself (and he is speaking in English, a language that he is not supposed to know—learning it is the pretense for the "virginia straunger" to enter Laura's company), then this disavowal of tears means that they belong to the fictional Indian. Both interpretations could be true. Iaspero's words draw attention to his ambiguous, divided self. Only when his Indian make-up is removed can he reveal who he is. When his father realizes that the Indian is an "impostor," he states that "I love too truly to deserve that name [of impostor] / Iaspero was neuer such" (19.122–3). Iaspero's maintaining of the fiction of his Indian identity, his self-naming as a "prodigious monster," and his confusion as to who is producing "teares" suggests that to some degree he has trouble distinguishing himself from his Indian identity. Only when the axe comes down and the Indian side of him is excised and "the tawny that soild ouer his face comes of" does he separate himself from his disguise and articulate his own name.

## "MORE NAKED IS THEN NAKED INDIAN": LONDON'S IDOLATORS

Like Greene's *Historie of Orlando Furioso* and *The Fatal Marriage*, Philip Massinger's *The City Madam* employs the theatergram of characters adopting Indian shapes in order to resolve their difficulties. However, while the subtext of Greene's play is that the Indian shape metaphorically defeats the Spanish aggressors, and while Iaspero's adoption of an Indian shape confuses his own sense of self, Massinger's subtext is far more targeted towards Indian aggressors and what to do with them—a response, I argue, to recent events in Virginia and to changes in colonial policy. *The City Madam* employs the trope of the naked Indian to play with ideas of clothing, disguise, innocence, and deceit—all of which are resolved once the Indian guise is discarded at *The City Madam*'s conclusion, a gesture which takes with it the Indian presence in the play's household.

The play revolves around the fortunes of the family of Sir John Frugal, a London merchant whose wealth and reputation have been forged in overseas trade in commodities such as "Tissue, gold, silver, velvets, satins, taffetas" (2.1.72). His knighthood gives his wife, the eponymous City

Madam, and his daughters, Anne and Mary, "hopes above their birth and scale" (1.1.17): they follow the latest courtly fashions rather than behave as respectable, and soberly dressed, city wives; the daughters demand luxuries from their suitors Lacy and Plenty such as "A fresh habit / Of a fashion never seen before, to draw / The gallants' eyes that sit on the stage upon" them (2.2.119–21). Sir John is less than happy with their conduct, and he withdraws from the household to a monastery in the Netherlands, while the suitors depart for "three years travel" (3.2.73). He leaves in charge of the household his brother Luke, a reformed bankrupt.

Sir John's exile is, however, a ruse, as his real intention is to "minister" some "physic... / To my wife, and daughters," and to test whether his brother has really changed his ways (2.3.3–4). Sir John returns to the household, along with the suitors, disguised as "Indians / Lately sent... from Virginia" who have arrived in London to continue their Christian education that was begun in the colony (3.3.73–4). These "Indians," or fake Indians, soon reveal that they have no intention of converting to Christianity. They are in league with the Devil and have come to London to procure "Two Christian virgins" and "a third... Married" to sacrifice to him (5.1.36–9). Lady Frugal, Anne, and Mary fit the bill nicely. The Virginians tell Luke of their diabolical intentions and enlist his help with the promise of limitless New World wealth. He is all too willing to be converted to their cause, showing that despite his pronouncements about his reformed character he hasn't forgotten his spendthrift ways. Luke persuades Lady Frugal and her daughters to travel to Virginia, hiding what is intended for them by telling them that they will become queens to Indian "Kings of such spacious territories and dominions, / As our great Britain measur'd will appear / A garden to't" (5.1.115–17). In the final scene of the play, when the women are on the verge of transportation, and when Luke has let his new-found power go to his head—he too has begun to dress in an extravagant manner—the Indians stage an entertainment, a masque depicting "*The Story of Orpheus in the Underworld.*" During the festivities Luke is offered several opportunities to change his villainous ways and be moved, as Hades was in the Orpheus myth, but he shows no pity. Sir John then removes his disguise, reveals his plot, and regains control of the household. As a result, Lady Frugal and her daughters abandon their extravagant ways and promise to "move / In their spheres" and to alter "their habits, manners, and their highest port," so as to maintain "A distance 'twixt the city and the court" (5.3.153–6). The daughters vow to become "humble wives" and dress in their "own natural shapes" (5.3.157; 4.4.50). The now-penitent Luke is speechless— "Guilt strikes me dumb" (5.3.112)—and is proclaimed to have been "stripped... bare" (5.3.115). He is threatened with a variety of punishments, including being packed off "to Virginia, and [to] repent; not for / Those horrid ends to which thou did'st design these," i.e. not for sacrifice (5.3.145–6).

Even though upon the Virginians' arrival Luke is disgusted by the idea of extending charity to his visitors, neither he nor anyone else seems at all surprised by their presence in London, an indifference not shared by critics of the play who, undeterred by T. S. Eliot's dismissal of "the extravagant hocus-pocus of supposed Indian necromancers," have tried to figure out what they are doing in the Frugal household.[64] Critics have been divided as to the Indians' function within the play and their significance to Caroline audiences. Martin Butler sees them as "bring[ing] to bear . . . a consciousness of the godly citizen ideal underlying the North American trade," which operates "as a framework within which Luke's actions may be judged." Luke, of course, fails to live up to this ideal—rather than converting the diabolical Indians, he is converted by them—and the Indians look less like the innocent natives of much early colonial propaganda and more like the murderous child-sacrificers of later reports; but, contends Butler, Massinger was acutely aware of the citizen contingent in the otherwise elite, aristocratic audience at Blackfriars, who would have applauded both Sir John's charitable code of conduct and the citizenly "pious project to convert to Christianity some unfortunate heathens."[65] For Claire Jowitt, however, *The City Madam* does not present a secure and coherent "godly citizen ideal," as "Sir John's descriptions of indigenous Americans' desires for white women reveal the level of anxieties concerning miscegenation and the threat that black male sexual access to white females represents to British males." *The City Madam*, then, unstitches the "potent British manhood" that was assumed and required for the successful establishment of empire in the New World.[66] Jean Howard, by contrast, sees the play less in terms of English conduct in the New World and more in terms of London's emergence as a global city. She places *The City Madam* within the "cosmopolitan and decidedly global genre" of the London comedy, in which "foreign commodities" are circulated (commodities such as the exotic fabrics that Sir John trades in), "rendering them familiar, domesticating them," and erasing the "labor

---

[64] See T. S. Eliot, "Philip Massinger," in T. S. Eliot, *The Sacred Wood: Essays on Poetry and Criticism* (London: Methuen, 1964), 123–43, at 142. Although Eliot showed little interest in the Virginians, he did hold up *The City Madam* as one of only two saving graces in the Massinger canon (the other being *A New Way to Pay Old Debts*).

[65] Martin Butler, "Massinger's *The City Madam* and the Caroline Audience," *Renaissance Drama*, 13 (1982): 157–87, at 178.

[66] Jowitt, *Voyage Drama and Gender Politics*, 213.

expended in their production, transportation, and refashioning."[67] This process came "to define the essence of the cosmopolitan Londoner, the kind of Londoner likely to patronize the Blackfriars Theatre" to see *The City Madam*.[68] Massinger's play takes this facet of London comedy one stage further by reducing Indians to the "'signifiers' of the exotic" that constitute them rather than "actual exotica," as they amount to no more than properties attached to the three white English characters.[69]

I concur with Howard's emphasis on the play's appeal to the cosmo-politan Londoner and to the ways in which the Virginians become part of the fabric of daily life. But despite, in Howard's phrasing, "the insubstan-tiality of these New World figures," their presence (if "presence" is quite the right word) amplifies Massinger's satirical swipes at contemporary London, even as the play is implicated in the fashioning of the Blackfriars Theatre as the destination of choice for the city's fashionable crowd.[70] As Michael Neill has contended, the London of *The City Madam* finds its "true mirror" in "the colonial dystopia conjured by Sir John Frugal and his fellow Indians—Virginia," a point worth elaborating and complicating.[71] Luke's conduct links the household to Virginia, in so far as he behaves like the worst kind of colonist. Not only is he like the "Condemned wretches / Forfeited to the law" that according to Lady Frugal inhabit Virginia (5.1.107–8), but also his conduct once the Virginians arrive and tempt him recalls the oft-expressed fears about "white Indians." The play also encourages comparison between the Frugal women, the play's other female characters, and Virginia's first female settlers. In its first decade Virginia was an overwhelmingly male settlement. As Chapter 2 of this book points out, early attempts to rectify the gender imbalance of James-town were regarded as failures because of the rumored "qualities" of the women. Many years on, *The City Madam* continues to play with these associations. When Lady Frugal, Anne, and Mary find out that they are due to be transported across the Atlantic, they complain that "Strumpets and bawds, / For the abomination of their life, / [are] Spew'd out of their own country" and "shipp'd thither" to Virginia (5.1.107–10). Yet London as represented in the play is hardly much better than the Virginia described here. The city has its own "strumpets and bawds," the prostitute Shave'em and her bawd Secret. What's more, Shave'em bears a distinct

---

[67] Howard, "Bettrice's Monkey," at 336, 325.
[68] Howard, "Bettrice's Monkey," 336.
[69] Howard, "Bettrice's Monkey," 337.    [70] Howard, "Bettrice's Monkey," 337.
[71] Michael Neill, "'The Tongues of Angels': Charity and the Social Order in *The City Madam*," in Michael Neill, *Putting History to the Question: Power, Politics, and Society in English Renaissance Drama* (New York: Columbia University Press, 2000), 99–125, at 116.

resemblance to the Frugal women, as she too revels in sartorial and cosmetic excesses, taking pains to track down the latest fashions and making sure that her "colors are well laid on" (4.2.16) to attract her clients in a manner not dissimilar to the daughters' desire to attract "The gallants' eyes" (1.2.122). A further parallel between the Frugal women and the "strumpets" they despise is evident in the fact that they are also to be shipped to Virginia.

The signifying function of the Virginians is more nuanced than simply acting as a mirror between the colony and the capital. The multiple meanings operative through their presence onstage become apparent if we focus on the play's evocations of sartorial appropriateness and excess and its use of the temporary bodies of the Indians to bring out these various significations. For Neill, the "extravagant and melodramatic... idolatry" of Sir John's Indians gives "a horridly literal cast to the proceedings by which Massinger's City world is governed"; throughout the play "Massinger's London ... is repeatedly shown as an idolatrous society," in which both men and women worship material possessions, most especially clothing.[72] Lady Frugal, Anne, and Mary attempt to fashion a place for themselves at court by dressing in the latest styles and are described by Luke as indulging in "idolatry / Paid to a painted room" (i.e. the court; 4.4.117–18). Early in the play Luke displays a taste for fine clothing that hints at his own predilection for deception and hypocrisy. Before his "conversion" by the Virginians, he extols what "ravishing lechery it is to enter / An ordinary, cap-a-pe, trimm'd like a gallant" (2.1.80–1). Even Sir John, who despairs at the abuses of his family, relies on this idolatry to make his fortune, as he imports the "velvets, satins, taffetas" that spur it on.

While the Londoners and the Virginians are united in their idolatrous tendencies in the play, in one significant respect they couldn't be more different. By contrast to the English in London and in Virginia, Indians were famously indifferent to clothes, a "fact" which a number of commentators used to imply that they were preferable to the ostentatious English. In *A Key into the Languages of America* (1643), Roger Williams moralized that "The best clad English-man, / Not cloth'd with Christ, more naked is: / Then naked Indian." He disliked the Indian propensity for body art and argued that "It hath been the foolish Custome of all barbarous Nations to paint and figure their Faces and Bodies." Yet Williams included England in his list of barbarous nations because English women wore "Jesabell's face." And however "Fowle" Williams found "the

---

[72] Neill, "'The Tongues of Angels,'" 115–16.

*Indians* Haire and painted Faces," more foul still was "such Haire, such Face" in England.[73] Williams' disgust seems to come down to his sense that the English, as a civilized, Christian nation, should know better than New World savages. Other commentators argued that, unlike the English, the Indians did not take pride in their appearance, despite a predilection for body ornamentation. In his conduct book *The English Gentleman* (1630), Richard Braithwaite reported that "the *Russian, Muscovian, Ionian*, yea even the barbarous *Indian*... [are] loth, it seemes, to introduce any new custome, or to lose their antiquitie for any vainglorious or affected Noveltie." By contrast, it was only the English who "idolatrize our owne formes."[74]

Thus, while the Indians of *The City Madam* trigger comparison between the idolatrous heathen and idolatrous English, and while they encourage Luke by promising material gain, their want of clothing differentiates them, a lack that this play amplifies, ironically enough, through the use of disguise, a motif which usually involves the covering of the body but which here involves both covering and uncovering. Their nakedness, however staged, would have contrasted with the ornate, foreign clothing worn and idolized by Lady Frugal, Anne, Mary, and Luke, even if the costumes resembled, and may even have been, the ornate designs of Inigo Jones for *Tempe Restord* (Figure 4.2).[75] The play seems to contend that, for all their murderous intent, in terms of apparel idolatry, the Indians put London society to shame. At the end of the play, Lady Frugal and her daughters agree to adopt more sober attire befitting their social status and to alter "their habits" (5.3.155). More pertinently, Luke is "stripped... bare," and comes, at his moment of self-abasement, to resemble the naked Indians with whom he thinks he has been dealing (5.3.114). As much as the Virginian Indians mirror the conduct of the English, they also stand in relief to the Londoners' excessive self-fashioning, their very presence embodying Luke's belief that they "are learn'd Europeans, and we worse / Than ignorant Americans" (3.3.127–8). While the Frugal women and Luke once desired to be "best clad" English men and women, the play reveals them to be "more naked... / Then naked Indian," a trait which Sir John's Indian "physic" conjures out of them.

[73] Roger Williams, *A Key into the Languages of America* (Carlisle: Applewood Books, 1997), 193.
[74] Richard Braithwaite, *The English Gentleman* (London: for Robert Bostock, 1630), 16–17.
[75] See Gibson, "Introduction to *The City Madam*," in *The Plays and Poems of Philip Massinger*, 5.

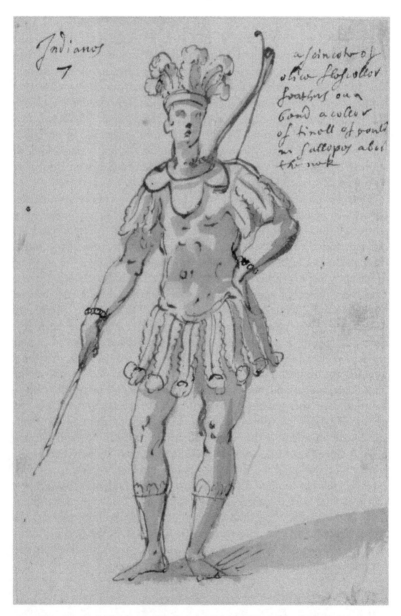

**Fig. 4.2.** An Indian, from *Tempe Restord*, designed by Inigo Jones, 1632. © Devonshire Collection, Chatsworth. Reproduced by Permission of Chatsworth Settlement Trustees.

## "APPARELL & HOUSEHOULDESTUFE": CLOTHING AND CONVERTING THE NAKED INDIAN

Thus far I have considered the ways in which the naked Indian disguise adopted by Sir John and his aides stands in relief to the excesses of the London characters, who in turn incarnate the accusations of corruption that tainted Virginia's early settlers. But this doesn't account fully for the employment of alterity as disguise in *The City Madam*. After all, the effects I've been describing could have been achieved by having Indian characters actually onstage, albeit the use of disguise calls especial attention to differences in attire (and attitudes toward attire). While I agree with Jean Howard's argument that as a result of the play's use of disguise the "native figures have been representationally deracinated," I also think that something else is going on here with this dramaturgic choice, not just in terms of the symbolic relationship between London and Virginia—as we have seen throughout the drama I have been addressing in this book—but also in terms of the relationships between naked Indians and clothed English *within* the colony, and most especially within the English colonial home. These sets of relationships come to a head at the moment when the disguise is removed at the end of *The City Madam* and the Indian presence is erased.

To try to understand these sets of relationships, it is worth exploring the function of clothing (both literal and metaphoric) in the English Atlantic colonies. Clothing was crucial to transatlantic relations, in terms of how it structured both the imaginings of adventurers and the quotidian life of settlers and Native Americans.[76] By the late sixteenth century the English cloth trade was in decline, and many observers expressed the belief that America offered an outlet. Richard Hakluyt encouraged Robert Cecil in the dedication to the second edition of *The Principal Navigations* to support enterprise in the "Westerne Atlantis or America," in particular

---

[76] On the importance of clothing to early English colonialism, see Timothy J. Shannon, "Dressing for Success on the Mohawk Frontier: Hendrick, William Johnson and the Indian Fashion," *William and Mary Quarterly*, 3rd series, 53(1) (1996): 13–42; Joan Pong Linton, "*Jack of Newberry* and Drake in California: Domestic and Colonial Narratives of English Cloth and Manhood," in *The Romance of the New World*, 62–83; Jill Lepore, "Habitations of Cruelty," in *The Name of War: King Philip's War and the Origins of American Identity* (New York: Vintage, 1999), 71–96; Beth Fowkes Tobin, "Cultural Cross-Dressing in British America: Portraits of British Officers and Mohawk Warriors," in *Picturing Imperial Power: Colonial Subjects in Eighteenth-Century British Painting* (Durham, NC: Duke University Press, 1999), 81–109; Roze Hentschell, "'Vente for Our English Clothes': Promoting Early New World Expansion," in *The Culture of Cloth in Early Modern England: Textual Constructions of a National Identity* (Aldershot: Ashgate, 2008), 75–102.

the Northwest Passage, through which "the best utterance of our natural and chiefe commoditie of cloth is like to be."[77] America was also viewed as a potential destination for cloth exports. *A True Declaration of the Estate of the Colonie in Virginia* asked its readers (and potential backers of the Virginia Company) "whither shall wee transport our cloth" and concluded that the new-found settlement would be ideal, as, once "peopled," it would serve as an excellent trading partner: "*mutabit vellera merces*, we shall exchange our store of cloth for other merchandize."[78] In *Nova Britannia*, Robert Johnson pointed out to potential investors that it was not just the English colonists who required clothing. The Indians wore "skinnes of beast, but most goe naked." They too might be cajoled into entering trade agreements for cloth, which "will cause a mighty vent of English clothes, a great benefit to our Nation, and raising againe of that auncient trade of clothing, so much decayed in England."[79]

The belief that the Indians would readily wear English clothing had its basis in anecdotal evidence prior to settlement in the seventeenth century. In his *History of the World* (1617), Walter Raleigh described how the original name given to Virginia by the English, the native word "*Wingandacon*," was a mistranslation attributed to the Roanoke natives' interest in what the English settlers wore. When the party "sent vnder Sir *Richard Greeneuile* to inhabite *Virginia* asked the name of that Countrie, one of the Saluages answered, *Wingandacon*, which is as much to say, as, *You weare good clothes*, or gay clothes."[80] Only after the mistake had been made apparent did Raleigh change the area's name to Virginia in honor of Elizabeth I. Other Englishmen sent to Roanoke wrote about how the Indians were fascinated with English clothing. Ralph Lane, governor of the first colony, reported that they were "very desirous to have clothes, but especially of course [coarse] cloth rather then silke."[81] Lane's news about the Indians' clothing preferences implied that English cloth might prove to be a viable commodity in Virginia and that the natives, in rejecting silk, had simple tastes. Other reports indicated that the Indians understood the English to be superior to them precisely because they wore clothing. The account of Sir Francis Drake's encounters in California in 1579 included in *The Principal Navigations* reports how the English met the Indians of

[77] Richard Hakluyt, "To the Right Honourable Sir Robert Cecil Knight," in *The Principal Navigations*, vol. 9, lxxiv–lxxx, at lxxviii and lxxx.

[78] *True Declaration of the Estate of the Colonie in Virginia*, 64.

[79] Johnson, *Nova Britannia*, 11, 22.

[80] Walter Raleigh, *The History of the World* (London: for Walter Burre, 1617), 175–6.

[81] "An Extract of Master Ralph Lanes Letter to M. Richard Hakluyt Esquire, and Another Gentleman of the Middle Temple, from Virginia," in Hakluyt, *Principal Navigations*, vol. 8, 319–20, at 320.

"Nova Albion" and "liberally bestowed on them necessarie things to cover their nakednesse." So amazed were they that "they supposed us to be gods, and would not be perswaded to the contrary."[82]

The belief that Indians might be interested in wearing English cloth was not just founded on trade. Apparel was understood as central to the broader purpose of colonization, namely, the establishment of a Christian commonwealth in the New World. Promotional literature regularly employed clothing as a metaphor for civility and conversion. A tract circulated to engage the support of the merchants of the Muscovy and the East India Companies in 1609 outlined the Virginia Company's intention "to communicate to [the Indians] first (as has been said) divine riches, and after that, to cover their nakedness and relieve their poverty by using human clothing and human food."[83] William Crashaw outlined the work of the settlers as regards the conversion of the Indians. They were to institute

> 1. Ciuilitie for their bodies, 2. Christianitie for their soules: The first to make them men: the second happy men; the first to couer their bodies from the shame of the world: the second, to couer their soules from the wrath of God: the lesse of these two (being that for the bodie) will make them richer then we finde them.[84]

Civility was to be worn as well as learned: covering the Indians' bodies would result in the salvation of their souls. Not that this would be easy. Alexander Whitaker voiced his belief that the Indians would resist being "clothed" but argued that this should be no deterrent. Taking a lesson from Paul, he stressed that "we must feed and cloath our enemies and persecutors" as well as friends, and argued that "the miserable condition of these naked slaues of the diuell [should] moue you to compassion toward them."[85] John Rolfe, writing to Thomas Dale, justified his marriage to Pocahontas in similar terms. He argued that while marrying an Indian might be deemed an abomination, if it resulted in her conversion, then it could be deemed an act of charity: after all, asked Rolfe, could he be "so vnnaturall, as not to giue bread to the hungrie? or vncharitable, as not to couer the naked?"[86]

---

[82] "The Course which Sir Francis Drake held from the haven of Guatulco in the South Sea on the backe side of Nueva Espanna, to the North-west of California as far as fourtie three degrees," in Hakluyt, *Principal Navigations*, vol. 9, 319–26, at 321.

[83] "New Britain: with a Statement of the great advantages which must follow the Colonizing of Virginia. Addressed (Dedicated) to the chief Treasurer of this Colony and of the Merchants of the Moscovite and the East India Company," in Brown, *Genesis of the United States*, 266.

[84] Crashaw, *New-Yeeres Gift*, D4.

[85] Whitaker, *Good Newes from Virginia*, 20, 23–4.

[86] "John Rolfe to Thomas Dale, 1614," in Hamor, *True Discourse*, 66.

Although cloth was central to a great many fantasies of the New World, tobacco (in Virginia) and the fisheries (in Newfoundland) proved to be the staples of trade, and the hope that America would save the cloth trade proved unfounded. However, cloth became important in English attempts to structure social life in the colonies. In 1621, George Thorpe, deputy of the college lands in Virginia, encouraged the Virginia Council that if it distributed "apparell & householdestufe" among the Native Americans "it woulde make a good entrance into their affections."[87] The project of clothing the Indians extended beyond the distribution of actual items of clothing to a systematic approach intended to engender civility and Christianity. Not only was "householdestufe" distributed under Thorpe's program; clothed, converted Indians, in particular children, were to be welcomed and even incorporated into English households, thus counteracting another sense of their nakedness, namely, their placelessness and nomadism. As a result of Thorpe's enthusiasm, the Virginia Company and Council permitted and encouraged Native Americans to live among and even with the English. In his 1622 tract *A Declaration of the State of the Colony and Affaires in Virginia*, Edward Waterhouse reported how Thorpe had ordered "a fayre house" to be built for the Powhatan chief Opechancanough, "according to the English fashion" to replace his "cottage, or rather a denne or hog-stye, made with a few poles and stickes, and couered with mats after their wyld manner." The house was designed explicitly "to ciuilize him."[88] The Virginia Company and Council also launched a policy to resettle Native American children in English homes. A report of a meeting of the Virginia Council dated August 2, 1619, records that it was "enacted [ . . . ] that for laying a surer foundation of the conversion of the Indians to Christian Religion, eache towne, citty, Borrough, and particular plantation do obtaine unto themselves by just means a certine number of the natives' children to be educated by them in true religion and civile course of life."[89] In May 1620 it was decided that children should be placed in the care of the Puritan separatists who were due to arrive in Virginia later that year—a plan that never reached fruition because the Puritans landed at Plymouth instead.

---

[87] "George Thorpe to Edwin Sandys, May 15, 1621," in Kingsbury, *Records of the Virginia Company*, vol. 3, 446.

[88] Waterhouse, *Declaration of the State of the Colony*, 16.

[89] "Report of a Meeting of the Virginia Council, August 2, 1919," in Kingsbury, *Records of the Virginia Company*, vol. 3, 165–6.

## "THE SURPRISE OF THOSE NAKED PEOPLE":
## INDIAN DISGUISE, MARCH 22, 1622

Reports from the colonies boasted of the success at clothing Indians. Thorpe believed that the Indians "begin more and more to affect English ffassions."[90] In Maryland in 1634, Father Andrew White wrote with much confidence that the Indians "exceedingly desire civill life and Christian apparrell."[91] According to the pamphlet *New Englands First Fruits* (1643), "Divers of the *Indians* Children, Boyes and Girles we have received into our houses, who are long since civilized." One of their number, William, "would not goe naked like the *Indians*, but cloathed just as one of our selves."[92]

However, English confidence in their success at clothing Indians was often misplaced. For example, Captain Christopher Newport's "Coronation of Powhatan" in 1608, which involved not just a crown but a "scarlet Cloke and apparel," was far from the proof of Wahunsenacawh's obeisance toward James I that the English interpreted it to be. John Smith, who was an eye witness to the event, described how Wahunsenacawh refused to kneel, despite "many perswasions, examples, and instructions," and proclaimed that "I also am a King, and this is my land."[93] The crown and the clothing exchanged failed to solidify an alliance between the Powhatan and the English. Instead, Wahunsenacawh used the crown to symbolize his own alliances with the various Native American tribes that formed his confederacy. According to Helen Rountree, "from 1609 onward," he thanked his people for planting corn "while wearing the paste-jewel crown that James I of England sent him in the fall of 1608."[94] Karen Kupperman has illustrated how the incorporation of the Chickahominy of Virginia by Thomas Dale in 1614, marked by their counselors consenting to wear "a suit of red cloath, which did much please them" and caused them to pronounce "them selues English men, and King Iames his men," was a fantasy of the English.[95] Instead of affirming the ascendancy

[90] "Thorpe to Sandys," in Kingsbury, *Records of the Virginia Company*, 446.
[91] Andrew White, *A Briefe Relation of the Voyage unto Maryland*, in Clayton Colman Hall (ed.), *Narratives of Early Maryland, 1633–1684* (New York: C. Scribner's Sons, 1925), 44.
[92] Anonymous, *New Englands First Fruits* (London: for Henry Overton, 1643), 3–4.
[93] Smith, *The Generall Historie of Virginia*, 358. Smith also recorded Wahunsenacawh's resistance in *The Proceedings of the English Colonie of Virginia* (1612), but without the detail of the Powhatan's declaration of sovereignty (possibly an embellishment on Smith's part).
[94] Helen Rountree, *The Powhatan Indians of Virginia: Their Traditional Culture* (Norman: University of Oklahoma Press, 1992), 110.
[95] "Thomas Dale to Mr D. M., June 18, 1614," in Hamor, *True Discourse*, 56.

of the English, "the entire relationship was shaped and managed by the Chickahominies... [and] the negotiations actually produced an alliance and trading pact under which the Chickahominies governed themselves as before."[96]

Even though clothing was central to English imaginings of the New World and significant in the structuring of English–Native American relations in the early years of settlement, the clothing project stumbled and stalled. In part this was the result of a lack of sufficient clothing to go around the colonists, let alone possible Native American converts. A dearth of supplies necessitated actions such as "An Act that No Cloath Be Sould to the Indians," passed in Virginia on August 16, 1633, which stipulated that no settler could "trade or trucke any such cloathe, cotton or bayes, unto any Indians which is or shall be bought into this colony, as marchandize intended to be sould to the planters here."[97] But, most of all, the project failed because of the inability of the English to get across what to them clothing signified. Roger Williams attempted to convince the Narragansett of Rhode Island that clothes were God-given and even managed to circulate clothing among them. Nevertheless, he found there to be limitations in using apparel as a civilizing tool. Williams observed that the Narragansett thought "Our English clothes are so strange." When they wore "an English mantle... all else [was] open and naked." Rather than use clothing to protect themselves against the elements, they preferred "in a showre of raine... [to] expose their skins to the wet then their cloaths, and therefore pull them off, and keep them drie." They also would wear "the English apparel" when meeting with the English, but "pull of[f] all, as soone as they come againe into their owne Houses, and Company."[98]

It is important that Williams notes the difference in behavior of the Narragansett in English homes and when they left English homes. While his observations suggest that the Narragansett held English clothing in high esteem (their word for "Englishmen" literally translated as "Coatmen, or clothed"), in a sense they also suggest that the Narragansett displayed a flair for performance and for dressing up.[99] John Smith had earlier noted this theatrical flair when he observed a "Mascarado" of Virginian women, painted and wearing various forms of ceremonial costumes, who "singing and dauncing with most excellent ill varietie, oft falling into their infernall passions, and solemnly again to sing and daunce;

---

[96] Kupperman, *Indians and English*, 72.
[97] "An Act that No Cloath Be Sould to the Indians, August 16, 1633," in Hening, *The Statutes at Large*, vol. 1, 219.
[98] Williams, *Languages of America*, 121.    [99] Williams, *Languages of America*, 59.

having spent neare an houre in this Mascarado, as they entered in like manner they departed."[100] The Indians, it seems, were as adept at acting as the English, and used forms of clothing (both their own and European) to enact various roles depending on the audience's needs and their own.

This Indian ability to dress up (rather than wear clothes) was especially significant in Virginia on Good Friday, 1622. Edward Waterhouse's official report of the attacks on March 22 described how the Opechanca-nough's forces "came unarmed into our houses, without Bowes or ar-rowes, or other weapons...sate downe at Breakfast with our people at their tables" and then "immediately with their [i.e. the settlers'] owne tooles and weapons, eyther laid downe, or standing in their houses, they basely and barbarously murthered, not sparing eyther age or sexe, man, woman or childe; so sodaine in their cruell execution, that few or none discerned the weapon or blow that brought them to destruction."[101] Accounts of the attacks stressed that the way that the settlers resided (in the words of John Chamberlain writing to Dudley Carleton in July 1622) "in scattered and stragling houses far asunder" had made them vulnerable to "the surprise of those naked people."[102] William Wynn, a Welsh law student in London, wrote to his father on July 12, 1622, "In Virginia, the savages have by a wile come (as they weare wonte) to traffique into our englishe howses, and with our owne weapons slew 329 of our men."[103] On the same day a letter (author unknown) informed Joseph Mead that the settlers had "been murthered by the Natives...under pretence of freindship."[104] Mead himself noted in September that the Virginia Company in London had branded the attacks "most barbarous & in the very midst of kindnes on our part &c."—that is, the English attempts to save the souls had been turned against them.[105] Mead appears to have received a slightly garbled account of the attack, writing to a friend that "the Indians" had invited "our men to their Feasting & merriment" in order to trap them and kill them.[106] While the details have been reversed, the point remains the same: the Indians had violated the rules of hospitality in the most bloody way possible.

---

[100] Smith, *The Generall Historie*, 357. On Smith's response to the masque, and the deployment of the language of theatrical form in colonial and ethnographic writing, see Jonathan Gil Harris, "Becoming-Indian," in Henry S. Turner (ed.), *Early Modern Theatricality* (Oxford: Oxford University Press, 2013), 442–59. My thanks to Gil for sharing this essay with me prior to publication.

[101] Waterhouse, *Declaration of the State of the Colony*, 14.

[102] "John Chamberlain to Dudley Carleton, July 13, 1622," in *Letters of John Chamberlain*, vol. 2, 446.

[103] Quoted in Johnson, "Notes," 107–8.

[104] "Indian Massacre of 1622," 408.

[105] "Indian Massacre of 1622," 409.    [106] "Indian Massacre of 1622," 408.

In the accounts of the events of March 22, the following common threads predominate: the Indians entered English homes as converts or potential converts, "without Bowes and arrows," weapons signifying their Indianness; the attacks happened because the Virginians had developed a keen sense of disguise; they had used their "wile" to be welcomed into the home so that they might be made members of the household "under pretence of freindship"; and they used the disguise of being "naked people" ("innocent," "unarmed") as the springboard for their assault. Pretending to be guests of (or, in Mead's version of events, as hosts to) the English settlers, the Indians used their nakedness as the best kind of disguise.

## "THIS WASHED OFF": VIRGINIA CLEANSED

Although performed a decade later, *The City Madam* can be seen as a response to the 1622 attacks, and in particular to the recurring motif of the household threatened and undone by naked Indians. Three Indians arrive in disguise at an English home, pretend to be willing Christian converts, and then attack the household from within. The parallels between the play and the attacks even extend beyond the plot, and there are some notable verbal echoes. Upon hearing that the Indians are about to arrive at the house, Luke objects, believing that it is hardly "Religious charity ... to send infidels, / Like hungry locusts, to devour the bread / Should feed his family" (3.3.78–80). Bread has obvious religious connotations. It was part of the Communion, which the Indians would have to take in order to convert. Luke's allusion to the eighth of the ten plagues in the Book of Exodus suggests that the Indians would devour and destroy the bread rather than consume it in the correct manner. In addition to these biblical connotations, bread was linked to the 1622 attacks in a more material way. As Waterhouse reported, the attacks began when the Indians "sate downe at Breakfast with our people at their tables."[107] Bread would almost certainly have formed part of the breakfasts that were laid out when the Indians appropriated the English weapons.[108] We can see it on the table in the foreground of Matthaeus Merian's depiction of the 1622 attacks, which was engraved and published by Theodor de Bry in 1628 (Figure 4.3).

---

[107] Waterhouse, *Declaration of the State of the Colony*, 13.
[108] "The morning meal was a simple affair, because women rarely had time to prepare anything elaborate. Leftover bread, cheese, and cider usually sufficed." Dorothy A. Mays, *Women in Early America: Struggle, Survival, and Freedom in a New World* (Santa Barbara, CA: ABC Clio, 2004), 104.

peranr?

**Fig. 4.3.** De Magna Clade, Quam Angli Anno 1662. 22 Matiiij in Virginia Acceperunt, from Theodor de Bry, *America Part XIII*, 1634. Courtesy of the John Carter Brown Library at Brown University.

*The City Madam* not only alludes to events in the Virginia colony's recent history; it also echoes the policies adopted by the Virginia Council in the aftermath of the attacks. Governor Francis Wyatt believed that the restoration of the colony required drastic offensive action against the Indians: "[our] first worke is expulsion of the Salvages to gaine the free range of the country for encrease of Cattle, swine &c which will more then restore us, for it is infinitely better to have no heathen among us, who at best were but as thornes in our sides, then to be at peace and league with them."[109] Others proposed even bloodier forms of retaliation than removing the Indians from the environs of Jamestown. A letter dated August 1, 1622, from Virginia Company members to Governor Wyatt and the

[109] "Letter of Sir Francis Wyatt, Governor of Virginia, 1621–1626," in *William and Mary Quarterly*, 2nd series, 6(2) (1926): 114–21, at 118.

Council in Virginia expresses the hopelessness of the prior policy of converting the Indians, "the saving of whose Soules, we haue so zealousy affected," and couples this assessment with fresh resolve to exact revenge and wipe them out: "we must advise you to roote out from being any longer a people, so cursed a nation, vngratefull to all benefitts, and vncapable of all goodnesse."[110] As Alden T. Vaughan argues, judgments such as these were "widely shared by the London Company and by... fellow colonists," and it "forecast Virginia's posture for the remainder of the century": "For ten years after the massacre, the colony, abetted by the company and the crown, waged merciless war against its neighboring tribes, whether or not they had participated in the uprising... All prospects of an integrated society had vanished."[111]

It seems to me not a coincidence that *The City Madam* was first staged as the decade-long fighting between the forces of Opechancanough and the English was coming to a close, nor that the play concludes with the removal of an Indian threat from an English household that in turn results in the reformation and restoration of that household. At the end of the play the Frugal women and Luke redress their ways by reforming their sartorial intemperance, and both Virginia and the Frugal home are amended. Sir John is restored to his position as head of the household. Virginia, imagined up until the close of the play as a place of drunkards, traitors, strumpets, bawds, and murderous Indians who pretend at conversion, becomes a place where Luke can "repent" (5.3.145). It is no longer a place where a villain might make hay, but rather one where he might be able to find salvation, and Luke's admittance of guilt for his actions implies that he will be a good penitent. That is, for the first time in early modern drama, Virginia is imagined as a transformational place where it seems possible to transform oneself from the prodigality of corruption and penury and become the hardworking subject of colonial endeavor. Several years too late it seems for the Virginia Company— which dissolved at the end of James I's reign—but finally theater seemed to be at least entertaining the possibility that the colony could effect lasting and positive transformation for its colonizers, for London, and for England.

All of these reformations occur when the Indians disappear. In the play's final scene Sir John, having given his brother enough rope with

---

[110] "Treasurer and Council for Virginia to Governor and Council in Virginia, August 1, 1622," in Kingsbury, *Records of Virginia Company*, 671.

[111] Alden T. Vaughan, "'Expulsion of the Salvages': English Policy and the Virginia Massacre," in *Roots of American Racism: Essays on the Colonial Experience* (Oxford: Oxford University Press, 1995), 105–27, at 106–7.

which to hang himself, announces his identity with the words "This wash'd off" (5.3.110). With this one line of dialogue, and with one physical movement of taking off the disguise, the Indians are removed from the scene. *The City Madam* features Indians who reject religious teaching and threaten the lives of the Frugal family, but by contrast to the bloody attacks of a decade ago that it evokes, it stages their expulsion or their rooting "out from being any longer a people" as an almost effortless act.

It is significant that the moment of revelation occurs at the conclusion of the play's masque. *The City Madam* appropriates the logic of those court masques in which foreigners not only convert and show their loyalty to the English crown but are also transformed into willing subjects by removing the prostheses that constitute their alterity. The moment of Sir John's washing away of his Indian disguise occurs at the end of "*The Story of Orpheus in the Underworld*," which the Virginians put on to celebrate Luke's new-found wealth (and also to test him further, as the subtext of the masque is charity). This sequence echoes less the Indians participating in the anti-masque of *Tempe Restord* (even if they wore similar or even the same costumes as their court masque counterparts) but instead the conclusion to Jonson and Jones' *The Irish Masque at Court* (1613) and *The Gypsies Metamorphosed* (1621). *The Irish Masque at Court* features gentlemen who perform a dance while wearing Irish mantles. The Irish presence is subsequently removed when "*the masquers let fall their mantles and discover their masquing apparel*," at which moment they are transformed as "new-born creatures all" (155 and 155SD).[112] This act of divestiture represents the "end [of] our countries most unnatural broils" (130). The gypsies in *The Gypsies Metamorphosed* undergo a similar transformation. As Mark Netzloff argues, the masque re-imagines contemporary concerns about England's border regions, as is evident in the head gypsy Patrico's declaration that he is a "bringer / Of bound to the border" (WIN 76–7). Writes Netzloff, "The border counties presented a threat to civil order and ideas of cultural unity because of the ease with which the cultures of gypsies, vagrants, and reivers could interact and mix together, even forming the possibility of an alternative community."[113] The masque resolves this threat to national stability when the gypsies undergo a "transformation" (WIN Ep. 14), "Assisted by a barber and a tailor" (Ep. 20), and their rags and complexions are changed. The "ointment"

---

[112] Ben Jonson, *The Irish Masque at Court*, in Bevington et al., *The Cambridge Edition of the Works of Ben Jonson*, vol. 4. All citations are from this edition.

[113] Mark Netzloff, "'Counterfeit Egyptians' and Imagined Borders: Jonson's *The Gypsies Metamorphosed*," *English Literary History*, 68(4) (2001): 763–93, at 763.

that "dyed our faces" (Ep. 9) to make it seem as if they had "tawny faces" (WIN 67) "was fetched off with water and a ball" (Ep. 13). Thus both masques stage a potential threat to James' sovereignty, represented by troublesome subjects wearing prostheses (cloaks, "tawny-face") that signify their alterity, only for said threat to be abated through the removal of the very accoutrements that mark out their difference. Furthermore, the bloody colonial project is reformulated not just as a simple act of acquiescence (as it is, for example, at the end of Chapman and Jones' *The Memorable Masque*, where the Virginians renounce sun worship to devote themselves to God and James I). At the conclusion of both masques the raggedly dressed Irish and tawny-faced gypsies become well-dressed masquers. The disruptive elements unsettling the English imperial cause are expelled and ultimately discarded, and courtiers take their place—a place that both masques suggest was always theirs anyway.

To follow on from this masque logic, we might conclude that the moment of "washing off" in *The City Madam* presents the triumph of (to borrow from Winthrop Jordan) white over black.[114] As Ian Smith claims, racial cross-dressing highlights the ironic distance between the blackness of the character and the whiteness of the actor: references to Othello's "sooty bosom" (*Othello* 1.2.70) or his face being "begrimed and black" (3.3.392) both wink at the actor's white body beneath the racial prostheses and promote a sense of whiteness' superiority over blackness.[115] It is not clear what Sir John washes off when he reveals his true identity, but whatever is removed at this point, what is revealed is the white skin of the character (and actor) beneath. However, something slightly different, and perhaps more complex, seems to be at work, and the fact that (unlike the other Indian plays) *The City Madam* does not name the color of what is being "wash'd off" presents us with opportunities to consider further what is at play here. The pigmentation of Native Americans was understood to be a cultural artifact rather than a natural phenomenon. Virginians were, in the words of William Strachey, not "naturally borne so discoloured" but became dark-skinned because "the Mothers cast them . . . with a kind of Arsenick-stone (like redd Patise, or Orpement,) or rather with redd tempered oynementes of earth, and the iuyce of certayne scrused rootes, so sone as they are borne." Like numerous other observers, these dyeing practices reminded him of his British ancestors, who "died themselues redd with woad."[116] Implicit in these comparisons

[114] Winthrop D. Jordan, *White over Black: American Attitudes toward the Negro, 1550–1812* (Chapel Hill: University of North Carolina Press, 1968).
[115] Smith, "White Skin, Black Masks," 36.
[116] Strachey, *Historie of Travell into Virginia Britania*, 70.

was the belief that the Indians could be led to civility, just as the Britons had been: that is, they could be returned, or washed back, to their state of native whiteness prior to its savage recasting, a process that might go hand in hand with their becoming clothed, civilized, and Christian.

Sir John's taking off of his Indian disguise could be seen to parody the various beliefs about the possible relationships between Indians and English (past, present, and future), which were enthusiastically endorsed by prominent colonial advocates such as Richard Hakluyt, Robert Johnson, William Crashaw, Alexander Whitaker, John Rolfe, Ralph Hamor, and George Thorpe—beliefs which *The Historie of Orlando Furioso* appears to be an early incarnation of (even though Greene was thinking about New Spain rather than Virginia); beliefs which the events of March 1622 had compromised severely. *The City Madam* rejects the promise of conversion in Sir John's pretend project, depicting it as something that fails before it has even begun. In the moment of washing off at the conclusion of "*The Story of Orpheus in the Underworld*," the play reiterates the emerging realization that the Indian could not and would not be clothed, and also it stages the fantasy that the Indian threat could be rooted out easily and washed away.

However, even though the transformation of the Indians into converts is rebutted, another transformation, seemingly abetted through the adoption and then discarding of Virginian Indian disguise, does seem to occur instead. By the end of the play Virginia has turned into a place of possible transformation—where Luke and other ne'er-do-well Londoners can go to reclaim their souls (and not to get rich and satisfy their desire). As a result of this possible transformation, London itself is disburdened of its unwanted elements, shipping them out so they can be of better service to the country as a whole through their redeeming of Virginia's wild territory and as a result the redeeming of themselves. But this transformation can only occur after the Indian presence has been removed. Sir John washes off his Indianness, and thus washes away the Indians; indeed, they were never really there in the first place, and served only as fleeting apparitions that can be easily dispelled. By washing away the Indians, Sir John can begin to re-imagine Virginia as a possible colony. By so doing he also reclaims his own rightful position, removing the Indians' threat from his own small plantation and placing in their stead a rightful, white, and now appropriately attired master.

# Afterword

### "Scene: Virginia": America and Heroic
### Drama on the Restoration Stage

None but those of the meanest quality and curruptest lives go
[to Virginia]

Governor William Berkeley, 1663

I look upon Virginia to be the happiest part of the World

Timorous Cornet, J. P., in Aphra Behn,<br>The Widow Ranter

This study has attempted to bring into presence hitherto absent figurations of America, Virginia, the New World, and the Indies—figurations
which were absent from early modern drama in the sense that they were
not directly represented on the early modern stage, and which have been
absent too in the sense that early modern critical studies have either glossed
over or waxed hyperbolical over their importance, without adequately
theorizing theater as a site of absences and substitutions. It has argued
that early modern playhouses were situated within networks through
which news and rumors about colonial life were circulated, to be devoured
by Londoners' hungry ears. This unregulated speech, voiced at the margins
of drama through the medium of the theatergram and theatermeme in plays
often seemingly uninterested in the New World, was powerful precisely
because of its marginality, as this was the space where playgoer met player
and where the real world met the world of the stage. Moreover, the disquiet
experienced by Virginia Company advocates was not unfounded: the
picture of America being circulated within and without the playhouse was
very much of the warts and all variety. Not only did drama's theatergrams
and theatermemes characterize the colony as a bad investment and its
adventurers as dissolute desperadoes; it also undermined the claims made
by the colony's promotional machine that this was a transformational space,
where Indians became Christian and the prodigal English were "made
men," and instead proposed the impossibilities of conversion and the radical

unmaking of men who were, in a sense, already unmade as a result of their prodigal Englishness. That London comedy employed Virginia reference points with most frequency is telling precisely because one of the hallmarks of the genre is its questioning of the transformational possibilities of mobility (physical, social, economic, spiritual)—and these were the key selling points of Virginia.

Advocates of the Virginia Company were astute playgoers, attuned more so than we both to the mockery emanating from the lips of the players and the potential effect of those words on the playgoers. They were also keen students of dramatic genre. In *A True Declaration of the Estate of the Colonie in Virginia* (1610), the Virginia Council described how "the honor and prosperity of this so noble an action, is eclipsed by the interposition of clamorous & tragicall narrations"—narrations such as "the tragicall historie of the man eating of his dead wife in Virginia" (discussed in Chapter 2).[1] If any genre fitted the story of Virginia, the Council seemed to favor "tragicall Comædie," which, in the words of its most famous proponent, John Fletcher, "is not so called in respect of mirth and killing, but in respect it wants deaths, which is inough to make it no tragedie, yet brings some neere it, which is innough to make it no comedy."[2] The Jamestown story featured travel, shipwrecks, near deaths (and many actual ones), but also the triumphant recovery of things thought lost, and, in the manner of all comedy, the promise of married life. How disappointing, then, for the Virginia Company, that the genre that attached itself to its enterprise was London comedy. While tragicomedy's dramatic arc tends towards some form of transcendent transformation borne out of near-death experience, London comedy reveals the baseness of such transformational efforts: if transformation occurs, it is frequently downward and, if not, inherently theatrical, which for the anti-theatricalists registered as morally compromised.

What happened, then, when America became present in plays from the late interregnum and Restoration era? The genre that may have suited Virginia Company tastes even more than tragicomedy would not emerge on stage until the Restoration, namely "heroic drama," defined by John Dryden in his preface to *The Conquest of Granada* (1670) as the dramatic corollary of epic poetry. For Dryden, heroic drama's subject was honor, its rhetoric was heightened (prose was not permitted), and its plotting revolved around rises (and sometimes falls) of historical figures—figures imbued with a sense of heroic masculinity—and the rises (and sometimes

---

[1]  *True Declaration of the Estate of the Colonie in Virginia*, 2.
[2]  *True Declaration*, 11; John Fletcher, "To The Reader," *The Faithful Shepherdess*, in Bowers, *The Dramatic Works in the Beaumont and Fletcher Canon*, vol. 3, 497.

falls) of the societies or nations over which they ruled.[3] According to *The Conquest of Granada*'s epilogue, while the "mechanique humour" of Ben Jonson befitted an earlier age "When men were dull, and conversation low," in this age "love and honour now are higher raised."[4] For Dryden, the prototype of this drama emerged in the interregnum in the work of William Davenant, who was forbidden "in the rebellious times to act tragedies and comedies, because they contained some matter of scandal to those good people, who could more easily dispossess their lawful sovereign, than endure a wanton jest." Hence Davenant "was forced to turn his thoughts another way, and to introduce the examples of moral virtue."[5] Such examples of dramatic "moral virtue" included *The Cruelty of the Spaniards in Peru* and *The History of Sir Francis Drake*, operas which were performed in 1658 and 1659 and then included in Davenant's portmanteau piece for the Drury Lane Theatre, *The Play-House to Be Let* (1663). Dryden too extended heroic drama's reach to the Americas in *The Indian Queen* (1664; with Robert Howard) and *The Indian Emperour* (1665). By the 1660s, then, the New World seemed to have found the mode of dramatic representation appropriate to its early promoters' ambition. In *A True Declaration of the Estate of the Colonie in Virginia* the Virginia Company claimed to have modeled its endeavors on the "heroicall actions . . . undertaken by so mighty states and Princes" of ancient empires.[6] In his sermon of 1610 William Crashaw praised the "heroicall aduenture" of the departing Lord de la Warr.[7] It took a later generation to realize this ambition and mount plays capable of matching "heroicall actions" with heroic action.

The presence of America on the Restoration stage can be attributed to a range of material factors. By 1660, Virginia had been a colony for five decades, and a crown property for over three. The population of the Chesapeake region rose dramatically, quadrupling from 1650 to 1670 to 41,000 settlers—a far cry from the 350 inhabitants of Jamestown and the surrounding areas in 1616.[8] The British presence in the Americas expanded geographically—New England was extensively settled, with 33,000 settlers by 1660.[9] And the Americas had become integral to the

---

[3] John Dryden, "To His Royal Highness the Duke," and "Of Herioque Plays: An Essay," *The Conquest of Granada Part I*, in John Loftis, David Stuart Rodes, and Vinton A. Dearing (eds), *The Works of John Dryden: Plays*, vol. 11 (Berkeley: University of California Press, 1978), 3–18.

[4] Dryden, "Epilogue to the Second Part of Granada," *The Conquest of Granada Part I*, in Loftis et al., *The Works of John Dryden*, 201.

[5] Dryden, "Of Herioque Plays: An Essay," 9.

[6] *True Declaration of the Estate in Virginia*, 4.     [7] Crashaw, *New-Yeeres Gift*, I.v.

[8] Figures from Alan Taylor, *American Colonies: The Settling of North America* (Harmondsworth: Penguin, 2001), 134–6.

[9] Taylor, *American Colonies*, 166.

British economy: Virginia became the principal source of tobacco, producing three million pounds just before the outbreak of the English civil war (a fifteenfold increase from when the colony became a crown possession); Barbados and Jamaica, meanwhile, were fast becoming the most lucrative of all of the overseas possessions, thanks in particular to sugar production enabled by the transportation of 260,000 African slaves.[10] The Americas, no longer the strange New World, were integrated in the daily life of Britons on both sides of the Atlantic. Moreover, the Americas now had a theater that could hold them: perspectival scenic design, influenced by the court entertainments of the earlier half of the century, was imported into the Restoration theaters, giving playwrights space to set their imperial imaginings with a greater degree of verisimilitude than that afforded the playwrights of the commercial theater pre-1642.[11]

As Bridget Orr has argued, the Restoration stage engaged with British imperialism in general, and not just as a way of allegorizing domestic politics but also as envisioning, celebrating, and expressing skepticism towards foreign policy.[12] In particular, it was heroic drama, which, to quote Ramesh Mallipeddi, "sought to dramatize the founding moments of Eurocolonial (especially peninsular) expansionist projects in Old and New World settings."[13] We can even see examples of heroic drama performed with the expressed intention of shaping British foreign policy. Thus John Dryden's *Amboyna*, which dramatized the very events in Indonesia about which the Privy Council had issued a ban on representation in 1625, was mounted in 1673 both to capitalize on anti-Dutch sentiment during the Anglo-Dutch conflict and to agitate for continued English aggression.[14] As stated in Dryden's prologue to the play, it was "The dotage of some Englishmen . . . / To fawn on those who ruine them; the Dutch"; Dryden attempted to counter this sentiment, both in public opinion but also in government, by encouraging the audience to "View then their Falsehoods, Rapine, Cruelty; / And think what once they were [in the 1620s], they still

---

[10]  Taylor, *American Colonies*, 134, 221.
[11]  Perspective scenery seems to have first been introduced to the professional stage in John Suckling's *Aglaura* at Blackfriars in 1637—designed by Inigo Jones—but it did not become widely used until the Restoration. See William Grant Keith, "The Designs for the First Movable Scenery on the English Public Stage," *Burlington Magazine for Connoisseurs*, 25 (1914): 29–39 and 85–98.
[12]  Bridget Orr, *Empire on the English Stage 1660–1714* (Cambridge: Cambridge University Press, 2001).
[13]  Ramesh Mallipeddi, "Spectacle, Spectatorship, and Sympathy in Aphra Behn's *Oroonoko*," *Eighteenth Century Studies*, 45(4) (2012): 475–96, at 476.
[14]  On the formation of anti-Dutch (and subsequently anti-French) public opinion, a project of which Dryden was part, see Steven C. A. Pincus, "From Butterboxes to Wooden Shoes: The Shift in English Popular Sentiment from Anti-Dutch to Anti-French in the 1670s," *Historical Journal*, 38(2) (1995): 333–61.

would be [in the 1670s]."[15] Foreign policy, then, was matter for the stage, and was addressed in polemical fashion by the playwrights, in a way that it had not been in the pre-Civil War era (with a few notable exceptions from the drama of the 1620s).[16]

Heroic drama's engagement with empire was serious business, but its emergence as a genre did not entirely dispel Jonson's "mechanique humour" from the Restoration stage—and not simply because Restoration comedy inherited much Jonsonian DNA. Heroic drama was the subject of much dramatic mockery, with George Villier's *The Rehearsal* being the most famous example: the quick and confusing scenic changes of *The Indian Queen* and *Indian Emperour*, along with the general bombast of Dryden's heroic lines of verse, were satirized through the character Bayes and his William Burrough's-esque cut-up approach to classical epic poetry to construct a fast-moving, entirely nonsensical work of phony epic grandeur. Early modern drama imagined the impact of the New World on English masculinity to be detrimental, yet even the heroic drama had difficulty upholding its central figures' heroic masculinity. Almanzor, the hero of *The Conquest of Granada*, is characterized by Dryden as "not absolutely perfect, but of an excessive and overboyling courage," imperfections gendered as feminized blemishes "which hinder not a face from being beautifull; though that beauty be not regular; they are of the number of those amiable imperfections which we see in Mistresses: and which we pass over without a strict examination, when they are accompanied with greater graces."[17] Without transgression there is no heroic action—as Dryden argued, "a tame Heroe who never transgresses the bounds of moral vertue, would shine but dimly in an Epick poem"—yet by transgressing the heroic body becomes distempered, a condition closely aligned to the prevalent discourses of gender in which disordered bodies are imagined as feminine.[18] The Virginia Company may have wanted to cast their enterprise in terms of "the honor and prosperity of this so noble an action," but to have their enterprise staged, even "heroically,"

[15] Dryden, *Amboyna*, in John Loftis, David Stuart Rodes, and Vinton A. Dearing (eds), *The Works of John Dryden: Plays*, vol. 9 (Berkeley: University of California Press, 1978), 7.

[16] On the topical plays of the 1620s, especially those relating to the Spanish match, see Jerzy Limon, *Dangerous Matter: English Drama and Politics 1623–1624* (Cambridge: Cambridge University Press, 1986); and Margot Heinemann, "Drama and Opinion in the 1620s: Middleton and Massinger" in J. R. Mulryne and Margaret Shewring (eds), *Theatre and Government under the Early Stuarts* (Cambridge: Cambridge University Press, 1993), 237–65.

[17] Dryden, "To His Royal Highness the Duke," 6.

[18] Dryden, "To His Royal Highness the Duke," 6. See Gail Kern Paster, *The Body Embarrassed: Drama and the Disciplines of Shame in Early Modern England* (Ithaca, NY: Cornell University Press, 1993).

opened up its population to accusations of the very kinds of transgressions that dramatic plotting required as the motor of its action.[19]

Perhaps most intriguingly the presence of America on the Restoration stage went hand in hand with the absence of the English colonist. Davenant's heroic dramas of the late interregnum celebrate English imperialism, but do so without representing English colonialism. *The Cruelty of the Spaniards in Peru* (1658) concludes with a combined English-Peruvian army putting the Spanish to flight. Yet as the stage directions intimate, the dramatic action "*may pass as a vision,*" because "*The imaginary English forces may seem improper because the English had made no discovery of Peru in the time of the Spaniards' first invasion there*"— nor had they since, Davenant did not add.[20] The combined forces' extirpation of the Spaniards, and the play's closing dance, with "*a Spaniard, who...pays lowly homage to the English...whilst the English and Indian, as they encounter, salute and shake hands, in sign of their future amity,*" forms a prophetic imagining of events that never came to pass, at least not in Peru.[21] Similarly, Davenant's *The History of Sir Francis Drake* (1659) stages the fall of the Spanish as a result of an English-led slave insurrection at Nombre de Dios in Panama. While Davenant here represents historical events—Sir Francis Drake did indeed lead real, and not imaginary, English and Cimarrón/Maroon forces against the Spanish in 1572—the events themselves are distinctly skewed in favor of English triumphalism. The closing scene, featuring a successful attack on a Spanish mule train, contradicts the historical record—the English attacked a mule train heading to not from Panama, meaning that it had not yet collected gold and silver. The play's concluding dance between the English, the Cimarrón/Maroon, and a Peruvian "*intimating, by their several interchange of salutations, their mutual desires of amity,*" is a distinctly fantastical final flourish.[22] Even though in the wake of 1572 English colonial advocates drew on the example of the English–Cimarrón/Maroon alliance as proof that the inhabitants of the Americas would rise up with the English against the Spanish (as we have seen in Chapter 4), there was no future amity between the groups. The random Peruvian, presumably included in the final moments to remind Davenant's audiences of the Peruvian theme from his opera of the previous year (both operas used the same scenery), and presumably intended to promote a pan-American–

---

[19] *True Declaration*, 3.

[20] William Davenant, *The Cruelty of the Spaniards in Peru*, in Janet Clare (ed.), *Drama of the English Republic, 1649–1660* (Manchester: Manchester University Press, 2002), 258.

[21] Davenant, *Cruelty of the Spaniards*, 260.

[22] Davenant, *The History of Sir Francis Drake*, in Janet Clare (ed.), *Drama of the English Republic, 1649–1660* (Manchester: Manchester University Press, 2002), 294.

English alliance, was in many ways more wish than reality. Davenant's operas promoted Oliver Cromwell's Western Design and the increased colonizing and imperialistic agenda of the English Republic; tellingly they did so not by celebrating more recent English colonial history (by the late 1650s England's transatlantic reach included Virginia, New England, and the Caribbean) but by reaching back into a heroic, barely historical past, re-envisioning English heroism against the Spanish foe or outright imagining this heroism altogether by parachuting English armies into other nations' war zones.

We find similar Anglo-prophesying in Dryden and Howard's *The Indian Queen*. The play's prologue stages an Indian boy and girl who recall "ancient Prophesies" concerning how "Our world shall be subdu'd by one more old." This "World" has "already hither come" in the form of the English audience, who, unlike the Spanish, "came not here to Conquer, but Forgive."[23] Yet the prophecy is never staged—the English remain an offstage presence both in *The Indian Queen* and *The Indian Emperour*, its sequel. The second play concludes with Guyomar's intention, following the Spanish conquest and the death of his father Montezuma, to lead his people "Northward" from Mexico "beyond the Mountains" where "Love and Freedom we'l in Peace enjoy," where "We to our selves will all our wishes grant," and where "[we] nothing coveting, can nothing want" (5.2.368–75). However, Guyomar's wish may not prove as triumphal as first seems, as Dryden's first audiences would have known.[24] His description of the northward climes, where "The Sand no Gold, the mine no Silver yields" (371) recalls the disappointed descriptions of Virginia, whose first English settlers found no gold in them thar hills. The promise of "Love and Freedom" and autonomous living for the Indians was, even by 1665, distinctly compromised by the presence of English colonies, and would become even more so in the decades that followed Bacon's Rebellion in Virginia (1676) and King Philip's War in New England (1675–78). If *The Indian Queen* begins by imagining the British as the future saviors of the Indians of Spanish America, *The Indian Emperour* concludes on a strangely ambivalent note about the possibilities of Indian freedom as they migrate north and (presumably) come into contact with British North America, a place founded on principles of conversion—which may make Guyomar's desire for self-determination

[23] Dryden and Howard, *The Indian Queen*, in Loftis et al., *The Works of John Dryden*, vol. 8, 184.

[24] Dryden, *The Indian Emperour*, in Loftis et al., *The Works of John Dryden*, vol. 9. All citations are from this edition.

difficult—and commercialism—which may make Guyomar's desire to "nothing covet" and "nothing want" impossible (375).

Davenant, Dryden, and Howard staged their heroic dramas in New Spain: indeed, as Adam R. Beach has pointed out, Dryden expressed distaste for Atlantic colonial society, hence perhaps why he chose never to set a play there.[25] But what would the heroic drama of British North America look like? We might now imagine a play featuring John Smith and Pocahontas, or a play drawing heavily on the accounts of the attacks of 1622 and their aftermath; but the first plays about the former event date from the late 1700s (Johann Wilhelm Rose's *Pocahontas* in Germany) and the early 1800s (James Nelson Baker's *The Indian Princess* in Philadelphia in 1808) and the latter has never been staged (other than the lost tragedy *The Plantation of Virginia* of 1623). The first play set in a British North American colony, Aphra Behn's Virginia-set *The Widow Ranter*, does not draw on these stories that have now become so foundational for the Anglo-American experience. Instead the play carries with it memories of Virginia that survive from the first half of the century, which we have seen voiced in London city comedy or plays which drew on that genre. Behn's colony is filled with "transported Criminals" who have found social advancement and personal wealth to elevate themselves far above their natural standing (215)—figures like the corrupt, cowardly justices Timorous Cornet, Whimsey, Whiff, and Boozer.[26] Only Nathaniel Bacon—based on the real Nathaniel Bacon, who led an uprising against Governor Berkeley in Virginia in 1676, because of the Governor's pro-Indian stance—is considered "a man above the common Rank" (215). We find the admiration of Indians and their physique also present in the play, as well as anxieties about what happens when Englishmen spend too much time in their presence. Bacon has been spending time among the Indians, some of whom fear that "under pretence of killing all the *Indians*... [he] means to murder us, lie with our Wives, and hang up our little Children, and make himself Lord and King" (220). The native Virginians are characterized by the settlers as violent, rapacious, even threatening to "ravish... us all" (220)—ravish, we might remember from Chapter 2, was a key word in Fletcher and Massinger's *The Sea Voyage*. But the play draws also on memories of the starving time of 1609–10, because it is the colonists who give themselves over to cannibalism: Bacon's "rabble" threaten to "barbicu this fat rogue,"

---

[25] Adam R. Beach, "Anti-Colonist Discourse, Tragicomedy, and the 'American' Behn," *Comparative Drama*, 38(2–3) (2004): 213–33. Dryden's distaste is evident in his prologue and epilogue to Behn's *Widow Ranter*.

[26] Aphra Behn, *The Widow Ranter*, in Maureen Duffy (ed.), *Behn: Five Plays* (London: Methuen, 1915, reprinted 1991). All citations are from this edition.

Wellman, one of Virginia's (very corrupt) justices (218). Thus, while the turn against the Native Americans that we witnessed post-1622 is in evidence in this play, so too are the cannibalistic urges of the English settlers, albeit several generations removed from the plight of the powdered wife.

The play itself, however, is curiously hybrid, combining elements of the heroic drama, through its depiction of Nathaniel Bacon, its outsized hero, and elements of the London comedy of the early 1600s where we have found most of our Virginia reference points. As Orr points out, Bacon is "a thoroughly heroic figure."[27] In contrast to the saltiness of the majority of Virginians, Bacon's language is heightened (albeit he does not speak in verse, even though Dryden stipulated the hero must). He is motivated, at least at first, by nation and honor rather than self and money. He is also involved in a romantic plot with the Queen, Semernia—which the real Bacon, an avid racist whose rebellion revolved around Governor Berkeley's refusal to drive out the local Native American tribes, most definitely was not. Even in his death, he delivers a message of peace and reconciliation to his followers: "never let Ambition,—Love,—or Interest make you forget as I have done, your Duty and Allegiance" (289–90) (again, it is doubtful that the real Bacon, who died of dysentery, would have had the motivation, or presence of mind, to speak such words). However, not only is Bacon a doomed figure—many heroes are—but he is a traitor, and a very famous one at that. While, as Orr and others have pointed out, Behn turned to Bacon as an elegy for the lost Stuart line—Behn's play is heavily informed by the Glorious Revolution—his rebellion was the act of a traitor whose actions against the English crown foundered.[28] That is, Behn's heroic male is an enemy of the English state; and he is an Englishman who does not inherit the colony but one who is cast out from it.

For all that the settlers fear Indian "ravishing," throughout most of the play Behn also characterizes Indians as heroic figures, their nobility standing in relief to the baseness of the Virginian settlers. Even though Bacon has animosity towards the Indians, when faced with the Indian King, Cavarnio, in battle, he gives him a "Soldiers chance . . . for your Life" (268), such is the respect between them. Their lengthy fight is punctuated by expressions of their mutual admiration ("That's nobly said"; "You're not behindhand with me, Sir, in courtesy"). Upon vanquishing his foe, Bacon

---

[27] Orr, *Empire on the English Stage*, 234.

[28] See also Daniel Gustafson, "Cultural Memory and the Royalist Political Aesthetic in Aphra Behn's Later Works," *Restoration: Studies in English Literary Culture, 1660–1700*, 36 (2) (2012): 1–22.

compares himself to Brutus: "now, like *Caesar*, I could weep over the Hero I myself destroyed" (269). The Queen, Semernia, meanwhile, is brave, noble, the "fairest creature" (235). As such, Behn not only looks back to heroic figures like Montezuma from Dryden and Howard's work a few decades earlier, but to the emergence of the Indian as tragic hero, a trope which would become much in vogue in the American theater of the early 1800s.[29] Yet the Indians overall lose their noble strain: prior to battle they turn to blood sacrifices, the Indian King and Queen leading a dance around the Temple "*Idol with ridiculous postures*" in rituals that will also include human "Sacrifice against the Evening" (although there is no indication that these practices involve consuming the flesh of the fallen) (264–5). And of course they are on the losing side, "*beaten back*" and turned to "fugitive slaves" (267) in the face of the colonists' aggression. The last we see of them is in their removal of the dead bodies of their king and queen: there is no talk of them after this point, only of Bacon's nobility after his fall. Having been a catalyst for much of the play's action, and symbolic of the very qualities which the settlers lack, the Indians end up being little more than a footnote to the story.

Virginia, it seems, was no place for heroes, even in the age of heroic drama. Instead, the Virginia memes which we have seen originally voiced in the drama of the early seventeenth century and to which Restoration comedy owes a considerable debt, are attached to characters who, for all their dissolute, uneconomic, unmanly behavior, emerge as the true inheritors of the Virginia colony. The play ends with multiple marriages between the settlers—between characters who prove their mettle in wartime, like Friendly, Hazard, Daring, and Fearless, and between those whose character may be less than virtuous, like Mrs Flirt and Dunce—and the promise of some form of stability. Even if some of the marriage dyads leave a little to be desired, they are not like the troubling, interracial matching of Bacon and Semernia.[30] Even though figures profit who maybe should not, like Timorous Cornet, who enjoys tobacco planting primarily because it affords him leisure time ("I'll to my old Trade again, and drink my Punch in Peace" (293)), the play depicts Virginia as having a booming economy, troubled only by the outbreak of war. The play, that is, ends like a London city comedy. Its characters who seem to embody honor (Bacon, the Indians' king and queen) are removed from the stage

---

[29] See Gordon Sayre, *The Indian Chief as Tragic Hero: Native Resistance and the Literatures of America, from Montezuma to Tecumseh* (Chapel Hill: University of North Carolina Press, 2005).

[30] See Margo Hendricks, "Civility, Barbarism, and *The Widow Ranter*," in Margo Hendricks and Patricia Parker (eds), *Women, "Race," and Writing in the Early Modern Period* (London: Routledge, 1994), 225–39.

and removed from the colony at its end. The remaining figures include the well-born Friendly, Hazard, and Daring, gentlemen from England, whose couplings with Virginian women Ranter, Chrisante, and Surelove go some way towards establishing a "well-born race" in the colony. But the cost is not only to the indigenous inhabitants, as Bridget Orr has argued.[31] It is to the very idea of Virginia as a place of heroic action, as the English gentlemen, although capable in battle and surely more capable in govern-ance than the hapless previous incumbents, including the aptly named Timorous, have come to Virginia to seek their monetary fortunes rather than their virtuous ones.

Timorous Cornet perhaps stands as the ultimate symbol of this old/new Virginia. A few scenes earlier, Timorous robs the body of a dead Indian, entering "*with Battle-Ax, Bow and Arrows, and Feathers on his Head*" and claiming, Falstaff-like, to have "kill'd him hand to hand" (271): while Trinculo of *The Tempest* recalls how much an Englishman would pay to see a dead Indian, Timorous steals the clothes off of one. His presence in the final scene, as a man wearing a (very unconvincing) Indian disguise, recalls the Indian disguise plays analyzed in Chapter 4. It also points us towards the fact that, even eighty years after the foundation of Jamestown, it was difficult, impossible even, to imagine English heroism in the New World: the heroes are either noble Englishmen who fall tragically or noble Indians who fall tragically too—or who were in Dryden's and Davenant's work imagined to be the saviors of the Indians from the Spanish at some unspecified future juncture. The inheritors of the New World, however, are Virginians, outcasts banded together on the outskirts of civility, driven by the promise of money, marriage, and freedom, through whom we trace dramatic lineage back to characters like Petronel Flash, Seagull, Scape-thrift, and Spendall, and all of the other figures from London city comedy to whom Virginia was attached in late sixteenth- and early seventeenth-century drama.

---

[31] Orr, *Empire on the English Stage*, 237.

# Bibliography

Acosta, José de. *The Naturall and Morall Historie of the East and West Indies*, translated by Edward Grimestone (London: for Edward Blount and William Aspley, 1604).

Adelman, Janet. *Blood Relations: Christian and Jew in The Merchant of Venice* (Chicago, IL: University of Chicago Press, 2008).

Agnew, Jean-Christophe. *Worlds Apart: The Market and the Theater in Anglo-America Thought, 1550–1750* (Cambridge: Cambridge University Press, 1986).

Akhimie, Patricia. "Travel, Drama, and Domesticity: Colonial Huswifery in John Fletcher and Philip Massinger's *The Sea Voyage*." *Early Modern Travel Writing*, special issue of *Studies in Travel Writing*, 13(2) (June 2009): 153–66.

Anonymous. *The Mariage of Prince Fredericke and the Kings Daughter, the Lady Elizabeth, vpon Shrouesunday Last* (London: for W. Wright, 1613).

Anonymous. *The Actors Remonstrance* (London: for Edward Nickson, 1643).

Anonymous. *New Englands First Fruits* (London: for Henry Overton, 1643).

Anonymous. *Good Newes from Virginia*. Reprinted in *William and Mary Quarterly*, 3rd series, 5(3) (1948): 351–8.

Anonymous. *The Wasp or the Subject's Precedent*, edited by Julius Walter Lever (Oxford: Malone Society, 1974).

Arber, Edward, ed. *A Transcript of the Registers of the Company of Stationers of London 1554–1640 A.D*, 5 vols (London: privately printed, 1875–94).

Arens, William. *The Man-Eating Myth: Anthropology and Anthropophagi* (Oxford: Oxford University Press, 1979).

Ariosto, Lodovico. *Orlando Furioso*, edited by Lanfranco Caretti (Torino: Einaudi Tascabili, 1991).

Axtell, James. *The Invasion Within: The Contest of Cultures in Colonial North America* (Oxford: Oxford University Press, 1985).

Bach, Rebecca Ann. *Colonial Transformations: The Cultural Production of the New Atlantic World 1580–1640* (New York: Palgrave, 2000).

Bach, Rebecca Ann. "Foreign Travel and Exploration." In Julie Sanders (ed.), *Ben Jonson in Context*, 263–70 (Cambridge: Cambridge University Press, 2010).

Bacon, Francis. *Instauratio Magna* (London: for John Bill, 1620).

Bacon, Francis. *Sylva Sylvarum: Or a Natural Historie in Ten Centuries* (London: for William Lee, 1635).

Bacon, Francis. "Of Plantations." In Brian Vickers (ed.), *Francis Bacon: The Major Works*, revised edition, 407–9 (Oxford: Oxford University Press, 2002).

Bailey, Amanda. *Flaunting: Style and the Subversive Male Body in Renaissance England* (Toronto: University of Toronto Press, 2007).

Baker, David J. *Between Nations: Shakespeare, Spenser, Marvell, and the Question of Britain* (Stanford, CA: Stanford University Press, 1997).

Banerjee, Rita. "Gold, Land, and Labor: Ideologies of Colonization and Rewriting *The Tempest* in 1622." *Studies in Philology*, 110(2) (2013): 291–317.

Barbour, Philip L., ed. *The Jamestown Voyages under the First Charter, 1606–1609*, 2 vols (London: Hakluyt Society, 1969).

Barbour, Philip. *Pocahontas and Her World* (Boston, MA: Houghton Mifflin, 1970).

Barbour, Richmond. *Before Orientalism: London's Theatre of the East, 1576–1626* (Cambridge: Cambridge University Press, 2003).

Barish, Jonas. *The Anti-Theatrical Prejudice* (Berkeley, CA: University of California Press, 1985).

Barker, Francis, Peter Hulme, and Margaret Iverson, eds. *Cannibalism in the Colonial World* (Cambridge: Cambridge University Press, 1998).

Bartels, Emily C. *Speaking of the Moor: From* Alcazar *to* Othello (Philadelphia: University of Pennsylvania Press, 2008).

Bawcutt, N. W., ed. *The Control and Censorship of Caroline Drama: The Records of Sir Henry Herbert, Master of the Revels 1623–73* (Oxford: Oxford University Press, 1996).

Beach, Adam R. "Anti-Colonist Discourse, Tragicomedy, and the 'American' Behn." *Comparative Drama*, 38(2–3) (2004): 213–33.

Beaumont, Francis and John Fletcher. *The Loyal Subject*. In Fredson Bowers (ed.), *The Dramatic Works in the Beaumont and Fletcher Canon*, vol. 5 (Cambridge: Cambridge University Press, 1992).

Behn, Aphra. *The Widow Ranter*. In Maureen Duffy (ed.), *Behn: Five Plays* (London: Methuen, 1915; reprinted 1991).

Bell, Sandra. "The Subject of Smoke: Tobacco and Early Modern England." In Helen Ostovich, Mary V. Silcox, and Graham Roebuck (eds), *The Mysterious and the Foreign in Early Modern England*, 153–69 (Andover, DE: University of Delaware Press, 2008).

Bellamie, John. *A Iustification of the City Remonstrance and Its Vindication* (London: Richard Cotes, 1646).

Bennett, Edward. *Treatise Concerning the Importation of Tobacco* (London: MS, 1620).

Benson, George. *Sermon Preached at Paules Crosse the Seaventh of May, M.DC.IX* (London: for Richard Moore, 1609).

Bentley, G. E. *The Jacobean and Caroline Stage*, 7 vols, vol. 5 (Oxford: Oxford University Press, 1956).

Berglund, Jeff. *Cannibal Fictions: American Explorations of Gender, Race, Colonialism and Sexuality* (Madison: University of Wisconsin Press, 2006).

Bevington, David. "*The Tempest* and the Jacobean Court Masque." In David Bevington and Peter Holbrook (eds), *The Politics of the Stuart Court Masque*, 218–43 (Cambridge: Cambridge University Press, 1998).

Bevington, David, Martin Butler, and Ian Donaldson, eds. *The Cambridge Edition of the Works of Ben Jonson* (Cambridge: Cambridge University Press, 2012).

Bliss, Lee. "The Wheel of Fortune and the Maiden Phoenix in Shakespeare's *King Henry the Eighth*." *English Literary History*, 42 (1975): 1–25.

Bly, Mary. *Virgin Queers and Virgin Queans on the Early Modern Stage* (Oxford: Oxford University Press, 2000).

Bowers, Fredson, ed. *The Dramatic Works of Thomas Dekker* (Cambridge: Cambridge University Press, 1961).

Bowers, Fredson, ed. *The Dramatic Works in the Beaumont and Fletcher Canon* (Cambridge: Cambridge University Press, 1976).

Bradshaw, Brendan, Andrew Hadfield, and Willy Maley, eds, *Representing Ireland: Literature and the Origins of Conflict, 1534–1660* (Cambridge: Cambridge University Press, 1993).

Braithwaite, Richard. *The English Gentleman* (London: for Robert Bostock, 1630).

*A Breife Declaration of the Plantation of Virginia duringe the first Twelve Yeares, when Sir Thomas Smith was Governor of the Companie, & downe to this present tyme. By the Ancient Planters nowe remaining alive in Virginia* (1894; reprinted Baltimore, MD: Genealogical Publishing, 1973).

Brenner, Robert. *Merchants and Revolution: Commercial Change, Political Conflict, and London's Overseas Traders, 1550–1653* (Princeton, NJ: Princeton University Press, 1993).

Bristol, Michael D. *Big-Time Shakespeare* (London: Routledge, 1996).

Brooke, Christopher. "A Poem on the Late Massacre in Virginia." Reprinted in *The Virginia Magazine of History and Biography*, 72(3) (1964): 259–92.

Brookes, Kristen G. "A Feminine 'Writing that Conquers': Elizabethan Encounters with the New World." *Criticism*, 48(2) (2006): 227–62.

Brookes, Kristen G. "Inhaling the Alien: Race and Tobacco in Early Modern England." In Barbara Sebek and Stephen Deng (eds), *Global Traffic: Discourses and Practices of Trade in English Literature and Culture from 1550 to 1700*, 157–78 (New York: Palgrave MacMillan, 2008).

Brooks, Jerome E. *The Mighty Leaf: Tobacco through the Centuries* (Boston, MA: Little, Brown, 1953).

Brooks, Jerome E., ed. *Tobacco: Its History Illustrated by the Books, Manuscripts, and Engravings in the Library of George Arents Jr.*, 2 vols (New York: Rosenbach Company, 1958).

Brotton, Jerry. *The Renaissance Bazaar: From the Silk Road to Michelangelo* (Oxford: Oxford University Press, 2002).

Brown, Alexander, ed. *The Genesis of the United States*, 2 vols (New York: Houghton Mifflin, 1890).

Brown, Paul. "'This Thing of Darkness I Acknowledge Mine': *The Tempest* and the Discourse of Colonialism." In Jonathan Dollimore and Alan Sinfield (eds), *Political Shakespeare: New Essays in Cultural Materialism*, 48–71 (Manchester: Manchester University Press, 1985).

Bruster, Douglas. *Drama and the Market in the Age of Shakespeare* (Cambridge: Cambridge University Press, 1993).

Burnett, Mark Thornton. *Constructing "Monsters" in Shakespearean Drama and Early Modern Culture* (New York: Palgrave MacMillan, 2002).

Burt, Richard. *Licensed by Authority: Ben Jonson and the Discourses of Censorship* (Ithaca, NY: Cornell University Press, 1993).

Burton, Jonathan. *Traffic and Turning: Islam and English Drama, 1579–1624* (Newark: University of Delaware Press, 2005).

Butler, Martin. "Massinger's *The City Madam* and the Caroline Audience." *Renaissance Drama*, 13 (1982): 157–87.

Butler, Martin. *Theatre and Crisis 1632–1642* (Cambridge: Cambridge University Press, 1987).

Butler, Martin. "Reform or Reverence? The Politics of the Caroline Masque." In J. R. Mulryne and Margaret Shewring (eds), *Theatre and Government under the Early Stuarts*, 118–56 (Cambridge: Cambridge University Press, 1993).

Butler, Martin. "The Invention of Britain and the Early Stuart Masque." In Malcolm Smuts (ed.), *The Stuart Court and Europe: Essays in Politics and Political Culture*, 65–85 (Cambridge: Cambridge University Press, 1996).

Butler, Martin. "Courtly Negotiations." In David Bevington and Peter Holbrook (eds), *The Politics of the Stuart Court Masque*, 20–40 (Cambridge: Cambridge University Press, 1998).

Butts, Henry. *Dyets Dry Dinner Consisting of Eight Seuerall Courses* (London: for William Wood, 1599).

*By the Counsell of Virginia* (London: for William Welby, 1611).

*By His Maiesties Councell for Virginia* (London: for Thomas Snodham, 1617).

C. T. *An Advice How to Plant Tobacco in England* (London: for Walter Burre, 1615).

Callaghan, Dympna. *Shakespeare without Women* (London: Routledge, 1999).

Casas, Bartolomé de las. *The Spanish Colonie*, translated by M. M. S. (London: for William Brome, 1583).

Castillo, Susan. *Performing America: Colonial Encounters in New World Writing, 1500–1786* (London: Routledge, 2006).

Cefalu, Paul A. "Rethinking the Discourse of Colonialism in Economic Terms: Shakespeare's *The Tempest*, Captain John Smith's Virginia Narratives, and the English Response to Vagrancy." *Shakespeare Studies*, 28 (2000): 85–119.

Chamberlain, John. *The Letters of John Chamberlain*, 2 vols, edited by Norman McClure (Philadelphia, PN: American Philosophical Society, 1939).

Chambers, E. K. *The Elizabethan Stage*, 4 vols (Oxford: Clarendon Press, 1923).

Chaplin, Joyce E. *Subject Matter: Technology, the Body, and Science on the Anglo-American Frontier, 1500–1676* (Cambridge, MA: Harvard University Press, 2001).

Chapman, George. "De Guiana, Carmen Epicum," in Lawrence Kemys, *A Relation of the Second Voyage to Guiana* (London: Thomas Dawson, 1596).

Chapman, George. "A Hymn to Hymen: For the Most Time-Fitted Nuptials of Our Thrice Gracious Princess Elizabeth," in Thomas Marc Parrott (ed.), *The Plays and Poems of George Chapman*, vol. 1 (London: Routledge, 1914).

Chapman, George. *The Memorable Masque*. In David Lindley (ed.), *Court Masques: Jacobean and Caroline Entertainments 1605–1640* (Oxford: Oxford University Press, 1995).

Chew, Samuel. *The Crescent and the Rose: Islam and England during the Renaissance* (Oxford: Clarendon, 1937).

Clark, Robert L. A. and Claire Sponsler. "Othered Bodies: Racial Cross-Dressing in the *Mistere de la Sainte Hostie* and the Croxton *Play of the Sacrament.*" *Journal of Early Modern and Medieval Studies*, 29(1) (1999): 61–87.

Clubb, Louise George. *Italian Drama in Shakespeare's Time* (New Haven, CT: Yale University Press, 1989).

Cohen, Walter. "The Literature of Empire in the Renaissance." *Modern Philology*, 102(1) (2004): 1–34.

Cooke, John. *Greenes Tu-Quoque, or The City Gallant* (New York: AMS Press, 1914).

Copland, Patrick. *Virginia's God Be Thanked* (London: for William Sheffard and John Bellamie, 1622).

Cornwallis, Charles. *Discourse of the State of Spain, Written by My Lord about the Beginning of this Yeare 1607*. BL MS Cotton, Vespasian C X, ff 1–35r.

Cox, John D. "*Henry VIII* and the Masque." *English Literary History*, 15 (1978): 390–409.

Craig, D. H., ed. *Ben Jonson: The Critical Heritage* (London: Routledge, 1990; 2005).

Crashaw, William. *The Sermon Preached at the Crosse* (London, 1609).

Crashaw, William. *A New-Yeeres Gift to Virginea* (London: for William Welby, 1610).

Craven, Wesley Frank. *Dissolution of the Virginia Company: The Failure of a Colonial Experiment* (Oxford: Oxford University Press, 1932).

Crouch, Patricia. "Patronage and Competing Visions of Virginia in George Chapman's *The Memorable Masque* (1613)." *English Literary Renaissance*, 40(3) (2010): 393–426.

Curran, Kevin. *Marriage, Performance, and Politics at the Jacobean Court* (Farnham and Burlington, VT: Ashgate, 2009).

D'Amico, Jack. *The Moor in English Renaissance Drama* (Tampa: University of South Florida Press, 1991).

Daileader, Celia. *Racism, Misogyny, and the Othello Myth: Inter-Racial Couples from Shakespeare to Spike Lee* (Cambridge: Cambridge University Press, 2005).

Daunce, Edward. *A Briefe Discourse of the Spanish State* (London: for Richard Field, 1590).

Davenant, William. "The Cruelty of Spaniards in Peru." In Janet Clare (ed.), *Drama of the English Republic, 1649–1660* (Manchester: Manchester University Press, 2002).

Davenant, William. "The History of Sir Francis Drake." In Janet Clare (ed.), *Drama of the English Republic, 1649–1660* (Manchester: Manchester University Press, 2002).

Davies, Sir John. *Epigrammes and Elegies* (Middleborough, 1599).

Davies, Sir John. *Microcosmos: The Discovery of the Little World* (Oxford: for Joseph Barnes, 1603).

Dawkins, Richard. *The Selfish Gene* (Oxford: Oxford University Press, 1976).

Deacon, John. *Tobacco Tortured* (London: Richard Field, 1616).

*A Declaration for the Certaine Time in Drawing the Great Standing Lottery*. In *Three Proclamations Concerning the Lottery in Virginia, 1613–1621* (Providence, RI: John Carter Brown Library, 1907).

Degenhardt, Jane Hwang. *Islamic Conversion and Christian Resistance on the Early Modern Stage* (Edinburgh: Edinburgh University Press, 2010).

Dekker, Thomas. *The Gull's Horn-Book* (London: for R. S., 1609).

Deloria, Philip. *Playing Indian* (New Haven, CT: Yale University Press, 1998).

Dillon, Janette. *Theatre, Court, and City 1595–1610: Drama and Social Space in London* (Cambridge: Cambridge University Press, 2000).

Dimmock, Matthew. *New Turkes: Dramatizing Islam and the Ottomans in Early Modern England* (Aldershot: Ashgate, 2005).

Dolan, Frances E. "Taking the Pencil out of God's Hand: Art, Nature, and the Face-Painting Debate in Early Modern England." *PMLA*, 10(2) (1993): 229–30.

Donne, John. "A Sermon Preached to the Honourable Company of the Virginian Plantation, November 13, 1622." In Neil Rhodes (ed.), *John Donne: Selected Prose* (Harmondsworth: Penguin, 1987).

Drew-Bear, Annette. *Painted Faces on the Renaissance Stage: The Moral Significance of Face-Painting Conventions* (Lewisburg, PA: Bucknell University Press; London: Associated University Presses, 1994).

Dryden, John. *Amboyna*. In John Loftis, David Stuart Rodes, and Vinton A. Dearing (eds), *The Works of John Dryden: Plays*, vol. 12 (Berkeley: University of California Press, 1978).

Dryden, John. *The Conquest of Granada Part I*. In John Loftis, David Stuart Rodes, and Vinton A. Dearing (eds), *The Works of John Dryden: Plays*, vol. 11 (Berkeley: University of California Press, 1978).

Dryden, John. *The Indian Emperour*. In John Loftis, David Stuart Rodes, and Vinton A. Dearing (eds), *The Works of John Dryden: Plays*, vol. 9 (Berkeley: University of California Press, 1978).

Dryden, John and Robert Howard. *The Indian Queen*. In John H. Smith, Dougland MacMillan, and Vinton A. Dearing (eds), *The Works of John Dryden*, vol. 8 (Berkeley: University of California Press, 1978).

Duxfield, Andrew. "Introduction." In *The Fatal Marriage*, at <http://extra.shu.ac.uk/emls/iemls/renplays/fatalintro.htm>.

Duxfield, Andrew. "'That Horse that Runnes Vpon the Toppe of Powles': Middleton, Dekker and the Anonymous *The Fatal Marriage*." *Notes and Queries*, 54(3) (2007): 264–5.

Dyson, Jessica. *Staging Authority in Caroline England: Prerogative, Law and Order in Drama, 1625–1642* (Aldershot: Ashgate, 2013).

Elias, Norbert. *The Civilizing Process: Sociogenetic and Psychogenetic Investigations.* Revised edition, translated by Edmund Jephcott (Oxford: Blackwell, 2000).

Eliot, T. S. "Philip Massinger." In T. S. Eliot, *The Sacred Wood: Essays on Poetry and Criticism*, 123–43 (London: Methuen, 1964).

Elliott, J. H. *Empires of the Atlantic World: Britain and Spain in America, 1492–1830* (New Haven, CT: Yale University Press, 2006).

Evans, Kasey. *Colonial Virtue: The Mobility of Temperance in Renaissance England* (Toronto: University of Toronto Press, 2012).

Evans, Kasey. "Temperate Revenge: Religion, Profit, and Retaliation in 1622 Jamestown." *Texas Studies in Literature and Language*, 54(1) (2012): 155–88.

Ezell, John. "The Lottery in Colonial Virginia." *William and Mary Quarterly*, 3rd series, 5(2) (1948): 185–200.

Farmer, Alan B. "Play-Reading, News-Reading, and Ben Jonson's *The Staple of News*." In Marta Straznicky (ed.), *The Book of the Play: Playwrights, Stationers, and Readers in Early Modern England*, 127–58 (Amherst: University of Massachusetts Press, 2006).

Feerick, Jean. *Strangers in Blood: Relocating Race in the Renaissance* (Toronto: University of Toronto Press, 2010).

Field, Nathaniel. *A Woman Is a Weather-Cocke.* In William Peery (ed.), *The Plays of Nathan Field* (Austin, TX: University of Texas Press, 1950).

Fisher, Will. *Materializing Gender in Early Modern English Literature and Culture* (Cambridge: Cambridge University Press, 2006).

Fletcher, John and Philip Massinger. *The Sea Voyage.* In Anthony Parr (ed.), *Three Renaissance Travel Plays* (Manchester: Manchester University Press, 1995).

Florio, John. *World of Words* (London: for Edward Blount, 1598).

Floyd-Wilson, Mary. *English Ethnicity and Race in Early Modern Drama* (Cambridge: Cambridge University Press, 2003).

Forman, Valerie. *Tragicomic Redemptions: Global Economics and the Early Modern English Stage* (Philadelphia: University of Pennsylvania Press, 2008).

Freud, Sigmund. *The Future of an Illusion*, edited by Todd Dufresne and translated by Gregory C. Richeter (Peterborough, ON: Broadview, 2012).

Freud, Sigmund. *Totem and Taboo: Resemblances between the Mental Lives of Savages and Neurotics*, translated by James Strachey (London: Routledge, 1950; reprinted 2001).

Fuchs, Barbara. "No Field Is an Island: Postcolonial and Transnational Approaches to Early Modern Drama." *Renaissance Drama*, 40 (2012): 125–33.

Gair, W. Reavley. *The Children of Paul's: The Story of a Theatre Company* (Cambridge: Cambridge University Press, 1982).

Garner, Shirley Nelson. "'Let Her Paint an Inch Thick': Painted Ladies in Renaissance Drama and Society." *Renaissance Drama*, 20 (1989): 123–39.

Gaspar, Julia. "The Reformation Plays on the Public Stage." In J. R. Mulryne and Margaret Shewring (eds), *Theatre and Government under the Early Stuarts*, 190–216 (Cambridge: Cambridge University Press, 1993).

Gibson, Colin. "Introduction to *The City Madam.*" In Colin Gibson (ed.), *The Plays and Poems of Philip Massinger*, vol. 4 (Oxford: Clarendon, 1976).

Gillies, John. "Shakespeare's Virginian Masque." *English Literary History*, 53(4) (1986): 673–707.

Gillies, John. *Shakespeare and the Geography of Difference* (Cambridge: Cambridge University Press, 1994).

Glapthorne, Henry. *The Tragedy of Albertus Wallenstein* (London: for George Hutton, 1639).

Glapthorne, Henry. *The Lady's Privilege* (London: for Francis Constable, 1640).

Goodman, Jordan. *Tobacco in History: The Cultures of Dependence* (London: Routledge, 1993).

Gordon, Andrew and Bernhard Klein, eds. *Literature, Mapping, and the Politics of Space in Early Modern Britain* (Cambridge: Cambridge University Press, 2001).

Gordon, D. J. "Chapman's *Memorable Masque.*" In Stephen Orgel (ed.), *The Renaissance Imagination*, 194–202 (Berkeley: University of California Press, 1975).

Gorges, Sir Ferdinando. *A Briefe Narration of the Originall Undertakings... of New England* (London: for N. Brooke, 1658).

Gray, Henry David. "Some Indications that *The Tempest* Was Revised." *Studies in Philology*, 18(2) (1921): 129–40.

Gray, Robert. *Good Speed to Virginia* (London: for William Welby, 1609).

Green, Mary Anne Everett, ed. *Calendar of State Papers, Domestic Series, of the Reign of James I. 1623–1625, with Addenda* (London: Longman, Brown, Green, Longmans, and Roberts, 1859).

Greenblatt, Stephen. *Renaissance Self-Fashioning: From More to Shakespeare* (Chicago, IL: University of Chicago Press, 1980).

Greenblatt, Stephen. *Shakespearean Negotiations: The Circulation of Social Energy in Renaissance England* (Berkeley: University of California Press, 1988).

Greenblatt, Stephen. "Learning to Curse: Aspects of Linguistic Colonialism in the Sixteenth Century." In *Learning to Curse: Essays in Early Modern Culture*, 22–51 (New York: Routledge, 1992).

Greenblatt, Stephen. *Marvelous Possessions: The Wonder of the New World* (Chicago, IL: University of Chicago Press, 1992).

Greenblatt, Stephen, Walter Cohen, Jean E. Howard, and Katherine Eisaman Maus (eds). *The Norton Shakespeare*, 2nd edition (New York: W. W. Norton, 2008).

Greene, Robert. *The Spanish Masquerado* (London: for Thomas Cadman, 1589).

Greene, Robert. *The Historie of Orlando Furioso, One of the Twelve Pieres of France*. In J. Churlton Collins (ed.), *The Plays and Poems of Robert Greene*, 2 vols, vol. 1 (Oxford: Clarendon Press, 1905).

Greer, Margaret R., Maureen Quilligan, and Walter Mignolo, ed. *Rereading the Black Legend: The Discourses of Religious and Racial Difference in the Renaissance Empires* (Chicago, IL: University of Chicago Press, 2008).

Greg, W. W. *Two Elizabethan Stage Abridgements: The Battle of Alcazar and Orlando Furioso* (London: Malone Society, 1922).

Griffin, Eric J. *English Renaissance Drama and the Specter of Spain* (Philadelphia: University of Pennsylvania Press, 2009).

Gurr, Andrew. *The Shakespeare Company* (Cambridge: Cambridge University Press, 2004).

Gustafson, Daniel. "Cultural Memory and the Royalist Political Aesthetic in Aphra Behn's Later Works." *Restoration: Studies in English Literary Culture, 1660–1700*, 36(2) (2012): 1–22.

Habel, J. William, ed. *The Works of Michael Drayton* (Oxford: Blackwell, 1931).

Hakluyt, Richard. *Discourse of Western Planting*, edited by D. B. Quinn and A. M. Quinn (London: Hakluyt Society, 1993).

Hamor, Ralph. *A True Discourse of the Present Estate of Virginia and the Successe of the Affaires There till the 18 of Iune. 1614* (London: for William Welby, 1615).

Harris, Jonathan Gil. *Sick Economies: Drama, Mercantilism, and Disease in Shakespeare's England* (Philadelphia: University of Pennsylvania Press, 2004).

Harris, Jonathan Gil. *Marvelous Repossessions:* The Tempest, *Globalization, and the Waking Dream of Paradise* (Vancouver: Ronsdale Press, 2012).

Harris, Jonathan Gil. "Becoming-Indian." In Henry S. Turner (ed.), *Early Modern Theatricality*, 442–59 (Oxford: Oxford University Press, 2013).

Hart, Jonathan. *Columbus, Shakespeare, and the Interpretation of the New World* (New York: Palgrave Macmillan, 2003).

Hattaway, Michael. "Seeing Things: Amazons and Cannibals." In Jean-Pierre Maquerlot and Michèle Willems (eds), *Travel and Drama in Shakespeare's Time*, 179–92 (Cambridge: Cambridge University Press, 1996).

Healey, Thomas. "History and Judgment in *Henry VIII*." In Jennifer Richards and James Knowles (eds), *Shakespeare's Late Plays: New Readings*, 158–75 (Edinburgh: Edinburgh University Press, 1999).

Heinemann, Margot. "Drama and Opinion in the 1620s: Middleton and Massinger." In J. R. Mulryne and Margaret Shewring (eds), *Theatre and Government under the Early Stuarts*, 237–65 (Cambridge: Cambridge University Press, 1993).

Hendricks, Margo. "Civility, Barbarism, and *The Widow Ranter*." In Margo Hendricks and Patricia Parker (eds), *Women, "Race," and Writing in the Early Modern Period*, 225–39 (London: Routledge, 1994).

Hening, Waller William, ed. *The Statutes at Large, Being a Collection of All the Laws of Virginia*, vol. 1 (New York: R. and W. and G. Bartow, 1823).

Henslowe, Philip. *Henslowe's Diary*, 2nd edition, edited by R. A. Foakes (Cambridge: Cambridge University Press, 2002).

Hentschell, Roze. *The Culture of Cloth in Early Modern England: Textual Constructions of a National Identity* (Aldershot: Ashgate, 2008).

Herrmann, Rachel B. "The 'Tragicall Historie': Cannibalism and Abundance in Colonial Jamestown." *William and Mary Quarterly*, 68(1) (2011): 47–74.

Highley, Christopher. *Shakespeare, Spenser, and the Crisis in Ireland* (Cambridge: Cambridge University Press, 1997).

Holinshed, Raphael. *Holinshed's Chronicles of England, Scotland, and Ireland,* 5 vols (London, 1808).

Hollings, Marion. "Spenser's 'Men of Inde': Mythologizing the Indian through the Genealogy of Faeries." In Jonathan Gil Harris (ed.), *Indography: Writing the "Indian" in Early Modern America, Asia, and England,* 151–68 (New York: Palgrave MacMillan, 2012).

Horn, James ed. *Capt. John Smith: Writings with Other Narratives of Roanoke, Jamestown, and the First English Settlement of America* (Washington, DC: Library of America, 2007).

Horn, James. *A Land as God Made It: Jamestown and the Birth of America* (New York: Basic Books, 2005).

Hornback, Robert. "The Folly of Racism: Enslaving Blackface and the 'Natural' Fool Tradition." *Medieval and Renaissance Drama in England,* 20 (2007): 46–84.

Howard, Jean E. *The Stage and Social Struggle in Early Modern England* (London; New York: Routledge, 1994).

Howard, Jean E. *Theater of a City: The Places of London Comedy, 1598–1642* (Philadelphia: University of Pennsylvania Press, 2007).

Howard, Jean E. "Bettrice's Monkey: Staging Exotica in Early Modern London Comedy." In Jyotsna Singh (ed.), *A Companion to the Global Renaissance,* 326–39 (Oxford: Blackwell, 2009).

Hulme, Peter. *Colonial Encounters: Europe and the Native Caribbean 1492–1797* (London: Routledge, 1992).

Hulme, Peter and William H. Sherman, eds. The Tempest *and Its Travels* (Philadelphia: University of Pennsylvania Press, 2000).

Hulme, Peter and Neil L. Whitehead, eds. *Wild Majesty: Encounters with Caribs from Columbus to the Present Day* (Oxford: Clarendon Press, 1992).

Hutchings, Mark. "Shakespeare and Islam: Introduction." *Shakespeare,* 4(2) (2008): 11–120.

Hutner, Heidi. *Colonial Women: Race and Culture in Stuart Drama* (Oxford: Oxford University Press, 2001).

James I. *A Counterblaste to Tobacco* (London: Robert Barker, 1604).

Jardine, Lisa. *Worldly Goods: A New History of the Renaissance* (London: MacMillan, 1996).

Jardine, Lisa and Jerry Brotton. *Global Interests: Renaissance Art between East and West* (London: Reaktion Books, 2000).

Johnson, Odai and William J. Burling, eds. *The Colonial American Stage 1665–1774: A Documentary Calendar* (Cranbury, NJ: Associated University Presses, 2001).

Johnson, Robert. *The New Life of Virginea.* In Peter Force (ed.), *Tracts and Other Papers* (New York: Peter Smith, 1947).

Johnson, Robert. *Nova Britannia*. Reprinted in Peter Force (ed.), *Tracts and Other Papers* (New York: Peter Smith, 1947).

Johnson-Haddad, Miranda. "Englishing Ariosto: *Orlando Furioso* at the Court of Elizabeth I." *Comparative Literature Studies*, 31(4) (1994): 323–50.

Jones, Ann Rosalind and Peter Stallybrass. *Renaissance Clothing and the Materials of Memory* (Cambridge: Cambridge University Press, 2001).

Jones, Eldred. *Othello's Countrymen: The African in English Renaissance Drama* (Oxford: Oxford University Press, 1965).

Jonson, Ben. *The Alchemist*. In David Bevington, Martin Butler, and Ian Donaldson (eds), *The Cambridge Edition of the Works of Ben Jonson*, vol. 3 (Cambridge: Cambridge University Press, 2012).

Jonson, Ben. *Bartholomew Fair*. In David Bevington, Martin Butler, and Ian Donaldson (eds), *The Cambridge Edition of the Works of Ben Jonson*, vol. 4 (Cambridge: Cambridge University Press, 2012).

Jonson, Ben. *Epicene, or the Silent Woman*. In David Bevington, Martin Butler, and Ian Donaldson (eds), *The Cambridge Edition of the Works of Ben Jonson*, vol. 3 (Cambridge: Cambridge University Press, 2012).

Jonson, Ben. *Every Man out of His Humour*. In David Bevington, Martin Butler, and Ian Donaldson (eds), *The Cambridge Edition of the Works of Ben Jonson*, vol. 1 (Cambridge: Cambridge University Press, 2012).

Jonson, Ben. *The Irish Masque at Court*. In David Bevington, Martin Butler, and Ian Donaldson (eds), *The Cambridge Edition of the Works of Ben Jonson*, vol. 4 (Cambridge: Cambridge University Press, 2012).

Jonson, Ben. *The Staple of News*. In David Bevington, Martin Butler, and Ian Donaldson (eds), *The Cambridge Edition of the Works of Ben Jonson*, vol. 6 (Cambridge: Cambridge University Press, 2012).

Jonson, Ben, George Chapman, and John Marston. *Eastward Ho!*. In David Bevington, Martin Butler, and Ian Donaldson (eds), *The Cambridge Edition of the Works of Ben Jonson*, vol. 2 (Cambridge: Cambridge University Press, 2012).

Jooma, Minaz. "The Alimentary Structures of Incest in *Paradise Lost*." *English Literary History*, 63(1) (1996): 25–43.

Jordan, Winthrop D. *White over Black: American Attitudes toward the Negro, 1550–1812* (Chapel Hill: University of North Carolina Press, 1968).

Jowitt, Claire. "'Her Flesh Must Serve You': Gender, Commerce and the New World in Fletcher's and Massinger's *The Sea Voyage* and Massinger's *The City Madam*." *Parergon*, 18(3) (2001): 97–113.

Jowitt, Claire. *Voyage Drama and Gender Politics 1589–1642: Real and Imagined Worlds* (Manchester: Manchester University Press, 2003).

Kamps, Ivo. *Historiography and Ideology in Stuart Drama* (Cambridge: Cambridge University Press, 1996).

Kareem-Cooper, Farah. *Cosmetics in Shakespearean and Renaissance Drama* (Edinburgh: Edinburgh University Press, 2006).

Keith, William Grant. "The Designs for the First Movable Scenery on the English Public Stage." *Burlington Magazine for Connoisseurs*, 25 (1914): 29–39.

Kelso, William, J. Eric Deetz, Seth Mallios, and Beverley Straub. *Jamestown Rediscovery*, vol. 8 (Richmond, VA: Association for the Preservation of Virginia Antiquities, 2001).

Kezar, Dennis. "Shakespeare's Addictions." *Critical Inquiry*, 30 (2003): 31–62.

Kilgour, Maggie. *From Communion to Cannibalism: An Anatomy of Metaphors of Incorporation* (Princeton, NJ: Princeton University Press, 1990).

Kingsbury, Susan M., ed. *Records of the Virginia Company*, 4 vols (Washington, DC: United States Government Printing Office, 1933).

Klein, Bernhard. *Maps and the Writing of Space in England and Ireland* (New York: Palgrave MacMillan, 2001).

Knapp, Jeffrey. *An Empire Nowhere: England, America, and Literature from Utopia to The Tempest* (Berkeley: University of California Press, 1992).

Knutson, Roslyn. *The Repertory of Shakespeare's Company, 1594–1613* (Fayetteville: University of Arkansas Press, 1991).

Kolodny, Annette. *The Lay of the Land: Metaphor as Experience and History in American Life and Letters* (Chapel Hill: University of North Carolina Press, 1984).

Kupperman, Karen Ordahl. "Fear of Hot Climates in the Anglo-American Colonial Experience." *William and Mary Quarterly*, 41 (1984): 213–40.

Kupperman, Karen Ordahl. *Indians and English: Facing off in Early America* (Ithaca, NY: Cornell University Press, 2000).

Kupperman, Karen Ordahl. "Angells in America." In Phillip Beidler and Gary Taylor (eds), *Writing Race across the Atlantic World: Medieval to Modern*, 27–50 (New York: Palgrave MacMillan, 2005).

Kupperman, Karen Ordahl. *The Jamestown Project* (Cambridge, MA: Belnap Press, 2007).

Lake, Peter and Michael Questier. *The Archbishop's Lewd Hat: Protestants, Papists and Players in Post-Reformation England* (New Haven, CT: Yale University Press, 2002).

Lee, Sir Sidney. "The American Indian in Elizabethan England." In *Elizabethan and Other Essays*, 263–301 (Oxford: Clarendon, 1929).

Lefebvre, Henri. *The Production of Space*, translated by Donald Nicholson-Smith (Oxford: Blackwell, 1991).

Lemmi, Charles. "The Sources of Greene's *Orlando Furioso*." *Modern Language Notes*, 31(7) (1916): 440–1.

Lepore, Jill. *The Name of War: King Philip's War and the Origins of American Identity* (New York: Vintage, 1999).

Léry, Jean de. *A History of a Voyage to the Land of Brazil*, translated by Janet Whatley (Berkeley: University of California Press, 1992).

Lesser, Zachary. *Renaissance Drama and the Politics of Publication: Readings in the English Book Trade* (Cambridge: Cambridge University Press, 2004).

Lesser, Zachary. "Tragical-Comical-Pastoral-Colonial: Economic Sovereignty, Globalization, and the Form of Tragicomedy." *English Literary History*, 74(4) (2007): 881–908.

Lestringant, Frank. *Cannibals: The Discovery and Representation of the Cannibal from Columbus to Jules Verne*, translated by Rosemary Morris (Berkeley: University of California Press, 1997).

Lévi-Strauss, Claude. *Mythologiques: Volume 4: The Naked Man*, translated by John and Doreen Weightman (Chicago, IL: University of Chicago Press, 1981).

Lewis, Anthony J. "'I Feed on Mother's Flesh': Incest and Eating in *Pericles*." *Essays in Literature*, 15(2) (1988): 147–63.

Limon, Jerzy. *Dangerous Matter: English Drama and Politics 1623–1624* (Cambridge: Cambridge University Press, 1986).

Lindley, David. "Courtly Play: The Politics of Chapman's *The Memorable Masque*." In Eveline Cruickshanks (ed.), *The Stuart Courts*, 42–58 (Stroud: Sutton Press, 2000).

Linton, Joan Pong. *The Romance of the New World: Gender and the Literary Formations of English Colonialism* (Cambridge: Cambridge University Press, 1998).

Little, Ann M. "'Shoot that Rogue, for He Hath an Englishman's Coat on!': Cultural Cross-Dressing on the New England Frontier, 1620–1760." *New England Quarterly*, 74(2) (2001): 238–73.

Loengard, Janet S. "An Elizabethan Lawsuit: John Brayne, His Carpenter, and the Building of the Red Lion Theatre." *Shakespeare Quarterly*, 34(3) (1983): 298–310.

Lost Plays Database. *Amboyna*, at <http://www.lostplays.org/index.php/Amboyna>.

Lost Plays Database. *The Conquest of the West Indies*, at <http://www.lostplays.org/index.php/Conquest_of_the_West_Indies,_The>.

Lost Plays Database. *The Hungarian Lion*, at <http://www.lostplays.org/index.php/Hungarian_Lion,_The>.

Lost Plays Database. *The New World's Tragedy*, at http://www.lostplays.org/index.php/New_World%27s_Tragedy,_The.

Lost Plays Database. *The Plantation of Virginia*. <http://www.lostplays.org/index.php/Plantation_of_Virginia,_The>.

Lott, Eric. "White Like Me: Racial Cross-Dressing and the Construction of American Whiteness." In Amy Kaplan and Donald E. Pease (eds), *Cultures of United States Imperialism*, 474–95 (Durham, NC: Duke University Press, 1993).

McClintock, Anne. *Imperial Leather: Race, Gender and Sexuality in the Colonial Contest* (New York: Routledge, 1995).

McInnis, David. "Lost Plays from Early Modern England: Voyage Drama, a Case Study." *Literature Compass*, 8(8) (2011): 534–42.

McInnis, David. "Shakespeare and the Atlantic World." In Trevor Burnard (ed.), *Oxford Bibliographies in Atlantic History* (New York: Oxford University Press, 2014), at <http://www.oxfordbibliographies.com>.

MacLean, Gerald. "Introduction: Re-Orienting the Renaissance." In Gerald MacLean (ed.), *Re-Orienting the Renaissance: Cultural Exchanges with the East*, 1–28 (London: Palgrave MacMillan, 2005).

MacLean, Gerald. *Looking East: English Writing and the Ottoman Empire before 1800* (New York: Palgrave MacMillan, 2007).

McLuskie, Kate. "Making and Buying: Ben Jonson and the Commercial Theatre Audience." In Julie Sanders with Kate Chedgzoy and Susan Wiseman (eds), *Refashioning Ben Jonson: Gender, Politics and the Jonsonian Canon*, 134–54 (London: MacMillan, 1998).

McLuskie, Kathleen E. "Politics and Aesthetic Pleasure in 1630s Theater." In Adam Zucker and Alan B. Farmer (eds), *Localizing Caroline Drama: Politics and Economics of the Early Modern English Stage, 1625–1642*, 43–68 (New York: Palgrave MacMillan, 2006).

McManus, Clare. "*Epicene* in Edinburgh (1672): City Comedy beyond the London Stage." In Robert Henke and Eric Nicholson (eds), *Transnational Exchange in Early Modern Theater*, 181–96 (Aldershot: Ashgate, 2008).

McMillin, Scott and Sally-Beth MacLean. *The Queen's Men and Their Plays* (Cambridge: Cambridge University Press, 1998).

McMullan, Gordon. *John Fletcher and the Politics of Unease* (Amherst, MA: University of Massachusetts Press, 1994).

McMullan, Gordon. "'Thou Hast Made Me Now a Man': Reforming Man(ner)liness in *Henry VIII*." In Jennifer Richards and James Knowles (eds), *Shakespeare's Late Plays: New Readings*, 40–56 (Edinburgh: Edinburgh University Press, 1999).

McMullan, Gordon. "Introduction." In Gordon McMullan (ed.), *Henry VIII or All Is True* (London: Thomson Learning, 2000).

McNulty, Robin, ed. *Ludovico Ariosto's Orlando Furioso, Translated into English Heroical Verse by Sir John Harington, 1591* (Oxford: Clarendon, 1972).

Magnusson, A. Lynne. "Interruption in *The Tempest*." *Shakespeare Quarterly*, 37 (1) (1986): 52–65.

Mallipeddi, Ramesh. "Spectacle, Spectatorship, and Sympathy in Aphra Behn's *Oroonoko*." *Eighteenth Century Studies*, 45(4) (2012): 475–96.

Maltby, William. *The Black Legend in England: The Development of Anti-Spanish Sentiment, 1558–1660* (Durham, NC: Duke University Press, 1971).

Maquerlot, Jean-Pierre and Michèle Willems, eds. *Travel and Drama in Shakespeare's Time* (Cambridge: Cambridge University Press, 1996).

Mardock, James. *Our Scene is London: Ben Jonson's City and the Space of the Author* (New York: Routledge, 2008).

Marlowe, Christopher. *Doctor Faustus A-Text*. In David Bevington and Eric Rasmussen (eds), *Christopher Marlowe: Doctor Faustus and Other Plays* (Oxford: Oxford University Press, 1995).

Marshall, Tristan. "*The Tempest* and British Imperium in 1611." *Historical Journal*, 41(2) (1998): 375–400.

Marshall, Tristan. *Theatre and Empire: Great Britain on the London Stages under James VI and I* (Manchester: Manchester University Press, 2000).

Massinger, Philip. *The City Madam*, edited by Cyrus Hoy (Lincoln, NE: University of Nebraska, 1964).

Matar, Nabil. *Islam in Britain, 1558–1685* (Cambridge: Cambridge University Press, 1998).

Matar, Nabil. *Turks, Moors, and Englishmen in the Age of Discovery* (New York: Columbia University Press, 1999).

Matar, Nabil. *Britain and Barbary 1589–1689* (Gainesville: University Press of Florida, 2005).

Mayne, Jasper. *The City Match*. In Isaac Reed and Octavius Gilchrist (eds), *A Select Collection of Old Plays*, vol. 9 (London: Septimus Prowett, 1825).

Mays, Dorothy A. *Women in Early America: Struggle, Survival, and Freedom in a New World*. (Santa Barbara, CA: ABC Clio, 2004).

Mead, Joseph. "The Indian Massacre of 1622: Some Correspondence of the Reverend Joseph Mead," edited by Robert C. Johnson. *Virginia Magazine of History and Biography* 71(4) (1963): 408–10.

Melnikoff, Kirk and Edward Gieskes, eds. *Writing Robert Greene: Essays on England's First Notorious Professional Writer* (Basingstoke: Ashgate, 2008).

Middleton, Thomas and Thomas Dekker. *The Roaring Girl*, 2nd edition, edited by Elizabeth Cook (London: Methuen, 1997).

Montaigne, Michel de. "Of the Cannibals." In Stephen Greenblatt and Peter G. Platt (eds), *Shakespeare's Montaigne: The Florio Translation of* The Essays*: A Selection*, translated by John Florio, 56–71 (New York: New York Review of Books, 2014).

Montrose, Louis. "The Work of Gender in the Discourse of Discovery." *Representations*, 33(Winter) (1991): 1–41.

Morgan, Edmund S. *American Slavery, American Freedom: The Ordeal of Colonial America*, 2nd edition (New York: W. W. Norton, 2003).

Morrison, Morris Robert. "Greene's Use of Ariosto in *Orlando Furioso*." *Modern Language Notes*, 49(7) (1934): 449–51.

Morrissey, Mary. *Politics and the Paul's Cross Sermons, 1558–1642* (Oxford: Oxford University Press, 2011).

Mullaney, Steven. "The New World on Display: European Pageantry and the Ritual Incorporation of the Americas." In Rachel Doggett, Monique Hulvey, and Julie Ainsworth (eds), *New World of Wonder: European Images of America*, 105–13 (Washington, DC: Folger Shakespeare Library, 1993).

Mullaney, Steven. *The Place of the Stage: License, Play, and Power in Renaissance England* (Chicago, IL: University of Chicago Press, 1988; reprinted Ann Arbor: University of Michigan Press, 1995).

Mulready, Cyrus. "Romance on the Early Modern Stage." *Literature Compass*, 6(1) (2009): 113–27.

Munro, Ian. *The Figure of the Crowd in Early Modern England: The City and Its Double* (New York: Palgrave MacMillan, 2005).

Munro, Lucy. *Children of the Queen's Revels: A Jacobean Theatre Repertory* (Cambridge: Cambridge University Press, 2005).

Munro, Lucy. "Marlowe on the Caroline Stage." *Shakespeare Bulletin*, 27(1) (2009): 39–50.

Münster, Sebastian. *A Treatyse of the Newe India*, translated by Richard Eden. Reprinted in Edward Arber (ed.), *The First Three English Books on America*, 3–42 (London: Archibald Constable, 1895).

Neill, Edward D. *History of the Virginia Company of London*. (Albany, NY: Joel Munsell, 1869).

Neill, Edward D. *The English Colonization of America during the Seventeenth Century* (London: Strahan and Co., 1871).

Neill, Michael. "'Mulattos,' 'Blacks,' and 'Indian Moors': *Othello* and Early Modern Constructions of Human Difference." *Shakespeare Quarterly*, 49 (1998): 361–74.

Neill, Michael. "Material Flames: The Space of Mercantile Fantasy in John Fletcher's *The Island Princess*." *Renaissance Drama*, 28 (1999): 99–131.

Neill, Michael. "'The Tongues of Angels': Charity and the Social Order in *The City Madam*." In *Putting History to the Question: Power, Politics, and Society in English Renaissance Drama*, 99–125 (New York: Columbia University Press, 2000).

Neill, Michael. "Turn and Counterturn: Merchanting, Apostasy and Tragicomic Form in Massinger's *The Renegado*." In Subha Mukherji and Raphael Lyne (eds), *Early Modern Tragicomedy*, 154–74. (Woodbridge: D. S. Brewer, 2007).

Netzloff, Mark. "'Counterfeit Egyptians' and Imagined Borders: Jonson's *The Gypsies Metamorphosed*." *English Literary History*, 68(4) (2001): 763–93.

Newstock, Scott L. and Ayanna Thompson, eds. *Weyward MacBeth: Intersections of Race and Performance* (New York: Palgrave, 2009).

Niayesh, Ladan. "Shakespeare's Persians." *Shakespeare*, 4(2) (2008): 137–47.

Nicholls, Mark, ed. "George Percy's 'Trewe Relacyon': A Primary Source for the Jamestown Settlement." *Virginia Magazine of History and Biography*, 113(3) (2005): 212–75.

Noble, Louise. *Medicinal Cannibalism in Early Modern English Literature and Culture* (New York: Palgrave MacMillan, 2011).

O'Brien, Robert Viking. "Cannibalism in Edmund Spenser's *Faerie Queene*, Ireland, and the Americas." In Kristen Guiest (ed.), *Eating Their Words: Cannibalism and the Boundaries of Cultural Identity*, 35–56 (Albany: State University of New York Press, 2001).

O'Neill, Stephen. *Staging Ireland: Representations in Shakespeare and Renaissance Drama* (Dublin: Four Courts Press, 2007).

Orgel, Stephen. *The Illusion of Power: The Political Theater in the English Renaissance* (Berkeley: University of California Press, 1975).

Orgel, Stephen. "Shakespeare and the Cannibals." In Marjorie B. Garber (ed.), *Cannibals, Witches, and Divorce: Estranging the Renaissance*, 40–66 (Baltimore, MD: Johns Hopkins University Press, 1987).

Orgel, Stephen and Roy Strong. *Inigo Jones: The Theatre of the Stuart Court*, 2 vols (Berkeley: University of California Press, 1973).

Orr, Bridget. *Empire on the English Stage 1660–1714* (Cambridge: Cambridge University Press, 2001).

Parker, John. "Religion and the Virginia Company, 1609–1610." In K. R. Andrews, N. P. Canny, and P. E. H. Hair (eds), *The Westward Enterprise: English Activities in Ireland, the Atlantic, and America*, 245–70 (Detroit, MI: Wayne State University Press, 1979).

Parker, Patricia. *Literary Fat Ladies: Rhetoric, Gender, Property* (London and New York: Methuen, 1987).

Parr, Anthony ed. *Three Renaissance Travel Plays* (Manchester: Manchester University Press, 1995).

Parry, Graham. "The Politics of the Jacobean Masque." In J. R. Mulryne and Margaret Shewring (eds), *Theatre and Government under the Early Stuarts*, 87–117 (Cambridge: Cambridge University Press, 1993).

Paster, Gail Kern. *The Body Embarrassed: Drama and the Disciplines of Shame in Early Modern England* (Ithaca, NY: Cornell University Press, 1993).

Patterson, Annabel. *Censorship and Interpretation: The Conditions of Writing and Reading in Early Modern England* (Madison: University of Wisconsin Press, 1984).

Pincus, Steven C. A. "From Butterboxes to Wooden Shoes: The Shift in English Popular Sentiment from Anti-Dutch to Anti-French in the 1670s." *Historical Journal*, 38(2) (1995): 333–61.

Platter, Thomas. *The Travels of Thomas Platter*, translated by Clare Williams (London: Jonathan Cape, 1937).

Pollard, Tanya. "The Pleasures and Perils of Smoking in Early Modern England." In Sander L. Gilman and Zhou Xun (eds), *Smoke: A Global History of Smoking*, 38–45 (London: Reaktion, 2004).

Potter, Lois. "Topicality or Politics?: *The Two Noble Kinsmen*, 1613–34." In Gordon McMullan and Jonathan Hope (eds), *The Politics of Tragicomedy: Shakespeare and After*, 77–91 (London: Routledge, 1992).

Price, Daniel. *Saul's Position Staid, or the Apprehension, and Examination of Saule* (London: for Matthew Law, 1609).

Price, Merrall L. *Consuming Passions: The Uses of Cannibalism in Late Medieval and Early Modern Europe* (London: Routledge, 2003).

Pritchett, Stephen and Robert Cornwall, eds. *The Bible: Authorized King James Version* (Oxford: Oxford University Press, 1997).

*Proceedings of the English Colonie in Virginia, The*. In James Horn (ed.), *Capt. John Smith: Writings with Other Narratives of Roanoke, Jamestown, and the First English Settlement of America* (Washington, DC: Library of America, 2007).

Prynne, William. *The Vnlovelinesse of Lovelockes* [ . . . ] *Proouing: The Wearing, and Nourishing of a Locke, or Loue-Locke, to Be a Altogether Vnseemely, and Vnlawfull vnto Christians* (London, 1628).

Purchas, Samuel. *Purchas His Pilgrimage* (London: for Henry Fetherstone, 1617).

Purchas, Samuel. *A Discourse on Virginia* (1625). In *Hakluytus Posthumus, or Purchas His Pilgrimes*, 20 vols, vol. 9 (Glasgow: MacLehose, 1906).

Quinn, D. B. "'Virginians' on the Thames in 1603." *Terrae Incognitae* (1970): 7–14.

Raleigh, Sir Walter. *The History of the World* (London: for Walter Burre, 1617).

Raleigh, Sir Walter. "The Last Fight of the Revenge." In Richard Hakluyt (ed.), *The Principal Navigations, Voyages, Traffiques, and Discoveries of the English Nation*, vol. 7, 93–105 (Edinburgh: E. and G. Goldsmid, 1888).

Raleigh, Sir Walter. *Discovery of the Large, Rich, and Beautiful Empire of Guiana, by Sir W. Ralegh: With a Relation of the Great and Golden City of Manoa (which the Spaniards call El Dorado), etc. Performed in the Year 1595*. Hakluyt Society, First Series, vol. 3 (Farnham; Burlington: Ashgate, 2010).

Raman, Shankar. *Framing India: The Colonial Imaginary in Early Modern Culture* (Stanford, CA: Stanford University Press, 2002).

Rankin, Hugh. *The Theater in Colonial America* (Chapel Hill, NC: University of North Carolina Press, 1960).

Ransome, David R. "Wives for Virginia, 1621." *William and Mary Quarterly*, 3rd series, 48(1) (1991): 3–18.

Reese, Jack E. "Unity in Chapman's *Masque of the Middle Temple and Lincoln's Inn*." *Studies in English Literature, 1500–1900*, 4(2) (1964): 291–305.

Ribeiro, Aileen. *Fashion and Fiction: Dress in Art and Literature in Stuart England* (New Haven, CT: Yale University Press, 2005).

Rice, Raymond J. "Cannibalism and the Act of Revenge in Tudor-Stuart Drama." *SEL Studies in English Literature 1500–1900*, 44(2) (2004): 297–316.

Rich, Robert. *The Lost Flocke Triumphant* (London: for John Wright, 1610).

Robertson, Karen. "Pocahontas at the Masque." *Signs: Journal of Women in Culture and Society*, 21(3) (1996): 551–83.

Robinson, Benedict. *Islam and Early Modern English Literature* (New York: Palgrave MacMillan, 2007).

Rountree, Helen. *The Powhatan Indians of Virginia: Their Traditional Culture* (Norman: University of Oklahoma Press, 1992).

Ruge, Enno. "Preaching and Playing at Paul's: The Puritans, *The Puritaine*, and the Closing of Paul's Playhouse." In Beate Müller (ed.), *Censorship and Cultural Regulation in the Modern Age*, 33–61 (Amsterdam: Rodolpi, 2004).

Rustici, Craig. "The Smoking Girl: Tobacco and the Representation of Mary Frith." *Studies of Philology*, 96(2) (1999): 159–79.

Rustici, Craig. "Tobacco, Union, and the Indianized English." In Jonathan Gil Harris (ed.), *Indography: Writing the "Indian" in Early Modern America, Asia, and England*, 117–32 (New York: Palgrave MacMillan, 2012).

S. S. *The Honest Lawyer* (New York: AMS Press, 1914).

Said, Edward. *Orientalism: Western Conceptions of the Orient* (New York: Vintage, 1979).

Sanders, Julie. "Print, Popular Culture, Consumption and Commodification in *The Staple of News*." In Julie Sanders with Kate Chedgzoy and Susan Wiseman (eds), *Refashioning Ben Jonson: Gender, Politics and the Jonsonian Canon*, 183–207 (London: MacMillan, 1998).

Sanders, Julie. *Caroline Drama: The Plays of Massinger, Ford, Shirley, and Brome* (Plymouth: Northcote House Press, 1999).

Sanders, Julie. *The Cultural Geography of Early Modern Drama, 1620–1650* (Cambridge: Cambridge University Press, 2011).

Sayre, Gordon. *The Indian Chief as Tragic Hero: Native Resistance and the Literatures of America, from Montezuma to Tecumseh* (Chapel Hill: University of North Carolina Press, 2005).

Schoenfeldt, Michael C. *Bodies and Selves in Early Modern England: Physiology and Inwardness in Spenser, Shakespeare, Herbert, and Milton* (Cambridge: Cambridge University Press, 1999).

Seed, Patricia. *Ceremonies of Possession in Europe's Conquest of the New World 1492–1640* (Cambridge: Cambridge University Press, 1995).

Shahani, Gitanjali. "Of 'Barren Islands' and 'Cursèd Gold': Worth, Value, and Womanhood in *The Sea Voyage*." *Journal for Early Modern Cultural Studies*, 12 (3) (2012): 5–27.

Shannon, Timothy J. "Dressing for Success on the Mohawk Frontier: Hendrick, William Johnson and the Indian Fashion." *William and Mary Quarterly*, 3rd series, 53(1) (1996): 13–42.

Shapiro, James. *Shakespeare and the Jews* (New York: Columbia University Press, 1997).

Sharpham, Edward. *The Fleer*, edited by Lucy Munro (London: Nick Hern Books, 2007).

Shirley, James. *The Constant Maid*. In William Gifford and Alexander Dyce (eds), *James Shirley: The Dramatic Works and Poems*, vol. 4 (New York: Russell and Russell, 1966).

Sigalas, Joseph. "Sailing against the Tide: Resistance to Pre-Colonial Constructs and Euphoria in *Eastward Ho!*." *Renaissance Papers* (1994): 85–94.

Smith, Ian. "White Skin, Black Masks: Racial Cross-Dressing on the Early Modern Stage." *Renaissance Drama*, 32 (2003): 33–67.

Smith, Ian. "Othello's Black Handkerchief." *Shakespeare Quarterly*, 64(1) (2013): 1–25.

Smith, John. *A Map of Virginia* (Oxford: for Joseph Barnes, 1612).

Smith, John. *The Generall Historie of Virginia, New England, and the Somer Isles*. In James Horn (ed.), *Capt. John Smith: Writings with Other Narratives of Roanoke, Jamestown, and the First English Settlement of America* (Washington, DC: Library of America, 2007).

Stallybrass, Peter. "Patriarchal Territories: The Body Enclosed." In Margaret Ferguson, Maureen Quilligan, and Nancy J. Vickers (eds), *Rewriting the*

*Renaissance: The Discourses of Sexual Difference in Early Modern Europe*, 131–42 (Chicago, IL: University of Chicago Press, 1986).

Stallybrass, Peter and Allon White. *The Politics and Poetics of Transgression* (Ithaca, NY: Cornell University Press, 1986).

Steggle, Matthew. *Richard Brome: Place and Politics on the Caroline Stage* (Manchester: Manchester University Press, 2004).

Steggle, Matthew. "Placing Caroline Politics on the Professional Comic Stage." In Ian Atherton and Julie Sanders (eds), *The 1630s: Interdisciplinary Essays on Culture and Politics in the Caroline Era*, 154–70 (Manchester: Manchester University Press, 2006).

Stevens, Andrea R. " 'Assisted by a Barber': The Court Apothecary, Special Effects and *The Gypsies Metamorphosed*." *Theatre Notebook*, 61(1) (2007): 2–11.

Stockwood, John. *A Sermon Preached at Paules Crosse* (London: for George Bishop, 1578).

Stone, James. "From Lunacy to Faith: Orlando's Own Private India in Robert Greene's *Orlando Furioso*." In Jonathan Gil Harris (ed.), *Indography: Writing the "Indian" in Early Modern America, Asia, and England*, 169–81 (New York: Palgrave MacMillan, 2012).

Strachey, William. *For the Colony in Virginea Britannia, Lawes Diuine, Morall and Martiall* (London: for Walter Burre, 1612).

Strachey, William. *The Historie of Travell into Virginia Britania*, edited by Louis B. Wright and Virginia Freund (London: Hakluyt Society, 1953).

Strassler, Robert, ed. *The Landmark Herodotus: The Histories* (London: Quercus, 2007).

Stubbes, Philip. *The Anatomie of Abuses* (London: Richard Jones, 1583).

Sullivan, Garrett A., Jr. *The Drama of Landscape: Land, Property, and Social Relations on the Early Modern Stage* (Stanford, CA: Stanford University Press, 1998).

Sutherland, Julie. " 'What Beast Is This Lies Wallowing in His Gore?': The Indignity of Man and the Animal Nature of Love in *The Sea Voyage*." *Modern Language Review*, 107(1) (2012): 88–107.

Sylvester, Joshua. *Tobacco Battered* (London: for Humphrey Lownes, 1615).

Symonds, William. *Virginea: A Sermon Preached at Whitechapel* (London: for Eleazar Edgar and William Welby, 1609).

Tailor, Robert. *The Hog Hath Lost His Pearl*. In Lloyd Edward Kermode (ed.), *Three Renaissance Usury Plays* (Manchester: Manchester University Press, 2009).

Taylor, Alan. *American Colonies: The Settling of North America* (Harmondsworth: Penguin, 2001).

Taylor, Gary and John Lavagnino, eds. *Thomas Middleton: The Complete Works*. (Oxford: Oxford University Press, 2007).

Test, Edward M. "*The Tempest* and the Newfoundland Cod Fishery." In Barbara Sebek and Stephen Deng (eds), *Global Traffic: Discourses and Practices of Trade in English Literature and Culture from 1550 to 1700*, 201–20 (New York: Palgrave MacMillan, 2008).

Thompson, Ayanna, ed. *Colorblind Shakespeare: New Perspectives on Race and Performance* (London: Routledge, 2006).

Tobin, Beth Fowkes. *Picturing Imperial Power: Colonial Subjects in Eighteenth-Century British Painting* (Durham, NC: Duke University Press, 1999).

Tourneur, Cyril. *The Atheist's Tragedy.* In Katherine Eisaman Maus (ed.), *Four Revenge Tragedies* (Oxford: Oxford University Press, 2008).

*A True and Sincere Declaration of the Purpose and Ends of the Plantation Begun in Virginia* (London: for I. Stepneth, 1610).

*True Declaration of the Estate of the Colonie in Virginia, with a Confutation of Such Scandalous Reports as Have Tended to the Disgrace of So Worthy an Enterprise* (London: for William Barret, 1610).

Tyler, Lyon Gardiner, ed. *Narratives of Early Virginia, 1606–1625* (New York: Charles Scribner, 1907).

Tynley, Robert. *Two Learned Sermons, The One, of the Mischeuious Subtiltie, and Barborous Crueltie, the other of the False Doctrines, and Refined Heresies of the Romish Synagogue* (London: for Thomas Adams, 1609).

Van Renen, Denys. "A 'Birthright into a New World': Representing the Town on Brome's Stage." *Comparative Drama*, 45(2) (2011): 35–63.

Vaughan, Alden T. "Shakespeare's Indian: The Americanization of Caliban." *Shakespeare Quarterly*, 39(2) (1988): 137–53.

Vaughan, Alden T. "Early English Paradigms for New World Natives." In *Roots of American Racism: Essays on the Colonial Experience*, 34–54 (Oxford: Oxford University Press, 1995).

Vaughan, Alden T. "'Expulsion of the Salvages': English Policy and the Virginia Massacre." In *Roots of American Racism: Essays on the Colonial Experience*, 105–27 (Oxford: Oxford University Press, 1995).

Vaughan, Alden T. *Transatlantic Encounters: American Indians in Britain, 1500–1776* (Cambridge: Cambridge University Press, 2006).

Vaughan, Alden T. and Daniel Richter. "Crossing the Cultural Divide: Indians and New Englanders, 1605–1763." In Alden T. Vaughan (ed.), *Roots of American Racism: Essays on the Colonial Experience*, 213–52 (Oxford: Oxford University Press, 1995).

Vaughan, Virginia Mason. *Performing Blackness on English Stages, 1500–1800* (Cambridge: Cambridge University Press, 2005).

Vecellio, Cesare. *Habiti Antichi et Moderni di Tutto Mondo* (Venice: Giovanni Bernardo Sessa, 1598).

Virginia 350th Anniversary Celebration Corporation. *The Three Charters of the Virginia Company of London* (Williamsburg, VA: Virginia Historical Society, 1957).

Vitkus, Daniel. *Turning Turk: English Theater and the Multicultural Mediterranean, 1570–1630* (New York: Palgrave, 2003).

Warren, Michael. "Greene's *Orlando*: W. W. Greg's Furioso." In Laurie E. Maguire and Thomas L. Berger (eds), *Textual Formations and Reformations*, 67–91 (Newark: University of Delaware Press, 1998).

Waterhouse, Edward. *A Declaration of the State of the Colonie and Affaires in Virginia* (London: for Robert Mylbourne, 1622).

Webster, John. *The Devil's Law-Case*, edited by Francis Shirley (Lincoln, NE: University of Nebraska Press, 1971).

Weimann, Robert. *Shakespeare and the Popular Tradition in the Theater: Studies in the Social Dimension of Dramatic Form and Tradition*, ed. Robert Schwartz (Baltimore, MD: Johns Hopkins University Press, 1978).

West, William N. "Introduction: Italy in the Drama of Europe." *Renaissance Drama*, 36/37 (2010): ix–xiv.

Whitaker, Alexander. *Good Newes from Virginia* (London: for William Welby, 1613).

White, Andrew. *A Briefe Relation of the Voyage unto Maryland*. In Clayton Colman Hall (ed.), *Narratives of Early Maryland, 1633–1684* (New York: C. Scribner's Sons, 1925).

Williams, Roger. *A Key into the Languages of America* (Carlisle: Applewood Books, 1997).

Willis, Deborah. "Shakespeare's *Tempest* and the Discourse of Colonialism." *Studies in English Literature*, 29(2) (1989): 227–89.

Wilson, Bronwen and Paul Yachnin. "Introduction." In *Making Publics in Early Modern Europe: People, Things, Forms of Knowledge*, 1–22 (New York: Routledge, 2010).

Worden, A. B. "Literature and Political Censorship in Early Modern England." In A. C. Duke and C. A. Tamse (eds), *Too Mighty to Be Free: Censorship and the Press in Britain and the Netherlands*, 45–62 (Zutphen: Walburg Pers, 1987).

Woudhuysen, H. R. "Introduction." In H. R. Woudhuysen (ed.), *Love's Labour's Lost* (London: Thomson Learning, 2000).

Wright, Louis B. *Religion and Empire: The Alliance between Piety and Commerce in English Expansion, 1558–1625* (Chapel Hill, NC: University of North Carolina Press, 1943).

Younghughes, S. Brigid, Harold Jenkins, and F. P. Wilson (eds), *The Fatal Marriage, or The Second Lucretia* (Oxford: Malone Society, 1958).

Zucker, Adam. *The Places of Wit in Early Modern English Comedy* (Cambridge: Cambridge University Press, 2011).

Zucker, Adam and Alan B. Farmer. "Introduction." In Adam Zucker and Alan B. Farmer (eds), *Localizing Caroline Drama: Politics and Economics of the Early Modern English Stage, 1625–1642*, 1–15 (New York: Palgrave MacMillan, 2006).

Zwierlein, Anne-Julia. "Shipwrecks in the City: Commercial Risk as Romance in Early Modern City Comedy." In Dieter Mehl, Angela Stock, and Anne-Julia Zwierlein (eds), *Plotting Early Modern London: New Essays on Jacobean City Comedy*, 75–94 (Aldershot: Ashgate, 2004).

# Index